FACE to ƎƆA'H

with

GIFTEDNESS

edited by
Bruce M. Shore   Françoys Gagné
Serge Larivée   Ronald H. Tali   Richard E. Tremblay

© 1983

The World Council for Gifted and Talented Children

ISBN: 0-89824-042-5

No part of this publication may be reproduced, translated, or transmitted in any form without permission in writing from the publisher, except by a reviewer who wishes to quote brief passages in connection with a review written for inclusion in a magazine, newspaper or broadcast. Copyright to individual texts remains with the authors and The World Council for Gifted and Talented Children, and for the entire volume with The World Council. Requests for reproduction should be made, in the first instance, to the publishers.

Anyone requesting further information on these matters is asked to contact the publisher:

Trillium Press, Inc.
Box 921
Madison Square Station
New York, New York, U.S.A. 10159
(212) 684-7399

Printed and Bound in Canada
by the McGill University Printing Service, Montreal

ii

First Yearbook of The World Council for Gifted and Talented Children

developed from

Selected Presentations at the Fourth World Conference on Gifted and Talented Children Montreal, 1981

PREFACE

The thirty-two chapters of this Yearbook are selected from the 369 papers, symposia, and workshops accepted for presentation at the Fourth World Conference on Gifted and Talented Children held in Montreal in August, 1981 under the auspices of The World Council for Gifted and Talented Children.

The theme of the conference was "Many views of the gifted for the advantage of all children." Under this guiding principle were brought together an unprecedented range of perspectives from education, psychology, history, mathematics, sociology, criminology, neuroscience, computer science, futurology, androgogy, and political science. Topics included gifts and talents in the relatively unfamiliar contexts of adulthood, retirement, handicap, and higher education. The theme expresses a commitment to the benefit of all children through attention to the highly able.

The articles include keynote and other invited presentations, as well as others which for the most part either treat unfamiliar material or express attention to the gifted in places not previously represented in the literature on giftedness. These selected presentations have a dual challenge in that they are intended, on one hand, to add to the now extensive literature on giftedness already available in the English language, and on the other, to add to the literature available in French. A world view quickly makes it apparent that not everyone has direct access to the accumulated experience published in English. For example, there are only a half dozen books or monographs in French on giftedness, and only two of these are commercially published and widely distributed. A French edition of this volume is therefore the third and this requires the inclusion of a small amount of material which readers of the literature in English may consider familiar. However, it was selected in response to questions that are now being asked in new contexts, and, in that understanding, will hopefully be of interest to all.

One of the major outcomes of this international meeting of over 1200 people from some 40 countries was the need for all of us to see our work and interests as others see them. Such a perspective is often challenging. From this experience comes the title of this book, **Face to Face with Giftedness.** There is a need to pause, take stock, hear our critics, and assess new and future directions. We have attempted to do this with regard to the social context and meaning of giftedness and of some of its measures, to situations in which giftedness is unfulfilled, to cultural variation in the meaning of giftedness within and among countries, and to refinement in thinking about curriculum for the gifted. These five topics comprise the sections of this book, and each includes a brief introduction.

Some of the topics which have previously been rarely considered in the literature on giftedness include Canadian and American native peoples, the People's Republic of China, Africa, parental interaction with infants, the computer as an extension of intellectual ability, secondary education, and delinquency. In addition to directing attention to these topics, the conference organizers also sought keynote and invited speakers who had not yet addressed a major conference on giftedness, but were well known for their other contributions which were most relevant to the topic.

We hope that this selection will enable readers who attended to recall the depth and scope of exchange, and for all to share the theoretical and practical content of the conference.

The Editors
Montreal, April 1983

ACKNOWLEDGMENTS

The production of this volume and its French edition was made possible by the financial support of the Government of Canada (Secretary of State) whose financial support for the conference included provision for the publication of proceedings, and a further grant by McGill University from a fund provided by the Government of Quebec (FCAC Program) for the dissemination of the results of research.

The efforts of several people must also be acknowledged. Martha Kovacs, Vivian Rabinovitch and Arlene Doheny typed the manuscript onto the McGill University System for Interactive Computing from which it was directly prepared for printing, using a Xerox Diablo terminal and Canadian Roman print wheel at the Centre for Teaching and Learning Services. Support staff at the Centre, Anne Sage, Marie LaRicca, and Jayne Millett assisted frequently in helping to organize the computer input, and were especially tolerant as we monopolized their printing terminal for two weeks. We are grateful to Mary Lou Arnold, for reading the entire manuscript several times at various stages of production. Shawn Carey, Arlene Dover, Meeta Goel, Marcella Grenier, Linda Ross, and Martha Wright also helped ensure that the variety of types of presentations, spelling conventions, and referencing styles have been given some uniformity without detracting from the personal styles of the contributors. We are also grateful to the Lakeshore School Board, in particular to Louise FitzGerald, for assistance in translating articles from French to English, and to the McGill University Translation Service for their participation. Paste-up was done by Patrice Atwell. Finally, we thank Max Stiebel, graphic artist at the Instructional Communications Centre, McGill University, for the cover design.

NOTE

Editing a book that gathers contributions from persons scattered over five continents requires an enormous amount of work. We never imagined how much until we plunged into this endeavor.

As our work unfolded, Bruce M. Shore assumed not only the leadership of the group, but also a major role in the numerous tasks related to this edition. Bruce initiated the contacts with authors, technical staff, the World Council, printers and publishers, to name a few. Were it not for his perseverance, this book might not have been born, at least not on schedule.

As co-editors, we are aware of the crucial role that he has played in developing this text. We hereby acknowledge his involvement in the total project. For all of us who will benefit from the reading of **Face to Face with Giftedness,** we give special thanks to Bruce who has been the skipper of the ship, acting with competence, humor and democracy until our successful landing.

Françoys Gagné
Serge Larivée
Ronald H. Tali
Richard E. Tremblay

CONTENTS

Preface   v

Acknowledgments   vii

Note   viii

PART 1: SOCIAL CONTEXTS   1

1. **Burton L. White,** The Origins of Competence   3

2. **Martin Dishart,** Psychosocial Facilitators, Enhancers, and Inhibitors of Gifted Children   27

3. **Dewey Gene Cornell,** The Family's View of the Gifted Child   39

4. **Dorothy Coleman,** The Identification and Understanding of Very Young Gifted Children   51

5. **David Willings,** The Gifted at Work   56

PART 2: THE MEANING OF GIFTEDNESS   75

6. **Albert Jacquard,** Highly Gifted, or People?   77

7. **Joan Freeman,** The IQ as a Measure of Intellectual Giftedness   91

8. **Alan Kramer,** The Gifted Child as Freak; Giftedness as Handicap   97

9. **Klaus K. Urban,** A Comparison of Attitudes toward the education of "Normal," Handicapped and Gifted Children   111

10. **Glenn F. Cartwright,** Symbionic Minds for the Gifted   130

11. **Earl C. Joseph,** Expert Systems and People Amplifiers   138

PART 3: GIFTEDNESS DEFLECTED   155

12. **Alyce Faye Eichelberger & Tom Greener,** A View of the Gifted Child in a London Day School for the Maladjusted   157

13. **Margaret Parker,** Bright Kids in Trouble with the Law   179

14. **Margot Lagesen King,** Environmental Availability, Giftedness, and Delinquency Proneness   186

15. **Arthur Robinson,** Personality Growth: Emotional and Intellectual Understanding   193

16. **Richard E. Tremblay,** Bright Juvenile Delinquents in Residential Treatment: Are they Different?   199

PART 4: CULTURAL PERSPECTIVES   211

17. **Alanis Obomsawin,** Children of the Earth   213

18. **Karlene George,** Native American Indian: Perception of Gifted Characteristics   220

19. **Nava Butler-Por,** Giftedness Across Cultures   250

20. **Susan R. Butler,** The Talented Child in the People's Republic of China   271

21. **John Dunstan,** Attitudes to Provision for Gifted Children: The Case of the USSR   290

22. **Henry Olajide Oluyele Coker,** The Gifted in a Developing Society: The Nigeria Case   328

23. **Ahmed Yussufu,** Giftedness in Context   346

24. **Danica Adjemovitch,** Reaching the Unreached: A View from the UNICEF Perspective   358

PART 5:   CURRICULAR CONSIDERATIONS   369

25. **Bette Stephenson,** Legislative Leadership and the Education of the Gifted   371

26. **A. Harry Passow,** The Four Curricula of the Gifted and Talented: Toward a Total Learning Environment   379

27. **Pierrette Massé & Françoys Gagné,** Observations on Enrichment and Acceleration   395

28. **D. T. E. Marjoram,** The Secondary School Curriculum and the Gifted Child   414

29. **H. Gilbert Nicol,** Restoring a Challenge to Secondary Education   426

30. **Edward de Bono & Norah Maier,** Teaching Thinking to the Gifted   438

31. **Harold Don Allen,** Extracurricular Mathematics: Incentive for the Talented   448

32. **Véronique Rossillon & Marguerite Castillon du Perron,** A French Approach to Education for Gifted Children   460

Contributors   483

Editors   487

The World Council for Gifted and Talented Children 488

PART 1

SOCIAL CONTEXTS

These five chapters explore relationships among children, parents and community. The critical role of parents unites the first four, while the fifth looks at the gifted as adults themselves. Burton White, author of books on the raising of young children, shares his decades of experience in the development of childhood competence. Parents are a child's first teachers, and their contribution between the seventh month and third year is critical to a child's intellectual and social development. Martin Dishart, psychotherapist, family counselor, educator, focuses on the gifted child's need for other gifted children, partly for relief from the inadequacies of relationships which exist without choice at home and school. Clinical psychologist Dewey Cornell explores the dangers of parents reifying labels such as "gifted." In an original piece of research, Cornell describes how parents understand the term "gifted" when they are told it applies to their child, and highlights the discrepancies within the family, especially the impact on a sibling not recognized as gifted. Dorothy Coleman, active in the United Kingdom's National Association for Gifted Children describes how her association has attempted to directly assist parents in understanding and coping with the giftedness of any of their children. In reading her article, it is important for professionals to remember that she is describing parents helping parents. Finally, David Willings, a professor of management and organizational talent in adults has brought him actively into the study of the development of giftedness in general, especially creativity. On completing his paper one cannot fail to ask, what happened to all the beautiful competence we were developing in the first chapter?

We urge the reader not to be pessimistic or to wrongly generalize from this selection of papers.

1

Some, indeed many, gifted children mature marvelously and lead happy and productive lives. These papers point out vividly, however, that a special obstacle course exists for gifted children. Our task is not to lament it, but to overcome it, and this may require a diversity of approaches: the traditional emphases of pedagogy and developmental child psychology are only a part of the solution. The resolution of some of the problems will, as several of these chapters illustrate, be to the benefit of others as well: siblings, parents, employers, and classmates, to suggest a few. Other perspectives as are elaborated in the four other sections of this volume.

THE ORIGINS OF COMPETENCE

Burton L. White

In thinking about this particular conference and its sponsoring organization, it seemed to me that some people might equate "competence" with "gifted," but other people might not. So I began to explore the issue, and ask the question, "Are all competent children gifted?" and the mirror question, "Are all gifted children competent?" This led me to one of my favorite resources, Webster's dictionary. Webster has this to say: **"gifted:** having a natural ability or aptitude, or talented"; **"talent:** any natural ability or power, natural endowment, or a special superior ability in art, mechanics, learning, etc."; **"gift:** suggests of a special ability that is bestowed upon one as by nature, and not acquired through effort." Then I turned to a psychological dictionary and found the following definitions: "possessing one or more special talents or abilities of a high order, for example, in music, painting, or math"; "possessing a very high degree of brightness, sometimes stated as an IQ of 140 or above." I don't know whether any of that illuminates anything for any of you, but for me it helps clarify things a little bit. It seems to me that Webster's definition places a fair amount of emphasis on genes, on what you bring into the world, and tends to imply that the special talent that is involved will surface no matter what. It also seems to me that the psychological dictionary definition tends to avoid confrontation with the classical nature-nurture controversy, and indeed only talks about possession at some stage in life of a special ability. It says nothing to the issue of how it got there. Now, my role, therefore, may be somewhat next door to what some of you were expecting to concentrate on at this conference, although "next door" is not too far away and is probably appropriate. I would raise the question at this early point that perhaps what is required for the development of competence may not be compatible with what is required for the development of the gifted or the very talented, and I would like that to be thought about a little bit as we go along.

I would like to give you a little background for my declarations. (I think anybody who speaks to a group about an important topic has an obligation to set up the context.) Since I was a teenager, I have been interested in well developed, decent people. This is not merely an intellectual interest; it just seems to me that making the most out of my life seemed to get me involved with this question of why life seemed richer when I interacted with fully developed and lovely people than with other kinds of people. That hooked me on a deeply personal level in my late teens. A brief stint in the army led me from a career in mechanical engineering (which wasn't really getting anywhere anyway) to the field of psychology, and soon to the work of Abraham Maslow. Maslow, as many of you must know, was very much interested in human potential and in the self-actualization of people. It seems to me that the concept of human potential is one thing that allows us to bridge whatever gap might exist between the concepts of competence and the concepts of giftedness and talent. It surely relates to both, and what most of us here would regret, and do regret repeatedly, is the degree to which human potential simply is not realized.

This exposure to Abraham Maslow's work led me to begin a research career with children between birth and six months of age exclusively, focusing on the role of early experience in the surfacing of the first human abilities. That work lasted from 1958 to 1967-68. In approximately 1965, the United States in particular (and many other parts of the world in general) began a really unprecedented assault on the question of why some children get through the first six years of life well prepared to enter formal education, while many others are already headed to failure and gross underachievement. The key program in the United States was the Head Start Program, but the Head Start Program which focussed on children from poor families who were between three and five years of age was only one of many types of programs that began, for the first time (certainly in psychological research), to look seriously at the putting together of a human being in the preschool years. Because of circumstances, I was offered by the School of Education at Harvard basically a blank cheque to study the first six years of life. This was absolutely irresistable, although I felt that from a scientific standpoint it was absolutely hopeless . . . far too complicated. But it was still irresistable. At the time, I had to make a judgment. The trend of the day in early childhood educational research and child development research in the preschool years was to tackle directly the question of underachievement of children from poor families and minority groups. I felt that of all places, Harvard was one of the few that could go beyond that subsection of the large question of human potential to ask the question "How does one help any human being who enters the world make the most of whatever potential he brings into that world?" So I convinced the powers at the time to let us study that question, which in many ways is a very different one from the question of avoiding failure.

So we began to study the first six years of life with that in mind. We learned fairly soon that the child who looked outstanding at six (the child who coped with the day long tasks of living better than 95% of the other children) had a pattern of special abilities which, under the best of circumstances, we found present in the three year old as well as the six year old. Indeed it was our judgment (and it was not a precise, thoroughly validated one, but a concensually agreed upon one) that development between three and six, in the case of a child who got off to a wonderful first three years, was more a case of modification of a precious complex collection of abilities than it involved the emergence of a collection of other abilities. Right or wrong, this particular judgment led us to concentrate on the first three years of life. This work, in the first five or six years of the Harvard Preschool Project, also led to the following kinds of conclusions:

1. Very few people out of all of us ever make the most of their innate potential. There is tremendous waste of human potential, day in and day out.

2. Experiences play a very significant role in the realization of innate potential. They are no after-thoughts of minor significance.

3. The maximum development of abilities is much more likely during the first seven months of life than from then on.

4. Poor levels of achievement sometimes begin within the first seven months, but are much more often first noticeable shortly after the first birthday. Our judgment is that children begin to strike their colors routinely between their first and third birthdays, whether they are falling back, or whether they are leaping forward, in a substantial way. With all due credit to the concept of "the late bloomer," this is still a generalization that I would advance to you.

Sources of Evidence about the Importance of Early Development

There are three sources of evidence that I would like to address in relation to these particular judgments. First of all, wide scale worldwide testing of the development of abilities in the first years of life, especially those of language and intelligence, consists of monitoring a wide array of abilities, especially emphasizing mastery over the body (which is quite an achievement in the first year of life) and primitive social skills (primitive problem solving skills). I am referring to the kinds of testing done on the broad gauge tests like the Gesell, the Bula, the Cattell, the Denver, the Bayley - general tests of human achievement whose principal and proper application is for crude screening of growth normality and nothing more. What we have seen over and over again is that there are two groups of human beings that can be widely separated out. One group is the child who either starts life in terrible difficulty with pathology of a substantial kind (physical pathology) or who quickly gets there during the first year of life. These are children who, by the end of the first year, are repeatedly testing out at below 85 on general tests with an average level of 100. Especially in the work of people like Noblock and Passimanick, it has been seen that for such children, these test scores are indeed predictive. A child who repeatedly scores more than a standard deviation below the mean in the first year does indeed generally look weak in the second year and beyond.

The general understanding within child development research is that infancy tests are not predictive. It is not true for the group I have just mentioned. But it is true for the others, and this is so hard for practitioners and parents to accept. A child with a Bayley Mental Index score of 135 at the first birthday is no more likely to be above average at three on a Stanford-Binet (or some other language or intelligence test) than a child with a score of 95 at the first birthday. So for the vast majority, indeed for 85 to 90% of all children, testing in the first year of life does not tell you where you are going. It is only for the children who are in very substantial difficulty during that period of time. As for testing beyond the first year of life, predictability of later intellectual and linguistic skills (the area in which we have done our best work) begins to become functional late in the second year of life, complicated by the fact that children get very "testy" during the second half of the second year and make very poor subjects. If your read a report that says "thirty-five two year olds scored 'x' and thus . . . " and it doesn't have an asterisk that says "we don't trust our data," be suspicious. At any rate, by the age of two, scores on the Bayley Mental Index will correlate quite nicely with scores on the McCarthy, the Binet, and the WISC over the next three, four, or five years. That prediction never reaches a very high level. It rarely goes beyond +.4, or +.45, depending upon the population and so forth, even in years to come. But it starts to be useful, especially for special groups of children and for the extreme children, late in the second year; by the third year it is quite stable.

The second source of evidence is educational programming experiences. It has been found over and over again, at least in the United States, that the status of a child at six with respect to school readiness is indeed predictive of where that child is going to go at the very least in the next few years of schooling and, indeed, probably further on. The child who comes at six years of age to a formal curriculum raring to go, enthusiastic about learning, talented in language and intelligence, and not a social cripple, is a child whose learning rate is such that each year she stays in school, the gap between her and the average will get larger. The other side of the coin also had long been found to be true. The child who looks unprepared at six, who has the skills of a four to five year old, and has a lower learning rate, tends to fall further behind. This is what is meant by the concept of "a widening of the gap." Since 1968 or so, a phenomenal amount of money and effort in the United States has been devoted to doing something about that relatively sad state of affairs. We have had special enrichment programs for underachieving six, seven, and eight year olds, and their track record is nothing to write home about. The only people that think they are effective are those that are directing such programs, and even most of them are not really big fans of them. So, sad to say, special remedial education for children between six and ten has not had marked success. It seems as if the patterns that are established in the first years are not that easily moved around. Exactly why we don't know. Since 1965, similar efforts have also been addressed to the three to six year old range, and that is what the bulk of the Head Start activity has been focussed on. We have learned that many of the children who do very poorly when they are ten years old are not only identifiable at the sixth year, but that they are identifiable at the third year; a gap has already developed. We have also found that it is extraordinarily difficult to do an awful lot about such problems from the third birthday on. There has been newspaper publicity about the occasional short-term success and there has been a propaganda campaign by the United States Government to suggest that long-term gains from these early programs were substantial. However, overall, the track record is really quite disappointing.

Third, we hit studies stimulated in the mid 1940s by a psychiatric researcher named Renee Spitz on the question of the vulnerability of children in the first years of life when the primary affectional bond between parent and child either did not get a chance to grow, or was interrupted for varying periods of time. They went under the general label of "maternal deprivation studies" and generally their findings were quite interesting, even though much of the quality of the research left much to be desired. They have left us with several interesting findings, notably, that from six months on, an interruption in that basic bond of three months or longer seems to lead to profound, lasting damage. Gaps of less than three months do not seem to cause anywhere near the problem; a week or two doesn't amount to anything, thereby relieving lots of anxious parents and giving them a chance to take a vacation. The finding I want to point to here is that if a child is five and a half months old and has spent those five and a half months in a situation where there wasn't any typical, extraordinarily loving, one-to-one relationship (even in an institution), and was then placed into a good, solid milieu with a good deal of personal attention, no lasting harm was ever detected. Now, it could be that there is some harm; given our only partially effective ways of assessing development, it is quite possible that there are some lasting deficits that people could find. But on the whole, there was a marked difference between the effects of what happened to interrupt the experiences (and the bond in particular) after the six month period (between six months and three years) as compared to the impact of this unusual experience picture in the first six months of life. Those who wish to talk about the vital importance and risk involved in unusual experiences in the first weeks of life have to incorporate such general findings on thousands of children into their picture. My judgment on it is a little different from some. I think that getting through the first six or seven months of age (getting through it well) has been basically worked through in the process of evolution; it is a relatively easier job to make the most of your learning in the first six or seven months than it is in the period that follows the first half year of life.

The fourth source of information comes from basic research on human developmental processes, especially language and intelligence. First of all, I would like to point out something from psychological studies of child development and some closely related ones. Detailed studies of the process of development in the normal or, for that matter, any human being between birth and three are only very recent, with the conspicuous exception of the work of Piaget, among others. It really intrigues me. I happen to be a fan of Piaget's (in fact, a devout admirer of Piaget). I think he stands alone. If Piaget had not been interested in the origins of intelligence, or if he didn't have three children, or if he had never lived, where would the field of the development of intelligence be? Maybe I am provincial, but where I come from, nobody else has really done anything resembling the kind of work he has done in explaining the origins of object permanence, causality, thinking ability, or memory. At any rate, it is only since 1965, in the United States at least, that there has really been a serious look at the details of development in the first three years of life. It sounds crazy, but I think I can back that up if anyone wants to talk about it. There has been an awful lot of interest, an awful lot of talk; but serious scientific study has been remarkably missing. The best sources of information (the most reliable and useful ones) that young parents had until 1965 were Dr.Spock and Gesell. And the reason they had some information is because they were obliged to. They were in medicine and had the responsibility of (a) seeing to it that a child was developing normally, and (b) calming the anxieties of young parents (which took up much more of their time). A psychologist, and in fact most people teaching child development, wouldn't have recognized a normal two year old if they tripped over her. Not only were detailed studies of the first three years very, very rare, but detailed longitudinal studies, where you saw the same child over a period of many months, were even more unusual. We have had a host of hugely expensive longitudinal studies (including Terman's studies of the gifted) starting off in the 20's and 30's in the United States, and they left a bad taste in the mouth. Virtually all of them cost a fortune and the field wasn't judged to be terribly commensurate; so they fell out of favor. Nevertheless, most of us in the field feel that you cannot properly study the evolution (the ontogenesis) of the human being - any creature so complicated and changing - without doing repeated studies on the same subject over a long period of time. It just has not been done; there is very little of it. In the case of gifted children you are generally going to find that it is a relative who is writing about one child more often than anything else (at least in the past). In addition, detailed longitudinal studies of children in the first three years of life who were developing well were also very, very scarce. It is interesting that we have failed to take advantage of nature's successes, because out of any thousand children being born any day of the week, some fraction of them will get off to a marvellous start in life. You don't have to dream up the answers to those questions. We're not obliged to do that, but we can at least begin by looking at some of these successes. And indeed that is what we have tried to do.

ORIGINS OF COMPETENCE

The Harvard Project

From 1965 to 1978, with about fifteen to twenty people working with me, we studied a fair number of children developing very well. I won't say it was among the thousands; it was among the hundreds. The first chore we assigned ourselves was the definition of a beautifully developed six year old. We couldn't find such a definition in the child development literature. We found lots of studies of children in trouble, a good number of studies that came ultimately from Freud's ideas about infantile sexuality. But we couldn't find much work on a beautifully functioning six-year-old child. There was one study that Lois Murphy had done at Sarah Lawrence College which was a delightful exception. Collin was her subject, a boy they studied from two and a half to five and a half years of his life, primarily while he was at nursery school, never in the home (which is another exception and typical of the field). Collin was interesting. He wasn't a genius. He was a child whose IQ was about 140, but he was grossly free from any difficulties or abnormalities. His favorite activity was engaging in role play, coming in each day with some new identity and challenging the teachers to figure out who he was. His nickname for himself was Bob Important, which I really think is a telling nickname.

The way in which we did our own work was not to invite children by the hundreds into the laboratory of the University. All seventeen or eighteen of us went out, one at a time, to nursery schools, kindergartens, day care centers, and homes, stood quietly ten feet or so away, and carefully recorded and observed what these children were doing as they went about their ordinary business. We did extensive field observations to get a feel for that one child in about twenty-five to thirty whom everybody agreed coped with life better than the average child. We noticed, through our approach to the problem of what a nicely developed six year old was, the following considerations. We found that in the area of sensory skills, vision and hearing, there were no appreciable or marked differences between these outstanding children and most others. We found no substantial differences in perceptual-motor abilities, like tossing balls back and forth or hopping on one foot. We found no appreciable differences in general control over their bodies, nor even in their humor or their likeability. So these outstanding children were not totally different from their peers. But we felt that they were different to a substantial degree in the following areas.

First of all, their whole approach to social interchanges was very special, not totally different from others, but markedly well developed. They were unusually able to get and hold the attention of adults in socially acceptable ways. They had a variety of mechanisms of doing that and chose the appropriate ones for the situation. They were very good at using adults as resources after first determining they could not do something for themselves. There were other children who were not used to using adults as resources to complete tasks; there were others who tended to overuse them. By the way, we have been able to pinpoint when this talent first surfaces in the human life. It is in the behavior of the ten-month-old or so child, give or take only about a month under ordinary circumstances. As he crawls about, and may be running low on a cookie or a cracker, he may from time to time go "uh,uh" while gesturing toward the adult who is nearby. By this he means to say "Pardon me, there, I seem to be running low on this substance, and I understand you can help me . . ." and so forth.

Parents enjoy their children more when they have a sense of what is coming and can watch for it. It is very, very exciting. These children were very comfortable and sure of themselves, and they were able to express affection or mild annoyance to adults quite comfortably. They could say "I like you" and give somebody a hug or they could say "Would you leave me alone . . . you're bothering me now . . . go away." These children were very proud of their achievements and spontaneously remarked about it. In one of the films that we have done, a three year old

13

says "I'm doing a good job." This is a characteristic of the capable young child. They engaged in role play much more than the average child, make-believe behavior, pretend behaviors, and the roles that they adopted generally were roles pointing to the future rather than to the past. Some children at six could lead other five and six year olds, but were uncomfortable when asked to follow. Others can follow, but are uncomfortable when asked to lead. These outstanding children can do both.

Competition, at least in eastern Massachusetts, another distinguishing characteristic of the nicely developed six year old, is the capacity and the desire to compete. "I can do better than anybody else." (We have found, by the way, in subsequent work that certain cultural groups do not like this characteristic in their children.) Also, there is the ability to express affection and mild annoyance to adults. Altogether this collection of social abilities characterizes a child who is comfortable with adults, who doesn't treat them primarily as fear objects or purveyors of authority, who treats them almost like peers and has the expectation that they are anxious to help, that they are interested in what they are doing, and that they are more capable than themselves. Yet it doesn't bother them.

In the realm of nonsocial abilities, the language abilities of these children obviously were advanced. In intellectual areas, we noticed that they had an unusually well developed capacity to sense discrepancies or differences. These ranged from simple differences in appearance (like a new haircut on another child) to perceptions of differences in temporally organized sequences (such as noticing when somebody went out of turn) and also to errors in logic (on the part of teachers, for example). They spot those things better than others. They live in a longer slice of time than other children. They anticipate consequences that might be coming in the future. They are, of course, very capable of dealing with abstractions as compared to the average. They are capable of taking the perspective of another. In Piaget's system, seven to eight-year-old children become less egocentric in their thinking style. They start, for the first time, to want very much to make themselves understood to somebody else, and they get into rehearsing what they are going to say habitually in an attempt to make themselves understood. This is absent in the typical two and three-year-old child; it is rather well developed in the outstanding six year old. They were characteristically capable of making interesting associations. I avoid the concept of creativity because I have never figured out how to define it. But I can tell you that these children made very interesting associations, many of which appeared to be original. They have the capacity to plan and carry out complicated activities, the capacity to use resources effectively, and an interesting perceptual style: the ability to maintain focus on what they were doing up close and, at the same time, keep track of what was going on in a busy room. They could cope with more information per unit of time and still know what was going on. Whereas most children at around six still have occasional difficulties with distractability, these children can focus their attention well in spite of a busy scene. This particular collection of behavioral characteristics is one that experienced teachers of three to six year olds recognize and generally endorse. We found, as I said earlier, that three year olds developing well exhibited all of these characteristics (maybe not in this polished a form, but that was their style of behavior).

We then went on, in our research, to examine the day-to-day lives of one to three-year-old children in the hopes that we would watch this process in action. We were looking for the kinds of experiences regularly associated with the emergence of such style. And we did this by visiting homes of children specifically identified to be children who were either likely to be outstanding at three, in the positive sense, or to fall back substantially. This likelihood was determined by looking at the performance of the slightly older child, or the older child in the home. We went to homes for up to fifty-two visits over a two year span. I would point out that if you're interested in the process of education, you cannot make a very small investment do it properly; and you cannot avoid going to where the child lives. This is one of the limitations of university-based research. It is also one of the limitations of pediatrically based research. The process is an ongoing affair - you cannot study child rearing or very early education if you do not become thoroughly familiar with where the child is growing up. Even in this day and age, with our growth of substitute care, most children still grow up in their own homes. Although it is an awkward place to do research, it is mandatory to do so if you are going to really be familiar with this particular phenomenon. Very few people have ever done it, and it is not going to happen very frequently in the near future as far as I can tell.

We then went on to experimental work with average families trying to test hypotheses about effective child-rearing practices and the development of competence. With respect to these first three years we came to the judgment that a distinction had to be made between the first seven months and the balance of the period. The human abilities acquired in the first seven months are primarily the following.

Partial body control: the newborn is basically inept with respect to his body, but the seven month old has head control, can turn over (stomach to back and so forth), can reach accurately for nearby objects to bring them close for exploration, and has a little arm and leg strength. Still, she ordinarily cannot usually get up to a sitting posture on her own, nor can she walk or climb, or any of those things. She does, however, have partial body control, especially including reaching. In terms of sensory adequacy, as far as we can tell, the normal newborn (in fact, even the best of them) is neither blind nor deaf, but does not have precise and mature visual or hearing abilities. The six month old, for all practical purposes, is indeed a mature creature with respect to seeing and hearing. The visual process is ninety percent complete by three and a half to four months; for hearing, it would appear to be comparable. The first-problem solving skills, according to the work of Piaget are likely to have been acquired. They have nothing to do with thinking ability (the manipulation of ideas). It is the primitive ability to move object or obstacle A to the side in order to deliberately reach for and procure object B. That is the first intentional behavior of consequence, and it is the limit of the problem solving skills of a seven-month-old child.

The first social skill: gaining attention through one means only - making noise. Of course, no meaningful language of any consequence exists. There are debates among our linguistic researchers as to when language learning starts. I take the kind of simple minded view that if a child can understand the meaning in a single word, that is language. If it is something simpler than that, I consider it prelinguistic; however, that is a matter for debate.

What we and others seem to have been finding is that the average expectable environment, the wide range of styles of experience of children under seven months of age, ordinarily contains all that is needed for the achievement of all of those abilities. Given the wide range in the way untutored people (as most parents are) structure the experiences of their babies, most children get through these first achievements quite nicely.

There is, however, reasonably good evidence that the rate of achievement of abilities in the first seven months of life is pliable. Children could, for example, learn to use the hand as a reaching tool by a little over three months of age rather than five, and this could in the future lead children to other cumulative achievements that might encourage higher levels of skill very early on; but a serious attack on that question has not been pursued.

What kind of a being are we dealing with at seven months of age? Well, first of all we are dealing with a being whose torso is in the vertical much more than that of a newborn. This is a primitive notion; the reality is that the child, for the first three and a half months of life, is a horizontal creature unless being toted around all the time. Even then they are not comfortable about being in the vertical orientation. Your seven month old is a vertical creature who can see and hear quite well, and who has, more than any other animal in the world, a tremendous interest in what is out there, a tremendous curiosity and urge to learn and explore, but no locomobility. He cannot get there on his own. I would guess (and nobody really knows) that as a result most seven month olds are somewhat frustrated. And some confirmation of that concept comes in what happens when a child learns to crawl, or is given a walker to move with. You don't have to induce them to go out and explore the world; they take off. The child is generally a friendly creature at that stage of life. The child is also socially an uncomplicated creature, and not a manipulator. The child is adventurous and persistent. That is the seven-month-old student.

What will she acquire by the third birthday? Complete body control, complete sensori-motor intelligence, and higher mental abilities, or thinking, toward the end of the second year; a full array of social skills that I have listed for you, and apparently something like three quarters of all the language she'll ever use in ordinary conversation for the rest of her life, including a receptive vocabulary of about a thousand words, (this is a highly flexible outcome) as well as all the primary grammatical elements in her own native language. But I believe there is good reason to think that higher mental abilities - language, social skills, and intrinsic interest in learning - are all "at risk" and really receive the input that would allow maximum fulfillment of potential during this particular time of life. Unlike the abilities acquired in the first seven months of life, I believe these precious abilities that distinguish us from other animals - our special capacities in thinking, in language, in social skills, and in lifelong intrinsic interest in learning - undergo critical development in the seven to thirty-six month period and are remarkably sensitive to environmental differences. Given the fact that we do not prepare the structures of the world of these children for this task, and given the luck of the draw, I do not think that more than one in ten of our children, conservatively speaking, get the kind of learning opportunities in this time span that would allow them to move forward as well as they might. Combine that with what I said earlier about the degree of permanence, or fixity, of patterns of the three-year-old child; given our experience in turning human beings around when they get a bit older, you begin to see why some of us are so committed to getting children off to a good start in the first years of life, rather than to waiting around until they get to be six or seven.

Input Favorable to the Development of Competence

What is the kind of input that would help children really move ahead, fulfilling much of their opportunity for growth more during this time period? What are the requirements for, and the impediments to, the realization of full potential during this period of time? This is necessarily a crude picture I must sketch. First, they need physical normality and good health. There are common impediments, aside from obvious pathology like Downs Syndrome or total deafness at birth, etc. Most conspicuously, I would like to point to one: undetected mild to moderate hearing losses. In the last fifteen years or so, it has become increasingly clear that one really amazingly simple problem that gets in the way of good development of children in great numbers is the fact that small and slightly larger hearing losses are reasonably common. They are not necessarily permanent; they are sometimes intermittent during the first three years of life. Yet, for an interesting set of reasons, they are not detected very often until the child is six or seven years of age. The deaf child is spotted at birth, because when there is a loud noise everybody jumps except the baby. Almost any medical practitioner or parent will spot the child with a profound loss. But the mild to moderate loss, the ten to fifty unit loss, is much more common statistically at birth (though still small) and much more likely to develop in the course of infancy because of smaller respiratory passages and the proneness to infection of the young child. Runny noses and babies are synonymous. Autitis medium (infections of the inner ear and associated fluid) is an extraordinarily common affair. Now what happens when that occurs? Very commonly, even the naive parent will notice that the child does not behave quite right, doesn't respond quite right at six, eight, or nine months. They will then often bring this up to a medical person and say something to the effect that they are worried about the child: "Perhaps the child doesn't hear quite well." Medical people more often than not when given that sort of complaint, will say: "Don't worry about it . . . Not to worry, she'll grow out of it". This is heard over and over again. Now what we have learned from close inspection is that even naive parents are generally correct when they sense these small hearing losses. We also know how to cope with them. We have ways of screening in the first five months of life, ways of correcting these problems; the difference in human learning is phenomenal. The child who does not hear terribly well at six or seven months of life, as they are about to enter major language learning shows less interest in language. If you do not acquire language optimally within the first three years of life, I do not believe you can acquire higher mental abilities optimally. If you do not acquire both optimally in the first three years, you will be a different kind of social animal, because we tame, civilize and socialize our children to relations with other people through speech in that period of life - perhaps more than in any other period. We do not grunt and groan at them; we explain things. This is why the hearing lossed six year old is very commonly a socially awkward creature as well. So again, I am always playing with the two sides of the coin: the things that lead to underdevelopment and failure, and the things that are implied about the best possible development in a young human.

Second, children need sufficient opportunity to practice mastery of body skills. Motor control is not at risk with most children in the first years of life, but it plays an enormously important role in the overall economy of the development of the best talents in the very young child. Common impediments to the fullest development of body skills, and fullest enjoyment of that development, is the prevention of practice by anxious parents and the objective danger of most homes. The learning environment of most homes is suited for adults, not to newly crawling, naive babies, and there is no concerted effort on the part of society (and the educational establishment in particular) to conceive of the learning environment of the home in that way. The fact is, we have more broken bones and fractures in early childhood in the ten to twenty month period than at any other time, and we also have more accidental poisonings. So if a parent is not concerned about safety at that point, they are oblivious . . . there is something wrong with them. They should be concerned. But if, on the other hand, they are coached and taught, they can redesign the home and make it a safe and interesting place. They can put a gate on the third step rather than at the bottom or the top, and find children practising. In the first years, children characteristically move very rapidly through motor development and it means a great deal to them. Watch them practice when they are starting to climb; they do it over and over again until they get it right. They get a tremendous thrill out of it, and nothing reinforces that thrill and achievement more than somebody standing seven feet away who is crazy about that child. For the parents and grandparents (six people only), that achievement of the child is the most exciting thing that happened that month. If you are not there, you do not give it. We believe that pride in achievement has its roots in the normal motor achievements (from pulling to sitting to walking) in the seven to eleven month age range for most children. These are the origins of reality-based pride in achievement. Every normal child has the capacity to go through that learning experience.

Third, they require sufficient and appropriate linguistic input. Common impediments, aside from undetected hearing losses, are lack of awareness of language learning and the teaching process by parents. Some of our most delightful parents were poor language teachers because they did not speak to the child until the child spoke, and children who are bright may not do any speaking until they are a year and a half to two years old. They are capable of learning enormous amounts of language from six to eight months on, but the normal adult does not ordinarily talk to creatures who do not answer. So a natural tendency interferes with the best possible language learning; chatter boxes make better language teachers. What we have found is that there is a kind of **style** of child rearing that is most conducive to topping the scale at three with language learning: The home is made as safe as possible for the newly crawling seven or eight month old. The child is turned loose and encouraged to explore this marvellous new world, even if it is a poor home. (You don't need money . . . everything is new to the baby.)

The child then gets into three kinds of situations that cause the child to come towards an adult. One is that something hurts them (they pinch a finger or fall down) and they want to be comforted. Second, they are frustrated by something (maybe a door will not come unstuck, or two toys will not come unstuck). Third, they find something very, very exciting (such as an old ashtray) and they want to share it with somebody. Under those circumstances, in the homes of children leaping forward in development, they turn to the adult and ask for attention. It is very easy at that point to read the mind of the baby; they are not complex creatures. So, you have a motivated student and you know the subject. This is a far more pregnant situation than taking Dolman Delecato reading materials and chasing the eleven month old baby around the room.

Next they need clear consistent guidelines for relating to other people. Typical impediments are the lack of awareness of the details of social development, and fear, on the part of adults, of losing some or all of the baby's love and therefore a reluctance to control, to set limits, to say NO. It is very hard to "turn off" a baby in your own home. They absolutely must create a very solid attachment to some older person; it is built into us as creatures. Even if you beat them once in a while (though I am not advocating it) they will still love you; it is essential to their survival. They need time and attention from totally committed adults. In our research, and suggested in the work of others, the single key ingredient for the nurturing of the best possible development, is an awful lot of time during the course of the day with somebody who, between the time you are seven to twenty-four months of age, is crazy about you. (This is probably advisable for us at all ages, but in terms of the very young child, it seems especially appropriate.)

One of the ways in which this does not happen with many children is when children are closely spaced. My guess is that you need a good two and a half years with one person, who is doing a fine job teaching you, in order to get the best possible curriculum. If, at the end of the year, you are in the middle of your development of language and a close attachment to another person, and an interloper arrives who gets attention before you, I just do not think it is as likely that you are going to get the most out of those first years. We have found that two-year-old children actively dislike their one-year-old siblings. It is a little bit like what you would find in the mind of a younger husband whose wife one day announced: "Honey, I have wonderful news for you. Next week I'm going to bring someone home to live with us. He's going to be a little younger than you, a little better looking than you, and naturally, I'm going to pay more attention to him than you because he's new and he needs to be shown around. But you'll get used to it, and I want you to love him . . . he's going to be **OUR** new husband." This is precisely what is expected of a two year old when there is a one year old in the family. Two year olds cannot handle that; the best giveaway to the reality in the home is when you ask a parent how the little girl likes her one-year-old brother and the parent pauses and then says, "She loves her younger brother . . . but there seem to be times when she doesn't seem to know her own strength."

Generally speaking we see three teaching functions of adults. The first is in providing appropriate learning oppportunities (opportunities that are appropriate for the emerging interests and skills of the child). Children change so rapidly in these first years that you know what you are doing in order to do that best. The second is serving as a personal consultant for the child: facilitating learning, encouraging it, sharing enthusiasms, and comforting the baby when the baby doesn't feel so well. The third function (and one which is just as important if you are interested in a child whom you can enjoy in life as well as admire) is maintaining firm control and guidance with respect to social relations - teaching the child that she is extremely special, but no more so than anybody else in the world.

The primary hazards to the proper performance of all of this are, first of all, lack of knowledge. The teachers of these children are not prepared for the job, and the notion that all you need in order to be a mother is to be a solid, normal woman is preposterous. There is nobody in this room that can handle two children under three (with the younger one being over seven months) with ease; it is a hell of a tough job. Men do not know that because they are not around and no matter what they hear from the women it is not enough; just be there for a while and you can see how tough it is.

In addition to lack of knowledge, the stress of the sort I just implied, there is also lack of support. The underlying assumption is respect for the privacy of the family. We leave these things to the nuclear family, and in most, or in many, many homes, it is still the case that the man leaves it to the woman. That is not fair, and it is not promising for the outcome of the process. What is needed is systematic professional guidance of development from birth (universal education programs from birth) with the family treated as the first and probably the most important educational system to which the child will ever be exposed.

To address the issue of competence versus giftedness, I would say that special talent by very young children is an enduring interest and will likely continue to be so. Currently, for example, I am repeatedly exposed to enthusiasm about the Suzuki method in early music training, about math and reading precocities (especially advocated by people like Dolman and the Montessori advocates), and of course, the inevitable precocities in sports (tennis, ice skating, and swimming). I will put a question before you: Is the development of a special talent, often referred to as giftedness, compatible with the full development of all important human attributes? I think that question demands attention. That full array includes motor skills, humor, imagination, intelligence, social skills, and intrinsic interest in learning. When people ask me about the programs to nurture special development, asking whether this is a good one or that is a good one ("Shall I do it or shan't I?"), I cannot deny that the possibility of precocity is there. It has been proven; there is no question about that. Children can acquire talents in the first years of life that they ordinarily do not. Anybody who denies that has not been around lately. However, I suggest that they take care in the choice of the methods they follow, and especially the people they work with, in whose care they put their children, and that they evaluate the costs in regard to the total development of the child before they make any such judgment. Sometimes the costs are just too great.

For the future, I see developing (unfortunately slowly) a much clearer picture of early human development, especially relationships among innate potential and early experiences. Second, I envision much higher levels of human achievement from three months on. Our current norms, I think, will be exceeded systematically year in and year out (and I do not think it is merely a matter of diet). Thirdly, I anticipate better decisions on whether or not to aspire to "giftedness" for a child, and how to help each new child develop into the most fully developed human being that her innate potential will allow.

2

PSYCHOSOCIAL FACILITATORS, ENHANCERS, AND INHIBITORS OF GIFTED CHILDREN

Martin Dishart

As a psychotherapist, as well as an educator and researcher, I will talk about a universal need of all gifted children, a need that exists in proportion to the degree of their giftedness. I will also talk about the extremely gifted and some very important needed research.

There is good reason to believe that the one thing, the one universal thing, that all gifted children need, and to a large extent in proportion to the degree of their giftedness, is other gifted children, chronological peers who have approximately similar degrees of giftedness, preferably in related fields or areas. They need gifted peers for at least four special reasons. They need them (1) for reality verification, (2) for special communicative feedback, (3) for their own self-image, and (4) to learn contexts, relationships, and applications for their capacities as well as for what they know. These needs are so important because how the gifted child learns and develops is ultimately much more important than what he learns or knows. If a child receives response and feedback to only a portion of his realities, that child will find it difficult to know what is reality and what is fantasy and after a while is likely to respond to only that portion of his own realities to which other people respond. Gifted and talented children are different. They must know that what they are able to perceive, think, reason, and create can also be experienced and responded to by other people, especially other children because the response of a child to a child is more congruent, is a better fit, than the response of an adult.

The response of a gifted child to a gifted child - if it is spontaneous and not structured by adults - has a fulfilling quality and is experienced differently from the same verbal or body language from an adult. This is most easily observed with extremely gifted children. Those of you who have been as fortunate as I in being able to work with and personally relate with extremely gifted children and their families, as close friends and in their homes, know what I mean. The adult can relate to the very gifted child within the child's full ranges, and communicate that if the child chooses to reach out further within his range or even try to touch the outer edges of his capacities, there will be positive response and reciprocal feedback; and a very special relationship can be established between the child and the adult.

Yet, when the same relationship can be established with another child there is something extra-special which transcends any child-adult relationship. I do not know all the reasons but think it has to do with the fact that the two children have lived, experienced, and processed information for similar amounts of time and that as a result something different and more congruous is communicated from child to child. The ages do not have to be exactly the same, nor the type or degree of giftedness. But each child does have to be able to either comprehend or account for the other child's ranges and capacities in order to provide the necessary reality verification, communicative feedback, support for each other's self-image, and context of what is being related to. The gifted child is another child, who, unlike an adult, is also small and physically undeveloped. From that perspective he can perceive and reason like the other child and is able to learn and discover more about what really exists.

It is like the opposite of what would happen if the average or bright normal person had to live in a community and go to school with people who were intellectually, academically, socially, and artistically retarded. It is the opposite of what the very gifted child ordinarily experiences in a regular classroom or with older people who know what he knows but have lived longer, are bigger, more experienced and are really very much different. It is important for the child to experience others like himself. If you're eight years old you don't find this in grade ten and if you're twelve years old you don't find it in a university - unless there are others like yourself in the same place.

For mental health reasons also, gifted children need feedback to verify the reality of their perceptions, thoughts, reasoning, and creativity. If others respond to only parts of the gifted child's realities, it can cause more than merely boredom and turn-off. At the very least the child will doubt or withdraw from that part of his reality to which others do not respond. He will treat his gifted capacities as unreal because they are like fantasies to which no one else responds. The child may hide and suppress his giftedness.

He will teach himself that reality is not what is tangible and real to him but is rather what other people respond to. If this is further reinforced by stigma, ridicule, and other peer and even teacher pressures, the giftedness can be functionally lost.

If every day you were in a room with 25 other people who said that an unreachable 15-inch line was the same length as a 12-inch line, not only would you soon agree but after awhile the two lines would look the same to you. How long can anyone maintain his reality in an environment where everyone else's reality is different? And how about a child who has never experienced human feedback responses to his thinking, reasoning and creative realities? No, the result is more than boredom or turn-off. One lets die or kills that part of the self that others deny. It can affect mental health, lead to denial through alcohol or other drugs, or even cause mental illness.

Children generally become less creative when they enter school. Their creativity continues to diminish until it is significantly lower by the age of ten. In some cases the child is never again as creative as just before entering school.

What happens is that the child is taught to conform with right behavior and right answers and eventually concludes that anything that isn't right is wrong. The textbooks, teachers, grades, and report cards all reward right answers and right behavior. There are few or no rewards for good reasoning which yields a different answer. Too many questions are discouraged, not responded to, rejected, or even punished. It can be so very tempting to use one's giftedness to hide one's giftedness.

There is too often a conflict between relating to and saying what is true and relating to and saying what other people want to hear. The very bright child frequently finds that if he uses his energies to seek the intrinsic joys that come with discovering reality, he will be denied the also needed approval and affection that accompany compliance and conformity. So the conflict that we all face between seeking and expressing truth versus seeking approval can be much greater for the gifted child as is the enabling brightness itself.

An eight year old is day-dreaming about Star Wars and formulates a relevant question. He can hardly wait to ask his teacher - unfortunately just as math begins. "If nothing travels faster than the speed of light, will man ever be able to get to stars that are hundreds or thousands of light years away?" How many teachers will consider the quality of the question, how her response will affect the way that other children in the class relate to this child, or even what a golden opportunity to relate the question to math and science? How many teachers will not feel threatened by not knowing the answer? How many have enough personal security to ask for a little time to think about it, thereby modeling behavior that teachers are human and need time to think and that it's okay to not know. The child in question was told to not interrupt with his weird questions. That afternoon he tried to listen to other children stumble over words in the third grade reader even though his reading level exceeded the eighth grade. By the next morning his new name was "Weirdo."

Teacher rejection of creativity, coupled with peer rejection, can be lethal to any amount of talent. Gifted kids are more sensitive to peer pressures than the general population. The same sensitivity of the gifted child also applies to situations where he loses his identity as an individual and becomes "the gifted one" and is expected to always be perfect in everything, never to make mistakes, never to goof. The stress, whether from parents, peers, or teachers can be intolerable and devastating. The gifted child needs to be himself and accepted as an individual.

The emotional tone of a classroom is determined to a large degree by the behavior of the teacher. How a pupil feels, especially about himself, is more important than what he knows. And social approval and acceptance as a worthy person encourages self-acceptance which in turn increases one's ability to accept others. The child who is able to influence other children and even adults to feel at ease, to cooperate, to relate together and work toward common goals shows true gifted "leadership" rather than just who will follow whom.

Gifted students need a time in class to discuss what is important to them, to express and test out ideas, to learn how others think and feel. In all of this the teacher should be a guide, a resource, as well as a fellow human being who also has ideas and feelings and can make mistakes and be afraid.

Now in a school situation where there is only one gifted child in an average class of general students, with no special programs, it is absolutely impossible for any teacher to fully meet either the educational or personal needs of that child. And that is exactly the situation faced by most teachers in most of our school systems, where two out of every three classes of 30 students will have one child with an IQ of 130 or above along with seven children who have IQs of 89 or below. This is unfair as well as impossible for most teachers even though they try their best.

Gifted children should be grouped, "tracked," "streamed" by their gifted capacities for at least the subject areas of their high talents. They do not necessarily have to be in separate schools. This would enable their teachers to receive special in-service training in understanding and meeting the needs of gifted and talented children. Such programs should exist from primary or Kindergarten, where it is most important, through high school graduation.

It has always existed to some extent in the universities except that many gifted children never reach university while other children attend who might be much better off anyplace else.

There should be curricula which are designed for gifted children in the first place. An enrichment supplement does not really correct a curriculum that is weak, dull or redundant for the learner. And such a curriculum pushed faster does not correct its faults even if the learner achieves content acceleration. There are curricula which are simplified enough and slow enough for handicapped learners. We need to develop curricula which are enriched enough and accelerated enough for gifted learners.

So far I have given examples of enhancive, facilitative, and inhibiting factors as they relate to the psychosocial aspects of three special needs of gifted children: reality verification, communicative feedback, and self-image.

There is a fourth need, namely for gifted children to learn contexts, relationships, and applications for their capacities as well as for what they know.

Where there is inadequate research information, as it is in this case, it can be most revealing to observe examples of extreme giftedness; one often observes discrepancies between high capacities and the child's ability to understand either the contexts or applications for those capacities. This is especially true for children with mostly adult contacts such as "only children" or where the child is educated out of school by adult private teachers and tutors.

The most likely reason is that if a child uses his capacities to learn from adults, even gifted adults, without other children present, the adult has had many more years to learn from trial, error, and experience the same information that the much younger child has the capacity to learn all at once. So, for example, an eight year old with a Stanford-Binet IQ well above 200 is discussing some laboratory research that she read about which involves rats. She reads at university level with good comprehension, does high school math, can even read and write in several languages fluently, and understands the research she is discussing, yet cannot answer the question: "Why do you suppose that most research laboratories that use animals use rats?" Not even when asked: "What if they were to use elephants or tigers?" could the child come up with any logical answer such as pertains to cost, size, or ease of handling. There are too many such examples to simply ascribe it to some special deficit of the individual children.

Because they can take in so much new information, gifted children, especially the highly gifted, seem to need not only communicative feedback for their realities, but also communicative feedback from approximate age peers who are also learning to utilize the information with trial, error, and experiential contexts and applications. Of course, the adult teacher should actively facilitate such communications since the mere presence of other gifted children will not act as a panacea for constricted learning. It may be that teachers with special training in what to do, using such approaches as Bloom's taxonomy at the level of "Application" and higher could also facilitate the desired learning for the gifted child without other gifted children. But unless there is a special focus, the adult is most apt to attend to what the child learns and how fast he learns it rather than how the child learns to relate and manipulate the information.

It is not the amount of time during which a gifted child's learning took place but rather what took place during the learning and how it was learned.

An analogy would be someone who spent seven years learning a language, with high grades, in high school and college but can't order a meal or buy something in a department store in the foreign country, then goes to another foreign country whose language he has never studied and after living there for six months can get along very well using the foreign language.

Even a tutor relationship is apt to focus upon subject content, speed of learning, and information retention rather than relationships, contexts and applications for what was learned. One sometimes sees the same thing happen after some parents are told that their child has an extremely high IQ. They feed more and more information to the child, as if the high IQ nutritionally required it, usually from adult tutors, private lessons, and resource books, and sometimes even shunning other children with lesser IQs, with the result that the originally bright child becomes less bright in conceptually understanding and being able to utilize the newly accumulated information even though achievement test scores go up with it. Even reading, for the gifted child whose parents boast about the number of books that their child reads with comprehension each week, can become as addictive and meaningless as endless television watching is for the less bright child; the content is experienced with current comprehension but not internalized with reflection, relatedness, or application.

What the gifted child needs in the classroom and in the home is to learn contexts, relationships, and applications with other children who can reach out with similar ranges and degrees of giftedness. The child also needs adults who can facilitate this by including conceptual learning along with new data.

Gifted children tend to be "loners." They may need each other more than they need the education. They need the feedback, the reality verification, the atmosphere, the security and support of their intellectual and talent peers. They need to be able to work together toward quality, excellence, and extended ranges. They need to play together and fantasize together. They also need adults, especially parents and teachers, who will facilitate and enhance the fulfillment of these needs. Now all this may sound idealistic, but our achievements are not likely to be any better than our goals.

Parents have perhaps the most important roles of all. First and foremost, they should enjoy their bright children. Too often parents are worried by brightness, afraid of doing the "wrong thing." Case histories show that many parents suspect giftedness by age three but fear both the stigma of saying so and the stigma in the culture of anyone being too bright.

Parents have to be reassured supportively that it's okay and good for a child to be talented or gifted. If they can enjoy their child's learning and development, that is the first step for a good learning environment. A safe place for the baby to crawl, explore and do things; fenced rooms instead of a playpen; a mattress near the floor instead of a crib; learning to identify and share vicariously in the small ecstasies that accompany a child's discoveries; rewarding with recognition a child's good thinking even if it leads to wrong answers; understanding and responding to their child's thinking and what things mean to the child and the logic of his logic from his viewpoint.

We also need some good research because we are only at the beginning of learning about giftedness. Our best programs are based mainly on acceleration for the precocious and that was being done hundreds of years ago.

As soon as we consider a child's giftedness as precociousness, we are placing that child in a rather narrow convergent channel of learning and development. We are enriching and accelerating those opportunities which will enable the child to achieve at an earlier age what is ordinarily achieved in later adolescence and early adulthood. Then after he achieves it and reaches adulthood, we lose interest and focus our attentions upon another precocious child. This is because there is a double standard for giftedness.

When we say a child is gifted, we usually mean he is precocious, like people who are older, not like the individual child that he is. But when we say an adult is gifted, we are considering the person's qualitative and quantitative abilities, productivity, and accomplishments as an extraordinary individual. It could be very helpful to more often consider the gifted child in the same way.

Giftedness does not come into being all at once when the child is old enough to take a Wechsler or Stanford-Binet test. Aspects of it were there as long as the child was there. But we have yet to learn how to reliably discover it, what to do about it, and when to do it. Are there perceptual and sensory as well as cognitive and creative capacities which, like the olfactory, are culturally suppressed by either no communicative feedback or restrictive taboos? Are there mental capacities which, like vision, will never develop fully unless there are certain kinds of stimuli at certain developmental stages of infancy and early childhood? Are there special capacities for empathy, for the awareness and control of bodily processes, and for the focusing of subliminal stimuli? All of this has been largely unresearched. We assume the readily obvious. But the process by which a gifted child reasons or creates may be the resultant of more than just the obvious. It may be more like the myriad of factors and stimuli, some subliminal, which guide a migrating bird thousands of miles to its nest of the previous year.

Where have all the gifted gone? What happens to the large majority of gifted children when they become adults? And conversely, how many adults recognized as gifted were gifted as children; and were they gifted in the same areas? To what extent do gifted children come from parents who were gifted children? And were the parents gifted in the same areas and at the same ages? We need much earlier, as well as much better, identification of gifted capacities. Considering the amount of human development that takes place before the age of four, it makes little sense that most gifted children are not identified until after the age of eight and most programs for the gifted begin in the junior high schools after the age of twelve.

We need to learn more about the gifted from the gifted, children as well as adults. We have largely ignored input and feedback from the gifted themselves while we plan around them, test them at things we are good at, and do things for them and to them. Yet we do not really know their ranges, what if any other factors coexist with giftedness, when and how it first occurs, when it can first be predicted if at all, or even what happens to giftedness after adulthood.

We should know more about the nonprecocious gifted and how to identify and help them. We should know at what ages the various kinds of giftedness can be identified and which interventions can enhance and facilitate the development of each type of giftedness. More specifically, how will early interventions affect the maximal development of giftedness in the adult?

We need research in which gifted children teach

us about their ranges and the nature of their giftedness in their own language rather than having to translate into the "Esperanto" of our taxonomies and models. Then perhaps we will be able to help them learn within their ranges and capacities rather than seeing how fast they can learn within ours. The goal should be to teach gifted children what we know in such a way that they can eventually leave us behind and learn within their own ranges and capacities.

3

THE FAMILY'S VIEW OF THE GIFTED CHILD

Dewey Gene Cornell

In our efforts to identify and educate the children with superior abilities, we have found it convenient to group them under the label of "gifted." As Nicholas Hobbs (1975) has pointed out, labels are necessary for practical reasons, like identifying children for special educational programs (or in organizing a conference), but labels also present some problems. There are dangers of reifying the label into something more concrete, leading to stereotypes, misconceptions, popular myths, and so on. It is ironic that we often say that gifted children are neglected in schools geared to serve the norm when in fact the group of children we call gifted is by definition one of the most diverse groups we could compose and no single program could meet all of their needs. This conference recognizes this problem in its theme "Many views of the gifted." However, issues of education and program I will leave to others. My purpose in mentioning this all too familiar problem is to underscore how much more difficult it must be for parents to make sense of our research and understand what we mean when we tell them their child is gifted. What does this mean to them and how does it affect their perception of their child?

My concern is not research on the ways in which gifted children actually differ in their abilities but rather the ways in which parents perceive children labeled as gifted, regardless of their abilities - the psychology of perceiving a child as gifted rather than the psychology of gifted children themselves. There are two main reasons to study the family's view of the gifted child. First, knowledge of how the family perceives the child is essential to understanding how family members relate to the child, and the way in which the family environment influences the development of the child's gifted abilities. Second, we have a responsibility to the children we label gifted to investigate how our intervention affects the child and the child's family.

Parents involved with the gifted education movement can easily misinterpret research findings that report group characteristics of gifted children. When various studies report that gifted children as a group are psychologically better adjusted, more creative, sensitive, inquisitive, or socially mature in comparison to the norm, it is too easy to assume this means that every child labeled as gifted must share all of those admirable qualities. Frierson's (1966) study of upper and lower status gifted children nearly 20 years ago emphasized the idealized view of gifted children which the research literature has inadvertently promoted. More recently Joanne Whitmore (1981) has used the phrase "the Terman myth" to refer to the positive stereotypes of gifted children which seem to have replaced the negative ones Terman was instrumental in overturning. However, fixed notions of the gifted child, whether positive or negative, are unrealistic and misleading.

For example, recently a parent I've never met called me long distance (and got me out of bed) one Saturday morning to ask about my study. I told her I had interviewed families with gifted children and explained my concern that the term "gifted" is often misused as a stereotype. She told me she couldn't agree more, saying "Every gifted child is a unique individual." Then she asked me whether I had studied children who were "academically talented" or children who were "gifted." I asked her what she meant. "Well," she said, "there's a big difference. An academically talented child and a gifted child are like night and day. Gifted children are very sensitive to their environment, they see things in different ways and they don't think the same way other children do. They're special." As with this mother, parents don't realize the extent to which they have adopted stereotypic views of gifted children. The term "gifted" has become reified to the point it no longer describes one area of the child's abilities, but the whole person.

My contention is that the perception of a child as gifted is a powerful factor in the family, shaping the quality of the parent's relationship with the child and influencing the entire family lifestyle. Parents often attach special psychological significance to the idea that their child is gifted - in some cases leading to an idealization of the child which is unrealistic and unfortunate for the child.

Theoretical Background

There are two theoretical approaches to these contentions. One approach is that of labeling theory and symbolic interactionism. We have recognized that the act of labeling a child itself has an effect on the child and everyone who deals with the child. The symbolic interactionists like Jerome Blumer and George Herbert Mead emphasize that the meanings which we assign to others will determine the nature of our relationship with them.

We know something about the effect of negative labels in creating stereotypes or self-fulfilling expectations for children who are emotionally disturbed or delinquent, but we have very little knowledge of positive labels, which is one way to consider the results of the study I am about to present (see also Fisher, 1978).

A second way to look at the gifted child in the family is from the point of view of family systems theory. Here again we know a great deal about emotionally disturbed children; the family systems model proposes that the child's emotional problems are a function of how family members interact as a system. The child's problems may serve some function in maintaining the family stability or homeostasis, but we know very little about the family system of gifted children. Specifically, we might ask whether a child's giftedness defines a particular role for the child in the family, and whether the child has a more favored status in the family than other children. The family systems point of view differs from the labeling approach in at least one important way. When we consider giftedness as a label we look at the consequences of the label - what happens to the family when the label is applied. However, the family systems approach adds an historical dimension. Now we ask: How did this child become labeled? What was this child's relationship to the family before and is it possible that the family system helped to produce this label as a role for the child in the family? Our aim, then, is to assess the family system of the gifted child to consider how the family differs from other families and how the parents' perception of the child as gifted affects the family.

Method and Design

First, we decided to study families, and not just gifted children. This was necessary to gain as complete a picture as possible of how the child fits into the family, and also necessary for a family systems approach. A basic methodological difficulty in studying families is the tremendous number of different family constellations created by family variables such as the number, sex and age of children, the parents' marital status, and so forth. Therefore, we limited the study to families meeting certain specifications.

We selected families with first and second-born children between the ages of 6 and 11. In all families the marriage is intact, both parents living at home. We selected equal numbers of families with boys and girls in both birth order positions to control for the interaction of sex and birth order. Families were contacted through the records of several school programs for gifted children. We identified 22 families with gifted children who fit our selection criteria and then added a control group of 20 or more families whose children were not in gifted programs. All of the families were middle to upper middle class and lived in communities where gifted education is well known - though still somewhat controversial.

In locating families with gifted children we only require that one of the two children be placed in a gifted program. In the sample of 22 families there are 10 families where both children are in gifted programs and 12 families where only one child is in a gifted program. In view of the research literature on first-born children, it should not be a surprise that in all of the families with only one gifted child, it is the first-born child who is in the gifted program and the second born who is in a regular classroom.

The gifted children had all been identified and labeled by virtue of their school placement in a gifted program. The average IQ of the gifted children was 135 and all of them were achieving very well in school. Again, our interest is not in these children's specific abilities, but in the fact that they have all been labeled as gifted.

The study was presented to parents as research on families, not giftedness. They were told that the study was concerned with the relationship between the family environment and school achievement. Both children and both parents were given equal attention in gathering data. The family assessment procedure used with each family consisted of 4 parts: (a) clinical interviews with both parents, together and then individually, (b) the Moos Family Environment Scale, (c) the Children's Personality Questionnaire, and (d) a series of family tasks used to observe the family in group interaction.

Results

I want to focus primarily on the data of the parent interviews. Each parent was asked a standard series of questions about each of their two children. Both objective and projective questions were used. Two clinical judges were trained to a criterion of 80% agreement in rating audio tapes of the parents on a series of scales. The results I will report are those significant beyond the conventional .05 level.

First, we analyzed the parent's perception of his or her child as gifted or not gifted. That is, we wanted to distinguish between the child's objective school placement in a gifted program and the parent's subjective perception of the child. We asked the parents to describe their child's abilities and talents and give their own assessment of whether their child was gifted or not. When we compared the mother's and father's perceptions of their children we found clear differences between the two parents. In approximately 50% of the cases where a (first-born) child was placed in a gifted program only one parent perceived the child as gifted. That is, the parents frequently do not agree in their perceptions of their gifted children.

In every family where the parents disagreed it was the mother who perceived the (firstborn) child as gifted and the father who did not. (In one family, though, the mother contended the first-born, not the second-born, child was gifted and the father contended just the opposite.) This difference between parents reflects a broad difference between the parents in their attitudes toward giftedness in their children. It is probably not surprising, in our society, that the mother is the one who is actively involved with matters of gifted education, since mothers are usually more involved in all school matters. But it cannot be overlooked that the fathers take a quite different view of giftedness. Often the father describes the mother's involvement with giftedness as "her cause" or "her crusade" which he prefers to take little part in. Even in those families where both parents perceived the child as gifted, more often than not the father attributed primary responsibility to the mother for first recognizing that the child was gifted.

If we as professionals only deal with the mother, we cannot assume the father will share the mother's views even on so basic a matter as whether the child is gifted or not. The parents' disagreement may even be a source of tension or conflict in the family. Certainly we cannot expect the same degree of cooperation from the father in any recommendations we make for the child. We must consider both parents in our work with the family and be willing to educate fathers as well as mothers.

As might be expected, the mothers and fathers have quite different conceptions of giftedness. We coded parents' definitions of giftedness into several categories and found that mothers tend to define a gifted child as someone with special learning abilities. In contrast, the fathers view a gifted child as a prodigy or genius. It seems that fathers' standards are more stringent, which is perhaps one reason why they do not perceive their child as gifted. The fathers tend to voice negative, rejecting attitudes toward the notion of giftedness. Fairly consistently the fathers say that a gifted child is socially or emotionally maladjusted, troubled, a social misfit, and so forth. Clearly the old negative stereotypes of gifted children that Terman and others tried to dispell remain among the fathers, though not the mothers.

Many of the mothers voice equally stereotypic positive attitudes and beliefs about gifted children. They describe gifted children as paragons of intellectual and social virtue. Often they tend to downplay or rationalize the child's weaknesses or problems, sometimes blaming the school. The child who is short-tempered, impatient, or simply impolite is described as a gifted perfectionist who is merely misunderstood by those who are "uninformed" about "the way gifted children are." Giftedness can become the explanation for the child's total personality and behavior.

Here I must be careful not to suggest stereotypes myself. I am stressing the problem areas and not characterizing all of the parents. However, we tend to dismiss the parents who seem over-invested in their children's giftedness rather than addressing this problem as a topic for research and intervention. Moreover, I think the extreme cases merely fall on a continuum so that there are many more moderate cases where giftedness is reified and the child is idealized.

The next step in our analysis was to consider how the parent's perception of giftedness influences their relationship with their children. Clinical judges blind to whether the parent perceived the child as gifted or not rated the parent-child relationship on a series of scales. We found that parents who perceive their child as gifted are higher on the measure of parental pride in their child than were those parents who do not perceive their child as gifted.

The parents of gifted children seem to take greater pride in their children's accomplishments and speak with greater enthusiasm about the child. Moreover, we found qualitative differences in the reasons parents gave for feeling especially proud of their child. Contrary to expectations, the parents who perceive their child as gifted are less often especially proud of their child for scholastic accomplishments and more often proud of their child's social skills and maturity. The parents who do not perceive their child as gifted are more likely to emphasize scholastic accomplishments.

Finally, we found that the parents who perceive their child as gifted are higher on the measure of parent-child closeness, describing a more intimate, affectionate relationship with the child. These findings are true for mothers and for fathers in separate comparisons, supporting our contention that the parent's perception of giftedness is a powerful factor in the parent's overall relationship with the child.

Many other studies (for example, Domino, 1969) have suggested special qualities to the parent's relationship with the gifted child. However, these studies generally fail to isolate the parent's perception of the child as gifted as a crucial factor. In our study we were able to compare mothers' and fathers' relationships with the same child when the mother perceived the child as gifted and the father did not. Here we found more confirmation for emphasizing the parent's perception over the child's actual abilities. The parent who perceives the child as gifted is higher on measures of parental pride and parent-child closeness than the parent's spouse who does not perceive the child as gifted.

However, in all of these cases it is the mother who perceives the child as gifted and the father who does not, so that we needed to rule out parent sex as a alternative explanation for the results. We were able to do this simply by comparing the mothers and fathers neither of whom perceive their child as gifted. Here there are no differences between mothers and fathers. Then we compared the fewer number of cases where both parents do perceive the child as gifted and still found no parent sex differences. So it seems reasonable to conclude that it is not parent sex but the parent's perception of the child as gifted which determined our results.

It seems that in many families the labeling of a child as gifted because of school performance is part of a much broader role the child plays in the family. Especially in families where both children are perceived as gifted the notion of giftedness can become an organizing force in the family, structuring family relationships and shaping much of the family's lifestyle. There is evidence of this from a variety of sources, which I will review only briefly.

The Family Environment Scale was administered to parents with gifted children as well as the parents in the control group whose children attend regular classrooms. The two groups were equated on three measures of socio-economic status: parent education, occupation, and family housing type. The families with gifted children were higher on the measure of cohesiveness in family relationships and lower on the measure of conflict in the family. Both these measures reflect positive qualities to the overall relationships among family members. It should not be surprising, though, that the greatest difference between groups was that the families with gifted children are much more strongly oriented toward intellectual-cultural activities. As the parents explained in their interview, they are extremely devoted to their children's intellectual and cultural development, providing the children with music and dance lessons, taking them on special trips and in general organizing the family lifestyle around activities for their children. Here giftedness seems to provide the parents with an orienting rationale and a sense of purpose which directs the family lifestlye. This is further reflected in the recorded observations of the family interacting during a standard series of family tasks. The tasks included the Plan Something Together task, a family Thematic Aperception Test (TAT), and a family statement task which required the family to reach consensus on specific items from the Family Environment Scale. All of the data analysis on the family tasks is not complete, but it is clear that the influence of giftedness is prominent in the family. The TAT stories contain many references to achievement, often with rather clear messages for the children.

On the tasks in general, it is surprising the extent to which the parents focus on their gifted children, usually relinquishing control of the family process to their children's direction, their ideas and decisions.

The transcripts of the family tasks were scored by an adaptation of the Bales Interpersonal Process Analysis coding system. Bales (1970) and others have used the number of statements an individual receives from other group members as an index of the individual's status or "power" in the family. In families, usually the parents are more powerful members of the group; but in the families with one gifted child, the gifted child has the highest status of any family member. To put it simply, families with a gifted child seem to focus on the gifted child during group interaction by directing more attention to the gifted child than to any other family member.

Finally, I want to mention the siblings of gifted children who are not themselves labeled as gifted. I call them the "not gifted" siblings guardedly because in fact many of them appear to be quite talented, achieve well in school, and have IQs comparable to their gifted siblings. However, the important point is that their parents do not perceive them as gifted and therefore they do not enjoy the same favored status in the family as their gifted sibling. We studied 12 of these not-gifted siblings and compared them to two other groups - families where both children are labeled gifted and control families where neither child is labeled gifted. We have found that with only a few exceptions the not-gifted siblings of gifted children seem to have lower self-esteem and less drive to pursue and develop their abilities than we would expect on their potential. On the Children's Personality Questionnaire we find that these children were significantly more anxious, less outgoing, more easily upset, and socially more inhibited.

I think that this is an area that needs more research and that it may indicate a serious problem area. When we label one child as gifted, we indirectly label the siblings as not gifted. This is especially true if the parents overvalue the term gifted and tend to idealize the gifted child. Another factor contributes to this problem. Frequently parents with first-born children who are gifted tend to associate the personality traits of their first-born child with giftedness. This makes it difficult for them to recognize giftedness in a second-born child whose personality may be quite different. For example, if their first-born child tends to be shy, serious minded, and perfectionistic, they have trouble perceiving a second-born child as gifted who is gregarious, light-hearted and outgoing. Again, there is a tendency to develop stereotypic notions of gifted children which we must resist ourselves and discourage in parents.

Now, I have covered a great deal of material, so let me summarize briefly. I have contended that the act of labeling a child as gifted has widespread impact on the family, the quality of the parent-child relationships, and influencing the family lifestyle. I believe there is a range of effects from positive to negative, adaptive to maladaptive in how families respond to the gifted child. I have touched upon some potential problems areas, cases in which one of the children is not perceived as gifted. I believe these kinds of problems originate in a tendency to idealize and stereotype the notion of giftedness, for which I recommend a renewed commitment to appreciating and respecting the individual differences and unique qualities of each child we label gifted.

References
Fisher, E. An investigation into the effects of positive labeling on the families of gifted children. Unpublished EdD Dissertation, Teachers College, Columbia University, 1978.

Frierson, C. Upper and lower status gifted children: A study of differences. Exceptional Children, 1965, 32, 83-90.

Hobbs, Nicholas (Ed.). The futures of children: categories, labels and their consequences. San Francisco: Jossey-Bass, 1975.

4

THE IDENTIFICATION AND UNDERSTANDING OF VERY YOUNG GIFTED CHILDREN

Dorothy Coleman

I should like to tell you about an experiment in communication undertaken by the National Association for Gifted Children in Great Britain, initially funded by the Department of Health and Social Security.

An increasing number of parents with very young gifted children contacted the National Association for Gifted Children (NAGC) as a result of publicity in the national press and on radio and television. Following the First World Conference in London in 1975, we realized that the problems encountered by these parents presented us with a whole area of unexplored territory. We felt it was important to alert the various ancillary sources to the problems of identifying exceptionally able children at a very early age and hoped, through our own extended knowledge and experience, to be better able as an association, to assist the parents who turned to us for information and help. As a registered charity, we were always attempting to obtain funds from private and public sources, through the efforts of our director Henry Collis. After prolonged negotiation we wrung a small annual grant from the Department of Health and Social Security to be used partly to fund the training of individual counselors recruited from our membership (some of you may remember an account of the work done by them, given by Felicity Seighart, our chairman, and NAGC members at the Third World Conference at Jerusalem in 1979) and partly to finance single day conferences concerned with the identification and understanding of the very young gifted child.

The location of these conferences was left entirely to our discretion and were spread about the

United Kingdom. They were held annually from 1976 and bi-annually from 1978 onwards - sometimes in areas with already flourishing NAGC branches, and sometimes where we felt that a stirring of interest and concern might be stimulated and encouraged.

Colleges of education, universities and teaching hospitals all offered accommodation, and until this year (when government funding dried up) we were able to offer the day conferences with morning coffee, lunch and tea provided at no cost to the participants. I need hardly tell you that the conferences - and the lunches - went down extremely well.

Initial organization was mounted from the London headquarters of the NAGC and involved very useful contact with a wide variety of supportive disciplines. Many of the professional people contacted confessed to never having heard of the NAGC or having considered the problem. However they subsequently showed a great deal of interest in our aims and objectives. These groups included the Association of Pediatricians, local Health Service officials in the chosen locality, the Professional Association of Midwives, health visitors, social workers, the national headquarters of the Pre-School Play-Groups Association, and the local education authority.

As a matter of interest, our links with the numerous local education authorities in the United Kingdom have become progressively stronger in the last five years. There are a mere handful who have failed to designate a particular member of their staff (often a deputy education officer, a senior inspector or one specifically appointed to advise or provision for gifted children within the authorities' schools) to be our contact officer. As a matter of courtesy, they are always invited to all NAGC functions in their area, as well as the conferences under discussion. We feel that nothing but good can come through this collaboration at all levels.

After the first two conferences, which covered the South London area, North London and the northern home counties, we established a speaker pattern. In each area, we attempted to involve an eminent pediatrician, an educational psychologist with knowledge of the locality, and an educationalist with wide experience in the recognition and teaching of gifted children, and always included at least two parents who had lived through the problems, so often formulated by the sometimes quite desperate mothers who got in touch with us, or were referred to the NAGC by clinics, schools, or their family doctors.

The conference was brought to a close summing up and giving news of what was offered by the NAGC locally and nationally, and although time for questions and discussion was allowed after each speaker's session, so much interest was aroused and discussion provoked that it was often late in the day when the meeting finally broke up.

The number of participants was limited to approximately 150. This proved to be a comfortable number to accommodate and feed. Mingling of disciplines and interests was encouraged during break periods.

Once the venue and program were fixed, invitations went out to pediatricians, general practitioners, nursing staff from the local hospitals, health workers, social workers generally concerned with family welfare, and preschool and nursery groups organizers and teachers. They were also sent, through the local education authority, to educational psychologists, the Primary Inspectorate, as well as nursery and primary school head teachers and staff.

Taking school holiday closures into consideration, we found March and October to be the most suitable months in which to hold the conferences.

At every meeting, huge amounts of literature about the NAGC were available, book-lists were printed and distributed, and as many books on relevant subjects that it was possible for the NAGC organizer to transport were on display so that people could browse at coffee and lunch time. If the meeting was held in an area with an already flourishing NAGC branch, a number of members came along to be on hand to give information about their local activities and, wherever possible, to recruit enthusiasts with specialty skills willing to involve themselves in the numerous activities organized by branch members.

These tended to vary according to expertise, enthusiasm, and time available; some branches organized activities for members and children on a weekly basis, whereas others did so less frequently.

As a result of these conferences held in widely differing areas of the United Kingdom, we have been much encouraged to find a marked rise in the degree of interest engendered in the work of the Association. Local newspapers have usually been anxious to report on the meetings and local radio stations have offered time for informative talks, or given opportunity for a talk-in/question-time type of program.

This has meant that parents have contacted the Association, their local authority, or area preschool groups and have often been able to alleviate the quite frightening sense of isolation and inadequacy that many parents do feel when faced with a preschool child who probably sleeps no more than five or six hours in the twenty-four, talks non stop when awake, asks incessant questions which may be beyond the parents' realm of experience to answer, and has a wide range of interests and hobbies that the children of neighbors and friends in the same peer group find totally bizarre or unacceptable.

Such a child often strains family relationships to a breaking point and a mother's patience and numerous energy beyond that. We were therefore more than concerned to learn that our modest financial help from the Department of Health and Social Services was to be discontinued because of financial stringencies at the end of 1980.

We felt very strongly that these conferences fulfilled a very important, and indeed a unique role in the dissemination of information, and in giving experts in many very different fields the opportunity to consider together a problem which very few of them had ever considered before. We were determined to continue to offer these conferences biannually. We realized that without the financial support that we had received from the DHSS it would not be possible for us to do so without cost to the participants. We also realized that we were probably the only association in the United Kingdom doing this anyway and that those interested would be quite prepared to pay a modest fee to attend.

After discussion in executive and finance committees, we made a careful budget, cut costs as finely as possible and decided that we could cover expenses if we charged a fee of 6 pounds - about $12 - to each participant. This, with rising costs of postage and food, will obviously have to be reviewed from time to time, but was wholly adequate for our last conference held in East Anglia at the Teacher's Centre in Norwich, during March of this year. Hopefully, colleges, hospitals and local education authorities will continue to offer free accommodations, speakers will, as before, donate their time and talents, and our work in this field will continue and flourish. Plans are already in hand, and locations have been chosen for conferences into 1983.

We hope, like "the pebble tossed into the pool," to extend our influence into ever widening circles.

5

THE GIFTED AT WORK

David Willings

Many of our countries are in the process of advancing from the idea that the gifted children will get ahead anyway and if they don't, they weren't really gifted. Our national associations still have a lot of work to do here but I think the appropriate attitude for the 1980s is one of cautious optimism. As Professsor Torrance (1980) has said, "gifted education is here to stay." I think many people here will share my concern over the contention of Hagen (1980) that there is no such thing as a gifted child; merely a potentially gifted child. It is not borne out by the facts as they impinge on the professional lives of many of us here at this time. Gifts and talents manifest themselves at an early age. On the other hand, the gifted child of today may be the gifted adult of tomorrow. Education is not, I believe, merely a process of preparing children for the world of work; that is altogether too narrow and too utilitarian. All of us who have taken upon ourselves a professional concern for education, at whatever level, have committed ourselves to the task of enabling our charges to find a role in society. I do not believe work is the central aspect of this but it is a significant force. If I say "my name is Willings," all this tells you about me is that my father's name was Willings. If I say "I am a Professor," then and then only have I in some measure identified myself. The gifted child, like any other child, will find a role in society partly through his work and, to a great extent, what he does will identify him. What is more, he is likely to take some of the problems he encountered as a gifted child into his adult life and the world of work. It is these problems I want to discuss. I think it is convenient to consider two categories, the intellectually gifted and the creatively gifted, and look at the problems some of these people encounter not only in business but in the world of work in general.

The Intellectually Gifted

D. W. Harding (1957) drew attention to the problems he described as "the recognition of excellence." Professor Harding suggested that teachers can go to considerable lengths to hide from themselves that a child is more intelligent than they are. The usual reaction is to take a dislike to the child. Tarkowski (1958) and I (1968) have found that precisely the same reaction takes place among managers when faced with a gifted subordinate. Managers and executives often hide from themselves the fact that a subordinate is more intelligent than they are by taking a dislike to him or her. Bridges (1973) points out that teachers are often motivated to cut the gifted child down to size. Tarkowski and I have found the identical motivation among managers often coupled with the belief that they are doing the gifted subordinate a favor. The gifted child is a threat to the adult ego. In working life of course, the gifted employee is perceived as a threat, not only to the ego of his superiors but also to their career prospects. The danger seems quite real that the gifted subordinate will overtake the manager of normal abilities.

There is nothing new in any of this. Bernard Shaw in his prologue to **Saint Joan** compares Joan of Arc and Socrates. Of Saint Joan, he says:

> She patronized her own king and summoned the English king to repentance and obedience to her commands. She lectured, talked down and over-ruled statesmen and prelates. She pooh - poohed the plans of generals leading their troops to victory on plans of her own . . . . As her actual condition was pure upstart, there were only two opinions about her. One was that she was miraculous; the other that she was

unbearable. . . . If Joan had been malicious, selfish, cowardly or stupid, she would have been one of the most odious persons known to history instead of one of the attractive. If she had been old enough to know the effect she was producing on the men whom she humiliated by being right when they were wrong . . . she might have lived as long as Queen Elizabeth . . . . she was naive enough to expect them to be obliged to her for setting them right and keeping them out of mischief. Now it is always hard for superior wits to understand the fury roused by their exposures of the stupidities of comparative dullards. Even Socrates, for all his age and experience, did not defend himself at his trial like a man who understood the long accumulated fury that had burst on him, and was clamouring for his death. His accuser, if born 2,300 years later, might have been picked out of any first class carriage on a suburban railway during the evening or morning rush from or to the city; for he had really nothing to say except that he and his like could not endure being shown up as idiots every time Socrates opened his mouth. Socrates, unconscious of this, was paralysed by his sense that somehow he was missing the point of the attack. He petered out after he had established the fact that he was an old soldier and a man of honourable life, and that his accuser was a silly snob. He had no suspicion of the extent to which his mental superiority had roused fear and hatred against him in the hearts of men towards whom he was conscious of nothing but good will and good service. . . . If Socrates was as innocent as this at the age of seventy, it may be imagined how innocent Joan was at the age of seventeen. Now Socrates was a man of argument, operating slowly and peacefully on men's minds, whereas Joan was a woman of action, operating with impetuous violence on their bodies. That, no doubt, is why the contemporaries of Socrates endured him so long, and why Joan was destroyed before she was fully grown. But both of them combined terrifying ability with a frankness, personal modesty, and benevolence which made the furious dislike to which they fell victims absolutely unreasonable, and therefore inapprehensible by themselves. . . . It is not so easy for mental giants who neither hate nor intend to injure their fellows to realise that nevertheless their fellows hate mental giants and would like to destroy them, not only enviously because the juxtaposition of a superior wounds their vanity, but quite humbly and honestly because it frightens them. Fear will drive men to an extreme; and the fear inspired by a superior being is a mystery which cannot be reasoned away.

Many gifted persons in working organizations have found precisely the same thing. Conscious only of a desire to do the best possible job, they are at a loss to understand the viciously hostile reaction they provoke.

Seagoe, quoted in Martinson (1981), outlines some of the problems the gifted child can experience as a result of being gifted. These will be so familiar to the present audience that I will merely outline the ones that are taken into the world of work. They are the following: (a) possible gullibility, (b) occasional resistance to direction, rejection or remission of detail, (c) difficulty in accepting the illogical, (d) invention of own system, (e) dislike for routine and drill, (f) lack of stimulation, (g) critical attitude towards others, (h) rejection of the known, need to invent for oneself, (i) stubbornness, (j) need for success and recognition, sensitivity to criticism - vulnerability to peer group rejection, (k) frustration with inactivity and absence of progress. All these add up to impaired promotability. Dalton (1959) and a number of surveys following Dalton have shown that job performance is not a significant factor in promotability. Social acceptability, the ability to fit in, the ability to think as the rest of management thinks; these are the factors which make a person promotable. The gifted employee is not readily promotable. This idea that the gifted will get ahead anyway and, if they do not, they were not really gifted, has no basis in fact. The fact of the matter is that we are living in an age when the gifted are among the least likely to advance. Tarkowski goes further and shows that such people often run the risk of dismissal because, although their work is excellent, they do not fit in. Who loses by this? The gifted themselves are certainly losers. However, the prime losers are our respective countries who are deprived of the contributions of these people.

The Creatively Gifted

I have already suggested (1972, 1980) that the creatively gifted can be divided into three categories: the adaptive thinker, the elaborative thinker and the developmental thinker.

The adaptive thinker is able to perceive relationships where no one has perceived them before. Koestler (1959, 1962) believes that all creativity is of this type and defines discovery as "the marriage of cabbages and kings." Examples abound. Many children before James Watt have watched a kettle boil over. James Watt related it to propulsion. The adaptive thinker not only perceives relationships but is preoccupied with them.

In England, Eric Donald of British Aerospace addressed himself to the problems of fractures in the bolts that hold aircraft together. They were difficult, if not impossible, to detect. Donald related this to the bleeding of a wound. He drilled a hole in the bolt and inserted a red dye susceptible to ultra violet light. Then he sealed up the bolt. By running an ultra violet light over the fuselage of an aircraft it is now possible to tell when a bolt is cracked and it can be replaced before it fractures. "Just like when a wound bleeds," Donald commented, and called his innovation the "bleeding bolt."

The elaborative thinker is motivated to research, refine and beautify. He takes someone else's idea and researches and refines it. Koch, who discovered tuberculin, pulled together and refined knowledge which had been available for seventeen centuries. Shakespeare stands out as an elaborative thinker. Often both in literature and science someone makes a breakthrough (probably an adaptive thinker) and then a number of elaborative thinkers refine and perfect the idea. McKellar (1957) suggests that the creative person is seriously receptive to previous thought processes but refuses to accept them as final. This certainly appears to be true of the elaborative thinker.

The developmental thinker internalizes and synthesizes his emotional and intellectual experiences and proceeds to translate them into a mission. Many eminent philosophers were in all probability developmental thnkers.

Based on the work of such writers as Dauw (1966), Hudson (1966) and myself (1980), it is possible to outline some of the problem areas for the creatively gifted at work. These are set out in Figure 1. Again, all of this adds up to impaired promotability and even the risk of dismissal. It is hardly surprising that Torrance (1971) finds that the creatively gifted tend to change jobs more frequently than people not creatively gifted. This makes them less acceptable to employers, and Torrance asks, "Is bias against job changing bias against giftedness?"

Paterson (1955) suggests that in our work we are motivated by two drives: the drive to be somebody and the drive to do something worthwhile. Where these two drives are not equally gratified, and it is useless for one to be gratified without the other being equally gratified, several problems invariably ensue. Morale decreases, a sense of frustration pervades every aspect of life, effectiveness decreases to a level where performance gives severe cause for concern. With the creatively gifted we must remember that they are perfectionists and have very high standards. So what would be worthwhile to a normal person in this respect

Figure 1
Problems Experienced by Creative Thinkers

ADAPTIVE	ELABORATIVE	DEVELOPMENTAL
"Why is everyone else so stupid?"	"Why is everyone else so stupid?"	"Why is everyone else so stupid?"
Rejected by peers.	Rejected by peers.	Rejected by peers.
Perceived as a threat by some colleagues and superiors.	Perceived as a threat by some colleagues and superiors.	Perceived as a threat by some colleagues and superiors.
Unacceptable leader.	Unacceptable leader.	Unacceptable leader.
Cannot perform effectively unless work itself is intellectually stimulating.	Cannot perform effectively unless work itself is intellectually stimulating.	Cannot perform effectively unless work itself is intellectually stimulating.
Perfectionist.	Perfectionist.	Perfectionist.
Difficult laughing at self.	Not able to laugh at self.	Takes self very seriously.
Self generator.	Highly independent.	Loner.
Concerned with how facts and ideas relate.	Unwilling to accept facts and ideas as final.	More concerned with "Is it satisfactory than "Is it right?"
Perceived as dilettante and/or undisciplined.	Perceived as moody and tempermental.	Perceived as remote and/or aloof.
Perceives others as narrow.	Perceives others as lazy or incompetent.	Perceives others as shallow or even
Sense of failure early in life.	Believes self a failure due to not	Sense of failure early in life. having met own standards.
	Withdraws into shell in face of frustration.	
Unconventional career goals.		Unconventional career goals.

		Cannot understand why others do not see things his way.
Frustrated by set procedure.		Frustrated by set procedure.
May fail at jobs those of lesser ability do well.	May fail at jobs those of lesser ability do well.	May fail at jobs those of lesser ability do well.
		Missionary urge.
		Tends to see life as a Socratic arguement.
Width of interests and activities not appreciated.		

alone is more prone to morale and performance problems for a gifted person: yet another reason why they fail at jobs a person of less ability would do well.

I have already (1972, 1980) drawn attention to the problem of labeling. Once a person establishes himself in a particular area, he is labeled there. He is expected to behave like someone in that area and confine himself to activities consistent with the label. The production person is expected to stick to production. The accountant must stick to accountancy and behave like an accountant. The lawyer must stick to law and behave like a lawyer. The creatively gifted have a wide range of interests and are the least able to stick within the constraints of a label. In vocational guidance quite the most difficult problem, sometimes insoluble, is to help the person who has displayed competence in a particular area but who now wants to change to another area; a frequent problem among the creatively gifted who often exhaust quite early in life the potential for fulfillment in a sphere of work which would last a normal person a lifetime. It is a penalty for displaying competence in an area that we are labeled in it and then we are not expected to concern ourselves in any other area. A director of a large executive selection organization told me "Business is very cautious. A firm making biscuit tins would far rather have a man who has made biscuit tins for ten years than a man who knows what he is doing in the whole area of production."

Paterson (1972) draws attention to a destructive trend in organizations. We tend to reward the satisfactory use of creative talent by promoting the person concerned into management. Engineers or scientists in an organization may spend a few years doing the job they are trained to do. If they do well they are promoted. Their administrative responsibilities increase. By the time they reach early middle age they are very probably functioning purely as administrators. This is not only the case in business. In social work, in teaching, to name but two, valuable service will be rewarded by an executive appointment. I do not wish to imply that there is no scope for creativity in administration. There may well be. However, administrative responsibility is not necessarily the best reward for the person whose creative work in research has been found acceptable. "Why," a company director recently asked me, "is it that innovative young chaps start off with a bang and invariably go to the dogs?" This could be the answer. Many of them cannot be creative in administration. Roe (1953), in a study of the behavior patterns of research scientists points out that from an early age they tend to pursue independent paths. She describes such people as "self-sufficient introverts." It must be added that in these days of emphasis on groupwork, the self-sufficient introvert has problems not only in business but in any sphere of work.

Hudson, on the other hand, points out that the creatively gifted person is a swashbuckler in his work. At first sight this may conflict with the idea of the self-sufficient introvert. The operative words are in his work. I have suggested (1980) that what we often have here is an introverted swashbuckler. An introverted swashbuckler is the archetypal horse of a different color and impairs his own social acceptability.

I have touched on the fringes but I hope I have said enough to explode the myth that the creatively gifted are not readily employable and among the least likely to advance. I would like to go on and consider another topic.

Attitudes to the Gifted

The president of a large international organization said at a conference, "The cold and brutal fact is that industry needs these people. If they cannot adjust to us than I suppose we must adjust to them." He was not very well received. I will quote a few remarks addressed to me by senior managers, directors, and vice presidents in England, Canada and the United States. "They want to do fundamental research. I'm f---ed if I'll entrust research to someone until he's proved himself." "Why do we hire these intellectuals? They're no damned use. They don't fit in. They cause trouble." "I would rather have twelve stable non-entities than one transient genius." "We have a very gifted young chap. He came up with two ideas which we have unashamedly stolen. But he never learned how to follow normal procedure. Couldn't fill in a form PY34 to save his life. He left us after seven months and I think it was for the best." "We had a research physicist, brilliant girl, but, do you know, she came to see me and said she couldn't work in her office. She actually wanted to work at home. I told her she'd better learn that this is the Civil Service. Maybe she'd like us to send her salary home to her."

R. E. M. Harding (1940) has shown, and I am in the process of following up, the diverse conditions for creative work. We have to consider the conditions for creative work. We have to consider the conditions under which people get their best ideas and the conditions under which they do their best work. We have to consider the time of day they are at their activity peak. A colleague of mine who is writing a two volume biography of a religious leader is at his activity peak between five and eight in the morning.

Personally, I pay lip service to the idea that there is such an hour. I am at my activity peak between seven and eleven in the evening. These conditions are enormously varied. A highly creative research engineer known to me gets his best ideas while driving. Having driven with him in London I am less than happy about him cultivating this. I get some of my best ideas while gardening. The conditions under which people do their best work are enormously varied. My colleague, to whom I have already referred, has to have the radio on while he is working. I cannot take distractions. I handwrite all my work because the noise of the typewriter disturbs me. There are also some people who can funtion well with several projects going at the same time.

The problem is that, with a few exceptions, employers require all their staff to be active between nine in the morning and five at night, to get their best ideas on the factory premises and to have a high distraction tolerance. This is not only an impossible demand but it is unnatural.

Harvey Schwarz, a practicing managing director for over twenty-five years, and one of the pioneers of the Decca Navigator, outlined his philosophy of the management of the creatively gifted in a personal communication (1978). He strongly criticizes the tendency in many organizations to have these people work together in groups. In his experience such people cannot work together and cannot be made to do so. At best one will get a semblance of team work, at worst distruptive conflict. Schwarz's practice is to have two people working in separate parts of the company on the same problem so that competition supplements evaluative dialogue. He is aware that this tends to frustrate the people concerned in the short term but believes it pays off in the long term. The creatively gifted cannot turn on at nine in the morning and turn off at five at night. He believes that it is essential to be flexible on hours; what is important is results. Schwarz emphasizes the need for the person at the top to be receptive to ideas. Indeed, the management of ideas has been the linchpin of his business practice. In many organizations a person who has an idea will even be fairly considered. Sometimes this can almost degenerate into a court martial or an inquisition for daring to have an idea. In the majority of organizations the burden of proof is on the person with the idea. Schwarz reverses that. He maintains that one must start with the basic assumption that the idea has potential and ought to be pursued. Thus, the person putting up the idea is not on the defensive and is open to consider possible defects and areas which need more investigation. Moreover, as Schwarz himself points out, the creatively gifted tend to be pessimistic and preoccupied with the things that could go wrong. Schwarz regards one of his functions in the management of ideas as providing a balance to that and looking at the potential of the idea. Of course, it would be absurd to suggest that all the ideas put to him are taken up - he is in business. He also believes that the essential in the management of ideas is the ability to take risks and a believe in the individuality of the person with ideas. He recalls the time when a problem was put to one of his research and development people. This person disappeared for several months and one day arrived back armed with the answer. it was after this that Schwarz decided that, while someone's physical presence at the factory was less important than the fact that they were delivering the goods, and there was no objection to research and development people working where they could best work, nevertheless, one of his personal assistants must know where they are.

One of his engineers was never seen in the laboratory before two in the afternoon but was rarely out of the laboratory before midnight. Different people function best at different times of the day. At the other end of the diurnal variation, another key person in Decca Navigator was usually on the company premises and functioning at five in the morning. By early afternoon, if he was still there, he was virtually incoherent. Schwarz recalls that another of his engineers always used to claim that he got his best ideas in his bath.

Indeed, Schwarz had realized before psychologists documented the fact, that there is an infinite variety of conditions under which the creative person does his best work. Schwarz had the courage to practice the idea that such people should be left free to generate the most conducive conditions. It must be added that this brought him into perpetual conflict with some of his fellow directors and, among the more conventional managers in his own company, bitter lamentations apropos Schwartz provided the common link without which no group can be cohesive. For the creatively gifted one of the dependent factors is the receptivity of the person at the top to their potential and individuality.

Prospects for the Future

I am preaching to the converted when I say that the gifted are a significant factor if not the significant factor in the national economy of any country, and that most of the countries with which I am acquainted are recklessly squandering this resource. The advancement of any country depends on its ability to attract and make use of potential innovators. There was a time when America led the world in this respect. In the 1960s, large numbers of creative people from Europe emigrated to America. In Europe this was called "The Brain Drain." In 1972 more than seven hundred PhDs emigrated from England to America. Editorials in **Business Week** and comparable publications show that Americans themselves feel they have lost this lead. In the past two years, politicians in England, France and Germany have said that they intend to induce the brain drainers to return to their native countries. I see no evidence of this being put into practice as yet but our associations can cash in on the emerging political awareness that the gifted are a national resource.

We could profitably look into ways of helping gifted children anticipate and work out strategies to overcome the problems they will encounter in the world of work. I have never been able to subscribe to the idea of self fulfillment through work. The gifted will find a measure of self fulfillment in a combination of their work and rewarding outside activities. In some respects, French is a much more functional language than English. Our French colleagues have several words for work including vocation, profession and metier. Gifted people must be helped to find all three. One will not suffice. They need to find a vocation, a profession and a metier and all three are highly likely to be different.

We must increase our public relations activities. In many countries, more and more lay people are becoming aware that to be gifted is not an unmixed blessing. However, this activity could be increased to make management, government (the largest employer in any country) and professional bodies aware that the gifted need help to develop their potential and that it is in the national interest to do so. Some circles in business pay lip service to the idea but that is all. It is going to be an uphill struggle. The country which can develop its gifted and talented will attract the gifted and talented from other countries.

In preparing the gifted child for adult life we have to take account for the fact that the problems do not find a lower level in adult life. The last thing we want is for the significant work we have done and will continue to do on behalf of the gifted child to be rendered useless when that child reaches adult life. Mr. Schwarz has shown that ultilization of the gifted and talented can be done but we are asking business and government to rethink employment policies.

However, we can pride ourselves on the fact that our national associations are not just another pressure group carrying a torch for a minority. We have concerned ourselves with the development of a resource at least as significant to our national economies as oil.

GIFTED AT WORK

Postscript

From 1970-1974, I was engaged in research on career aspirations and expectations among final year students. Of two thousand students questioned, thirty-five were identified as gifted. Biographical information was collected and I hoped to follow them up over a period of twenty years. I have lost contact with twenty of these respondents leaving me with a sample of fifteen which consisted of ten British and five Canadian respondents. Four of the British group and all of the Canadian group were women. While no firm conclusions can be drawn from such a small sample, which cannot even be considered representative, it does appear that several hypotheses merit investigation. For this reason some of the findings are given here.

First, everyone in the sample felt cheated at University and that University was an alienating experience. Seven respondents had transferred from science after first year. Two had transfered from law (an undergraduate program in Britain). One respondent transfered from engineering to geology. One took a number of science courses because her mother wanted her to go to medical school. After eighteen months in medical school she withdrew and is now completing a PhD in Italian. Only one has completed a PhD and he did this after several years working outside university. Three felt that some creative development had taken place at university, but attributed this not to the degree program but to an individual professor with whom they were able to develop a one-to-one mentor relationship. Ten considered going on for a higher degree but decided that they had had enough of full time education and could not take any more.

Second, radical career changes were frequently reported. Eight respondents have changed their career at least once. The changes are given below:

Accountant to Social Worker to Accountant
Teacher to Monk to Professor of Anthropology
Teacher to Film Director
Minister to Teacher to Probation Officer

Psychologist to Professional Photographer
Nurse to Clinical Psychologist
Publisher's Editor to Teacher to Literary Agent
Personnel Manager to Art Gallery Administrator
to Accountant.

It must be pointed out that the accountant who changed to social work was strongly opposed by his wife. He had difficulty finding a job in social work but it may well be his wife's influence which led him to return to accountancy which he hates. Only two respondents describe themselves as happy in their work.

Third, one respondent has not experienced problems in personal relationships. Eleven of the respondents have married but only two describe their marriages as happy and for one of these the happy marriage was her second marriage. Five of these marriages have ended in divorce. One respondent has been through two divorces. Broken engagements and broken relationships were frequently reported by the respondents. Twelve complained of boredom in personal relationships and three reported that the other person in the relationship felt "swamped" or "exhausted."

Fourth, eight of the respondents have felt the need for professional intervention over the past ten years. Five consulted a psychiatrist and none of them felt that they were helped. Three of these five concluded that they were more intelligent than the psychiatrist. Two others felt they benefited from a period of analytic psychotherapy. One consulted a professional counselor and felt herself to be in competition with him. This respondent had a radical conversion experience and after that discontinued meeting the counselor because she felt such a procedure would be incompatible with her religious beliefs that "the Lord will meet all my needs."

Fifth, the entire sample reported that they were talkative and outgoing as children but, as adults, seven of them now perceive themselves as shy and ill at ease in company. Five were frequently rebuked or teased by their parents for being talkative and outgoing. One of these five was given the nickname "chatterbox" by her parents at the age of three and this nickname stuck to her until she was a teenager. Two grew up in an atmosphere of conflict between their parents and believe they withdrew into themselves as a result. One was rebuked by her teachers for being talkative and teased and made to feel unacceptable by her peers because of this.

Sixth, one respondent felt safe with her parents and that her parents accepted her for herself, quite independently of her achievements. Both her parents listened to her ideas, at times offering guidance and criticism and she grew up feeling loved and accepted for herself independently of her achievements. She never felt pressured by her parents or that it was incumbent upon her to achieve. Her parents offered her and her sister, who also appears to be gifted, unconditional positive regard. It is tempting to draw inferences from this fact and the fact that only this respondent describes her first marriage as happy, feels entirely safe with her spouse and is one of the two respondents happy in her work. After leaving university with a degree in business administration, she had some difficulty finding a job in business. She went into journalism and is now on the staff of a monthly magazine. It is noteworthy that the other respondent who describes herself as happy in her work and in her marriage felt obliged to divorce her first husband and made a radical career change. The sample is admittedly small but there is a wealth of evidence that the child who feels loved and safe at home has the best chance of growing into a fulfilled adult.

Today's gifted child is tomorrow's gifted adult. No child can be given guarantees of a rewarding and fulfilling adult life but for the gifted there are a number of obstacles. I hope I have exploded the myth that the gifted will get ahead anyway and, if they do not, they were not really gifted. It has no basis in fact. I believe the myth is dying. A task which faces us in the gifted movement is to hasten its death and then bury it.

References
Bridges, S. I. Q. 150 London: Priory Press, 1973.
Dalton, M. Men who manage: fusions of feeding and theory in administration. New York: Wiley, 1959.
Dauw, D. C. Personality self description of original thinkers and good elaborators. Psychology in the Schools, 1966, 3.
Hagen, E. Identification of the gifted. New York: Teachers College Press, 1980.
Harding, D. W. Psychological problems in the recognition of excellence. Presidential address to Psychology Section of the British Association for the Advancement of Science, 1957.
Harding, R. E. M. An anatomy of inspiration. Cambridge: W. Heffer and Sons, 1940.
Hudson, L. Contrary imaginations. London: Methuen, 1966.
Koestler, A. The sleepwalker. London: Hutchinson, 1959.
Koestler, A. The act of creation. London: Hutchinson, 1962.
McKellar, P. Thinking and imagination. London: Cohen and West, 1957.
Martinson, R. A. The identification of the gifted and talented. Reston, Virginia: Council for Exceptional Children, 1981.
Paterson, T. T. Morale in war and work. London: Parrish, 1955.
Paterson, T. T. Management theory. London: Business Publications, 1972.
Roe, A. The making of a scientist. New York: Dodd-Mead, 1953.
Tarkowski, Z. M. T. Stress and strain in human relations. Engineering, November, 1958.
Torrance, E. P. Educating the gifted in the 1980's: removing limits on learning. Journal for the Education of the Gifted, 1980, 4 (1), 43-48.
Willings, D. The human element in management. London: B. T. Batsford, 1968.

Willings, D. The creatively gifted. Cambridge: Woodhead-Faulkener, 1980.

PART 2

THE MEANING OF GIFTEDNESS

The closest these five chapters come to a recapitulation of textbook definitions of giftedness is that the IQ is mentioned. World-renowned geneticist and demographer Albert Jacquard offers a stern warning to us that the words we use to talk about abilities and giftedness are heavily laden with connotations about hereditability and value which may ultimately and unduly constrain our understanding of giftedness. While users of English may be getting over the war of words (gifted, creative, talented, highly gifted, even severely gifted), perhaps as a result of battle fatigue more than any real solution, the spread of interest in giftedness to nonanglophone communities gives them a turn at the same task. In many cases the problem is exacerbated by the way the word gifted has become adapted in those other languages.

Nevertheless, Jacquard's points are not merely "their" issue; they go beyond the words. Joan Freeman, psychologist and researcher into the meaning of IQ scores, especially high scores, then points out that if there is a need or opportunity to use IQ scores in the selection of gifted children, this should be done with much more constraint than in the past. Her conclusion that only nonverbal IQ scores are to any extent relatively free of environmental contamination stands beside the frequently published support for individually administered general IQ measures in the identification of giftedness. Freeman also highlights the appropriateness of special educational services for the gifted. Alan Kramer provides a bridge to several of the other papers in this volume. The qualities which, in the minds of some, distinguish giftedness in a positive way, are handicaps elsewhere (witness David Willing's earlier portrayal of the world of work). Kramer puts a share of the responsiblity on the gifted, however, notably to respect the needs of those with whom they interact not to be blinded but aided by their brilliance. Special educator Klaus Urban reports that the teachers' and parents' perceptions of giftedness do not necessarily concur nor correspond to convention, but they do agree on the need to attend to accommodating individual differences in education generally. Urban suggests that this basic point may be the beginning point for a definition of giftedness satisfactory to a broad constituency. The final two chapters of this section may imply that we are spending too much time haggling over old questions and may fail to ask some new ones. Educational psychologist, futurist, and educational computer applications expert Glenn Cartwright proposes that we must take the computer into account in what may be meant by giftedness. The computer is not just a device but, on one hand, an environment; like other environments it must have an impact on the content and quality of thinking. On another hand, the computer is increasingly a prosthetic device and even an extension of the healthy body and brain. What could the mind not conceive until the hand had its extension in the hammer or pliers? What can we not yet conceive when the brain will have its computer? Futurist and scientist Earl Joseph's contribution may belong in several different parts of this volume. The technology of peace, his major theme, is a suitable curriculum topic. It also raises in counterpoint the fear acknowledged by Urban about giftedness married to evil. We suggest that Joseph's chapter poses a rhetorical question: Should our definition of giftedness include a moral component? If giftedness is to be highly valued, is it so without content? Joseph is talking about a curriculum for humanity and we are obliged to consider its place in our understanding of giftedness.

6

HIGHLY GIFTED, OR PEOPLE?

Albert Jacquard

I was most surprised to be invited to this conference. When it was confirmed that the shepherds really wished the wolf to enter the sheepfold, I realized that the organizers were courageous, and above all that they wanted to clarify ideas. This gives me certain duties, in particular that of being clear. Our task is not to get involved in a controversy, but rather, as much as possible, to derive precise concepts and to use words without ambiguity. My entire talk this morning will be about two words.

It might be imagined that arguments about words are vain, a little laughable. I do not believe this. I believe that words are tools, in fact the principal tool of the scientific researcher. Even more than pipettes and microscopes, the researcher needs words to express his thinking. Words are also weapons, terribly destructive weapons. And what I wish to show you is that the words that have united us here, that have called you together, in French "surdoué," in English "highly gifted,*" are disastrous words, horribly disastrous, destructive. Let us then discuss these words.

We imagine that each word has one meaning, and it is simply this meaning which we must evoke. But what the word really conveys, what it leaves, beyond

---

* The French word "surdoué" is sometimes translated simply as "gifted," but it has a narrower meaning. While "doué" is closer to the English terminology, "surdoué" (like "superdotado" in Spanish and "hochbegabt" in German) was used first and has gained priority in the lay language and therefore in the thinking about giftedness. The use of the word "gifted" in English has a similar history.

its explicit sense, as a track in the spirit of the interlocutor, is the implicit meaning resulting from all the preconceived ideas that have become attached to it. This double role of words is unfair; one can fight against what is explicit if one disagrees, while the implicit sense penetrates surreptitiously, underground; it marks us, and against it we fight poorly.

It is the implications of the words "highly gifted" that I wish to discuss. They are dangerous words. Why? Let us examine both components. The plan of my talk is thus ready made: first "highly" and then "gifted."

"Highly"

What does "highly" mean? It means that one is dealing with a concept that implies a hierarchy. When one puts highly before an adjective, it means that there is a scale of values. For an object on sale to be highly priced, means that it is above the normal price. To be highly gifted means to be above the others. But above the others in what respect? This remains implicit, but we know very well that it is intelligence. Trying to be clear, I thus ask the question: "What is intelligence?" Certainly there are a thousand replies, which means that there is no reply. Intelligence is creativity, it is imagination, it is comprehension, it is quickness, it is depth, it is all you wish it to be, it is a thousand characteristics of the mind. I react as a mathematician: "What, you say that intelligence is a whole and yet you wish to make of it a hierarchy?" Now, it is logically impossible to hierarchize wholes, to put them into some kind of order. The only order there may be is based on the order of numbers. To hierarchize objects, wholes, we would have, as we say in mathematics, an application of this whole on the whole of numbers. Therefore this quality which you call intelligence must be measured explicitly, not by some numbers, but by one number. As a result, the only thing that you can hierarchize and to which you can apply the term highly, opposite of lowly, is not the object itself, nor intelligence, but the parameter that you wish to slap onto it. Here a strange story unfolds, which I hope will end one day soon, the story of the parameter that we call the "Intelligence Quotient," the IQ, which for the most part is not a quotient and has not really very much to do with intelligence. IQ, two striking letters which are both often lies. Indeed, for this famous IQ to be linked to intelligence, we would have to define intelligence as Binet does: "Intelligence is what we measure by tests." This is facetious, but there is an important element of truth: it is logically necessary if IQ is to be a measure of intelligence.

But naturally, since this is a measurement, I ask questions, just as the physicist does when he takes a measurement: he questions its precision and its stability. Is the IQ precise? Is the IQ stable? You know very well that the answer to both questions is no.

The IQ varies. Thus yesterday, at one of the meetings I attended, someone mentioned the case of an IQ that jumped 50 points in one year. As for the precision of IQ, we know that it is poor. We are dealing with a measurement that is neither stable nor precise. By successive stages, we have completely forgotten the initial object, which was intelligence, and come to work on a parameter which represents we don't know what, a number. But this number has gone public. And the man in the street uses it as if it were as objective a characteristic as eye color or blood group: "My child has an IQ of 98." The verb "to have" presupposes that the IQ is an object, that it is something attached like a label. It is serious that we have thus reified a concept which in fact is undefinable. In this whole area we have the impression that we have replaced the pertinent question, "What is it?" to which no one can reply, with a completely useless question, "How can we measure it?" This is really intellectual cowardice, to replace the definition of an object by a measurement.

Psychologists have fallen victim to the fascination of numbers; they believe that to make their discipline more "scientific" it was necessary to introduce a number into it. Certainly psychology as a science today allows us to obtain credit and credits, but all at the price of betraying the object.

Let us imagine that the estheticians invent a beauty quotient, BQ, measured by computers, by dividing the circumference of the hips by the length of the nose, etc., etc. Why not? This would be an effective operational parameter. People would conclude: "Madame, your daughter has a BQ below that of Catherine Deneuve, but above that of Alice Sapritch. Your son is between Alain Delon and Michel Simon." You laugh at this idea, and you are right. Why do we not laugh when we hear about IQ?

I am not here to destroy, but to build. However, I think it is necessary first of all to dispel certain false ideas, and the idea that we can measure intelligence is one of these. Truly I do not understand why this number is so fashionable. I realize furthermore that each time that I argue with psychologists they say very quickly, "We are hardly talking about IQ. Everyone knows that that doesn't really mean much. We know that it is only one indication among others. Why do you wish to stop us calculating it?" Fine, but we must be aware of the damage done by thoughtless use of this number. Think of the sentence: "My child has an IQ of . . ." where the verb "to have" is meaningless.

Let us not deny the collective responsibility of those who have allowed this false idea to spread, and allowed a whole social mechanism to be founded on this false idea. It is in the name of IQ that in France children are "selected", which means eliminated and thrown in the waste basket. If the psychologists themselves admit that IQ has little meaning, why do we speak about it so much?

Finally, the syllables "highly" can signify nothing if the object that is evoked is this many-faceted concept which is intellectual activity.

"Gifted"

Are we gifted? That is to say, have we received

gifts? Certainly we have received gifts, or we would not exist at all. Each of us, each person, each living being, exists only because we have received gifts, but we must ask very precisely about what we mean by this term. Here we must take an elementary genetics course, and as I say to my students to get them to listen to me, we must know what it is that makes a baby. How to make a baby? Everyone knows how, but no one knows what happens. It is logically monstrous. It works out all right, but how does one explain that in sexed species it requires two individuals to make a third?

Gagne referred to the sexuality of the bacteria. That's a lot simpler. A bacterium transforms the other into itself by injecting its chromosome into it. We don't do that, however. We do not say to each other: "Come so that I can transform you into myself." We say, "We two, let us make a third." The schema is easy to sketch out: a gentleman, a lady, a child, and two arrows going from the first two to the third. But what do these arrows mean? In fact, they have no biological meaning. Remember, in Plato's time, the question: "Where does a child come from?" The answer was, "It comes from the father; the mother has no essential role. The child is completely formed in the man's semen." This idea was supported, at the beginning of modern science, when people began to look at objects under a microscope. People looked at semen and saw there spermatozoa. Then in each spermatozoon people saw, looking carefully, a baby. Ready made. That was one of the first discoveries of science. This idea was held for a long while. Now just because an idea is accepted, that doesn't mean that it is right. It only proves that it is useful to the society that uses it. Now this idea was wonderfully useful because it justified "scientifically" male domination of women.

It also justified at the time, and this is less well known, original sin, that is the idea that the child is stained from birth with sin. Theologians had trouble justifying this idea, but they were able to affirm: "It's scientific; science shows us that the baby is completely formed in the spermatozoon. If it is a girl, it is not important. But if it is a boy, he has, ready made, testicles in which there are, ready made, spermatozoon that he will emit, in the course of his life, and in each there is, ready made, the baby who will be born, and then . . . ." This was called the theory of "encasement." And at the time people even calculated the date of the end of the world by trying to find out how many generations could be nested in the testicles of a normal gentleman, Russian dolls in the form of children who will be his progeny. Going back into the past, we were all present, the nth Russian doll, in Adam's testicles. We were there when he disobeyed God. It is normal that we should be punished. And so original sin found a scientific basis.

I tell you this story only to show you how dangerous it is to use the phrase "It has been shown scientifically." We live at a time when the worst things are done in the name of science. In the name of science original sin was justified, and that is not too serious; but in the name of science racism and contempt have also been justified, and that is more serious.

It was believed also that the child was ready made in the ovum, for the ovum is a very large cell. For a century ovists and spermatists argued over whether the chld was ready made in the one or the other.

In fact, it was ready made in neither the one nor the other; but how to resolve the problem? The only way to escape out of this logical impossibility is to speak no more of this sketch, nor to evoke silhouettes of the father, the mother, and the child, but of the genes that they bear. Since Mendel, we no longer speak of apparent characteristics, but of the genes that govern these characteristics. And above all we know that for each characteristic we possess not one gene but two. My blood group ABO is unique, but it corresponds to two genes. This is a completely different vision, of which we have yet to realize the logical consequences. We have the appearance of singleness; I have only one skin color, only one intelligence, and one blood group ABO; but it is a dual collection of factors that govern these. We are beings not in a state of singleness but of duality.

The schema for procreation is thus simple. Each of the two genes that the child receives is drawn by chance from the parents. At the beginning of each being, there is the collection of genes; everything that will devolve in this individual depends on his genes. Even today, people say to me: "Can you deny that there is a genetic component to such and such a characteristic?" Certainly not. There are genetic components for everything, including my political opinions and my religion. Perhaps not as many for blood groups, but there is a genetic component for all characteristics. Without genes, I would have no religion, no political opinion, because I would not exist. Yet a gene is by nature mute. A gene cannot express itself all by itself. A gene is like an isolated word in a sentence.

In a discussion, meaning is given not only by the words but also by the grammar. If I say the sentence "The cat eats the mouse," everyone will understand me. Why? Because the words "eat," "mouse," "cat" are understood by everyone. But that is not enough. To understand me, one must also know the rule of grammar that has the subject before the verb, and the object, the victim, after the verb. The sense depends on words and on grammar; words without grammar are mute, and grammar without words is empty. We need both. It is exactly the same with genes. A gene is mute. It can only express itself because it has a relationship with its surroundings. These surroundings, in the beginning, are the maternal matrix, since, after birth, it is the environment that gives nourishment, information, affection, energy. A living being results from the interaction between the contributions of the environment and the contributions of the genes. It cannot exist without the one or without the others, just as a sentence has no meaning without vocabulary or grammar.

In this respect we ask a seemingly innocent question: "Since there are two series of causes, the genetic causes and the environmental, what is the role of the one and what is the role of the others?" We attempt to reply to this question by calling upon mathematics, by using computers, by applying famous techniques of variable analysis, by using big words like "correlation," "covariance," etc., and we obtain an evaluation of "heritability" that is believed to indicate the role of the genes in a characteristic studied.

But this seemingly innocent question is completely absurd. It can only have meaning in the very special case where genetic causes and environmental causes are joined. I have just sent an article to the journal "Biometrics" on this subject. Heritability, in the sense where it would represent the role of genetic factors in the determination of a characteristic, can be defined only if one makes the hypothesis, obviously false, that there can be addition of genetic effects and environmental effects. If one admits that the heritability of intelligence, for example, is, as had been written so often, equal to 80 per cent, that would mean that a child who has normal genes, but no education, no environmental support, would have an average IQ of 80 per cent of some total and that a child who had a normal education, but who had received no genes, would have an IQ of 20 percent of that value. It is highly unlikely that children without genes would have an IQ of 20 per cent of anything. This logical absurdity has been camouflaged by all the mathematical apparatus that was used. This is a most interesting area for epistemologists, where various disciplines, mathematics and biometrics on the one hand, and psychology, on the other, have borrowed concepts and words from one another without understanding them. It is sobering to think that certain psychologists speak, in good faith, of the heritability of the intellectual quotient, while a very famous mathematician, director of the statistics department of the University of Iowa, Oscar Kempthorne, a leader in genetic mathematics, wrote a few years ago: "In the realm of IQ, heritability cannot even be defined. How could one argue its value in this regard?"

There we are. On the one hand, people who have had the courage to define mathematical techniques to calculate heritability say, "These methods cannot be applied in the case of intelligence." On the other hand, psychologists use them and appeal to the key concept, heritability, but in their particular case it means nothing. You cannot give meaning to notions without reference to genes and to environment. You do not ask the question, "What is most important for giving meaning to a sentence? Grammar? Or words?" It is neither grammar nor words; it is their totality, their interaction. Genes are similar to the rules of grammar and the environment similar to these words. It contributes elements that the genes use to realize the individual.

This is true for all the living world, not only for people. Everything that lives results from the meeting, from the interaction of genetic factors received by chance, and from the environment. What is then specific to man?

From the biological point of view, under the microscope, man is similar to other animals. Their metabolisms are the same, but he doesn't behave like the others. He is the only species that discovered how to adapt his surroundings to himself, not himself to his surroundings. Man was probably born in the very hot and humid tropical climate of Africa. He can recreate that climate in the middle of Greenland, in an igloo; with a seal oil flame that he causes to burn, he obtains a hot and humid atmosphere. Man is the only animal who does not submit to his environment but is its coauthor. He has done even better; to the two sources of genes and environment, he has added a third source.

This third source is the collective indestructible memory based on writing. The child of man is born not only with the promises and threats of his genes, the promises and threats of his environment, but he also has at his disposal all the treasures of all the libraries of the world; he can have access to the experience of the whole species since the invention of writing. Only man has attained this. Why? Because he had the luck, thanks certainly to his genes, to have a cerebral structure extaordinarily richer than the cerebral structure of any other animal. In the brain there are, as you know, between 10 and 100 million neurons. In the course of its construction, during the nine months of pregnancy, a child lays down an average of 250,000 neurons à minute, and at certain periods, close to a million a minute; a factory with a fantastic output creates this fabulous tool which is the brain. Little by little, over his childhood, he puts in place 100,000 million cerebral interconnections, the synapses. To understand the fabulous riches implied in the enormous number, 100,000 million, I say to my students: Imagine that one day you need money and are tempted to sell your soul to the devil. Don't do it; offer the devil your synapses instead. And say to the devil, "I will sell you my synapses for one franc each." If the devil accepts, you will have 100,000 million francs. That will allow you to pay all the taxes of the French, including sales, and the direct and indirect taxes for more than a century, even if succeeding governments increase them. This, and even more than this, is the treasure of our brain.

This treasure is the source of extraordinary possibilities linked to a key concept, that of "complexity." Complexity is an ancient concept that has come into its own recently, not so much among biologists as among physicists and chemists. Let us recall what you learned around 16 or 18 years of age. From the beginning of the 19th century, our vision of the material world has been conditioned by the concept of entropy, corresponding to the famous second law of thermodynamics. This states that over time, energy can only run down. Progressively, all the universe is heading to a destiny of insipidity, destruction, a vast greyness sadder than nothingness. That is the law of matter. However, one part of this universe, the living, seems to be resisting this entropy. Instead of running down, the whole of living beings, over the course of evolution, have been enriched. We are no longer blue algae; we are richer in structure and in information than are the blue algae.

This paradox is resolved by the physicists who certainly accept the second law of thermodynamics, but take into account that this is of value only for isolated structures. But what we observe around us are nonisolated structures. In the words of Ylia Progogine, Nobel laureate in chemistry for 1977, we are interested in "dissipative" structures, that is structures which at their borders submit to the flow of energy, to disturbances. Now when such a structure is complex, it is capable of struggling against entropy by using the disturbances that it endures to enrich itself again; instead of being destroyed, it can become more complex. This is true of any structure, even an inanimate one. What is a living one? It is simply so complex that it is capable of struggling victoriously against the degradation of entropy. Thus there is no longer opposition between the inanimate and the living - there is a more or less complex continuity.

But in this scale of complexity, the champion is me, it is you, it is we humans. We have the medal for complexity with our 100,000 million nerve connections. We represent the most complex structure that has ever existed in the universe. As a result, we are capable, more than any other structure, of using the disturbances we endure to build ourselves, to self-create. In other words, to my sketch in which there were three arrows, the arrow coming from the genes, the arrow coming from the environment, the arrow coming from society, I must add a fourth arrow, that of self-creation. It begins with the individual and it returns to the individual. It is cofabrication of man by himself.

This is not the result of metaphysics. It is the logical consequence of the real physical world that gives us science. Man, thanks to his complexity, is a being capable of self-construction. Insofar as he is only the product of his genes, his environment, and society, he is a fabricated object. But thanks to this fourth arrow, he is a subject who has constructed himself. He is his own coauthor. We are coauthors of ourselves. One might give to this arrow (and here it is not the man of science who speaks) a name: liberty.

This is what a geneticist has in mind when he mentions gifts. I am the result of many sources, but in the end, I make myself. To attempt, in such a complex process, to isolate what is inevitable, that is to say what is genetic, is to fly in the face of reality. These famous gifts we speak of do exist. They come from everywhere, and they come also from myself. At a certain stage, I give myself my own gifts. Am I then gifted? Am I underendowed? Am I highly gifted? This is a question that really has no meaning.

You say to me: "We knew that already." This is exactly what is so discouraging; each time I discuss this with psychologists, they agree with me. But, what has passed into the public domain from their talk is completely different. What the public understood is that there are highly gifted people, people superior to others. And these others are victims. They accept being victims; they do not hesitate to say: "The highly gifted are the treasure of society." Why should a "highly gifted" person be more of an asset than an "underendowed" individual? If I am fighting, it is not, once again, to destroy, but to make people aware of the human demolition caused by these words. The vast majority of the population understands that it is not highly gifted, and thus that it us underendowed, destined, by nature, to be submissive.

I happened to go into the working class districts to speak to young people about genetics. Finally, in a high school in a poor suburb of Paris, one of the teachers said to me afterwards: "You have to come back. It is important. You can't imagine how many children come to us and say, 'I'm not worth anything,' because they have met with failure." That a young boy or girl of 18 years could say, and honestly believe, "I'm not worth anything," represents a total failure of the educational system. For it is false. This young person is not worth nothing, as you well know. But he believes it. And if he believes it, it is a whole social mechanism that has made him believe it. Why? Because it is really practical. A society where 95 per cent of the people imagine that they are worth nothing is a society easy to control. A society where, in contrast, people believe that they construct themselves, that they are capable of more, that they can be coauthors of themselves, this is a society which must accept a great number of (excuse the term) shit-disturbers, of nonconformists, of complainers. But this is the price that must be paid in order that each should have the option of becoming a Person.

I do not deny that the thirst to know is not the same in individuals. Certain children have an extraordinary appetite for knowledge. These children, it is true, are ill treated by society. You devote yourselves to them, and you are right, and I am trying to give you a bad conscience for doong so. We need reform in the school system to their advantage; this is certain. But why, to attain this, flatten all those who are termed underendowed?*

There are highly gifted people in this hall, but at the podium there is an underendowed individual. This is true. I am a former underendowed, and I feel a solidarity with all the underendowed that you, with the words you use, risk destroying. This conference has a wide following. A journalist said to me that he was surprised to realize how much of an audience there is for articles on this subject. Everyone is interested, for everyone asks the same question: "Am I intelligent?" In the beginning, most people ask themselves "Am I beautiful?" Most have had to answer "No." Then we make fun of ourselves and think of something else. But to the question "Am I intelligent?" we do not know

---

* In French, "sous-doué." The prefix "sur" means over, and "sous" means under.

how to reply. The only mirror in this area is the psychologist. And he will answer you, mechanically, with a number. He will say: "You are worth 130 or 98." As if that were an answer.

In the name of all those whose IQ classifies them as feeble-minded, I ask you to proclaim, you who have the power: "These words, highly gifted, we will not use them any longer. They were a linguistic mistake; these words do not mean what the public thinks they mean." All psychologists should take a vow that each time they allow themselves to say or write the words "gifted" or "highly gifted" they will do penance for eight days. More constructively, they should proclaim: "We are aware that every person is treasure, and that treasures cannot be arranged in a hierarchy." The gifts we have received are different, that is certain. But there was only one starting point. The role of society is to furnish everyone with surroundings, libraries, an education, and not to create children as we wish them to be, well built objects, but individuals capable of giving gifts to themselves, of becoming subjects. This is the price we must pay to create a society of Human Beings.

7

THE IQ AS A MEASURE OF INTELLECTUAL GIFTEDNESS

Joan Freeman

An assumption is always made, in the measurement of intelligence, that there are recognizable, quantifiable differences between children, even though the calculated proportion of environmental and genetic influences in the IQ are a matter of contention (Tobias, 1974; Scarr-Salapatek, 1976; Clarke & Clarke, 1976; Eysenck & Kamin, 1981). The more recent developments which have taken place in the calculation of those proportions are mostly statistical reanalyses of old data on, for example, twin studies. Thus old errors of measurement and the unconscious assumptions of those times must also be part of the reanalysis (Kline, 1980). Moreover, there is no evidence that children's intelligence functions in the same way at different levels. This paper describes research in England which has explored the nature and measurement by IQ of high intelligence in children.

Socio-economic Status and IQ

As part of the Gulbenkian Project on Gifted Children (Freeman, 1979), a comparison was made between 82 children who had scored IQ 141 or more on the Stanford-Binet Intelligence test - High IQ children - and 128 children who had scored between IQ 100 and IQ 140 - Moderate IQ children; 210 children altogether.

The most notable feature of the High IQ children, when compared to the Moderate IQ children, was their superior socio-economic status. All the variables, as shown in Table 1, were significantly different at the .01 level. (by analysis of variance and $\underline{t}$ test). IQ groups, in percentages of 82 and 128

Table 1

Variable	High	Moderate
Mother's high level occupation	57	27
Father's high level occupation	78	47
Mother's high level education	50	22
Father's high level education	50	30
Paternal grandfather's high level occupation	43	31
Maternal grandmother's high level occupation	20	8
Paternal grandfather's high level occupation	43	23
Maternal grandmother's high level occupation	18	11
High standard accommodation	49	42
Superior neighborhood	82	60

Both mothers and fathers of the high IQ group children were of a very high level of education and occupation in comparison with the moderate IQ group, and with the British population in general. Even the children's grandparents were of an exceptionally high occupational status. Thus the families of the high IQ children were seen to have had a two generation history of high achievement; it is very likely that they would also have had higher IQ scores than the moderate IQ group's families. Socio-economic status was thus seen to be related to high IQ in the children.

Educational Home Background and IQ

Further investigation was made to define the details of the children's home backgrounds which could have affected their IQ scores. Each step was then compared with every other step on the 102 rated home educational variables which had been described by parents and observed by the researcher.

A visible relationship could be seen between the children's IQ scores and their educational home backgrounds. It ran fairly smoothly in an inverted "U" curve from average to high IQ. The greatest number of home background differences occurred between the lowest and especially at the highest steps and the least between the middle steps that were closest together. Children of higher IQ were seen to have very different educational home backgrounds from children of lower IQs.

There appeared to be a change in the children's educational home backgrounds along the IQ range from 131 to 150. Children of IQ 130 or more were seen to have educationally more positive home backgrounds than children of lower IQ. It was probable that the children's home backgrounds had affected their scores.

Children Who Scored at the 99th Percentile Nonverbally

Of the 210 children in the sample, 65 had scored at the 99th percentile on the Raven's Matrices Test. They were then examined in terms of their IQ scores and educational home backgrounds. The mass of original variables was reduced by cluster analysis to a more manageable number of constructed variables for this purpose. The only significant differences (at the .01 level) to emerge between IQ and environment for them were the cultural milieu of the home and provision made for the children; that is, achievement-related facilities. In brief, it was what parents did at home and the provision they made for their children which affected the level of the child's IQ score. Parental attitudes were not found to make a significant difference, nor did social class per se, but parental behavior did. Significant environmental differences in the home backgrounds of Raven's 99th percentile children were contrasted for IQ above and below 140.

The Raven's 99th percentile child who scored highly on the Stanford-Binet test was seen to be from a much more favorable home with regard to its cultural milieu and the facilities provided for the child's scholastic achievement. Thus equally able children, measured nonverbally, from different kinds of homes were found to have significantly different IQ scores. For the 99th percentile children the average correlation for those home environment variables with IQ was r = 0.508 - their scores thus reflected a 26% environment to 74% heredity ratio. But, for the children of 50 to 99th percentile the average correlation of these home environment variables with IQ was r = 0.362, so that their IQ scores reflected a 13% environment to 87% hereditary ratio.

The IQ as a Measure of Intellectual Giftedness

Gifted children (measured nonverbally) appear from this study to be particularly able to benefit, more than other children, from a good educational environment. Because the IQ measure picks up a substantial proportion of those effects it is especially likely to define as its highest levels gifted children from the best environments. Intellectually gifted children from poor environmental circumstances may not score more highly than nongifted children from better circumstances. The gifted child's considerable potential to benefit from input would be expected to widen the gap in IQs between gifted children from good and poor educational environments. Less able children will be less dependent on the environmental effect on their IQs as they are less able to benefit from it. Hence, gifted children identified by IQ alone are almost inevitably from excellent home backgrounds (Reissman, 1962; Frierson, 1965).

Children who score at IQ 141 or more, within the top 1% of the Stanford-Binet, are considered here as gifted children who have, to a considerable extent, realized their potential. It would seem safe, at that very tiny percentage of the population, to assume that even were such high IQ children to be underachieving, they could be said to have such a high ability level that they could still be termed gifted. That children may achieve at this level because of their educationally supportive and providing environments, is not to say that they are less gifted; it is preferable to say that they are gifted children who are realizing their academic potentials and that children of the same ability who do not score appropriately on such a test are not realizing their academic potentials.

If the IQ test is regarded primarily as an achievement test at its higher levels, then giftedness may be measured with it on that understanding. But what the test may fail to do is to identify gifted children who are not sufficiently educationally well provided for or who are handicapped in their intellectual functioning. Because of that reserve it would be preferable to avoid the widespread use of the IQ as the sole means of identifying the intellectually gifted.

However, in the real world the IQ is used by nonpsychologists quite readily, as though it were a fixed quantity of ability, and by many psychologists too. As an adaptation for the probable continued use of IQ testing as a measure of giftedness, it would be useful to have a cut-off point to work from. The evidence from this study has shown that at IQ 130 to 150 the environmental effects begin to be particularly effective. It is therefore suggested that the lower level of IQ 130 be used as a base measurement from which giftedness may be further judged, which would involve about 3% of the child population. IQ points measured above that should then be considered.

It is also suggested that where an IQ test is used as a measure of giftedness then some other form of nonverbal or specific ability measure be used in parallel. Although it is recognized that a high score on a nonverbal test such as the Raven's also reflects some measure of achievement, it is relatively less influenced by educational environmental factors. It is clearly quite impossible to measure a child's intellectual ability independently of environmental influences, but it is possible to minimize their effects.

Conclusions

1. The IQ is an unsuitable measure of innate intellectual giftedness in children, as it is progressively more contaminated with environmental influences,

particularly from IQ 130 upwards.

2. Nonverbal tests are the fairest and best measures of innate ability and should be used in identification of the gifted along with other specific measures.

3. Gifted children are particularly able to benefit from educational provision.

References

Clark, A. & Clarke, A. D. B. Early experiences: myth and evidence. London: Open Books, 1976.

Eysenck, H. J. & Kamin, L. Intelligence: the battle for the mind. London: Pan Paperbacks, 1981.

Freeman, J. Gifted children: their identification and development in a social context. Lancaster: MTP Press, 1979.

Frierson, E. C. Upper and lower status gifted children: a study of differences. Exceptional Children, 1965, 32, 83-90.

Jensen, A. R. Educability and group differences. London: Methuen, 1973.

Kline, P. Burt's false results and modern psychometrics: a comparison. In H. Beloff (Ed.), A balance sheet on Burt. Supplement to the Bulletin of the British Psychological Society, 1980, 33, 20-23.

Reissman, F. The culturally deprived child. New York: Harper & Row, 1962.

Scarr Salapatek, S. An evolutionary perspective on infant intelligence. In M. Lewis (Ed.), Infant Intelligence. New York: Plenum, 1976.

Terman, L. M. The measurement of intelligence. Boston: Houghton Mifflin, 1916.

Terman, L. M. & Merrill, M. A. Stanford-Binet Intelligence Scale manual for the revision. Third Revision, Form L-M. London: Harrop, 1961.

Tobias, P. V. IQ and the nature/nurture controversy. Journal of Behavioral Science, 2, 5-24.

8

THE GIFTED CHILD AS FREAK:
BRILLIANCE AS HANDICAP

Alan Kramer

The Gifted Child in Context

The concept of giftedness is one of the oldest in the lexicon of Man as an intellective being. The ancients were convinced that their various gods bestowed unsolicited gifts of wisdom and insight on a small selection of worthies. We have come a long way since then. Having split the atom and unraveled the secrets of the DNA spiral, the study of human intelligence has joined the march of science, as we've touched, probed, and bifurcated the human brain. We know about synapses and neurons, hemispheric dominance, and where various pieces of information are stored and processed. Yet, in our fundamental conception of giftedness as a human phenomenon, we are still very much captives of the ancients' world view. We still maintain with uncritical conviction that extremities of mental endowment are automatically "gifts," to be appreciated and envied.

The reality, sadly, is sometimes at odds with this ideal. Human beings exist in contexts, within which behaviors and characteristics are honored or condemned, rewarded or punished based on their degree of conformity to a set of norms. Within different contexts there are different degrees of receptivity to specific forms of normative divergence, but all systems tend to be self-protecting and wary of idiosyncracy. The particular benefits or hazards of giftedness cannot be understood without reference to the one context within which all young people, gifted or otherwise, are found - the normative institution known as the school.

The typical school is an institution with all of the normative and hierarchical rules that categorize all institutions. Organizationally, it is an environment strictly divided between adults and children, with a separation of roles that is nearly total. Philosophically, it exists for the sole purpose of transmitting a certain catechism of attitudes, perceptions, skills, and pieces of knowledge from one generation to another. Whether it performs these roles well or poorly, with tyrannical rigidity or with warmth and flexibility does not change its basic character. The school is a value-laden place. It processes, judges, and molds, and, despite the fact that virtually everyone in the world must go there at some stage of his life, for some it really isn't the right place at all.

It is admittedly not the right kind of place, for example, for the severely retarded, handicapped, or emotionally disturbed. It is not that such children have no need for these same skills and bits of knowledge that are transmitted to the rest of the population. In many ways such children need them to an even greater degree. The problem lies in the normative nature of the manner of transmission in the school. Because of particular qualities of mind or body, the "match" between the nature and rate of acquisition of educational content on the part of these children and the nature and rate of transmission on the part of the school is inappropriate and often impedes rather than facilitates development.

This discontinuity between the problematic child and the traditional educational context is something that educators have come to understand, accept, and attempt to deal with in increasingly systematic ways. What they tend neither to understand fully nor to deal with is the comparible discontinuity that exists for a significant minority of the children at the opposite end of the intellectual scale. It is assumed as an educational axiom that gifted children, bestowed as they are with special capabilities, have the automatic potential to succeed at whatever challenges they face. Exceptions to this rule are written off as aberrations or as examples of lack of effort or "concentration" on the part of the children themselves. What is not truly considered is the possibility that giftedness can in some cases be just as much of a disruptive influence in a child's life as retardation or emotional disturbance.

Part of the problem is confusion of concepts. The very passivity of the term "gifted" encourages the most idyllic interpretations. That the "gift" received by the child might not suit him to the daily demands of his environment does not seem to be seriously considered. In our haste to categorize the gifted child, several crucial questions are ignored. It needs to be asked, for example, what type of "gift" the child has been given - a photographic memory, extraordinary analytical powers, exceptional linguistic or mathematical fluency, or a pension for intellectual creativity and divergent thinking. To what extent does this particular package of traits prepare the child to succeed in the normative environment of the school? How well adapted emotionally is the child himself to the unique intellectual and social pressures (not least of which is the discontinuity between his mental, emotional, and chronological ages) this gift imposes on him?

A Continuum of Psycho-Intellectual Stages

There are, broadly speaking, two areas within which such conflicts tend to manifest themselves among gifted children, in their relationship to the imposed learning structure of the school and to the matrix of social relations and norms that spring out of this structure. Both of these areas are directly and inextricably linked to each other, despite the existence of taxonomies that separate them into cognitive and affective domains. In fact, all children (as well as adults) perceive and experience their environment as a piece. The mental processes that allow them to see the world around them, define its boundaries and operations, and determine a place for themselves within it are essentially identical, whether the object at hand is a geometry proof or a set of peer relations. The notion that cognition can exist without reference to style of thinking, insight, personal receptivity to ideas and concepts, and the like is just as illusory as the notion that affect is unrelated to an individual's ability to intellectually understand the nature of the social milieu within which he must be able to function. That such an artificial separation of human operations into parallel taxonomies has gained such wide currency is more a testimony to the utter passivity of the average child within the educational framework than to any natural breakdown between these areas. In other words, it is the school that isolates affect from cognition and not the intrinsic nature of the human species.

With the gifted child, the artificiality of this division becomes even more obvious. For one thing, the concept of "task commitment" that is crucial to the realization of intellectual potential clearly demands both an in-depth understanding of the task and the personal commitment to carry it out. In addition, the extraordinary fluency of the gifted child interferes with any strictly linear notion of intellectual development. Whereas the average child in school tends to learn what he is taught in the order he is taught it, the gifted child tends to see resonances between ideas and concepts that go far beyond the immediate learning task. Within Bloom's taxonomy, he may leap from knowledge to synthesis in a given area, simply because he has already gone through all the intermediary steps on his own. He may devise his own problem-solving approach, thereby blocking out whatever "conflicting" rules he is being taught. He may project a given topic onto a related area about which he already has strong feelings, thus allowing his "personal viewpoint" to "interfere" with what he is supposed to learn.

Rather than by restricting it to distinct and essentially rather linear taxonomical structures, the functioning of the human mind (and especially of the gifted human mind) might better be understood as moving through a "Continuum of Psycho-Intellectual Stages." These are not sequential steps, but components of intellectual independence, which is, or at least should be, the goal of all learning. Each stage is not "prerequisite" to the next in the narrow sense, but each provides a foundation and starting point for movement upward. Finally, once a base-point is established on any level, an upward momentum tends to occur, where development through the continuum becomes self-generating, drawing an individual toward higher and higher stages, as follows.

Retention: absorbing, assimilating, and retaining specific facts, ideas, and concepts to be subsequently retrieved for appropriate use.

Application: performing operations based on learned or self-derived ("looping" withing the Continuum) principles or algorithms in specific situations and based on defined rules and procedures.

Analysis: assessing specific characteristics of given situations in relation to stated or derived principles.

Generalization: synthesizing disparate data in order to determine the underlying principles in a given situation.

Projection: applying conclusions derived from one area of study to a related area, another field of study, or different time frame (future projection).

Valuation: evaluating a given situation according to a system of principles, selecting a set of values appropriate to given situations, and applying those values within one's own area of operations.

Commitment: developing a confluence of attitudes and actions based on a system of values, beliefs, and intellectual and personal commitments.

Independence: achieving a level of personal autonomy based on clarity of thinking, flexibility, tolerance of ambiguity, and personal commitment.

The key to the understanding of this model lies in its "directionality." Progression within the Continuum is based not merely upon increasing levels of psycho-intellectual "sophistication," but on a natural flow between absorbing information, using it as a basis for making sense of the world around, drawing conclusions and judgments about the world, defining a personal posture within it, and defining a way of life based on an informed system of values. That such a construct represents an "ideal" rather than a description of normative human behavior should not be used as an argument against it. In truth, the fact that we have come to accept a dichotomy between thought and action as "normal" may be one of its strongest arguments. It is no coincidence that the school places almost all its emphasis on Retention and Application, with only the most superficial attention to Analysis and Generalization, and with a pronounced hostility to any translation of intellectual activity into informed action (the Back-to-Basics movement has virtually institutionalized such regressive attitudes). The lack of "parallelism" between, say, Application and Commitment present overwhelming problems within a school context but no contradiction whatever "in life." It is assumed as a given in the non-school world that information and understanding should manifest themselves in a system of values and should lead to a way of life that is consonant with all of them. Much of psychology is directed toward correcting problems caused by a breakdown in this natural continuum. It is fatuous to think that the school-confined human mind should be impervious to such a natural developmental process.

The Gifted Child as Freak

Whereas most children may not be aware of being excessively confined by the limited psycho-intellectual perspective of the school, it is precisely the gifted child who has the capability and the natural inclination to progress beyond narrow or "academic," who perceives the Generalization embedded in the analysis being presented in class, who can make the Projection into related areas of thought, who assigns meaning instinctively to the cold masses of information being doled out to him, and who seeks some form of commitment to activate his beliefs. This tendency of gifted children to stretch the moral and philosophical as well as the intellectual confines of the curriculum has been well documented by many in the field (Karnes & Brown, Freeman, Terrassier, and others). Because of this, he is faced with a fundamental dilemma: does he close his mouth (and his mind) and confine himself to the restrictive psycho-intellectual diet presented to him; or does he wade into the fray at his level of interest and commitment, thereby risking the opprobrium of teachers and fellow students alike?

If he chooses the first path, the cost in terms of wasted and potentially atrophied intellectual ability could be staggering. A mind unused, like an arm or leg confined to a rigid cast, loses its suppleness and tone. The longer it is confined the more severe and potentially permanent the damage. Within the limited universe available to the child, he may lack the rehabilitative opportunities to reverse the damage before it is too late. Worse, however, is the possibility that, faced with the certain knowledge his perception of the world must be "wrong," at least where it counts in school, he may lose confidence in himself altogether and simply shut off his brain, much as the autistic child appears to do in a different context. In this case, rehabilitation appears to be unnecessary, for the untapped potential of the child's mind is rigidly shielded from view by his own protective mechanisms.

Another possibility, of course, is that the child will persevere, demanding a fair hearing and insisting on the legitimacy of his perceptions. Here the risks can be even greater. Teacher and students alike know how to distinguish between "acceptable" and "unacceptable" behavior. Right answers or clever insight that don't make others feel stupid are "in." Digressions or irrelevant comparisons or challenges to the accepted order are "out." Students who indulge in such behavior are seen as distracted, troublesome, disruptive, or just plain weird. It is not a matter of intelligence as much as one of role. It is not so much the straight-A "brain" who is an outcast. It is more the "freaky kid" who insists on talking about Japanese-American collusion in the bombing of Pearl Harbor, "and just when we were having such a nice discussion, too." It must be remembered that class discussions are part of the "showcasing" function of the school, an opportunity for students to give the expected right answers, prove that they have read the required material, and appropriately impress the teacher ("Don't forget that class participation counts as part of your grade."). By introducing "irrelevancies," sensible only within his world-view and intellectual perspective, the gifted child disrupts the orderliness and predictability of the classroom, thereby threatening the entire intellectual reward and punishment system that is vital to the success and self-confidence of both student and teacher alike.

Even more threatening than the gifted child who outstrips his fellow students (and often his teacher) in psycho-intellectual sophistication, however, is the one whose patterns of thinking leap-frog through the supposedly immutable hierarchy of skills with an unnerving lack of sequentiality. Just as the formalized symmetry of classical Newtonian physics held out tenaciously against the heresies of Quantum and Relativity Theory, contemporary pedagogical theory holds fast to the concept that learning must by its nature be predictable and sequential. Little credence is paid to the possibility that the human brain might be capable of quantum leaps of understanding and insight fully as discordant with the Conventional Wisdom as Planck's concepts seemed to be eighty years ago. What happens to the child who is capable of bypassing entire sequences of carefully constructed curricula in order to reach his own understanding of Algebra (as both Planck and Einstein did) or language structure, or who simply finds a different sequence of steps more sensible to him?

What happens to the gifted child whose mental proclivities lead him in different directions, through different sequences of learning, or to different conclusions than his more "normal" classmates? For him, the issue is not one of either speaking his mind or maintaining silence. It may well be a matter of intellectual and emotional survival. However flexible the human mind, it is not a formless mass of clay. It cannot be contorted into configurations that are totally alien to it. A child who brings a different kind of logic to the study of mathematics or language or science or any other discipline may not be capable of discarding his entire mental apparatus, simply for the purposes of conforming to a set of externally imposed learning conditions. There are countless stories of mathematically gifted children, for example, who, having devised their own roadmaps through the complexities of long division or fractions, are thereafter simply not capable of seeing the logic in the elaborate sets of rules presented to them. This psychic "roadblock" prevents them from retaining and applying the "acceptable" procedures and creates a level of confusion from which they cannot extricate themselves. The imbedding of their giftedness within their unique mode of perception leaves them inept and "stupid" in the face of the meaningless rules that must be applied without thought or personal involvement.

The personal and social implications for this type of gifted child are enormous. Extremes of intellectual potential do not create infinite degrees of intellectual malleability. The capacity for quantum leaps in insight and understanding do not guarantee either the intellectual or psychic ability to "erase" those insights and to perform on demand like a well programmed computer. High levels of psycho-intellectual ability do not promise conformity within a system in which only the lowest levels are demanded or even accepted. The ability to use one's brain creatively and effectively in no way ensures that the spirit will prove equally effective at warding off the scorn and isolation that may be the natural concomitant of not "fitting in."

Concordant and Discordant Modes of Giftedness

To assume from this that all gifted children (or even most) are intellectual misfits would be a great error. The fact is, as Terman and many others have pointed out, that most gifted children do adjust well, even in environments where much of their unique capability is wasted or actively repressed. The point here is that giftedness is not a monolithic factor that affects all children the same way in all sets of circumstances. Under certain conditions, giftedness can enhance an individual's ability to function in the world, and does so in the great majority of cases. There are conditions, however, under which certain forms of giftedness can present serious handicaps to their recipients. In fact, giftedness as a concept can be sub divided along three different lines:

1. **Type** of giftedness - General Intellectual Ability, Specific Academic Talent, Leadership, etc.

2. **Degree** of giftedness - testable IQ level, degree of creativity, etc.

3. **Mode** of giftedness - Concordant or Discordant.

Concordant modes of giftedness are those forms of mental capability that tend to better prepare an individual to succeed within and surpass societal expectations. Discordant modes of giftedness, on the other hand, tend to provoke an individual into conflicting with and threatening those same societal expectations. The very contextual nature of this concept makes it clear that Concordance and Discordance will vary somewhat in terms of the particular norms and expectations of any given society. As Margaret Mead and other anthropologists have long pointed out, societies have their own codes of acceptable behavior that differ considerably. In general, however, Concordant modes of giftedness tend to include all forms of academic proficiency, fluency of memory, linguistic and computational facility, analytical and algorithmic ability, and virtually all types of psycho-motor, artistic, and psycho-social giftedness. This does not mean that such forms of giftedness guarantee success or even prohibit failure and lack of adjustment. It merely means that these forms tend to be more consonant with societal roles and thereby success-enhancing by their nature.

Discordant modes of giftedness include intellectual nonsequentiality, a propensity for divergent thinking, high creativity, virtually all forms of psycho-intellectual behavior that are not considered age-appropriate, and both idiosyncratic and iconoclastic orientations. It is important to emphasize that these are not intellectual "poses" which are freely adopted but rather ways of thinking and seeing the world that flow naturally from an individual's psycho-intellectual make-up. Why one individual's giftedness takes a Concordant turn while another's becomes Discordant is as unanswerable as why one becomes a mathematical genius and another not. It is clear, however, that an attempt to activate Discordant forms of giftedness within a normative environment such as a school is far less likely to prove "successful" than an attempt to employ more Concordant behaviors.

Learning the history of racial or religious prejudice, for example, drawing generalizations about it in terms of social and political institutions in past societies, even dramatizing it theatrically or artistically can all be Concordant activities at which gifted children can shine. When these perceptions are activated, however, when past injustices are related to present injustices, when basic suppositions are questioned, when contemporary social institutions are in any way challenged, or when the school is perceived as a heuristic for such social problems, Discordances are created. Are these latter perceptions less the product of a gifted mind then the former? Is the basic distinction one between a "good student" and a "trouble-maker?" Or, is it possible that the latter perceptions are as natural to one type of gifted mind as the former are to another? In short, are these approaches merely reflections of different modes of giftedness?

It is ironic to note that educators (even educators specializing in gifted children) are as much bedeviled by these questions as the general population. When asked to name gifted individuals, most educators would list at least some of the following: Albert Einstein, Winston Churchill, Isadora Duncan, Thomas Alva Edison, Max Planck, Franklin Delano Roosevelt, Ludwig Van Beethoven, and Pablo Picasso. In fact, such names are used with great frequency when justifying the need for special programming for gifted children. The truth is, however, that none of these individuals were viewed as particularly gifted during their childhoods. Most were perceived as strange, and many were even seen as stupid and lazy. The mode of giftedness each possessed - precisely what made each of them uniquely successful as an adult - was seen as Discordant and out-of-step with existing expectations. Interestingly enough, this notion of being out-of-step or ahead-of-one's-time is one of the clearest signs of genius among adults. Thus, the contradiction: Discordant modes of childhood giftedness, despite being recognized as potential precursors of adult genius, tend to be viewed as aberrations and indications of mental dysfunction, even among those educators otherwise most attuned to the educational needs of children. In this regard, it is interesting to note the number of gifted programs whose selection criteria contain provisions specifically constructed to screen out such children, through the use of intellectually limiting convergent testing devices, reliance on open-ended teacher recommendations, or the imposition of psychological criteria based on "adaptability to the program."

Brilliance as Handicap

It would be nice to think that this contradiction were subject to simple solution. Unfortunately, it is not. Societies are by their nature normative and conformist; that is, in fact, what is said to distinguish society from anarchy. The independent thinker, the mind "ahead of its time" will always seem strange and somewhat alien. The tendency of Man to resist change will always be directed against those who are viewed as different and threatening. The potential loss of human capability by the under utilization of creative talent, on the other hand, is so staggering, especially as societies become more technological and thereby more monolithic and centralized, that some new approach to the problem is mandatory.

The first part of any such solution, of course, is awareness, awareness of the fact that the differently-gifted "freak" does exist, not only in institutions of higher learning, but in the prisons, the mental institutions, the principals' offices, the unemployment lines, wherever society's "misfits" are gathered together. What to do with these gifted outcasts can perhaps best be perceived analogously.

Much of the metaphorical language applied to gifted individuals revolves around the imagery of light: the flame of intellect, the spark of fire of genius, bright-ness, brilliance. The analogy is not accidental. A brilliant mind, like a brilliant light, has a Janus-like quality: it can illuminate, or it can blind. The difference is one of "attitude," the directionality of the light itself and the perspective of the observer. To the extent that the brilliance can be directed in concert with the needs of the observer, to illuminate dark and unfamiliar territory, that brilliance can be tolerated and even appreciated. Yet, turn that brilliance into the face of the observer, and it engenders nothing but fear and anger. Many (if not most) gifted individuals have the capability, because of the mode of giftedness with which they are endowed, to direct or "modulate" that light to adjust to these external demands. Other modes of giftedness, however, are not so easily adaptable. It is doubtful that an Einstein, a Churchill, or an Edison could have been the kind of "beacon" each turned out to be had he been forced to "dim his lamp of genius" in order to survive in the world. It is toward such individuals that the "attitude" of educators must be directed. There are four basic things that need to be done:

1. We must search for these people wherever they are, in the schools, on the street, in the jails, in the mental institutions, and among the outcasts and loners of society.

2. We must resist the temptation to teach and mold them to our expectations; rather we must help them to accept the uniqueness of their gifts and the difficult but crucial role that each of their "different drummers" will lead them toward.

3. We must become their advocates in the world

outside, demanding greater tolerance for differentness of all kinds and insisting on the legitimacy of their place as society's problem finders as well as problem solvers.

4. Finally, we must help them understand how to control their tendency to blind those around them and to use their brilliance as a source of illumination for themselves and for others.

This may not seem like much, a bit perhaps like playing Sancho Panza to Don Quixote. But that too is an important role for educators: to cherish, protect, and champion the special qualities of the unique human mind. In the final analysis, there is no one else to do it. And for some potential Edison or Duncan or Einstein, living today in an artificial shell of self-doubt and isolation, it could make all the difference in the world.

9

A COMPARISON OF ATTITUDES TOWARD THE EDUCATION OF "NORMAL," HANDICAPPED AND GIFTED CHILDREN

Klaus K. Urban

Gifted children are a minority and all those people who care for the gifted are a minority, too. Minorities always have to battle against prejudices. Experiences and conversations do not often give you the feeling that the majority of the people have positive attitudes towards gifted children or their advancement. Giftedness produces insecurity. This can lead to anxieties.

But, oddly enough, you can find no explicit attempts in the literature to evaluate or to make those prejudices and attitudes a little more objective. Only in connection with other research or program evaluation does one sometimes find some corresponding statements (Butler & Butler, 1979; Mira, 1979). It may be that this problem is more relevant in our country than in other countries. Because our situation in the Federal Republic of Germany is different from other countries in several respects, I must provide some introductory information.

The Situation of Gifted Children

Some years ago almost no one in West Germany knew anything about gifted children and related questions. Germany was and is still an "underdeveloped country" concerning the gifted (Urban, 1982). In 1978, the "German Association for the Gifted Child" (GAGC), stimulated by the work of the British NAGC, was founded. Without any financial support its activities are very limited. Nowhere else is anything done for gifted children younger than 15 years. For the older ones there are some research and cultural competitions, some foundations supported by money, and counseling for gifted university students - defined by very high achievement at the "Gymnasium."

In 1980, for the first time at all, a high federal German civil servant, a State Secretary in the federal Department for Culture and Science, made some remarkable comments on gifted children: "There is no contradiction between equal chances for all and the furtherance of the gifted." To promote the "giftednesses" of as many pupils as possible is one aim of the state's policy. This policy says "Yes" to a kind of elite, dependent on the simple idea that the Federal Republic of Germany as a country poor with raw materials has to endeavor in a special way to raise all those "riches" sleeping in the heads of young people. We are still waiting to see possible consequences.

In addition, in the last two years a slowly increasing number of articles have been published in newspapers, magazines, and journals; some radio stations broadcasted interviews or short reports. It seems that step by step, the "taboo of giftedness" becomes broken. There is a lot of reserve among the people, especially the teachers. For the most part, the situation can be characterized in terms of ignorance, prejudices and lack of information.

The School System
In many ways we have an ambiguous situation in Germany. On one hand there is a strongly selective procedure to get access to some disciplines at the universities. Only the very best students defined by highest average points in a lot of very different subjects at the final school examination, the "Abitur," may study medicine, for example, one of the so-called "numerus clausus" disciplines. On the other hand, there is the partial and tentative establishment of "Gesamtschulen," comprehensive schools. But often the comprehensive education by opponents as well as by supporters is misunderstood as an equalization to the same level, neglecting the unique personality of every child.

It may be that the relative proportion of gifted

children in the "Gymnasium" is higher than in other parts of the three-part school system ("Gymnasium," "Realschule," "Hauptschule"); but, considering the university education of teachers, the curriculum and the pressure of the "numerus clausus" mentioned above, first of all the well adjusted, noncreative, nondivergent thinker, the rigid and assiduous learner will be successful. In spite of the relatively high achievement level called for, often the gifted potential is not challenged, resulting in frustration and deviant behavior.

As for handicapped children, there is a highly specialized school system under the term "special education." There are special schools, for example, for physically handicapped, visually impaired, speech disordered, learning disabled, hearing-impaired, mentally retarded, and multiple handicapped children. The recent discussion, especially among younger educators, argues against this separation, its stimulus word being integration. In contrast to the U.S.A., for example, gifted children are not classified under exceptional children. This may be because there have been no gifted children in the minds of educators and politicians up to now. While working at a Teachers College in special education, training teachers for speech-disabled children, I was specially interested in their opinion on the education of handicapped children as compared to "normal" and gifted.

Social, Political and Historical Background
The problem of equality and democracy has been mentioned above. People think that a relatively young democracy like ours may not provide privilege for only a few children, but do not consider that simultaneously there are still privileges for some social groups for socioeconomic reasons and that a lot of potentially gifted children are underprivileged. Another big problem is based on the specific German situation and history: the deep aversion to elitism. It was a terrible kind of elite which nearly half a century ago brought crime, murder and war into the world. Too often and

too quickly gifted education - as we think of it - is falsely put into connection with the term of "elite" and its bad connotations. But I think that identifying, helping, and furthering gifted children, considering their common, special and individual talents and needs is one essential condition which can prevent similiar events in the future and help to cope with the hard problems of mankind, too.

Seeing this situation described above, and considering the political, social, educational, historical background, it seems very important to have more and specific information about people's opinion on gifted questions in general, about the thinking and attitudes of teachers, educators, psychologists towards gifted children and their education. Among other things, this information is necessary to find correct and effective short and long term strategies to convince people, to get support from politicians, to alter opinions and attitudes. This study could be a first step towards a broad and profound evaluation.

Method

In order to have a relatively economic instrument a questionaire consisting of two different parts was developed. In the first part 17 statements are given (see Table 1). It seems important not to isolate reflections on the gifted from the whole educational context but to combine similar questions: statements on integration versus special schooling, of individualized teaching and enrichment, on teaching handicapped children, on possible consequences for schooling based on individual exceptionalities, gifts, or needs. Some of them are a little bit provocative. The statements were to be rated on a five-point-scale as to their correctness or worth to be supported. "Fully correct" is designated by "1"; "false or full rejection" is designated by "5."

Table 1

Overall Mean Ratings on Questionnaire Items

Number	Statement	Mean
1.	Concerning handicapped children it is important to discover and further their abilities.	1.06
2.	Children are so different individually that they should not be taught together in classes combined by age.	1.92
3.	Most speech-disordered children are of average intelligence.	2.55
4.	In contrast to less intelligent children the gifted to do need special educational and instructional attention.	4.03
5.	Segregation into special schools does not further - in any way - handicapped children.	2.72
6.	The earlier disorders and handicaps are recognized, the more children can be helped.	1.03
7.	An integrated education of all children - handicapped or not - in the schools would best fit the claims of a democratic education.	1.36
8.	Pedagogy and instruction in general could profit by theoretical and practical efforts at a special education for the gifted.	3.44

COMPARISON OF ATTITUDES

9. Speech-disordered children need more help than children with normal speech.   2.06

10. Every child needs an education in schools which is individualized to his needs, abilities, and interests.   1.41

11. Too early identification of gifted children can be rather detrimental.   2.39

12. Normal school handicaps children.   2.56

13. Like special schools for less able children there can be schools for the highly intelligent, too.   4.02

14. If "special education" means an an education which is oriented at comparable aims but works in a individualized manner, then pedagogy should mean a "special education," too.   1.70

15. An integrated education of all children together - handicapped or not - would best fit the needs of the children.   1.68

16. Gifted children should be helped in in a special way within the regular schools.   2.26

17. Children who cannot be taught or instructed adequately in regular schools - good conditions provided - can be labeled as handicapped.   3.34

The second part consists of 15 educational aims to be rated as to their relevance concerning three groups of pupils: "normal," handicapped, and gifted children:

1. independence
2. creativity
3. social adjustment
4. cognitive flexibility
5. sense of responsibility
6. tolerance
7. autonomy of thinking
8. diligence
9. decision-making ability
10. trustworthiness
11. political consciousness
12. orderliness
13. peace-making ability
14. contentment
15. ambition

The terms used are relatively abstract, at a high level of generalization. They refer to attitudes and to personality traits as well as to abilities in cognition and thinking. It can be assumed that all are more or less acceptable and relevant, but that they get different weights and rank positions for the different groups of pupils. "High relevance" is designated by "1"; "no or minimal relevance" by "5".

The questionaire was given to 126 people: 65 teachers and 61 students in special education. A short form of the first part with 6 items (2, 4, 5, 7, 10, 13) and the second part were given to 98 parents of children visiting a regular public school in the 5th and 6th grade (ages 11 to 13). The data of 120 responses from 91 persons could be evaluated.

Results

Not only will "pure" results be described, but also data in combination with short comments and attempts at explanations. A comprehensive interpretation will follow.

Statements rated by teachers and students. With two exceptions there are no general differences between teachers and students. Therefore, the combined results are described. Table 1 shows the average extent of agreement with or rejection of the statements. As can be seen, the highest agreement occurred on items 1 and 6, the first one as a kind of warming-up statement, the second one as a sentence with an expected high level of affirmation.

Let us concentrate on the special "gifted" statements. The two strongest rejections are items 4 and 13. At first glance there seems to be a contradiction. On the one hand 73% of the teachers fully or in part confirm that gifted children need special educational attention. On the other hand, 76% deny that there should be special schools for gifted children. Items 8 and 16 give the necessary completion. Because there shall not be special schools there can be no special pedagogy for the gifted by which the normal pedagogy could profit (item 8); therefore most of the teachers say that the gifted should be particularly furthered within the normal schools.

A high consensus exists on item 10 where a highly individualized school education is emphasized. This is supported by the result of item 2. Considering the strong agreement to items 7 and 15, a contradiction in terms seems to occur. How to solve the dilemma of a high individualization versus full integration? The combination of both demands seems to be utopian. (I can't see any presuppositions, either in our educational system, in political volition, in teachers' training, or at universities to make such a coexistence possible.) Substantial differences between teachers and students, which reflect at the same time age differences, and may be as such in study contents, too, are to be found at item 5 and 16. The students support item 5 (they doubt the positive effects of separation) whereas the majority of the teachers reject the statement.

Seventy-two percent of the teachers support fully or in part special provision for gifted children in regular schools (without separation), compared to only 28% of the students whose majority (54%) declines it. It seems that among the students the dilemma between the theoretical approach of individualization and integration and the practical translation is greater than among the teachers, maybe because of the students' lack of practical experience and greater idealism, not burn-out.

Attitudes and opinion of the parents. With one exception, the parents' ratings show quite another picture (see Table 2).

Table 2

Comparisons of Parents' (P) and Teachers (R) Ratings

Items	Ratings		(Percentage)			Mean	Mode
	1	2	3	4	5		
2 P	11	13	33	31	11	3.1	3
T	37	43	6	5	-	1.9	2
4 P	9	34	16	34	7	2.9	2/4
T	4	11	7	17	61	4.2	5
5 P	5	8	10	29	49	4.1	5
T	19	26	4	44	7	2.9	4
7 P	31	3	14	49	2	2.9	4
T	69	22	7	2	-	1.4	1
10 P	60	28	2	10	-	1.6	1
T	74	20	2	4	-	1.4	1
13 P	11	22	42	14	11	2.9	3
T	6	9	11	30	44	4.0	5

Though 88% think that each child needs an education set to its individual needs, abilities, and interests (item 10), only 24% decline fixed classes in which children are grouped by age (item 2). Their attitudes towards total integration are not unanimous, more negative than supporting (item 7). They appreciate the separation of handicapped children much more than the teachers of such children themselves (78% versus 51%; item 5). As to special provision for gifted children, their attitudes are split, but rejection and affirmation are moderate (items 4 and 13). In contrast to only 15% of the teachers, 33% of the parents say "yes" in general to special schooling for gifted children, but 35% decline their establishment. The parents answers seem first to reflect their own experiences and school socialization. Second, they reflect their responses to their children's situation, for, after the combined 5th and 6th grade, the so-called "orientation level," the children will attend one of the three different types of secondary schools, depending on achievement and parents' choice.

Ratings of the educational aims, by teachers and students. Table 3, left column, shows the order of the 15 educational aims after all the ratings of the teachers/students group for normal children have been weighted and summed up. The highest possible average weight was 1.0; the lowest possible weight was 5.0. On the basis of the estimated relevance, you can distinguish three groups: first, the first four aims with the very high similar weights from 1.14 to 1.22.

Table 3

**Rated Relevance of Educational Aims
by Teachers and Students**

Normal

1.	independence	1.14
2.	tolerance	1.16
3.	creativity	1.21
4.	social responsibility	1.22
5.	peace making	1.41
6.	decision making	1.43
7.	autonomy	1.51
8.	cognitive flexibility	1.59
9.	trustworthy	1.60
10.	political consciousness	1.65
11.	contentment	1.70

12. social adjustment	2.30
13. diligence	2.43
14. orderliness	2.51
15. ambition	2.79

Handicapped

1. independence	1.13
2. creativity	1.16
3. tolerance	1.21
4. social responsibility	1.35
5. peace making	1.44
6. contentment	1.56
7. decision making	1.57
8. autonomy	1.66
9. trustworthy	1.66
10. cognitive flexibility	1.89
11. political consciousness	1.89
12. social adjustment	2.19
13. diligence	2.43
14. orderliness	2.48
15. ambition	2.78

Gifted

1. tolerance	1.09
2. independence	1.19
3. creativity	1.19
4. social responsibility	1.22
5. decision making	1.32
6. peace making	1.37
7. autonomy	1.41
8. political consciousness	1.44
9. cognitive flexibility	1.48
10. trustworthy	1.71
11. contentment	1.71
12. social adjustment	2.35
13. diligence	2.37
14. orderliness	2.49
15. ambition	2.83

Mean weights are shown: 1 = highest weight; 5 = lowest.

COMPARISON OF ATTITUDES

These aims can be named personality traits which characterize a mature personality, with marked self-identity connected with a high level of social responsibility. The middle group reaches from position 5 to 11; with aims 9 and 13 it joins relatively closely and by content to the first aims representing the dialectics between individual and social competences. Remarkably lower are the weights of the third group which contains 3, 8, 12, and 15. It is astonishing that these abilities and traits, though rated positive to a small extent, and which seem to characterize the "normal," successful man of our days, are judged to be less relevant. It will be interesting to see if parents think the same way. As to the three groups and the relative position of the aims, there are nearly no substantial differences between teachers and students; the exceptions are items 11, 7, and 4. Political consciousness ranks some places higher for students than for teachers, and cognitive flexibility seems less relevant. This is the picture for "normal" pupils.

As shown by Table 3, this picture is, in general, valid for the handicapped as well as for the gifted children. The three groups are stable; only rank variations within the groups can be noticed. The last positions and rank weights for the last four aims seem to be fixed.

As for the handicapped, the grade of contentment increases; that of political consciousness decreases. As for the gifted, the latter is taken to be more relevant, like decision-making ability (item 9). It should be considered that the first place with the highest weight is held by "tolerance." This seems to be a cautious hint of the reservations and expectations towards the gifted students (the "lack of accepting others," cf. Burg, 1981).

Frequency statistics and order alone do not give sufficient information on possible congruence of the data. Therefore, a correlation analysis was computed. The majority of the 990 coefficients are significant or positive, thus demonstrating that there are no contradictory aims. The only exception is the low but significant negative correlation between "orderliness" and "creativity" (normal group, r = -.22; p = 0.044). A factor analysis described later will show something more about the relations and unity of aims.

Table 4 shows the correlation coefficients (Spearman-Brown) for each aim between the three groups of children.

Table 4

Correlations among the Aims for the Three Groups of Children

Group/Aim	1	2	3	4	5	6	7	8
N/H	.71	.81	.96	.72	.72	.79	.80	.92
N/G	1.00	.89	.96	.76	.84	.72	.70	.96
N/G	.71	.75	.88	.51	.67	.49	.64	.88

continued	9	10	11	12	13	14	15
W/H	.83	.80	.83	.91	.89	.88	.88
N/G	.76	.96	.82	.96	.89	.94	.92
H/G	.53	.79	.60	.86	.77	.82	.86

N: "normal"   H: handicapped   G: gifted

At first, all figures, are positive and significant, most of them high and very high. This confirms the first impression of relatively high conformity as to the assessment of the relevance of educational aims for different groups of children. The highest conformity exists for "normal" with gifted; "normal" with handicapped follows. Though substantial and significant, all the correlations for handicapped with gifted are lowest.

Four items in particular seem to be rated less uniformly than the others: cognitive flexibility (4), tolerance (6), decision-making ability (9), and political consciousness (11). Their worth for each group seems to be different. The highest coefficients and accordances in each of the three group combinations were for aims 3, 8, 12 and 15. Those aims were assessed lowest for each group.

Factor analyses can give useful information if the relations between the aims for each group have the same or another structure. The calculations of the factor analyses yielded different factor structures for each group. For the "normal" children, three factors emerged; for the handicapped, four, and for the gifted two (see Table 5).

Table 5

Factor Structure of Aims
for the Three Groups of Children

"Normal"
Common variance 67.2%

Factor 1		Factor 2	
decision making	.77	diligence	.90
trustworthy	.76	orderliness	.88
independence	.75	ambition	.77
peace making	.65	social adjustment	.58
autonomy	.61	trustworthy	.44
contentment	.55		
creativity	.52	**Factor 3**	
political consciousness	.46	tolerance	.81
		creativity	.61
		cognitive flexibility	.54
		autonomy	.51
		social responsibility	.51

Handicapped
Common variance 71.9%

Factor 1

orderliness	.86
ambition	.79
social adjustment	.58
trustworthy	.49

Factor 2

independence	.92
decision making	.64
contentment	.59
peace making	.51
trustworthy	.49

Factor 3

tolerance	.84
social responsibility	.70
cognitive flexibility	.63
autonomy	.46

Factor 4

political consciousness	.78
autonomy	.54
peace making	.53

Gifted
Common variance 64.9%

Factor 1

independence	.91
tolerance	.81
decision making	.80
creativity	.77
autonomy	.76
peace making	.74
social responsibility	.69
contentedness	.65
trustworthy	.63
political consciousness	.54

Factor 2

diligence	.89
orderliness	.87
ambition	.74
social adjustment	.61
trustworthy	.46

Factor loadings shown following each item.

In the last case, the structure of factors seems clear, though complex. The traits of the first factor, a kind of main factor (50% of variance) seem to be seen on the background of a mature personality with a marked self-identity, free from external determination, but strongly dialectical combined with social responsiblity, and connected together by the influence, challenge, possibilities and responsibilities of a generalized giftedness.

The second factor which can be described in exactly the same way for both other groups, too, contains those traits we found rated lowest; they can be named as more or less old-fashioned, traditional educational aims. Here, as for the normal group (17%), they play a relatively moderate role (14%). Not so for the handicapped group: here they constitute the main factor which accounts for 38% of common variance. For the handicapped the factor structure is more differentiated, which might reflect the more complex and difficult situation of the handicapped. The four factors can well be named by the respective first and highest loading variable of each factor: orderliness, independence, tolerance, and political consciousness. The distribution and constellation of variables within the factor structure for the normal group cannot be interpreted clearly.

Parents' ratings of the aims. As expected, the average ratings of the parents (for normal children) differ from those of the teachers. The correlation coefficient for the relation between the order of the aims is .42. That is not significantly different from zero. Agreement exists as to the first place: independence. The greatest amount of assessed relevance was lost by tolerance, from second to eleventh position. The highest rises (up to ranks 2 and 4) are found for aims 10 and 3. The list of the four most important aims, rated by the parents, looks quite different from those rated by the teachers and students: independence, trustworthiness, sense of responsibility and social adjustment. Least important are political consciousness, and autonomy of thinking; less important are creativity and, to a smaller extent, flexibility of thinking. This picture is valid for the handicapped children too, but not for the gifted, though the correlation is significant and relatively (r = .73). The substantial differences concern tolerance which, as for the teachers, is situated highly on the third rank, and diligence, which is placed down on the

14th rank.

Summary and Conclusion

Opinions and attitudes of teachers, students, and parents towards different groups of pupils do not fully conform, but to a relatively high degree are similar.

Concerning schooling, they differ in questions of integration versus segregation; as to the aims in only a few items, especially political consciousness and tolerance. It is surprising that the relevance of the aims for different groups of pupils in general is assessed so equally. This can lead to the conclusion that it is not the groups of pupils that are to be considered as different, but the ways, and means, and the extent by which and in which the different aims can be realized. But in the eyes of the interviewed people, this does not mean necessarily a splitting of schools into various sections, separating children from one another because of their exceptionalities.

No direct aversion to the gifted has been found, but a kind of cautiousness and reserve which can be interpreted as maybe a lack of information about or a sense and sensibility for giftedness. The factor analysis showed that there is no differentiated picture for gifted children, but that an equalizing and generalizing mantle of "giftedness" is laid over all the aims. At this point, both sides of the label "gifted" and our activity become obvious. On the one hand we try to direct the attention of the people, teachers and so on toward a group of exceptional children, toward giftedness and gifted children, but on the other hand, the danger of equalizing arises that is similiar to the "halo" effect. The whole individuality of each child is exclusively seen under this label.

But as the answers to the statements make clear, there is in general a high consciousness of the necessity of an education which is designed to an individual's needs, abilities, and interests. If this is no lip-service, this could give the starting point and way for deeper understanding of giftedness and the needs of gifted children, on the wide variety of facets of giftedness, which are as manifold as there are different individuals.

The assessment of the statements pointed out the discrepancy between a highly theoretical and desirable approach of individualization and the practical experiences, and chances to realize this within school education, especially within a relatively differentiated, but uniform and rigid educational system, as in Germany. Macro- and micro-changes would be necessary in various fields, from the self-understanding of the teachers and their role, to curriculum and general school directions; from the organization of schools, classes and teaching, to the attitudes of the involved people.

In connection with such outlines, it must be kept in mind that the alteration and development of the relation of the individual to his social and natural environment, and to himself. The direction points at an individual and social personality, an individuality which is the result of a reciprocal interaction process, in which the individual on one hand is dependent on surrounding historical and social conditions, and at the same time is acting independently. The degree of a handicap can be defined by the relation between independence and dependence, between self-determination or self-regulation and external determination. This interpretation of handicap is different from a traditional concept; it does not exclude that the so-called "normal" or even the gifted child can be or get handicapped.

An individualized education has to cope with the basic contradiction of the pedagogical process, that is, the realization of personalization as self-determination by external determination. At the same time it should be obvious that not only the life of a handicapped person is a life within limitations. Individual learning and internalization of knowledge always includes the systematic omission, if knowledge includes the "learning" of the renunciation concerning the conscious individual development.

Thus, the question seems justifiable if so-called

special education is in fact the normal education, and that education which thinks itself competent for the nonexistent "normal" case is in fact the special education. Under such premises all children could benefit from further development and evaluation of educational theories, concepts, and programs designed for "special" children, gifted or not. Thus the motto of the conference ("Many views of the gifted for the advantage of all children") may not be seen isolated from the reciprocal proposition; it is a dialectic, supplementary process. By the orientation of learning processes toward concrete activities, capabilities, and potential of real individuals (not at rigid social norms) and taking into consideration their social and natural environment, educational and pedagogical actions can be fruitful for a satisfying social and individual personalization of all children, fruitful for all "special normal" children, for the advantage of the gifted, too.

References

Burg, B., Special programs for the gifted in Israel: a study of attitudes. Presentation at the Fourth World Conference on Gifted and Talented Children, Montreal, Canada, August 22nd, 1981.

Butler, N. & Butler, R. Parents and children's perception of special classes for highly gifted children. In J. J. Gallagher, (Ed.) Gifted children: reaching their potential. New York: Trillium, 1979, 223-245.

Mira, H. Creative behavior of gifted children from a disadvantaged social background. Gifted and Talented Education, 1979, 1 (1), 93-96.

Urban, K. K. West Germany - a developing country concerning the gifted. Gifted International, 1982, 2 (1), in press.

10

SYMBIONIC MINDS FOR THE GIFTED

Glenn F. Cartwright

One problem in the education of the gifted has been that little attention has been paid to their special needs, and when these needs have been recognized, relatively little has been done to accommodate them (Telford & Sawrey, 1977). Teachers, parents, and others who work with the gifted have often found themselves frustrated, suspecting that the gifted children in their care were bored, and were wasting both their time and their talent. Unfortunately, up to now, little could be done about it, because of the lack of special facilities, and because of the general lack of knowledge on how best to meet the needs of the gifted. Yet the realization has been steadily growing that special facilities and special attention for the gifted are not unwise, nor unfair, nor necessarily unequal (Goldenberg, 1979). As de Bono (1980) asked:

Does the concept of equality demand that a big man be fed more than a small man or that both be equally satisfied with their food? So special attention to the gifted is not contrary to egalitarianism.

We might note in passing a parallel problem in the use of computers in education. If we did not know what to do with gifted children in education during past years, we knew even less what to do with computers. As Papert and Solomon (1972) observed:

How strange, then, that "computers in education" should so often reduce to "using bright new gadgets to teach the same old stuff in thinly disguised versions of the same old way."

It is incredible that the gifted with great human potential, and computers with infinite machine potential should both have suffered the same fate, historically, at the hands of educators. But the way seems clearer now, and there is little doubt that the emergence of inexpensive microcomputers in education will be a boon to the gifted, allowing them to extend their intellectual power in ways previously unimaginable.

Evans (1979) recognized this phenomenon with respect to calculators and projected it to computers:

> But there is a kind of bright child, usually coming from an educationally upmarket home, who takes to the calculator like a duck to water, exploring its myriad permutations for sheer pleasure and, in doing so, acquires an intuitive grasp of fundamental mathematical concepts. Math teachers are already familiar with this small but interesting breed who stand out so markedly from the rest of the class . . . . If this trend becomes at all strong, we could find ourselves with a generation of children sharply divided between those who have amplified their own brain power with that of the computer and those who remain wedded to the haphazard ignorance of the past. (pp. 143-144)

One can easily see that the role of the microcomputer in the education of the gifted will be great. But the purpose of this paper is not to dwell on the role of microcomputers in the education of the gifted, for that is the stuff of the present and the immediate future. The purpose of this paper is to provide an even deeper insight - a peek farther down the road. To do this will be to catch a glimpse, not only of the long term future, but perhaps of the very direction of humanity itself.

Symbionic Minds

Such a task is not a simple one, nor one taken lightly, but it is necessary if we are to sense the future in any meaningful way, in an attempt to better understand our role and direction in the present.

Marshall McLuhan (1965) pointed out that the media had become extensions of man's nervous system: that radio, for example, had become an extension of the ear and television an extension of the eye. These extensions, however, had two characteristics: not being wired directly to us they were somewhat external, and most involved only one way communication.

The next significant step on the human agenda might well be the direct extension of the human nervous system involving two way communication with the human cortex. Much evidence exists to suggest we are already proceeding in this direction. So let us begin by recapitulating some recent advances in four particular areas. They are: (a) indirect interfaces to the brain like "emgors," (b) brain pacemakers, (c) biocybernetic communication, and (d) artificial intelligence. The following summary is intended to present the flavor of this research.

Emgors (electromyogram sensors) are devices which are now used to pick up brain signals in the muscles of amputees to control artificial limbs. They represent one way of tapping into the brain using existing nerve pathways. Similar approaches of tapping into nerves to reach the brain have been used in other applications: for example, at the University of Florida research continues in an attempt to find ways of implanting up to 100,000 miniature photovoltaic cells to stimulate previously unused parts of the retina in cases of retinal blindness. At the Los Angeles Ear Research Institute electronic ear stimulators act on the auditory nerve to return some semblance of sound to certain patients with acute hearing loss.

The second is the development of brain pacemakers which have been used for certain patients to help avoid deep depressions, prevent epileptic seizures, and reduce intractable pain. They have been used with neurotics, schizophrenics, and others who have experienced the feelings of extreme anger often associated with psychosis or violent behavior (Heath, 1977). Other cerebellar stimulators have been implanted as brain pacemakers to help spastic patients and those with cerebral palsy.

In the area of biocybernetic communication, experimental work continues in an attempt to interpret brain wave patterns and link them to specific thoughts. Pinneo and his colleagues (1975) were able to have subjects hooked to computer screens move white dots about simply by thinking about them. The Defense Advanced Research Projects Agency (DARPA) has reported that it is now possible to distinguish on electroencephalograms (EEGs) motor responses from cognitive processes, and decision-making processes from action components. The U.S. Air Force has reported training subjects to control their alpha waves in order to send Morse code messages which could be picked up by a scalp-monitoring machine and fed into a computer. One obvious goal of such technological development would be to use thought to control a wide variety of appliances. Imagine the utility of a pocket calculator if we could operate it by just thinking about the numbers rather than pushing corresponding buttons. The extension of this kind of research might eventually result in mental communication between individuals and even between machines and individuals, in a manner similar to telepathy, but based on proven scientific principles and sophisticated technology.

The final area, and it is a broad one, is that of artificial intelligence. Though this sounds a strange term to anyone unfamiliar with it, scientists around the world working in the area of artificial intelligence are studying pattern recognition, problem solving, and voice comprehension with a view to reproducing these abilities in computers. The tiny chess-playing machines which can now be purchased in local stores are a spin-off of this research. This work is now becoming more publicized - a rather good popular summary was given by Stockton (1980).

SYMBIONIC MINDS

The handwriting is on the wall: these four areas have much in common. For the most part, they deal with the brain directly, with thought processes individually, and with intellectual activity primarily. They are steadily converging. When they merge, it may be possible to create tiny, auxiliary brain prostheses called "symbionic minds."

Symbionic (from the words symbiotic and bionic) minds will amplify intelligence, and perform a wide variety of functions that we now take for granted as comprising intelligent human activity (Cartwright, 1980a, 1980b). Taking this projection as a plausible scenario, then, the question we wish to explore here is "What will happen when such devices as symbionic minds become widely available, and how might the gifted and all of mankind profit from them?"

The Synergy of Symbionics

It has already been suggested that the creation of symbionic devices will greatly increase our intellectual function. But a symbionic mind by definition will be more than just another tool. It is likely that the interaction between individuals and their symbionic minds will be synergistic - each will act with the other to create a new effect greater than the sum of their individual effects. Thus may man and machine be wedded, and the offspring of their union may be a synergistic system unlike any other. We may find ourselves dealing, in the future, with a new level of intellectual functioning, and perhaps even a new level of consciousness. Far from being a crutch-like device, the symbionic mind will contain sophisticated technology with its own degree of machine intelligence designed to enhance human abilities, and to propel man far beyond his innate potential.

Exponential Acceleration

Now consider what the upper limits might be if such a symbionic mind were available to a person already gifted with superior intellect. On the surface one might expect, as we always do, a linear relationship: a symbionic mind of a certain size might be expected to increase brainpower by x times. But this may not be how it will work at all. The gifted who participate in such a synergistic union may experience an intellectual leap more exponential than linear. Such cortical prostheses may help the gifted soar to new heights of creativity, imagination, and invention with no upper limits in sight.

To illustrate the concept of exponential growth, Evans (1979) asks us to imagine taking a piece of paper and folding it over on itself fifty times. Ignoring the difficulty of doing so, how thick would the resultant wad of paper be? Because most of us, mathematicians and computer programmers included, are more used to linear change and are usually unaccustomed to thinking exponentially, we are surprised to learn that the "stupendous block of paper will have pushed far above Everest, right out of the atmosphere, past the moon, beyond the orbit of the planet Mars and into the asteroid belt. Human beings just do not have a conceptual experience of the exponential."

There is every indication that high technology in the hands of the gifted might well produce more than we expect, and more than we can even imagine at this point in history. As Christopher Evans (1979) has pointed out:

> it is a characteristic of any race which involves exponential acceleration that the man who gets off first continually pulls away from his opponent (p. 245).

It is suggested that in the future, the gifted may be those who "get off first" and who continually pull away because of their intellectual exponential acceleration.

The Future Beckons

To summarize, (a) current medical and technological progress suggests the eventual development of brain prostheses known as symbionic minds to amplify intelligence, (b) the nature of their interaction with the human cortex will be synergistic, and (c) the resulting leap in intelligence will be exponential rather than linear.

It would be unwise to place our hope for the future on existing technology, for we have had many false starts and have been let down so often in the past. But there remains the glimmer of hope that a radically new and qualitatively different technology is on the horizon whose potential for good may vastly outweigh apparent disadvantages. Those who experience it may come to know an intellectual freedom previously unheard of. They will communicate at levels previously unknown. They will share new knowledge previously unimagined. They will find a peace previously undreamt of. If they can use their improved talents to return to us some solutions to the problems left behind, then the circle will have been completed, and our minimal investment in these mind prostheses will have produced significant dividends for mankind. To be aware of the impact of this new technology is the path we must follow. To learn how to use this new technology wisely is the direction we must take. This is our challenge for today, and our hope for tomorrow. The future beckons.

References

Cartwright, G. F. Symbionic minds: the advent of intelligence amplifiers. Paper presented at the First Global Conference on the Future, Toronto, July 1980. (a)

Cartwright, G. F. And now for something completely different: symbionic minds. Technology Review, 1980, 83 (1), 68-70. (b)

de Bono, E. Future positive. New York: Penguin, 1980.

Evans, C. The micro millennium. New York: Washington Square Press, 1979.

Goldenberg, E. P. Special technology for special children. Baltimore: University Park Press, 1979.

Heath, R. Modulation of emotion with a brain pacemaker. Journal of Nervous and Mental Disease, 1977, 165 (5), 300-317.

McLuhan, M. Understanding media: the extensions of man. New York: McGraw-Hill, 1965.

Papert, S., & Solomon, C. Twenty things to do with a computer. Educational Technology, April 1972, 9-18.

Pinneo, L. R., Johnson, P., Herron, J., and Rebert, C.S. Feasibility study for design of a biocybernetic communication system. Menlo Park, California: Stanford Institute, August 1975.

Telford, C. W., & Sawrey, J. M. The exceptional individual (third edition). Eaglewood Cliffs, New Jersey: Prentice-Hall, 1977.

Stockton, W. Computers that think. New York Times Magazine, December 7 and 14, 1980.

11

EXPERT SYSTEMS AND PEOPLE AMPLIFIERS

Earl C. Joseph

Advances in technology can have an impact on our methodology for achieving peace to either extend (evolve) our present approaches or to offer entirely different (new and revolutionary) alternatives. The latter can be more appropriate for the future than the technology and methods tried in the past. If we research peace, educate for peace, design society for peace, create peace machines, manage for peace, and apply technology for peace, (i.e., "build" societal machinery for peace) could we not have peace?

What new insights do our newly gained knowledge from the anticipatory sciences, general system sciences, computer sciences, artificial intelligence or the space program offer that is transferable to other areas of society? Certainly one area of needed application is in our decisioning process relative to peace for the future. For example, what is the machinery for peace? Also, what are the autocatalytic initiating triggers for establishing new tunnels into time, through the space of alternative possible futures, of the type which lead to and achieve lasting world peace?

Today our society, in its issues, reactive and crisis management mode, is akin to mid-course guidance functions of a peopled rocket going to the moon or aboard a future flight of the space shuttle - but with a major difference. Our trip to the future is largely without visions of the goals of where we are headed. That is, there is a lack of goals, except for reactive and corrective decisions and actions for easing the problems or attempting to avoid a problem crisis.

Our incremental reactive problem-solving approach for marching into the future as a process for defining the path, and where we arrive for each new today, virtually guarantees that the farther along the path we go into the future, the more problems there will be to solve. This comes about since few efforts are expanded to decide ahead of time which desirable futures to design, initiate, and construct, other than to solve past problems. Of course we need such solutions, but we also need to drive into the future with goals and visions (that the results of the application of the anticipatory science could provide) of where to go, rather than reacting after the crash of each crisis to turn us in another direction.

Peace Alternatives

The economic, technological, societal and political bases of war are rooted typically 5, 10 and often more than 20 years in the past - prior to hot confrontations using war machinery, whereas the cultural, religious and moral rationales for war were typically planted hundreds of years in the past, and even thousands of years ago. We see this vividly, for example, in Iran and Ireland today. Thus one path leading to future peace is to shake off the shackles of the past via modernizations involving education, new laws, new technology, new goals (e.g., China's present turn toward industrialization). Of course, such a turning point for a nation or region must be designed and programmed very carefully or else reactionary reactions set in. That is, like Iran, a group entrenched in its past dogmas swell up as a backlash against modernization changes, causing a national U-turn toward recapturing their past.

In other words, one path to peace is to remove and release society from its heritage, its identifications with its past, its past dogmas and the like. Obviously such an alternative is not easily achievable, in the short range, without immense internal reactions or control, nor is it always practical, nor always desirable for either short or long range futures. Therefore, society must also look for, and set into motion, other pathways toward future peace, while it is in transition from its past solidifications.

This is not to imply that the past does not offer many desirable things, intuitions, heritages, dogmas, etc., that would or could enhance the future. Rather, the implication is that there are some things that were found to be operative and desirable in the past, which are not appropriate now or for the future. This is perhaps best visualized once one realizes that our society is constantly gathering new knowledge from the research we conduct. Therefore, obviously the past didn't know everything that we now know or will know in the future.

Further, the social, technological, political, cultural, and other environments will be at least as different in the future from what they are today, as they are different today from those in the past. Therefore, some things, especially values, which were found to be desirably useful in the past may not be so in the future. Moreover, some values which can be operable or could be desirable in the future could not be so in the past. Therefore, future values must be considered in the context of the future possible technio- socio-political environments.

Today the war drums are beating ever louder - in El Salvador, the Mid-East, Poland, Ireland . . . Is it possible that the next world war is already in the making? Can it be prevented? Since laws, technology, goals, aspirations and the like can be traced back in time as the culprits leading to war, then the way they are initially designed should become paramount considerations in any efforts toward maintaining lasting peace. This leads to the conclusion that the future consequences of what we do today in deciding or designing a new law and a new social or hardware technology must take into account the long-range impact and consequences (rather than just today's imperatives) of today's reactions, actions and decisions.

From such considerations, we are finding that we must learn how to become anticipatory (pro-active) and how to preplan the autocatalytic paths we intitiate and carve into the future. We are learning that reacting, after the fact, to the dastardly deed that has been done to a current set of negative symptoms caused by a design decision made years ago by a past today's decision, causes more problems than are solved. What we are learning is to redesign to make "things" go right. But actually, for the longer term we need to learn how to decide and design "things" to go right from the beginning, rather than depending on reactive "social debugging" redesigns. Usually, today, we allow the negative impacts to build to crisis proportions before taking reactive actions. As such, when we become deeply immersed in a crisis environment, causing considerable pain (economic, lack of freedom, deprivations, or other), we thus require and must implement short-range corrective solutions. But even short-range solutions take a long time to ease the pain of the crisis - many years and sometimes decades. Worse yet, there are few alternative solutions left for the short range other than conservative deprivations or war. That is, when we need short range corrective actions either we are forced to give up something or go to get more. Of course each of these alternatives (so called solutions) can not hasten the achievement of the solution to the root problem. At best, short of war, short range solutions can only band-aid and soothe the problem symptoms. Rather, the more likely impact is to widen the gap to their solution or to create many new problems needing more short range solutions. All of us are familiar with the old expression, any solution to a problem creates more problems to be solved later on.

The message of course is to attack ("the best defense is an offense") at the front end when societal and technological decisions are being made, to solve both short range and long range problems, but more importantly to create and design future opportunities. That is, we need to move from the "problem-solution" ethic to "opportunity generating" in what we do. Such a trend in our value system is underway - albeit as yet only a small trend - thus there is perhaps considerable hope for the longer range future. This means, as implied in the foregoing, that we must take a longer range view as well as a more holistic general systems view when attacking at the front end, decision making efforts using an opportunity-generating paradigm. To do so requires the application of the anticipatory sciences. Included are holistic anticipatory forecasting and anticipatory technology assessment for generating future opportunities of the positive desirable impact nature and for pre-preventing negative consequences from what we do as intitial decisions and design actions. That is, our task is to remove future anticipated problems before they can become real (negatively impacting) problems as one positive way to achieve lasting peace.

From such foregoing anticipatory science philosophy relative to peace considerations and application, one of the questions that looms large is: what are the social, cultural, religious, etc., hardware and software technologies for peace? In other words, what is the machinery of or for peace? Today, every school student and many adults, can quickly tell us what comprises the machinery of war. However, few if any of us can intuitively tick off a list of the machinery, or even the strategies, required for peace. Today we cannot cite a tool kit for peace because research hasn't been performed to inform us of what machinery is needed in such a peace tool kit. Secondly, and partially as a result, the study of peace, at all grade levels, as courses in the curriculum has not been a part of our education processes, world wide. Further, we do not have a Department of Peace - in any state nor at the national level. One of our forefathers, George Washington, wanted a Department of Peace. His bill has been in Congress, as of 1976, over one hundred and fifty times - and like the first time, Congress continues to vote it into nonexistence.

For example, Minnesota does not build war machinery like guns, tanks and bombers to wage a hot war with its neighbors, Wisconsin and Iowa. Rather, "war machinery" like laws, taxes (e.g., incentives for business to locate in Minnesota) and other social intruments are used to fight "economic battles" with neighboring states. That is, our current value systems today allow socioeconomic "wars" but not "shooting wars," within the boundaries of a nation in order to gain or equalize civil strife. From such observations, one obvious way for forever eliminating hot shooting wars with MXs, atomic bombs, tanks, and bombers is to get rid of nations; that is, to create one nation on earth. Such a solution (?) would at least remove the mechanisms for building shooting type war machinery. Of course this solution does nothing, however, to correct internal trends leading to "war" and thus society would still be left with other forms of civil strife (union strikes, widening gaps, regional deprivations, or lack of access, etc.). However, in at least one sense, from the carnage of war viewpoint, such remaining (non-shooting) forms of war could be more humane. That is, instead of quick death in war, the pain of economic deprivations could perhaps last longer. But, with the removal of the need to spend societal capital on war machinery, society, as in the Japanese case since World War II, would have more capital to spend on correcting the root problems and trends that would otherwise build up, forcing the need for war. Thus, history again points a way (solution) with at least one example alternative that could be applicable for the future.

Intuitions for Peace Futures

In applying the unique concepts, ideas, methods and techniques of the anticipatory sciences and general system sciences to the question and achievement of peace: the natural question is: What are these unique concepts? Further, if we ask what should be included in the curriculum or content of peace education, we are faced with a similar question. In what follows, an initial answer is presented (your suggestions, additions, and changes are solicited):
- Developing a futures perspective.
- Identification and education of trends to avoid or encourage, new alternatives to design and generate

proactivity processes, impact assessments, and time dynamics for achieving peace.

- Researching scenarios for future peace and the identification of ways to bridge the present to such futures, for creating possible, probable and preferable peace futures.

- Implementing general systems intuitives and techniques.

- Holistic future images, total system views (designs and assessments), complexity handling techniques, feedback systems and dynamics, cybernetic dynamics, which involve the total world rather than a couple sectors.

- Designing "All Win" open futures, futures wherein everyone wins, rather than closed zero-sum future scenarios wherein only a few win.

- Designing for anti-introgenetic (elimination of system-caused problems) futures which are crisis immunized and predisarmed.

- Developing opportunity-generating management philosophy, rather than a negative, reaction, action system - away from a problem-solution ethic toward opportunity generation ethics.

- Designing convivial (friendly, safe, nice, desirable, fun) and symbiotic (living peacefully together) type socio-pol-technio systems.

- Initiating peace macroprojects, total (world) societal cooperation and involvement projects for peace.

- Establishing peace information, education and government networks and links.

- Governing through integrated future-impact assessed decision making including: human, social, political, technological, institutional, energy, environmental, inter-and intranational dynamics and cost-benefit efficiency impact assessments.

- Initiating turning points, strategies, and trends for peace.

- Establishing long range peace via schooled visions and images, mediated and established goals, projects, and opportunities.

- Initiating reward systems for peace.
- Creating nonviolent alternative future scenarios for governments.
- Mapping peace cybernetic management and societal planning and control mechanisms.
- Doing open systems (rather than closed systems) design for establishing peace adaptable systems and evolvable systems.
- Researching and designing for scaled down and scaled up technology, ie., appropriate technology for peace futures.
- Developing peace languaging and its diffusion.
- Establishing peace (futures) engineering curricula.
- Educating for peace, growth of intuitions from peace education, hope, and cooperation, developing life-long educational institutions for peace.
- Propagandizing for interest convergence for global concerns, peace symbols, value changes towards peace, etc.
- Creating operative environments (designs) for peace (example: "pink rooms").
- Establishing rewards and positive reinforcements for individual peace-affirming behavior.
- Measuring and directing (governing) world societal trends towards peace.
- Developing on-going peace strategies, their implementation and management and research.
- Developing peace institutions (academies, governmental departments, etc.)
- Developing holistic global designs for peace which are compatible at local levels.
- Tracking (e.g., measuring) trends for societal movements toward continuing peace, that is, anticipatory measures indicating where our actions and decisions are taking us and society-establishing societal measures that are usable as yardsticks or thermometers for peace.

Further, can continuing global peace be our long range future without an intuitive base for peace? That is, until peace education, as a disciplined and mandatory study area which occurs at all educational

levels, occurs world-wide, can we as a society expect continuing peace? What would such courses of study consist of? Some possibilities besides those implied above are:
- Alternatives to war for conflict resolution.
- The tools and machinery of peace.
- Designs for peace.
- Peace research.
- Peace management and control systems.
- Peace taxonomies for the strategies, methods, techniques and technology for peace.

Of course such lists can go on and on as do the questions, such as:
- What is peace and how can it be maintained or guaranteed for the future, ie., what do we mean by peace and how do we get it?
- What institutions do we need to instill via education (in students and adult public world-wide) to achieve and desire peace?
- What other institutions of peace does society need, micro and macro, local and global, national and international?
- What futures concepts and general systems intuitions should education instill, and at what grade levels?
- What paths are we on taking us into the future, toward peace or war?
- What are the economic incentives implementable for maintaining peace?
- What social indicators do we need to give society measures as to whether or not we are headed toward continued peace?

Technology and Peace Machinery

Today, and for the relatively long range future, silicon chip semiconductor technology is expected to continue to grow in usage and expand into a wider range of applications. But what comes after silicon chip technology, farther out in the future? Can such technology be used for creating peace machinery and for amplifying an individual's use of society's amassed knowledge?

Answering the first question, which is being asked more often, takes us along many new technological avenues which are opening for the future. They include gallium, arsenide, and sapphire wafers (instead of chips) and bio-physical technology. For nonsilicon chip technology, ememplified by the first two listed above, higher circuit densities and higher performance (in speed or reliability) seem possible, thus allowing continuing evolutionary progress for electronic and computer systems. The latter two from the list suggest that for the future, however, step-function revolutionary advances are also possible and likely.

Today, on a single silicon chip it is becoming possible to integrate over a hundred thousand electronic circuits, and soon more than half a million using near submicron geometries. Each circuit consists of approximately two and a half transistors (micro logic switches), four resistors and four capacitors - all made in the silicon by imbedding (doping) other elements (etching or implanting impurities into the silicon) with layers of evaporated metal and resistive materials. Such complexity of circuits per silicon chip allows the design and implementation of complete machines into a single silicon component, and as evolutionary future advances occur, we should be able to integrate larger and larger (in capability) machines onto the silicon. Such "chip machines" or "component machines" become building blocks for bigger machines. For example, the advent in late 1971 of the "calculator chip" made possible the modern hand-held calculator which grew and evolved since then into the more complex models now in common use.

The small silicon chips are made by breaking up large silicon wafers three to six inches in diameter. Wafers are sliced from pure silicon crystals grown (manufactured) from sand.

It is expected from forecasts that before the end of this decade we could and will be using the full wafer as the component instead of breaking it up into little chip pieces. Today, this chip step is necessary in order to separate and to toss out the bad chips (bad areas of the wafer). As our semiconductor manufacturing technology further matures, allowing purer silicon with fewer inperfections, it will become increasingly unnecessary to break the wafer into chips.

As we begin to use major portions of wafers, and later total wafers, as larger components, we will be able to integrate many millions of circuits, perhaps hundreds of millions. When we reach such a period, in the late 1980's or early 1990's, on the agenda for the future then looms the ability to construct component institutions. Some possibilities are: component libraries, offices-on-a-wafer, component schools science-on-a-wafer, component peace machines, component robot simulators, and more. That is, we will be able to design, construct and manufacture "component machines" for making bigger and more capable and more intelligent machines.

The question is this: What is the architecture for a peace machine? Is it in the form of a people amplifier appliance (like a calculator) for peace? Or is it a cooperating ethnotronic people amplifier (see Futurics, 1980, Vol. 4, Nos. 3/4) to amplify our thinking decisioning and actions for peace?

But what comes after wafer technology? One possible next step in miniaturization, beyond submicron geometries, could be VSD (Very Small Device) with near nano-meter geometric features. That's two orders of magnitude, or 100 times, smaller than current silicon circuit element sizes and interconnection line widths, allowing for a factor of 10,000 increase in circuit density.

There are few materials capable of reaching these ultra-small circuit geometries. One candidate now in research is biophysical molecular switch technology. Such biomolecular switches can act as conductors, semiconductors of super conductors, and therefore, can be used like semiconductor silicon logic circuits or as electrical switches. One way these bioswitches operate is via the use of electron transporting enzymes in electractive polymers.

Since enzymes are living things, controlled by DNA, genetic engineering techniques are required for the subassembly process to build biocircuits. That is, recombinant DNA cutting, splicing, editing and transcription process technology would be used to assemble the circuits. The assembly of the switchable organic molecules is accomplished via genetically engineering DNA amino acid sequences or produce specifiable proteins as templates for the self-construction of larger molecules, for example, to grow computer, program and ethnotronic molecules. That is, one likely longer future involves "growing" our future computers and programs as living systems. Imagine the fun some future designers could have designing "live" peace machinery technology.

But what form would such highly capable peace machinery take? What architectures and functions should be incorporated? What positive and negative social impacts and consequences should we anticipate once such future peace machinery is in common use? Of course, until we do such design R & D and technology assessments, we will be unable to answer such quesions, except via pure speculation. Peace is too important to leave to speculation.

Robotic Peace Technology

As we cross the threshold into the post-industrial society, ushering in the information age, science and technology undergo a major metamorphosis. On one side there is the pragmatic framing of new clusters of specialized knowledge fields. Ample examples are blossoming and explosively growing, the computer and information sciences, cybernetics, new genetics . . . albeit, the emphasis is often more a branching into subdisciplines or a growth of specialized interdisciplinary and cross-disciplinary fields. On the other side are multidisciplinary holistic fields like the general system sciences, the anticipatory sciences and the assessment sciences. Thus, there is a splintering toward deeper divisioning into specialization, as well as trends towards the unification and synthesis of knowledge. Of course, what is needed to add to this list of emerging new science directions is the peace sciences.

Upon closer examination, what seems to be emerging is a mosaic or panorama of a vast amount of accumulated information that requires new tools like the computer to handle. For the computer to be a useful assistant in any science, efforts are required to reduce this vast growth of detail into something digestible. Thus, the trend is to squeeze partitionable discipline areas into specific frames or models. Such reductionalisms are marked by their integrative nature through the universal language of modeling which is fast taking over the role heretofore played by mathematics. The computer enters the picture as the tool allowing such real-world models to be simulated. Through computer simulation, scientific experimentation can occur and becomes possible without the attendant cumbersome laboratory equipment and mathematical procedures.

That is, through modeling and simulation, it is now possible for scientists to "play" serious experimental and mathematical "games" with the object of their research via the use of the computer. This is accomplished by the scientist without first needing to learn sophisticated laboratory techniques or mathematics. In other words, the detailed mathematical and detailed discipline-oriented experimental skills and procedures are imbedded within the computerized model. Such "robot-simulators" allow the scientist to concentrate upon the science being investigated rather than being buried within the mathematics and discipline "crafts" to perform the desired experiment. However, the scientist must first learn his or her field and also the computer simulation and modeling language. Thus, robot simulator assistants increasingly now do for the scientist what the calculator does for the average person. That is, they remove the need to perform bulky, precise and rate skill functions, allowing the researcher to get more quickly and more easily to the core matters of science, that is, the search for and acquisition of new knowledge.

Do we not need equivalent tools for peace? It is now possible to conceive and design such peace tools. With robot-simulators the researcher can ask questions of computer modeling and have simulated experiments performed, that otherwise are nearly impossible or too time consuming and costly. For example, the researcher can ask that all important question, "What happens if?" Then the computer gives an answer, after performing the simulated experiment, while the experimenter views the progress of the computerized experiment and intervenes when desired. Then the experimenter can ask the next question, "What happens if something else is done instead," to arrive at a different comparable answer from the robot-simulator. Through such interactive simulations the researcher can get right "into" the experiment as a surrogate participant. Surely computer simulation in this fashion is far more desirable than war as a social experiment.

Next, envision future robot-simulators in the form of advanced hand held calculators with voice dialoguing capabilities. Further, envision them in the form of a simulator for general decision making rather than for calculating. The utility of such future smart robot-simulators for managers, politicians, voters, and so forth become obvious when we think of them as ethnotronic people-amplifiers or as "electronic assistants." Or, consider a robot-simulation in the form of a smart doctor machine for enhancing an individual's health. One form might be worn as a watch in the future so that it could constantly monitor the body's functioning. In this case a constant simulation would be to warn the individual of pending conditions that need attention before they build to proportions that could harm the individual's health. Later forms might even deliver the necessary counteraction to "repair" the system, for example, genetic splicing intervention to fix a malfunctioning gland or to "band-aid" the problem (e.g., automatic injection of insulin for the diabetic).

Thus, in the not so distant future, computerized robot-simulators, could become every-day necessary adjuncts to be worn as part of our dress. They could assist us in many ways, to amplify our minds as well as our bodies, including our interactions with others. Further, envision a similar worn or carried peace robot-simulator that could constantly monitor the world, perhaps like a "peace thermometer" measuring the individuals and the world society peace QOL (Quality of Life). And as actions or decisions are made by individuals, they could be pretested (simulated in a "what if" mode) as to their expected future peace outcome. Moreover, such peace people amplifier appliances could warn of world trends (results of collective actions and decisions) towards maintaining peace. Such a peace appliance is now a feasible possiblity for the agenda of the future. Should we research and continue to design such tools?

As can be seen thus far, there are many possibilities for designing peace machinery and many other forms also are possible. Multiple peace machinery forms are required by society for amplifying what we do for peace, for example, for amplifying: communications, decision taking, education access (including real-time education occurring at the time of need), closing gaps via raising economic, food production, quality of life capabilities forecasting and assessing future consequences of what we are doing.

Robots in factories as yet are not intelligent. They are basically sophisticated machine tools combining many operations and are somewhat adaptable. So far, they are not human surrogates. However, they are computerized, allowing them to be programmed and reprogrammed to fit changing work roles. Artificial intelligence (AI) techniques are being introduced into robots and in modern computer assisted management systems, including ethnotronics. These AI techniques are processes and algorithms which imitate human brain functions.

Today's artificially intelligent management

systems and factory robots are largely applied to nonperceptual tasks. The AI techniques include such areas as knowledge representation, knowledge acquisition, knowledge base operations, planning strategies, learning algorithms, decision trees, problem-solving algorithms, model analysis, sense and actuate, and more. When AI is used in the office of the future, schools of the future, and factory of the future systems, the intelligent management systems and factory robots can sense, model, manage, manipulate, test, and optimize the running of the system such as the factory. Thus, such future AI systems will be able to operate at both the managerial and factory floor levels or in the classroom. Soon robots will have the added functionality for visual, noncontact sensing and recognition, giving them perceptual capabilities.

Some robots can learn. When teachable industrial robots are introduced into a factory, they can be taught to do such tasks as spray painting, machine parts, weld or mill, or to move and connect or attach parts. Such robots, through artificial intelligence, increase the intelligence level of machinery, and thus are capable of drastically increasing the productivity of factories. In addition, as AI technology and AI knowledge grow, society should henceforth be on a trajectory of increasingly intelligent machines and their application.

For the near term future, robots are getting microsensors, "ears" to listen, the capability to talk, capabilities to simulate and draw upon expert knowledge from knowledge bases, greater mechanical dexterity, sight, mobility, and much more. However, most of their operation is based upon classical knowledge of cybernetics, feedback and control, computers, mechanics, etc., that has existed for a long time which is now being applied in new ways in robotic systems. The dual advents of mini and micro computers have greater spurred on robot developments by giving them economically feasible and physically small electronic logic and memories to allow artificial intelligent techniques to be also employed. Thus, the future promised robotic systems which will be able to listen, sense, see, talk, think, learn and act, and soon. Therefore, future robotic machinery is forecastable to have primitive (but constantly advancing) human capabilities - but not cast in the image of humans. That is, for a long time in the future, robots will continue to look like complex and fancy factory machines, or like a computer terminal, or a calculator, not imitating the way humans or androids look, except perhaps for their TV or movie versions.

For more than 20 years, universities have had courses within their computer science departments called artificial intelligence. Now society is at the threshold of massive application of the theories and knowledge taught through the years in such courses.

Automation, applied in the form of artificially intelligent robots will greatly increase productivity, free workers from dull and dangerous tasks, produce more quality products, widen product diversity, and do such factory jobs more cheaply and with less energy inputs. Thus, from the economic standpoint, robots will be desired and, as a result, usage should be expected to expand rapidly not only in the factory, but also in offices, schools and as adjuncts for people for their amplification.

These expectations suggest massive impacts and changes for the infrastructure of society. Increased robot application will require careful attention to the new society being designed (in such an ad hoc fashion). Today we are expending considerable R & D on factory robots which will create future robot revolutionary advances. Needed are similar efforts for robots dedicated for peace efforts. As a result, if we are careful, robots can have a positive influence on our life including raising the quality of life at work, in the home and for leisure time activities and for assisting with peace. But we will need to be very careful, indeed, lest we end up designing in further societal problems for the future robots to solve, or to go to war for us as robot soldiers. In sum, certainly we need more efforts for researching, designing, constructing and using future peace machinery.

PART 3

GIFTEDNESS DEFLECTED

Not all gifted individuals succeed in life, or if they do, manage without a tremendous amount of help. This section examines two specific areas of the nonfulfillment of giftedness: emotional maladjustment and delinquency. Alyce Faye Eichelberger and Tom Greener describe two vivid case studies of gifted maladjusted children and their ordeals on the way to adulthood. If this is how gifted children "make it on their own," as some skeptics would say, it is a wonder that anyone "makes it" anywhere, as one of these children fortunately does. The remaining four chapters are from among the participants in a three-session seminar on delinquency and giftedness. Parent and advocate Margaret Parker organized the program and sets the scene with an overview of the problem and a description of an initial rescue operation. Researcher Margot King explores the relation of self-concept and support systems to the development of delinquency in gifted children. Psychiatrist Arthur Robinson explores the psychological make-up of delinquents, gifted or not, and in a particularly fascinating paragraph, notes the recollections of affective treatment, notably by parents, when clients were as young as two or three. Finally, Richard Tremblay describes a treatment program for young male offenders and notes that the treatment needs of gifted delinquents are not grossly different from those for delinquent boys in general. A critical variable is the delicately balanced social climate in the institution. What all five of these papers point out, vividly and even passionately, is that much of the deflection of giftedness and its masking by adaptive problems has its roots early in life and particularly in the relationships with adults, notably parents. For some children, school-based educational services for the gifted risk being too little, too late. These papers also point out that while giftedness can itself generate barriers to effective treatment, treatment can be effective, but at what appears to be an enormous cost to society and to the individual. If anyone should elect to read this section before Part 1, we urge that the latter be examined next.

12

A VIEW OF THE GIFTED CHILD IN A LONDON DAY SCHOOL FOR THE MALADJUSTED

Alyce Faye Eichelberger & Tom Greener

Most people's idea of a gifted child is of a brilliant person making his mark on an impressed world. However, it is a fact that such children may be buried amongst ordinary and dull children and display behavior which is emotionally disturbed. It has been our desire to create interest in and alert other disciplines to gifted and emotionally disturbed children.

The gifted children in London's day maladjusted schools have a difficult time, because of their giftedness and their patterns of emotional disturbance. The maladjusted schools in recent years, according to a survey by two English clinical psychologists, Mary Evans and Mary Wilson, are not necessarily meeting the needs of emotionally disturbed children. And of those, the only real determination of giftedness is perhaps a school psychologist's intelligence test. Really disturbed children present such an overlay on their emotions that the conduct-disordered child may take over the schools.

Mary Evans feels that governing bodies should be aware of this as there is a danger of filling the schools with children who behave badly but are not emotionally disturbed. This has come about partly because the maladjusted schools now come under the area health authorities. If schools are lucky they may still be run according to the guidelines set out in the Underwood Report of 1950. Details are given in the following section concerning the historical development of the schools.

Gifted children in a maladjusted school are those who are able to produce an exceptional performance, as measured by IQ, or the less precise yardstick of creativity. But because of negative factors, they

157

remain unrecognized for their true abilities. Instead, they are perceived as diverging from the norm because of extreme antisocial behavior.

The Inner London Education Authority (commonly referred to as the ILEA) which runs London's state school system does not have a definition for giftedness in conjunction with maladjustment. They describe maladjusted children in their pamphlet simply as those who "show evidence of emotional instability or psychological disturbance and require special educational treatment in order to effect their personal, social, or educational readjustment . . . ."
However, Mary Evans believes disturbance is an entity within itself.

Often we label children as handicapped, educationally subnormal, maladjusted, and then just leave them to struggle along as best they can. This is a problem. For the most part, educators have attempted to defy the immense variability of young people by conducting a single-standard schooling. To treat children and young people as if they shared a uniform capacity and sequence of development, which of course they do not, has drawbacks for all students. Gifted maladjusted children are frequently unable to communicate with their peers, teachers or, to some extent, parents. Such children could not only fail to fulfil the promise of their great talent, but remain utterly undeveloped in all aspects of living.

Recent research indicates that if giftedness is not identified at an early age, the children's intellectual capacities may go undetected until early adolescence because of their manipulative ability. A child's average capacity for abstract thought may precipitate feelings which need to be worked through at a very early age. If help is not forthcoming then a collapse may well happen in situations of stress. The child will learn early on to manipulate adults to suit his reasoning, and if guidance is not available may choose a maladjusted route.

We agree with Torrance who says that these children noticeably possess almost limitless energy and often get into trouble. What appears to be a strong tendency toward disruptive and attention seeking behavior may stem from boredom, or a strong desire to create novel diversions.

It is true that some children never give rise for concern and remain committed to many, or even all school activities, but fail to achieve anything like their true potential. Such children escape categorization as "maladjusted," while others appear at all levels of achievement to be maximizing their capabilities, but paradoxically to receive even less individual attention than those to whom attention is drawn because of their divergence from the expected norms. It is worthwhile to a student wanting real notice to be taken to become a hell-raiser and a nuisance to teachers, school, and peers. Our goal in the London maladjusted schools is to provide ways in which the child who opts for this pattern can be given every opportunity to develop in ways which are both socially valuable and useful to that child and to others.

In our work, we have found that delinquency springs from the emotions more than from the intelligence. A very bright child who is caught in an unlawful or naughty situation would say, "Would I be so stupid as to do that?" Yet, emotions may sweep aside the warnings of intelligence or even of common sense. The child remains fixed at the emotional age at which a damaging experience to self concept was suffered and the child's goal is to balance unequal levels of intellectual and emotional development.

This type of student is resistant to help from teachers and therapists trusting to cleverness to get by. A child cannot be maladjusted twenty-four hours a day. There may be times when that child is more sane than the teacher. It is only when these children lose control of their emotions that they lose their capabilities.

Development

In London today there are 12 day schools for maladjusted children. The most recent growth, is in the number of special units and classes. Until the 1950's a child needing special education would have been sent away to a boarding school. London opened the first day school for these children in 1954. Chalcot School, from which the two cases which are presented here are taken, was opened in 1965. May Evans was the headmistress. She came from a background of working with disturbed people in the Royal Maudsley Hospital. Freda Martin was the psychiatrist. She had been the consultant psychiatrist with Chalcot and was director of the Tavistock Children and Parents Department before her return to Canada. Mary Evans left after two years and the deputy head was placed in charge for 18 months. A temporary head was then appointed for one year. In 1970, Tom Greener, a special education teacher, was appointed headmaster and Ian Warbuton as assistant. They are both still there. The school had 50 to 60 pupils with a dual team of educational and part time specialists. The psychiatrist did not treat the children but a psychotherapist came 3 days a week. The psychiatric social worker, in this case Kate Whitaker, treated the parents.

The team felt that there were three disturbing factors to look for in potential pupils and if two were found then there was great possibility of the child breaking down in school. These were: (a) damaging environmental influences, (b) abnormal quality of relations with others, and (c) predisposal to disorders or emotional illness.

The team tried to make the child and parent feel accepted even though there had been trouble everywhere. The headmistress conducted a special interview with a technique which gained the family's trust and the team made a commitment to the family that the child would not be turned out unless there was total acceptance and agreement by all members of staff that it was best for the child.

The child accepted for Chalcot was offered psychotherapeutic treatment and rest from ordinary school and the world around him, but academics were not ignored.

The headmaster saw the psychiatrist for 40 minutes each week, a chance for the headmaster to unload the anxieties and pressures of the job. The psychiatrist kept an eye on the school pathology. In the case conferences, she made sense of the behavior of the children and she often gave ten minute talks on such subjects as anorexia nervosa, and wrote letters to convince parents and authorities that certain steps needed to be taken to help a child.

The psychiatric social worker involved the parents in school life, encouraging them to come to parents' evenings. This was very difficult as the parents were frightened of coming to an abnormal school. The psychiatric social worker reassured the parents that they had done as well as could be expected, considering that their child was disturbed.

Later in the year, after trust had been formed and in order to encourage the parents to meet the psychiatrist, it would be announced that this was no ordinary parents' meeting but a special seminar. The parents were invited to come and later in the evening the doctor would arrive and with the headmaster and psychiatric social worker they would answer all the questions they could answer. This worked extremely well and many intelligent questions were asked by the parents. However, one year the father of a particularly disturbed child stood and asked if he could address the meeting. He began slowly: "When we came here to this school we thought it was a very nice school but we knew it wouldn't work. I want to tell the new parents that it has. But, we as parents have paid a price. We have become a very psychiatric family. When our daughter returns home from school she no longer says I was awful and naughty; it is only that I had a bad day and so did the others. If I had a bad day at the office I used to hate people and it was easy. Now I have to understand them."

Maladjusted schools in London tend to have either a rapid turnover of staff or an unusually static one. The importance of affection and trust between the staff cannot be overemphasized. Teachers transferring to special schools are on probation for three months, one reason being that the schools do not want teachers who fancy themselves as amateur psychotherapists. It is easy to become discouraged and want to give up educating the children and when this happens the children openly resent it.

The maximum number of children now allowed is fifty. All schools believe that the children gain because the day school is run, even if imperfectly, as a therapeutic community. This is not the result of some accident but of deliberate planning. Such a therapeutic climate needs a staff who can suspend the usual structure of judgements and techniques of maintaining order in the limited setting of the school. Then, perhaps with staff help, a child can begin to venture into the outside world, with a great deal of support, through field trips, or sport. The staff must also be united in a continuous and consistent concern for the health of the child.

Aggressive, antisocial behavior is often part of a disturbed child's defense against what the child feels to be an intolerably painful world in which the child is disliked. Such a child wants to be liked, but cannot manage without the defensive behavior which makes that child so unlikeable. Paradoxically, before the child can be likeable the child has to be liked. The school may have to be accepting and tolerant for a long time before the child feels ready to show vulnerability. When that child achieves this the school has made an important step forward.

The child may also benefit because there are fewer educational demands made. This does not mean the child does nothing, but that one abandons, for a time at least, the battle to achieve standards of work compatible with the child's intelligence and age. At the same time, the child's activities are carefully chosen to enable the child to experience success within the school structure as quickly as possible. For a child who comes to the school stressed and anxious, perhaps with a long past experience of failure, this provides a welcome and necessary boost to morale. The child's problems are studied in depth and careful plans are agreed on to help the child and the child is included in these contracts. Close cooperation between the educational and psychiatric team is essential. However, perhaps the greatest gain to the child is having the chance to form previously unsatisfactory relationships with older and younger children.

We no longer blame all childhood disturbances on just immature and ineffective parents, broken homes, and early separation, but also include neurological abnormalities and biochemical variations. Whatever the causes, many children in the day schools have a grossly impaired ability to relate to others. They are at odds with themselves and other people; their emotional responses seem bizarre and this inhibits their development in all ways. It is therapeutic to work with mature, warm adults who show an understanding of their perhaps distorted behavior, and to have the opportunity to be dependent, to have needs met, and eventually to learn to be able to wait to have needs met, to be supported through anger and despair, and encouraged to progress.

Some may benefit from psychotherapy; for all, there is the chance that through the work of the psychiatric social worker their parents and family will become more understanding and tolerant. Certainly one of the potential lasting gains to the child is the insight the child acquires into himself and into other people.

In 1979, we had the opportunity to visit establishments dealing with maladjusted children in London and other parts of England, France, the Soviet Union and Israel. I found strengths and weaknesses within the schools and similarities between their programs. One common strength was a bond between the children and another person, whether perceived as guru, counselor, substitute parent or whatever. These people served as a sounding board or confidant to the children who felt secure.

Another strength was the opportunity given to the

students to express their creativity and individuality. Many children seemed to feel that a lot of their maladjustment had begun when they were nine or ten. Because they became bored and wanted to entertain themselves their behavior became extreme and disruptive.

For example, a 16-year-old interviewed at a private normal school in London was president of his student body. He handled all of the student's fund-raising projects. While working out a budget, he embezzled a substantial amount of money which he used to purchase drugs. He sold them to the students and then replaced the money, making a handsome profit.

In July, parents at the school received this letter from the headmaster:

"Dear Parents:
    It is with great concern and sadness that we find it necessary to inform you of a recent incident within our school. We first learned of the incidents concerning the drugs from the teachers who reported allegations being made by other students. While an investigation was in progress two senior boys informed their parents of their actions. Following the disclosures, the parents chose to withdraw their sons and make known to the administration each boy's involvement."

A boy at Peper Harrow, a state boarding school for maladjusted gifted children in England, had been very curious about drugs, and began to experiment with their chemical effect on his body. He was using various combinations of drugs and took his O level in Science while under the influence of mind-expanding drugs, but immediately went into a coma from an overdose. He was amazed at his skills as he had felt he had no intellectual abilities. He has since completed A levels and is entering Oxford in the autumn.

One of the boys at Red Hill, another boarding school for the maladjusted, was a fanatic about Hitler and World War II. He could recite items, places, and information and his room was covered with Nazi posters and materials. Yet, as a general observation his emotions carried him rather than his intellect. He could not discuss the subject rationally or without violence and anger.

A boy at Borstal, a regime of punishment and education for boys who are in trouble with the law, tending towards the penal rather than the educational, was an expert at picking locks and stealing cars. He had never been caught. At the age of 17 he was trying to instruct a friend in the same art with less success, and they were both arrested. He had been taught to read at Borstal and was amazed that he had accomplished this feat. His small room was lined with paperback books and he had devised a check out system to lend to the other boys. He had also completed the commercial art course and was due to be placed as an apprentice upon his release. This particular boy made a success of it in the end but many children become lost because of lack of early identification and response to their unusual abilities and talents.

Weaknesses

The first weakness was the schools were set up specifically to deal with one of the major predisposing factors - inadequate parental care. At the same time, one of the most difficult problems faced by schools is the lack of comprehension of progress made by the child at the school. The result may be a tension between the child's experiences at home and at school, which in the short term may become a new difficulty.

R. D. Laing has said in cases of schizophrenia the child has been elected by the family to carry the burden of the collective family problems, thus seeming to absolve the other family members of their responsibility or difficulties experienced in family life. Maladjustment is clearly not schizophrenia, but there are useful parallels between Laing's hypothesis and the cases we are considering here.

The second weakness was the high ratio of staff to children, which is a drain on the authorities' funds.

Third, almost all of the schools I visited had a central figure who had been involved in the program since its inception and they were the controling force behind its success or failure. If such a person left, the program tended to fail.

We will now turn to the two case studies which I will be presenting. These children are unique in the experience of the school because their problems were diagnosed early and we still have contact with them and have been able to follow their progress.

Melissa

"Who am I then, tell me that first, and then if I like being that person, I'll come up, if not, I'll stay down here till I'm somebody else." Lewis Carroll in **Alice in Wonderland.** "A thick pidgy round pudding in a pancho." "An apple with thick toothpicks for arms and legs."

These were the descriptions to the teacher at Chalcot and the Paddington psychiatric social worker of Melissa in January 1967, when she was seven. She was referred to the Paddington Clinic by her mother because she had refused school dinners and refused to go to school in the end. The clinic diagnosed a need to separate her from her parents.

Family history. The father was thirty-two years old, of Polish-Jewish origin, and had been diagnosed schizophrenic since Melissa's birth. He was both an inpatient and outpatient at psychiatric hopsitals. He received electrochemical therapy which the mother said Melissa had witnessed. He was employed as a tailor and cutter at the time of Melissa's referral, and was not receiving drug treatment. He was very deluded and "zombielike." His actual description was "burnt-out depressed schizophrenic." He had been raised in a children's home because his mother had died.

Melissa's mother was twenty-eight and worked as a part-time secretary. She laughed manically during interviews at the clinic, she was grossly overweight and very anxious about Melissa. She feared her daughter would catch her father's illness.

There was no previous history of schizophrenia although both families had shown neurotic disorders. There were no other siblings. Mother had a morbid fear of mental illness and did not want Melissa to be different in any way, which was difficult as the child was grossly overweight and constantly teased by other children. However, she was physically healthy.

Mother cut short her own education but showed artistic talent and was offered a place in art school. She refused the art scholarship to marry Melissa's father. Mother said her own mother was a difficult person, and died before she was 10. The psychiatric social worker remembers when she went for visits that the wedding picture was often brought out. Melissa's mother was incredibly beautiful and slim and father looked very handsome and not at all like the broken man he was then.

Melissa's mother had toxemia in late pregnancy and the birth was a forceps delivery. Melissa's birth weight was 8 pounds. Melissa's mother knew nothing about babies and raised her from books from the library. The baby was bottle-fed and took ages to feed with the bottle until mother discovered the hole was too small. Her mother trusted books, not people. Melissa just swallowed everything and made no protest. She was always overweight but a healthy neonate. She had an extra kidney but no worries were professed medically about it. She had a few respiratory illnesses but there was never any separation or hospitalization at an early age. Her first separation occurred at five when she attended Paddington Day Nursey. She began to display difficulties in relationships with other children and refused school. She was then referred to the Paddington Clinic.

The psychiatrist's report states that in 1967 Melissa was "the healthiest member" of the family and of superior intelligence but needed a school in which she could reinforce any ability shown and be as happy as possible. She felt that Melissa would not be able to manage the outside world until she was much older. Both parents were described as over-protective and over-anxious.

Melissa had a superficial adult vocabulary but very infantile speech and mannerisms. On psychological testing at 6 years 6 months she had a mental age of 8 years 8 months and an IQ of 136 on the Weschler Intelligence Scale for Children - Revised, althought this was believed to be an underestimation. Her performance skills were much lower than her verbal skills because she sucked her hand constantly. She would not persevere with things and gave up easily even though she knew the answers. Her vocabulary was that of a 10 year old. Melissa's father insisted on following her to the testing room. Holding her hand, she removed his hat and coat. She had a very high babyish voice which was at a great variance with her syntax and vocabulary.

The family felt very persecuted by the clinic and so the referral to a maladjusted school was made, although fortnightly meetings continued at the clinic. Melissa was to have weekly psychotherapy and this continued well into her teens with a gradual tapering off of sessions.

Melissa was referred to a diet clinic as she was acutely aware of her obesity or physical abnormality which was subsequently causing her emotional problems. The family's general pattern had been to avoid reality either by changing schools or by failing to attend meetings at the clinic. Melissa stayed at home so she could deny reality. There were also problems of jealousy in that Melissa felt her father was thin but ill, while mother was fat but well. One is reminded of the nursery rhyme, "Jack Sprat could eat no fat, his wife could eat no lean; so between them they licked the platter clean."

Psychotherapy. The doctor established precise goals and kept to them throughout treatment: (a) to preserve what was healthy in Melissa and place her where she would be accepted and contained (Chalcot School) without "breaking" the situation, (b) to create a situation so that she remained in psychotherapy for a long time, (c) to overcome fear of outsiders, (d) to achieve a radical change in mother's attitude as early as possible at least by adolescence, and (e) to determine what was educationally possible for Melissa and make things more simple for her.   Melissa's psychotherapist did not think she could get into ordinary school and that she would increasingly be unable to distinguish reality and create fantasies. Melissa felt that her mother should meet all of her demands in life.

Chalcot. Melissa liked the school from the start but her mother found it difficult to leave the child at school and was jealous of her new social activities and ties.   Melissa stopped refusing to come to school but mother had to be weaned away.   This was a common situation with this particular family.   They were all right except when other family members were present, which was most of the time.   She had several teachers but never really formed a lasting relationship until near the end of her time at Chalcot.   She found it very difficult to make contact with male teachers, perhaps because she didn't know what to expect from men. In fact, she seemed to wish they were not there. Surprisingly enough, the relationship she formed finally was with a male teacher.

In 1966 when Melissa first entered the school she was placed in the reception class and resented it deeply.   She felt superior and therefore demoted. Work was more important than play both to mother and child, although her standards of work were only average or below.   She was lethargic and reluctant to make efforts. She was always complaining, whining, and was very manipulative.   She sought attention and became jealous of attention given to others.   She described imaginary but ghastly experiences of mad people.   She said she liked being an only child, yet her illness was fed on the basis of not feeling wanted and thinking her family would prefer another child besides herself.   She was highly critical of adults, as well as children, using this as one of her defenses.

169

She had real periods of distress, accompanied by inconsolable crying especially near the end of the school day when her mother arrived. She was very untidy and messy and her speech patterns "got on the nerves" of the other children, causing open clashes with the middle school girls. This was difficult for the teacher as Melissa manipulated these clashes by being petulant and disobedient and always having the last word. She would become unnecessarily hysterical and deserved to be the victim of these attacks. Then mother would arrive and make the other children more angry. Yet, Melissa openly desired friendships and was eager to be accepted. At this point Melissa presented a confused but two-sided general picture: on the one hand, a mature, somewhat precocious, understanding individual; on the other, a very young, spoiled cry-baby.

In February of 1967, Melissa's teacher began to notice that she was settling down and even establishing a friendship with one of the other girls. She chattered endlessly but was still easily made hysterical. Mother hounded her to do harder work with which she certainly could not cope. Melissa began to ride the coach to school, but only if her father came too. He would take one step inside the school gate and then leave. Mary Evans said that his behavior was symbolic of his love and hate of the school. Melissa began to be more openly naughty and enjoyed siding with the wrong-doers. When she was in a hysterical or mischievous mood, she incited the younger children and created screaming mob-like situations. Towards the end of her second term, Melissa had her first screaming tantrum which lasted about ten minutes. Mary Evan's memories of the panic attacks were of trying to drag a fat body onto her lap and stroking an enormous thigh. Her anger seemed to be coming out and the weight problem diminished ever so slightly. She was becoming very involved in group antics and creating a general pitch of hysteria. In August, during the summer holidays, she was to go to the weight clinic at a hospital. Melissa returned in September after the 5 week holiday very "normal." She worked and behaved in a very ladylike way while regressing at home to complete infantile behavior. Her school friendships were renewed but she began to be "bitchy" according to her friends. As the term progressed, her distressed periods of crying became longer and more intense. She was accepted by the children but still teased about her obesity. At this time, she began to form a relationship with a young man in the school. Melissa began to produce work which fitted the quality of her intellect. The family moved to a new house with "lots ado about nothing." However, Melissa got a room of her own and was delighted. A surprising sense of humor was emerging in Melissa. Although she never referred to her obesity directly she could respond to the other children's taunts with jocular sarcasm. Melissa's father attended parents evening which was a real bonus for the school, family and Melissa. Melissa was able to discuss her family relationships in school. She formed a competitive relationship with others. French was included in her curriculum and orally she progressed rapidly (this was to help her later in her selection of a career).

In July 1968, a regression occurred and the psychiatrist kept very close contact with the school and attended numerous staff meetings concerning Melissa. There was a change to be made; Melissa was to have a male teacher. She accepted the situation superficially but began to have stomach aches just before school started every day. After much reassurrance that she could keep contact with her female teacher she got past the stomach problems but would still pretend someone had hit her in the stomach and the pain was still there. She also refused to use the school toilets with no understandable reason other than the change of teachers.

Out of school she was very lonely with no friends so she began to write stories about an imaginary sister. These she brought into school and shared with her female teacher. With her male teacher, she formed a confidential relationship by having small conferences. By this time, she had moved groups and had a friendship with a very tall, thin, stick-like girl named Linda (fantasies of her father?). Every Wednesday the three of them, Linda, Melissa and the teacher, went to a local park for an hour, their special time. Linda never said anything while Melissa prattled on continuously about a vague cousin who was a dancer on Top of the Pops, a television show. The fantasies were so detailed and minute that the teacher believed her. Everything she spoke of was a fantasy.

Melissa was manipulative of the other children and an organizer, calling the shots. She became the leader of a gang and told them what to do and then would moan at them when they didn't. She began to draw fashion models, little stick people, all of them posing in different attitudes with their feet and hands moving about. All had very long eyelashes with ballet characteristics. Over the long summer holidays she completely covered a lavoratory roll with these figures for her male teacher.

So there was a little round ball, in the description of her teacher, producing these fantastic drawings of elongated people. One could see if she slimmed down that there was an attractive girl underneath just like the drawings, but instead all the teacher and school witnessed was a rather sad and pathetic character who was verbally aggressive.

Her doctor seemed to think at this point that Melissa expressed her hopes and needs in fantasy by creating worlds which were not so painful. Therefore, she gave herself the potential to survive life. Melissa felt that her sickness was a sorrow that she covered up within herself and so built into her personality, but it could not be conveyed with words. Her only visible sign was the oral fixation of eating and obesity.

In 1971, the various support systems (i.e., psychiatrist, clinic, and school) made a big push for boarding school. The parents refused, so Melissa was transferred to a delicate school (one for children with health problems). There she progressed very well still, continuing her therapy with the clinic. In 1973, she managed a long holiday away from her parents and started at a normal girls grammar school. However, her attendance broke down and during this period the school obviously had great difficulty in maintaining contact. We do know that she attended a local theatre group which apparently built up her self confidence.

In 1980, Melissa came to the reunion at Chalcot but it was a very awkward situation for her and she appeared uncomfortable. She had a laugh about her attendance at the school and how silly she had been. She looked very attractive and slim.

In October 1980, the headmaster of Chalcot received this letter:

"Dear Mr. Greener,

I am sorry that I've taken so long to reply to your letter but I've been very busy at college. I hope you won't think me unkind if I request that you don't give Johnny my address, because I feel we wouldn't have very much in common any longer. I'm now at Saint Martins School of Art, In Charing Cross Road, in my second year of a B.A. course in fashion design - I really like it there, it's great fun and I'm the student union co-representative for my year: When I leave, I'd love to work in fashion public relations or journalism, because there are few good designer jobs available. This September, I visited New York with a girl from college, and had a really great time - it took me ages to save up enough money, but I can't wait to go back. This Thursday I leave for Paris for a week's trip with the college to see the fashion collections, which should be fun - I'm still a "nervy" person, but I force myself to go on these trips because unless I force myself, I'll let life pass me by, and it's only my ambition that keeps me driving myself on. Anyway, I'd best close, as I've loads of work to do. I'll try to keep in touch as regards to my progress. Best wishes, Melissa.

Melissa is now a fashion designer working in London and Paris.

The aim of Melissa's treatment was separation. The school was a key contributor in keeping the link between home, school and the social services. Melissa could not have functioned otherwise. At the beginning of such a treatment, it may seem hopeless, for we are confronted with a bright child and cannot give enough educational aid to help her reach her full potential. But in this case, and in many others, the support and containment of the school carries them on their way in life.

Reginald

We all disliked him, the students, staff. He was a clever nasty abusive little bundle of anger and he got under your skin. He looked like a miniature pop star.

Reginald was referred to the Great Ormond Street Children's Hospital, London, in 1971 at the age of eight. He was suffering from a severe behavior problem, characterized by aggression, swearing and a low tolerance for frustration. He was of superior intelligence but the family background had been extremely unstable. Before he was referred to the hospital he had been to a boarding school which refused to keep him.

Reginald's father was unknown but mother had remarried when he was a baby and he had a stepfather at the time of referral. The stepfather was twenty-one and English. He managed pop groups and at the time was financially successful. He was an immature man but had a good relationship with Reginald. He, in fact, wanted psychiatric help for himself.

The mother was Canadian and moved to England, it was believed, because of the stigma of an illegitimate child and family pressures. She is said to have shown personality difficulties at an early age and was very slow in maturing. Because of his early placement in boarding school, the mother and son had formed a rather good, although sporadic, relationship. She wrote very long letters to Reggie then, and while she was in prison after being convicted on a drug charge. Mother and son spent time together in deep discussion at a very adult level and then the rest of the time she ignored him completely. Reggie was an unwanted child and had to fit into his mother's life style.

The boarding school, in a letter to the hospital, said that when Reginald came to them at age four, he was very excitable and incapable of sitting still. Although they did not consider this unusual behavior for a four year old it persisted for the two years he was there, and became worse. He was a bed-wetter and this did not stop until well into his teens. He had great difficulty sleeping and always caused problems at bed time.

Reginald started attending the day unit at the hospital three times a week for psychotherapy. His mother began sessions with a psychiatric social worker. Reggie continued psychotherapy until September 1973. The doctor felt that mother had a great deal to offer Reggie and did not want them separated. The marriage was now in extreme difficulty due to bad management and finances. Mother had started a tourist agency called Two's Company which showed single men around London when they were visiting.

By 1974, Reggie was making such excellent progress that the headmaster recommended that he go to an ordinary school. However, mother's marriage broke down and she married again disastrously, creating stress and strain in Reggie and so he continued at Chalcot until 1970.

Mother's financial position deteriorated and her lifestyle became very erratic. She was now living with her two brothers who had come over from Canada to help run the business. They were Greg, age 22 and Sevin, 20. The family lived in Hammersmith, a London suburb, in a squalid flat which was quite a change from a luxury house in Hampstead where Reginald had all comforts and anything he desired. Sevin and Reggie clashed immediately, yet formed a close relationship that Reggie seemed to need, but it was a violent one. Greg, the other brother, was a very ineffectual and inadequate person in every way. Both the mother's brothers were into drugs quite heavily and Sevin was rapidly becoming an addict.

Reggie started to show definite signs of delinquency. Mother was arrested returning from Africa with a suitcase of drugs. At this point, Chalcot became of extreme importance to Reggie. He relied on the staff for comfort and help. The liaison between the school and the psychiatric social worker held this little boy together as his outside world fell apart even to the actual reality of the house burning down.

Mother was unrealistic about the drug charge and did not even think about the fact that she would eventually be sent to prison. She had no friends and those people she knew were unreliable. Money was running out; Sevin tried to kick his drub habit but became so ill that he had to be hospitalized. Reggie became very verbally aggressive about the lack of money as he felt that cash was a measure of love and caring. He formed a relationship with his school teacher. The teacher, not wanting to put pressure on Reggie to discuss his family situation, arranged for Reggie to come into school early each morning to do extra work, as Reggie had always enjoyed work and was better than the others in his class. Reggie saw that his teacher could help him get out of the disturbed school into ordinary school which he desired very much. He began to form friendships with other children, especially with one boy who was also keen to go to ordinary school. They would make up little dramas about what to say and do in ordinary situations.

The teacher remembers one field trip when they went to the Natural History Museum. Reggie selected a postcard he wanted by number. When he asked the sales lady for it she said that it was out of stock. Reggie became highly indignant and demanded the manager. "Why did they offer things for sale and not produce, etc?" It ended with the museum apologizing to Reggie. It struck me that one might wonder how Jesus Christ's parents felt when they found him preaching to the elders in the temple. How much of a child's behavior is bad, or is it our inhibitions as adults that stop the development of the child?

At this time the teacher began to go to visit Reggie's home. His description was: "Whenever I went round there were always all sorts of people everywhere in the house all knowing Reggie but in reality only casually. They had an enormous sheep-dog that sat all over you when you came in to sit down. The conversations were never about Reggie, only about mother and her problems. The house was gradually becoming uninhabitable from neglect. The visits stopped when mother went to prison.

Reggie lived with his Canadian uncles at first but they disappeared and in 1978, Sevin committed suicide, collapsing in the home in front of Reggie. Mother went into deep depression because of prison and her brother's death. She could only attend to her own problems. The psychiatric social worker took train journeys to see mother and wrote to her weekly, often taking Reggie with her or bringing him things from mother. The letters from mother were long and arduous but were answered very carefully each time by the school. Reggie often spoke with mother on the phone at school as she was allowed calls and he had no phone elsewhere.

Reggie was placed with a friend of mother's who had a son of the same age. This arrangement did not work at all so he then went to live with the cleaning lady who had worked for his mother when they had been financially stable. This relationship flourished and Reggie was quite happy.

In 1979, mother was released from prison and she and Reggie went to live with a friend in Hammersmith and Reggie went to ordinary school. However, he continued his relationship with the teacher from Chalcot. Mother and Reggie were living in a seedy hotel, mother on the second floor and Reggie on the fourth. The teacher and Reggie would go and get a hamburger and then return to his room for a chat. They discussed his mother and how he was doing in school. Reggie had formed a love of football and was quite good, and this gave him friends and an outside interest. However, the teacher had to stop the visits due to pressures from Chalcot as Reggie was really not a part of that school anymore.

Reggie is still attending school in Hammersmith and leaves this year. He has not accomplished what he was capable of academically, but he has survived school. We were not able to discover from Reggie his plans for the future.

In this case study one sees that even a short period of time can at least help a child move on in life. However, because of the lack of long term containment, his potential seems to have been lost.

13

BRIGHT KIDS IN TROUBLE WITH THE LAW

Margaret Parker

Why has an agency for gifted children concerned itself so deeply with kids in trouble with the law?

Throughout its history, the Kootenay Centre for the Gifted has tried to do jobs apparently not being done well by others. The cycle of recognition of a special need, information gathering, then sharing of knowledge and experience to help all do better has been gone through several times in the Centre's lifetime.

Over its many years' experience with gifted children, the Centre naturally has become very familiar with children in trouble. A counselor is not sought unless there is some kind of problem. However, this trouble has been educational, family or personal, largely with origins in misunderstood giftedness and seldom with serious legal or social consequences.

In the mid-seventies, kids in "real" trouble - trouble with the law - began to be brought for help, all of them very gifted. As the numbers of these children added up, the Centre became increasingly concerned with the social and human implications of such numbers and the seriousness of the problems these cases represented. If this many children with these kinds of problems were being brought to this small, private, nonfunded and virtually nonpublicized agency in the bush of British Columbia, what must be the real size and scope of the total picture?

As the need arose to do something more than simple individual counseling for kids in trouble with the law, the Centre's special-need cycle began again. The first step of course is always to get as thoroughly informed as possible.

In its usual way, the Centre searched many literatures, queried universities and governments, and asked both agencies and individuals of all kinds for information. Among the many people in correspondence with the Centre, including top professionals in many fields, those with any possible chance of interest or input were specifically called on to consider this problem. Many responded seriously and helpfully, some quite surprisingly.

At first, it seemed as if the very idea of a bright kid in trouble with the law was considered a contradiction in terms by most people. But over the months, as knowledge grew and papers were written and shared, responses studied closely, bits of information from varied sources pieced together and people who were most deeply concerned continually consulted, patterns began to emerge.

Recognition of the implications of those patterns finally led to general proposals for general agencies being made to try out new applications growing out of this knowledge, effort and insight in the light of the Centre's own experience. In the end, for the first time in history, the Centre proposed an association between a provincial ministry and itself to see whether its interdisciplinary, independent grasp of the unexpectedly broad and deep aspects of this serious problem could lead to more positive, creative retrieval of kids in trouble with the law, particularly bright kids.

At the beginning of 1980, after these years of preparation, the Executive Director of the Centre was given a desk and the use of a telephone and typewriter in the Special Services section of the Children's Services Division of the Ministry of Community and Social Services in Ontario. All expenses of the project were borne by the Centre. Four months later, the pilot project was concluded and on May 30, 1980, a final report was made with several recommendations. Another visit was made to the Division in Toronto in November of 1980 to respond to possibilities opened by inside publicity of the project (there was no outside publicity by mutual agreement). However, it is not known what effects the project had on anything done in Ontario since then, nor has there been any response of any kind to the final report and recommendations. The experience was one of the most frustrating but instructive the Centre has ever had. Inconclusive as it was, it certainly strengthened and deepened Centre conviction that a great gulf exists between those responsible for such children, and workers in other disciplines with extremely germane information and experience. Before, during and since the completion of the Ontario project, the Centre has dug out a number of efforts directly or indirectly affecting such children, some historically established but apparently either unknown to or ignored by ongoing agencies, some very recent with exciting results and collecting surprising information.

In its continuing effort to bring together commonly concerned but professionally disparate people, ideas and experience, the Centre, with the generous assistance of McGill University, called an invitational symposium on Bright Children in Trouble with the Law in Montreal at the end of May 1980. It is hoped that further meetings will be held to continue to bridge the barriers between people of various kinds involved in helping these particular children.

The literature on the subject, while somewhat circular, has been small but persistent in modern times. From its language and the remarks made about and conclusions drawn from the studies made, the attitudes and points of view of authors reflect the isolation so many professionals seem to work in. A book, **Delinquency and Difference,** is in preparation by the Centre, bringing together all the data now collected on the subject. While it is a first statement rather than a definitive and exhaustive work, it does bring together in one place and perhaps in somewhat different ways the varying experiences and ideas discovered up to now about such children.

This background is necessary to help explain the breadth and unusual recombination of information across disciplines involved, and to tell how this work came to be. If the picture were uniformly bleak, if there were no help to be found in any of the research, comment, experience and work over the decades, there would be no point in wasting time and effort to record any of this. But the picture is far from uniformly bleak and new combinations and approaches are very promising.

There is far more support than at first appeared for the original principles guiding the Centre when it had almost no solid data to rely on. Not all problems were successfully solved; but one of the first truths caring agency workers must face is that not all problems have a positive solution: not all kids can be saved. "Success" with many of these kids is an almost imponderable quality, metamorphizing over time, rather than the neatly limited, descriptive quantity statisticians would prefer. But what can be expected from a creature as unpredictable, as stubbornly individualistic, as constantly growing and evolving as man?

To those who care, anything that might help kids is worth learning more about.

As information about bright kids in trouble began to be assembled, and isolated people at work in various places began to communicate with one another, common patterns began to emerge, with problems surfacing which had not yet been recognized. Patterns noticed include traits common to practically all delinquent kids and treatment practices also common to practically all of them. These seem to be mismatched when the needs of the kids are considered. For example, delinquent kids are almost uniformly:
1. effectively nonparented,
2. well below most other groups of kids in exposure to and success in school,
3. far more learning disabled than most other groups of kids,
4. very strongly ego-centred,
5. deeply deprived of caring, either giving or receiving,
6. "runners" from most restraint situations where running is possible,
7. socially and emotionally deprived and isolated except within their own group, and

8. angry and rebellious, whether expressed by withdrawal or aggression.

The most casual glance at these traits shows that these kids lack positive human relationships, educational opportunities upon which to build any kind of successful adult life, and normal social experiences within which to express the give and take required to grow up socially and emotionally. Yet the treatment response to these needs that correction agencies have made historically and still make are placement and security-oriented rather than care-oriented. They are erratic, budget-restricted and convenience governed rather than consistent, need-directed and humanly governed. Kids who often reach institutions within two or three years of legal adulthood lose there whatever opportunities their already sterile environment provided for responsibility, decision-making and practice in positive human relationships; yet they face being released into a society which will punish them more severely the day after they are 16, 17 or 18 than the day before for lack of self-discipline, responsibility and success in dealing with other people well. Other agencies responsible for kids who are too young or whose misbehavior is not serious enough to warrant institutionalization do not treat them much differently.

An interesting observation about some of these traits is that they show strengths hardly suspected, much less considered bases for building positive futures. They demonstrate survival under conditions other kids succumb to - the suicides and dropouts who do not become delinquent. Yet the idea of a delinquent with positive strengths is a novel one.

The literature has changed considerably in the last five years or so, before which kids in trouble were seen as being more represented by slow kids. Ability-oriented treatment was built around that conception of potential rather than even an "average" one. Very recently, however, a few workers have stumbled upon surprising relationships between behavior which indicates delinquency, and ability differences. Others, by seeing old data in new lights, found the usual references to measured ability in delinquents questionable. At the same time, innovative ways of dealing with delinquents have been tried, built on direct response to the kinds of needs the traits listed before indicate.

New research suggests far more delinquents have high potential, and even are still performing at unusually high levels, higher than was once thought possible. The old limitation researchers complained about in the literature, of suspecting the validity of their own work because they could not measure the kids who don't get caught, does not affect this research. The findings were accidental in a standard school population. The suggestion of the small sample reported on is that from 25 to 30 percent or more of the kids found to be potential delinquents are able at the 98 percent level; and later statistics collected only as a side issue in a following study makes an even stronger picture, for far, far more really able kids were found among potential delinquents.

There are more questions than answers. Are all adjudicated kids to be considered in any serious discussion of positive treatment, or only those who are hurting themselves and society? Are kids who are caught to be considered gifted, even though they were dumb enough to get caught, and even to offend in the first place? How about all the kids who misbehave, some very seriously and some even well known to authority but not caught? Are they to be included in discussions and statistics? How are statistics to be collected on such a mixed and non-uniform group (or groups)? How can a uniform treatment, a uniform law accommodate to this very mixed set of groups of kids? And in a wider sense, but very pertinent to discussions about such kids, how can the balance be struck between protection of the public from wrongdoers and the need for the wrongdoers to learn to control themselves and make their own mistakes? How can another balance be struck between protection of the parenting function, the very foundation of society already at risk, and the need of kids to be protected against absent, indifferent or downright malicious parents? Sessions concerning the delinquent issue will not pretend to answer these questions, but they will certainly bring together some very thoughtful people who are considering them seriously and want to find positive answers.

14

ENVIRONMENTAL AVAILABILITY, GIFTEDNESS, AND DELINQUENCY PRONENESS

Margot Lagesen King

The attempt to measure a person's self concept has been of interest to many investigators. Coopersmith (1967), Rosenberg (1965), and Gallagher and Jenne (1967) have attempted to devise or use a self concept measurement to better understand how people internally value themselves and also how this may affect their intellectual abilities.

Coopersmith (1967) and Rosenberg (1965) found that boys with high self concepts were significantly higher in achievements and leadership abilities than low self-concept boys. Katzenmeyer (1976) found that when verbal abilities were high, self-concept scores tended to be high. This suggests that verbal performances may be an indicator of how the individual perceives himself. Maslow (1941) stated that if a person perceived himself in positive ways, there would be greater ability to use potential (intellectual, physical, and emotional) in self-actualizing ways. It has also been found in many studies of gifted children that their self concepts tend to be higher than nongifted children. A high self concept seems to associate with freeing a person's intellect to be used in many ways.

Briggs (1975), Coopersmith (1967), Rosenberg (1965), Neill (1960), and Horney (1950) contend that the self concept is a measure of how the person is accepted by significant others in the home environment. Coopersmith found four basic needs common to high self concepts which were highly related to the home environment: (1) respect, (2) acceptance, (3) limit setting from significant others, and (4) significant others also have high self concepts. However, Coopersmith (1967) as well as most researchers on self concept did not use female subjects and, therefore, caution should be exercised when making interpretations on female subjects.

Gallagher and Jenne (1967) found in their studies of gifted males and females, that when comparing self concept with various thinking abilities (divergent, convergent, evaluative thinking and cognitive memory) there are some differences between the sexes. When comparing males and females who had high IQs and were high divergent thinkers, they found that the females were perceived by their mothers as granting much independence, and boys were perceived by their mothers as controling and restrictive. When comparing environmental availability (activities in a given community which a subject perceives as accessible) for gifted males and females, King (1980) found that gifted females perceived more availability than gifted males. When correlating environmental availability and environmental support (perceived emotional, intellectual and physical and financial support), King (1980) found that the correlation was significant for both sexes at the .05 level, but the females' correlation was higher. This tends to suggest that gifted females perceived more activities available, thus the suggestion of more perceived independence while the males perceived less activities available and more support, thus possibly perceiving more restriction from significant others.

The purpose of this study was to investigate the relation between self concept and environmental support, environmental availability, giftedness and delinquency proneness. It was determined from the literature that high self concept females would be highly gifted, perceive high environmental support and high environmental availability, while the high self concept males would be perceiving high environmental support, low environmental availability and would be highly gifted. Coopersmith (1967) suggests that there may be some males who are highly gifted and perceiving high environmental support but are low in self concept. This may result from realizing their full potential, thus separating themselves from their peers, hence demanding more of themselves. They may also receive some social ostracism (Tannenbaum, 1960) which may cause the self concept to lower. Thus the low self concept males would be from two contrasting groups, the highly gifted, high environmental support, low environmental availability group, and the low gifted, low environmental support, high environmental availability, and delinquent prone group, King (1980). Furthermore, it was concluded from the literature that the gifted subjects would have a higher average self concept than the nongifted.

Method

The 95 gifted subjects were given an "environmental support/environmental availability" form and a self concept inventory to complete. The environmental support/environmental availability form consisted of 97 activities from which the subjects could identify those which they perceived as available in their community for their use. After each activity were three numbers: (1) self, (2) peers, and (3) parents. There were also three environmental support statements which the subjects were to relate to themselves: "who cares," "who helps," and "who is proud." If the gifted subjects perceived their peers were proud and helped, they circled the 2; if they thought their parents were proud, helped and cared, they circled the 3. If they felt both were proud, they circled both.

By totaling all activities the subject wanted to do and could do plus couldn't do but wanted to do, the number of desired activities was found. The possible activities was then subtracted from the total desired activities and divided into the total desired activities. This number was multiplied by 100 to find the percentage of environmental availability.

The percentage of support was determined by the three categories after each activity who cares, who helps, and who is proud. Each activity the subject perceived available was multiplied by three to find the total possible environmental support. The total actual perceived support was added together and from this score the percentage of environmental support was found.

The Coopersmith Self Concept Inventory was used as the self concept measurement. There were 50 questions and the subjects were to check whether the statement was like or unlike them. Within this inventory were three types of questions relating to self, social interactions, and parents. The self concept scores were divided into three groups: high self concept (38 and above); medium (29 to 37), and low (28 and below).

Results

It was found that as the female subjects perceived more environmental support and environmental availability they had higher self concepts and were perceived as more gifted. The female subjects with high self concepts perceived that their parents were proud of them, and answered parental questions on the self concept inventory positively. Also, the highly gifted males with low self concepts perceived their parents as proud of them and they answered the parental questions on the self concept inventory positively.

Males who were the lowest in self concept were from two contrasting groups. Eight were perceived as highly gifted with high IQ and achievement, high environmental support and low environmental availability while six were perceived as delinquent prone as determined by King (1980) with low giftedness, low environmental support and high environmental availability and high IQ. Why is the highly gifted, highly supported male low in self concept? As was suggested at the beginning of the paper, they are no longer judging themselves with their peers, but are perceiving their own full potential; thus, they tend to be more demanding of themselves, hence, lower in self concept.

The subjects that the teachers perceived as leaders were low in self concept. It was also found that the female subjects perceived as leaders by peers were low in self concept. Five of the seven gifted delinquent prone subjects were perceived as leaders.

It was noticed that there were fewer females in the high IQ range (130 and above) and high achievement range (99 to 95). It must be stated that the females as a group perceived lower amounts of support than the males. This lack of perceived support could be the reason for their lower signs of giftedness.

The gifted delinquent prone subjects (six males and two females) as determined by King (1980) were all low in self concept except for one female who was in the medium range. The delinquent prone males all had low environmental support, high environmental availability, low giftedness but high IQ or achievement scores, while the females had low environmental support, low environmental availability, low giftedness but high IQ or achievement scores.

It was found that the subjects who were perceived by teachers as scientific were low in self concept. The peers perceived a somewhat different group as scientific, and they had high self concepts. Peer judgment of scientifically gifted persons tends to choose those with high self concepts, while teachers choose subjects with low self concepts, both males and females.

When observing the 16 subjects with the lowest environmental availability, of the six females one was delinquent prone. The six males in low environmental availability were not delinquent prone and perceived high environmental support, while the females all perceived low support. From this, it can be suggested that males who perceive large amounts of freedom with no support become delinquent prone.

Discussion

It appears from this study that for females and males to use their full intellectual abilities, they must perceive much support from their parents. It also appears that females must perceive more independence than males, while males must perceive more structure than females in order to use their abilities.

When children first learn new activities it is sometimes frustrating because they know what they want to say or do but to make it happen has not become a reality. When children observe the parents as proud and behind their efforts, they tend to go beyond the frustration and are able to accept the challenge because it is rewarded. If children also see parents as accepting and dealing with their own challenges and frustration, they will realize this is part of growth. Self actualization does not come from contented, unquestioning, tranquil lives but from questioning, striving and challenging growth. Just as a baseball player must learn to go beyond the frustration of practicing over and over how to hit the ball further and faster, so must the gifted child practice with the intellect until ideas become more and more precise. These children need to be helped in their quest for intellectual growth just as the baseball player needs coaching.

Many people believe that gifted children can "make it" on their own, but this is not true. They must have someone who appreciates their intellect and such appreciation, encouragement, and guidance is what enables these children to use their full abilities.

References

Briggs, D. Your child's self-esteem New York: Doubleday, 1975.

Coopersmith, S. The antecedents of self esteem. San Francisco: Freeman, 1967.

Gallagher, J. J., & Jenne, W. C. The relationship of cognitive style to classroom expressiveness and associated variables. The Journal of Educational Research, 1967, 60, 273-279.

Horney, K. Neurosis and human growth. New York: Norton, 1950.

Jackson Stenner, A. & Katzenmeyer, W. Self concept, ability and achievement in a sample of sixth grade students. The Journal of Educational Research, 1976, 69, 270-273.

King, M. L.   Rural delinquency proneness: its relationship to giftedness, environmental support, and environmental availability.   Paper presented at the annual meeting of the Council for Exceptional Children, Philadelphia, 1980 (ERIC Document Reproduction Service No. ED 188-416).

Maslow, A. H., & Mittelman, B.   Principles of abnormal psychology: the dynamics of psychic illness.   New York: Harper, 1941.

Neill, A. S.   Summerhill.   New York: Hart, 1960.

Rosenberg, M.   Society and the adolescent self image.   Princeton: Princeton University Press, 1965.

Tannenbaum, A. J.   Adolescent attitudes towards academic brilliance.   New York: New York University, 1960, (ERIC Document Reproduction Service No. EC 032 731).

15

PERSONALITY GROWTH: EMOTIONAL AND INTELLECTUAL UNDERSTANDING

Arthur Robinson

I participate in this seminar feeling much like Hans Christian Andersen's "Ugly Duckling," as my experience with highly gifted persons is near-zero, while preliminary, albeit superficial reviews of available publications in the field together with a hasty study of the conference program indicated that I am surrounded by educationalists many of whom have been working in this field for a decade or more.

As a clinical practitioner of some 25 years standing with experiences from corrective institutions, mental hospitals, rehabilitation, child and social welfare institutions, a recurring factor has forced itself upon me: the prevalence of insufficient development of human resources in the clients referred and the official classification of these clients as "cases." I would emphasize that very few referred clients have been intellectually retarded, as in Denmark this diagnosis is for the majority of this type of "case" made inside the first few years of life and special measures have been taken to ensure maximum treatment and welfare facilities in special institutions.

In an index survey of the two journals: **Exceptional Children** (vols. 1-4, 1976-80) and **Review of Special Education** (vols. 1-4, 1973-80) there is to be found only one article which specifically names children's "Social and Emotional Needs." In both journals there is a massive concentration on studies dealing with school facilities and the development of programs and techniques.

A couple of articles suggest concern with obtaining parental satisfaction with a program or the effects of the teacher's personality in relation to the success of a program.

Analysis of the present conference program shows a slight progression in the attention paid, for example, to "social and emotional components of the gifted," "social adjustments and personal relationships," and the "social adjustment of the gifted child," etc. An approximate and maximum estimate of the 369 program items indicates that a mere 7 percent deal with a personality growth aspect, which is the main target of and my major concern in my professional everyday activity.

A small reminder would seem appropriate at this point. Look in your dictionary and see the conversion of the meaning of the word educe, - to bring out - develop from a latent or potential existence to the word educate: to give intellectual or moral training, to provide schooling for. And the definition of schooling could be seen as a near fascistic goal: to discipline, bring under control, deliberately train or accustom to, to induce to follow advice.

Thus schooling is a term in the language of school systems, while the teacher, however, is in a quandary here, as the word teach derives from the same root as token: a sign, symbol, evidence of affection.

Developmental psychological principles were characteristically acknowledged in the childhood of psychology as providing pointers for educators as to how to set up and carry through programs.

With the age of modern developments and the consolidations made in biological research and industrial engineering, rational principles were applied to, for example, child feeding; and meals of sufficient nutritive quality were suggested for use at regular intervals at different age-levels. "Avoidance of bad habits" from the Victorian moralistic attitude viewpoint now obtained a "scientific" flavor, while the strictly scientific, behavioristic learning models in teaching programs did, however, come to stress the value of positive reinforcement. The aims of educational programs were, however, and still seem to be designed for maximum utilization of the material (in this case human) to be "processed," while the more humanistic conceptions of affording nurture and support on an individual basis with due regard for personality growth have had little place in our grossly materialistic Western culture.

In the field of scholastic learning, rational fault-finding diagnostic methods and cures have led the school psychological field for many years, as though the aim was the production of "manuals" for servicing and repairing the item, as though we were dealing with our 10-year-old automobile. In child delinquency and criminal treatment the main keyword became "maladjustment," that is, to the goals of society, while the primary meaning, that the person concerned is badly adjusted, at odds with himself has been largely ignored. There are, indeed, pioneers in the field of personal growth, for example, Fritz Redl, Bettelheim and Rogers, and in the educational field, A. S. Neill, and lately John Holt; their views, however, seem to have made little impact as yet on educational systems.

"Understanding" - the gaining of new insight - comes normally through a multi-sensory perceptional experiencing process. Learning by hearing, seeing, and sensory experience of the world of human beings and objects forms the base for the "higher" more complex learning processes for use in our more adult, cognitive, rational world, which Piaget has demonstrated is not the world our children coinhabit before the age of 10 or 11, on average.

Piaget's model of developmental levels and processes - from the sensomotoric via the concrete (pre-operational) to the abstract (operational) level has proved fruitful for use as a model in work with cognitive functions. His key concepts, for example, coordination, assimilation, transformation, reversibility etc. are also, however, concepts which any therapist can use in assessment of personality growth. Piaget himself, however, stresses the enormity of the change ("a minor Copernican revolution") occurring when a child must lose the egocentric attitude to enter into the complicated world of extended physical and social relations: "partly in relation to objects, but furthermore in relation to other people" (my emphasis).

In deep therapy work it is remarkable how memories from this period (2-3 years) are evoked with such highly charged emotional clarity and with so strong a stamp of the original emotional feeling being recalled. It is never cognitive failures or disappointments that are remembered, but the injustices experienced from and the nonunderstanding shown by adults (usually parents) which lie behind psychological maladjustment. The learning child learns far more of the adult educator's hidden emotional messages and moral injunctions behind the verbal facade than the logical word or message meanings. And this learning process begins long before the child can make use of language as a helpful tool to support the organization of his perceptions.

Being "bright" at a mild or advanced level affords no intrinsic guarantee for experiencing emotional satisfaction and feelings of personal integrity.

Prisons and mental hospitals can always show a fair representative core of previously "successful" business men or academic clients to support the thesis that, with regard to the attainment of a feeling of personal satisfaction, intelligence in itself is of little help. Often, indeed, therapy work with such clients proves unsuccessful because they are so convinced about maintaining the position that their problems lie in the area of intellectual and not emotional understanding.

The normal child is highly sensitive. He "comes to his senses" prenatally and postnatally, long before he is enjoined by an adult to do so. In fact this expression used by an adult points out that the child is now required in fact to do exactly the opposite: the child is being instructed to give up his empathic, intuitive understanding and to adopt a "sensible" attitude, to be "reasonable," that is, to heed the adult's reasons.

It is with some apprehension that I now quote from Cyril Burt's **The Gifted Child** (1975), but it is in the context where Burt quotes from Terman's follow-up studies and the cause of failure, that is, highly gifted who have failed to fulfill the early promise. The failure causes are tabulated, and 32 percent of the "failures" are ascribed to the group under the heading: "Motivational conditions." "By far the most important factors arose from those emotional elements of personality, which underly motivation, in particular from their attitude to school. In many cases the school itself is largely to blame. Still more frequently the favourable or non-favourable attitude of the child is determined by attitudes prevailing in the home."

And it would seem to be in concordance with and an expansion of this factor that the next highest percentage (28%) of failure is ascribed to "unfavorable home conditions." On these two counts, then, these factors are seen as responsible for 60% of failures.

The use of precisely such terms as a promise and failure leave little doubt that the "promise" is an adult evaluation, and the "failure" consists of not living up to adult expectations.

These "objective" terms reveal the enormous investment adults (both professional educated and parents) make in attempts to fulfill through their children - both normal and more gifted - their own hopes and promises, seeking as it were to redress the balance of their own frustrated ambitions but clothing their children in a mantle of their aspirations. I see little reason to wonder at the quoted 60 percent of failures - failures to live up to others' expectations - nor am I surprised that Nixon found a resounding gimmick, when he gave status feelings and a sense of identity to the subdued population group he appealed to as "the silent majority" of personally unfulfilled voters with a stunted personality growth.

There is at present far too great a gap between the world of education and re-education, whether this takes place in institutions for delinquents or hospitals under the names of correctional treatment, rehabilitation or psychotherapy.

It is my hope that I may be able to help to

diminish that gap on the basic assumption that most behavior and learning disorders are primarily due to emotional problems in clients, who - whatever their age and intelligence level - lack the feeling of basic security acceptance, self-awareness, self-assuredness and integrity, which are necessary if they (and we) are to make full use of individual resources.

16

BRIGHT JUVENILE DELINQUENTS IN RESIDENTIAL TREATMENT: ARE THEY DIFFERENT?

Richard E. Tremblay

This paper addresses the problem of classifying juvenile delinquents with reference to their IQ. It is principally concerned with the differences between high IQ and average IQ juvenile delinquents in residential treatment.

Answers to three questions are sought in two longitudinal studies of juvenile delinquents treated at Boscoville, a residential treatment center in Montreal. The three questions are the following:

1. At the time of admission to the institution, are above average IQ juvenile delinquents different on psychological characteristics from average IQ juvenile delinquents?

2. Do above average IQ juvenile delinquents adjust better to treatment than average IQ juvenile delinquents?

3. Is the IQ of juvenile delinquents a good predictor of success in adjustment after residential treatment?

The first study used to answer those three questions is a longitudinal study of each boy who entered and left Boscoville between 1974 and 1977. The study included a two year follow-up of each of the boys after they had left the institution. This large scale evaluation research was done by the Groupe de Recherche sur l'Inadaptation Juvénile of the Université de Montréal directed by Marc Leblanc. Approximately thirty reports have been published to date on that project and readers are referred to the pertinent reports for details of the methodology.

The second study used to answer the three questions is also a longitudinal study of every boy at Boscoville, but during a shorter time span. The changes in behavior of boys during treatment was studied from February to October 1975, a 9 month time span. Methodological details of that study can be found in Tremblay (1976).

Boscoville

For those not familiar with Boscoville, a brief description of the institution, as it was at the time of both studies, follows. It is taken from Tremblay (1976). More elaborate descriptions can be found in Cusson & Leblanc (1980) and Gendreau (1966).

Boscoville admits adolescent boys who have been found guilty of breaking the law from anywhere in the province of Quebec, between the ages of 15 and 18, and with a minimum intelligence quotient of 90. The boys must have been diagnosed as having an antisocial character without any serious psychopathological problems and be able to read, write and compute at the ten-year old age level.

The physical organization of the institution is by house units (seven) with a central administration block and a sports block. Two house units are used for reception-assessment purposes, each catering to a maximum of eight boys at any one time. The other five house units are used for treatment catering to a maximum of 15 boys at any one time. Some staff members live on the premises, but all staff housing is at least a hundred yards away from the house units.

Each treatment unit staff team consists basically of one "Coordinateur" and four to six "Educateurs." All are graduates of a school of Psycho-Education either at the Université de Montréal or the Université de Sherbrooke (with either a Certificat, a BA or Master's degree). Each team also includes students studying for their Master's or BA degree, who assist a senior member of staff as part of their required degree work (with at least one female educator per team).

The social structure of the institution is meant to form a micro-city with each house unit being a borough. Each borough elects its representatives for internal purposes (e.g., a resident responsible for sports activities, a resident responsible for house duties, a resident responsible for classroom activities). Each borough also elects a representative to the city council which is responsible for the coordination of activities concerning the whole city. Each representative, in fact, becomes an assistant to the member of staff responsible for the given activity (classroom, arts, sports, house duties, etc.) and it is the responsibility of the staff member to support the resident in his task in such a way that it becomes a learning experience with regard to assuming responsibility in a social organization.

The residents in the two reception-assessment units are not considered citizens of the city, only acquiring their citizenship when they enter one of the treatment units. And citizenship can also be lost, for the system of rights and privileges attached to the status of citizenship forms a complex system of support and motivation to behave in a socially acceptable way. This system is based on continuous ratings by staff members of every boy's behavior and performance in each part of the program according to goals that have been agreed upon by the boy in question with staff members. These goals are based on the four stages of the psycho-educational model.

At Boscoville, instead of the customary central pool of teachers who see to the regular classroom or technical training activities in residential institutions for juvenile delinquents, members of each house unit staff team run the classroom, art and sports activities. In this way the boys of a given unit are constantly in contact with each other and with the staff of the unit, living in an intense group situation where they not only share routine and leisure but also learning activities. There are four types of activities for which there is at least one 90 minute period per day: classroom (e.g., mathematics, French), sports (e.g., gymnastics, athletics, football), projects (theatre productions, cinema, pantomime), and pottery.

The drawbacks of this type of organization are the heterogeneity of abilities and performances in learning activities and the need for specialists in any given activity in each unit. This has been dealt with by creating an individualized system of learning by written index cards ("fiches") and by having aspiring educators specialize in a given activity.

The learning and performance heterogeneity in the classroom is dealt with in the same way as the heterogeneity of individual potential and problems which characerize a group of persons. That is, the person must actualize his potential and solve his problems while the group must accept each person's problems and support him in actualizing his potential.

A weekly group therapy session for each house unit is conducted by two psychologists from the Université de Montréal. Also a weekly group discussion of current events is attended by all boys and staff members of each house unit. Individual counseling sessions are conducted weekly for each boy by an "educateur" of his choice, while constant use is made of life space interviews (Clinical exploitation of life events and emotional first aid on the spot, Redl, 1963).

Results

With reference to the first question: "At the time of admission to the institution, are above average IQ juvenile delinquents different on psychological characteristics from average IQ juvenile delinquents?", an assessment of 22 psychological variables showed no differences at admission between boys of above average IQ and boys of average IQ who stay in treatment for at least six months.

To answer the second question, "Do above average IQ juvenile delinquents adjust better to treatment than average IQ juvenile delinquents?" we present three different sets of results. First, a study of boys who leave treatment before one year shows that their average IQ is lower (mean=114.6). Second, a longitudinal study (9 months) of boys' behavior with peers, staff and in activities shows that boys with IQ of 130+ do not adjust better than boys with IQ of 90 to 110. Third, a study of changes on 22 psychological variables from admission to completion shows that both the above average IQ and average IQ groups make significant changes on almost all the psychological variables assessed. The gains made by the above average IQ group tended to be slightly larger than those made by the average IQ group, but when compared at the end of treatment both groups showed no significant differences on the 22 variables. It should be recalled that there were no significant differences between the two groups at the beginning of treatment.

To answer the third question, "Is the IQ of juvenile delinquents a good predictor of success in adjustment after residential treatment?" we have used four different criteria of success.

First, official recidivism in a two year period after treatment was studied. The above average IQ group (nonverbal scale and global scale) did not differ in recidivism rate from the average IQ group, but a classification of boys based upon the verbal IQ scale shows a difference between the two groups that is statistically close (at the level .06) to a level of confidence generally considered acceptable. "Return to an institution" was used as a second criterion of treatment success. The group of boys with an average IQ on the nonverbal and global scale were found to have a frequency of return greater than the group with an above average IQ on the nonverbal and global scale. The classification based on the verbal scale does not permit a valid prediction of return to the institution. Satisfaction with community adjustment as expressed by the boy himself was used as a third criterion. No difference was found between the group of boys with average IQ and the group with above average IQ.

Finally, our fourth criterion was psychological evolution between the time the boys left the institution and one year later. There are no differences found between boys with above average IQ and boys with average IQ on this criterion. Generally, boys tended to regress on these measures during the first year in the community.

BRIGHT JUVENILE DELINQUENTS

Discussion

Two general hypotheses are deduced from the results. First, if our treatment objective for juvenile delinquents is to reduce official recidivism and prevent a return to an institution, we can predict that residential treatment with a strong academic program such as Boscoville's will tend to succeed better with boys of above average IQ than with boys of average IQ. Second, if our treatment objective is the psychological evolution of juvenile delinquent (increased self-esteem and social maturity, decreased social anxiety and withdrawal) we can predict that residential treatment with a strong academic program such as Boscoville's will not succeed better with boys of above average IQ than with boys of average IQ. In both cases, whether we use official recidivism and return to the institution or use psychological evolution as a criterion of success, it is concluded that a classification of juvenile delinquents based on IQ for residential treatment purposes does not seem very useful. Knowing the IQ of an adolescent you are working with will certainly help adjust the program to his abilities, but this we should call an individualized approach and should be applied to each sphere of behavior. For example, it is as important to assess the physical abilities of each boy.

If juvenile delinquency (as defined by West & Farrington, 1977; Leblanc, 1980; Frechette, 1980) is related to a complex set of psycho-social factors the results we have presented show that boys with above average IQ are not different from boys with average IQ on these characteristics at the start of treatment, at the end of treatment and at a one year follow up after the end of treatment, although the treatment in question seemed to be better adapted to their needs than to average or below average IQ boys. Creating a separate group of juvenile delinquents based on IQ for residential treatment purposes does not only seem unnecessary but could also be harmful since treatment of juvenile delinquents is based largely on the use of group living.

By creating a group of bright juvenile delinquents for treatment purposes there seems to be a real danger of creating an artificial environment which will not have the necessary conditions for addressing the true problems of juvenile delinquents, that is, psycho-social adjustment. For example, one characteristic of delinquency is the exploitation of weaker individuals. A bright juvenile delinquent can probably learn not to exploit other less intelligent individuals only by living with them in a treatment oriented environment. From the study of Boscoville's drop-out clientele we can say that if there is a pressing problem related to IQ in the treatment of juvenile delinquents it is probably that average and low IQ boys are sacrificed for the sake of responding to the needs of above average IQ boys.

Conclusion

In my concluding remarks I offer a summary of residential treatment characteristics which appear to have a positive impact on juvenile delinquents. These characeristics have been extracted from a review of research on the treatment of juvenile delinquents in residential settings (Tremblay, 1980).

First, there does not seem to be any treatment model which is systematically more successful than another (e.g., behavioristic, psychodynamic, reality therapy). The most important characteristic of a successful treatment program seems to be that the staff share an "image of the world" and present it with conviction to the boys. This means a leader who can propose a set of values and unite staff members around them.

The social climate of an institution also seems to be a major characteristic of successful programs. The social climate is of course a result of other characteristics but since it can be measured (Moos, 1975) it is useful to present it as a characteristic which can be worked on. Moos (1975) proposes three main dimensions of the social climate: affiliation, goals and system maintenance. These three dimensions are closely associated to three basic qualities of educators of juvenile delinquents we have proposed elsewhere (Tremblay & Renou, 1980). The educator should be able to relate to individuals, he should be able to set goals and he should be able to organize an environment which helps in the attainment of the goals and can maintain itself when aggressed by delinquent behavior. Both the affiliative characteristics and the organizational characteristic should be recognized as means to attain the goals and should not be pursued as ends in themselves. From our experience it is difficult for educators not to mix up the fact that their personal qualities are means to ends and not ends in themselves. It is also difficult to find educators and, as a consequence, institutions which can maintain an equilibrium between affiliation and organization or control. Hence, residential treatment centers tend to be either too centered on affiliation, where it becomes an end, or too centered on organization where it becomes an end or too centered on goals, without attention to means necessary to attain them. Finally, it should be stressed that residential treatment will have an ephemeral impact if there is no strong follow-up treatment after boys have left residential treatment (Jesness, 1971; Moos, 1975; Bosse & Leblanc, 1980a).

References

Achille, P. A. & Leblanc, M. La personnalité des garçons de Boscoville. Montréal: Groupe de Recherche sur l'Inadaptation Juvénile, Université de Montréal, rapport technique no 18,1977.

Andry, R. G. The short term prisoner: a study in forensic psychology. London: Stevens, 1977.

Barbeau, G. L. & Pinard, A. Epreuve individuelle d'intelligence générale. Manuel. Montreal: Le Centre de Psychologie et de Pédagogie, 1951.

Barron, F. An ego strength scale which predicts response to psychotherapy. Journal of Consulting Psychology, 1953, 17, 327-333.

Bloom, B. S. Taxonomy of educational objectives: the

classification of educational goals. Handbook 1. Cognitive domain. New York: McKay, 1956.

Bossé, M. & Leblanc, M. L'adaptation sociale des anciens de Boscoville. Montreal: Groupe de Recherche sur l'Inadaptation Juvénile, Université de Montréal, Rapport final no 4, 1980.

Bossé, M. & Leblanc, M. La délinquance officielle des anciens de Boscovile six ans apres le début de la recherche. Montreal: Groupe de Recherche sur l'Inadaptation Juvénile, Université de Montréal, Rapport technique no 23, 1980.

Bossé, M. & Leblanc, M. L'évolution psychologique des garçons de Boscoville. Montreal: Groupe de Recherche sur l'Inadaptation Juvénile, Université de Montréal, Rapport final no 3, 1979.

Brooks, R. Bright delinquents: the story of a unique school. Windsor, England: National Foundation for Educational Research, 1972.

Cattell, R. B. & Sheier, I. H. Handbook for the IPAT - Anxiety scale. Champaign, Ill.: Institute for Personality and Ability Testing, 1952.

Clarke, R. V. G. & Cornish, D. B. The effectiveness of residential treatment for delinquents. Paper presented at the annual conference of the Child Psychiatry Section of the Royal College of Psychiatrists, London, March 1976.

Cusson, M. Délinquants pourquoi? LaSalle, Quebec: Editions H.M.H., 1981.

Cusson, M. & Leblanc, M. Boscoville: le milieu et la clientèle. Montreal: Groupe de Recherche sur l'Inadaptation Juvénile, Université de Montréal, Rapport final no 1, 1980.

Empey, L. T. American deliquency: its meaning and construction. Homewood, Ill.: Dorsey Press, 1968.

Eysenck, H. J. Crime and personality (2nd ed.). St. Albans, Herts.: Paladin, 1970.

Eysenck, H. G. & Eysenck, S. B. G. Personality structure and measurement. San Diego: Knapp, 1969.

Fitts, W. H. Tennessee Self Concept Scale: Manual. Nashville, Tenn.: Counselor Recording and Tests,

1965.

Folkard, M. S. Impact: intensive matched probation and aftercare treatment. Vol. 1. London: H.M.S.O., 1974.

Frechette, M. & Leblanc, M. La délinquance cachée à l'adolescence. Montreal: Groupe de Recherche sur l'Inadaptation Juvénile, Université de Montréal, Cahier 1, 1979.

Gengreau, G. L'intervention psycho-éducative. Paris: Fleurus, 1978.

Gendreau, G. Boscoville: une expérience en marche. Paper presented to the Centre de formation et de recherche de l'éducation surveillée, Vaucresson, France, 1966.

Gendreau, G. Les étapes de la rééducation d'après l'expérience de Boscoville. Paper presented at the au 2ième colloque de recherche sur la délinquance et la criminalité. Montreal, 1960.

Gough, H. H. Cross-cultural validation of a measure of asocial behavior. Psychological Reports, 1965, 17, 379-387.

Grittner, F. M. Individualized instruction: an historical perspective. The Modern Language Journal, 1975, 59 (7).

Guindon, J. Le processus de rééducation du jeune délinquant par l'actualisation des forces du moi. In l'Etude des Sciences de l'Homme, 1969, Vol. 7.

Hargreaves, D. H. Social relations in a secondary school. London: Routledge & Kegan Paul, 1967.

Hood, R. G. & Sparks, R. Key issues in criminology. London: Weidenfeld & Nicolson, 1970.

Jesness, C. F. The Preston typology study: an experiment with differential treatment in an institution. Journal of Research in Crime and Delinquency, 1971, 8 (I), 38-52.

Jesness, C. F. The Jesness Inventory Manual. Palo Alto, Calif.: Consulting Psychologist Press, 1969.

Krathwohl, D. R., Bloom, B. S., Masia, B. B. Taxonomy of educational objectives: the classification of educational goals. Handbook, 2. Affective domain. New York: McKay, 1964.

Leblanc, M.   La délinquance: un épiphénomène de l'adolescence. Paper presented at the Seminaire avance sur la justice des mineurs, Ste-Marguérite, Quebec, August 1980.

Mailloux, N.   Jeunes sans dialogue: criminologie pédagogique. Paris: Fleurus, 1971.

Moos, R. H.   Evaluating correctional and community settings. London: Wiley, 1975.

Redl, F.   The life-space interview in the school. American Journal of Orthopsychiatry, 1963, 33 (4).

Sullivan, C. E., Grant, M. Q., Grant, J. D. The development of interpersonal maturity: application to delinquency. Psychiatry, 1957, 20, (4).

Tremblay, R. E.   La formation de l'éducateur: le long chemin d'un idéal.   Paper presented at the Deuxieme Colloque Provincial sur la Formation de l'Educateur, College de St-Jérome, Quebec, March, 1981.

Tremblay, R. E.   Les caractéristiques des internats de rééducation susceptibles d'avoir un impact positif sur les mineurs en difficulté avec la loi: étude critique de resultats de recherche.   Paper presented at the Seminaire avance sur la justice des mineurs, Ste-Marguerite, Quebec, August, 1980.

Tremblay, R. E.   A psychoeducational study of juvenile delinquents during treatment.   Unpublished doctoral thesis, Institute of Education, University of London, 1976.

Tremblay, R. E. & Renou, M.   La formation des psycho-éducateurs à l'Université de Montréal. Revue Canadienne de Psycho-Education, 1980, 9 (2), 128-139.

Wagner, E. E.   The hand test manual (revised ed.). Los Angeles, Calif.: Western Psychological Services, 1969.

West, D. J. & Farrington, D. P.   The delinquent way of life. New York: Crane Russak, 1977.

PART 4

CULTURAL PERSPECTIVES

"We are gifted and very talented. But you're not going to find out the way you are asking us your questions." With that message, as well as two films and a song, Alanis Obomsawin closed the 1981 conference and a presentation which brought the audience to its feet. Obomsawin and Karlene George present the perspectives of North American native peoples, one the view of the artist, the other of the educator. We should not be surprised, however, at their concurrence. In another look at the understanding of giftedness within a culture, Nava Butler-Por examines different values in Israel, European and Oriental, Jewish and Arab. Switching from three of the world's numerically smallest communities, educator and frequent visitor to China, and political scientist and East-European expert John Dunstan present the situation in two of the world's giants, China and the USSR. The closing three chapters concentrate on the so-called third world. Political scientist Henry Coker and education ministry official Ahmed Yussufu look at policy questions about giftedness from the points of view of developing nations on opposite sides of Africa. How do we reconcile pursuing education of the gifted with socialist idealogies, the urgent need for basic education, or recent change from colonial status? What does education of the gifted mean when one hundred children and a teacher must share one book? Finally, former International Year of the Child official Danica Adjemovitch relates the efforts of UNICEF to help the development of all children.

The Soviet and Israeli examples have been reported before, but all eight chapters remind us that the most visible programs and services for the gifted, those which we might think of as mainstream or prototypical, are really highly exceptional and very

211

much products of their cultural, social and political environments. One challenge is to determine what is generalizable and under what circumstances.

17

CHILDREN OF THE EARTH

Alanis Obomsawin

I feel that every child when it's first born, is very gifted. I will speak of children of North American Indian ancestry - and I am one. I realize that I am speaking to people that are mainly in education. If I say anything that might hurt your feelings, I don't wish to apologize but I also want to tell you that I don't mean to be disrespectful. I am speaking out of experience - personal experience. I myself have not been in school for very long. I came out of school when I was fourteen years old and I began going to school when I was nine years old. The first year I spoke Indian only and I was put in a French school, in a French town. I remained there two years and it was not a good time. The reason I am here is because I have been very concerned about children - and for many years I have been going around the country, mostly Canada, to speak, to tell our history, to sing for children of all races, and a lot to our own people at the reserve level, at residential schools when they were still in existence. In the cities I have given concerts and I have been present in many schools and many universities - and, as I said before, it is not because I have any degrees or diplomas that I can speak to you. I am a bit nervous, but I am not afraid.

I went to the archives and read a lot there. I read many letters that sometimes came from the minister, sometimes from the priest, sometimes from the chief of police, who pleaded with the federal government, with Indian Affairs, to separate the children from the parents, because this was a way of making sure that they would learn another culture, another language, and that they would forget that they were Indians. I've read many letters where they praised themselves for the numbers of children that they took away. And they said that they had been very successful in what they were trying to do. I read letters where the chief of police in British Columbia was writing to Indian Affairs asking them to separate the tribes because there were too many tribes close together. When the time came that they came and they gave potlatches and they had their religious ceremonies, the priest and the Anglican minister had no power over the people, could not even be part or understand what they were doing. They wanted the people to not be in such large numbers in one place.

After a few years, this was granted and people were moved away - forty or fifty miles away - in smaller groups so that they would not gather in such large numbers. In 1969 the last residential school was closed, because of the fact that our people became aware of the terrible problems our children were faced with. While they were being taught a foreign culture and a foreign language and being kept away from their own parents, still they were being isolated from the white man's community, from the white man's way of being. As a result, our children, our young people, would end up in the cities, on Skid Row, in areas where the poorest people lived, where criminal people were living and were very poor in their minds and in their souls. Still today across this country you can go to many of our cities and you will find thousands and thousands of our people living in the cities that have been destroyed, diminished, and where they have lost themselves.

There were many programs to try and help in the city and also at the reserve level. We've seen them come and go. Some of the programs have been successful, and we find that the ones that have any success are the ones that are taken over by our own people, who have been there before. There are many communities and many reserves across the country that have taken over their own education. This is not the easiest thing to do. It means taking away a large number of children from the next town. It means taking away a large sum of money from the next town

- because the federal government pays for each child that goes to that particular school, which amounts to about $1500 to $2000 per child.

Our people have made their own research and their own investigation on why our children were always dropping out, and very few of them would go on to university or go to higher grades. They discovered many sad things that were happening to our children. I will give you some examples. I think the main problem is because the newcomers always felt superior to us. And they felt that we should learn their ways, their language, and that we should be like them, and that their god was the best. It never occurred to them that our people were very spiritual and highly religious people before they came, and that that was the main importance of our being.

When our children go to school and they speak only their mother tongue - even today they are classified as handicapped children. Now, to be a handicapped child in a school board means that you must go to a special class. A fine example in this province is on the north shore of Quebec, where the Montagnais children who came to school and spoke only Montagnais were classified as handicapped children. As a result of this, the school commission turns around to the federal government and asks double the amount of money for each child, for special classrooms - which comes to $3000 per child. Then these children are put into a classroom which is more like a nursery school, and because they are being taught with the same books that they used for the French classroom, our children are not able to understand very quickly. Therefore, they are immediately labeled retarded as they begin school. This is the beginning of the destruction of a human being.

When they get to sixth grade they have created a new program for them - this is happening now. It is called IAT, which means in French "initiation to begin to work" and we have teenagers that are in these classrooms. They are all Indians, and all they learn all day is how to bake cakes and how to read and write

215

French. They are about fourteen or fifteen years old at a school where all the rest of the children that are French Canadian are attending regular classrooms.

I don't think I have to explain any further than that. I'm sure that you understand what it means to our culture and to our nations. There is no way that a person or a people can survive without its language. Many of our languages have been lost, but still we have some tribes where the language is very much alive and we need to keep it. In these areas up North, some of the tribes have taken over their own school board, and they have a school at the reserve level from grade one to six. There the children are received by their own people - by teachers who speak Montagnais, or teachers' aides who can speak to them in their own language - which is a big amelioration. After grade six they must go again to the next town. The trouble is that in this particular area they're still teaching the same curriculum of the province. The teachers who are Montagnais feel greatly uncomfortable because they feel still that they are a tool to teach what the white man wants to be taught. In another place, in James Bay area, in a place called Rupert's House - this is also in Quebec - several years ago a new program was organized by the people themselves, which was very successful. It is called "Cree Way." They got their own press, and they printed their own books. They got the community very involved in telling the history of their own area, and they got some children to make drawings to illustrate these stories, and they began to teach this at the school level.

I, myself, have made some perception kits with two different reserves, which is a concentration of the history and the culture of a particular people. What a difference it makes with the child who sits at the school bench and sees officially his ancestors, his relatives, his parents being on the screen or being part of the curriculum. That child can grow up and feel good about himself and feel that it is all right to be an Indian, feel that his people, his ancestors, were great people, were wonderful people. They were good. They knew how to cure people. They knew how to survive in this country. They knew how to make snowshoes to travel to different parts of this country. They knew that you had to make snowshoes a certain way if it was a powdery snow, or if you were going up the mountain, or if you lived in a flat place. They knew all that.

And now, in many of our schools, these things are being brought back to our children. Right here very close to Montreal there is the reserve called Caughnawaga, or Kanawak - and two years ago, I think it was, they took their children from Chateauguay which is the area where all their teenagers were going to school. They took them out because they didn't want to be forced into a French government way of taking a license to go to the school you want. After being forced, doing this was the best thing that ever happened to them because the community got very involved. The mothers and the fathers had to become teachers overnight. You should see these kids today because they realized when those teenagers came back home, many of them didn't know how to read and write properly, although they were big boys and big girls. They hired their own teachers that they needed to do mathematics, or whatever subject that they wanted to hire people to do. And they got very involved themselves, in who they were. They threw out Quebec's curriculum. They say, "We start from here. First, the heart of our teaching way is our people here. Caughnawaga, who are we? What is our language? We teach our language, we teach our history - then we will go on to French and English and other people's history."

I was reading some reports on IQ tests that were given to some of our children. I read the exams and I read the questions - the oral ones and the ones that had to be written down, that our children had to answer. I'll give you some examples. Up North, again, there was a question that asked, "Why should you build a house out of bricks instead of wood?" All the children of that area skipped that thing. They didn't answer it. Now for children up North, on the North Shore, who live in wooden houses or in tents - at the age of five or six they would know what bush life is, and they would know what it is to live either in a log house or in a prefabricated house made of wood that perhaps Indian Affairs has built for them - but this is what they would know about. They would know about a tent when they go hunting and fishing with their parents, and that they camp out in the bush. With a question like that to be given to our children who have probably never even seen a brick house, how can we discover what that child has to offer as a gift?

There was another question that asked, "Lemons are sour and sugar is _____." They skipped that too because up North, again, the children are used to eating wild game; they are used to eating a lot of meat, and very few vegetables are part of their diet. They probably never even saw their mother using a lemon.

The reason why I say these things to you is that I ask to myself, "How are you going to find out if our children are gifted or not?" You have to look at us and find out who we are first. The trouble is that our children who come from a different culture, from a different way of being, when they leave home, know what it means to share because this is the basis of everything. They usually come from large families and no one will take a lot and keep it for himself. People always share with everybody - so anybody who has anything has a habit of giving it away. When a child gets into the city or to the school level, he starts behaving the same way. People think "he's trying to buy my affection", or "he's trying to buy my love", and it's because there's a clash in a way of being. You will see amongst our people, people having really hard times, and people are poor you will say, but they're all laughing, they have a sense of humor that is out of this world. You could have only bannock to eat for a week, but you'll kill yourself laughing at yourself because you'll say, "Look at you - you could only have bannock you think for today - maybe tomorrow. So what do you get? More bannock." There are jokes that go on all the time about ourselves. We are able to laugh at ourselves and our children are aware of this. They never leave their parents. The minute that they are born, a child is never left in a different room or has his own room someplace. He will sleep with his mother most probably for a few months, and later he will sleep in the same room and he will follow his mother and father until the age of six or seven. This is our way.

I thank you for hearing me, but I hope that when you go from here you will think of us and that we are gifted and very talented. But you're not going to find out the way you are asking us your questions.

18

NATIVE AMERICAN INDIAN: PERCEPTION OF GIFTED CHARACTERISTICS

Karlene George

In June of 1980, United Indians Of All Tribes Foundation received a $10,000 three-year grant from the Northwest Area Foundation (NWAF) of St. Paul, Minnesota as part of NWAF's gifted education funding program coordinated with Education Service District (ESD) 121 of Seattle.

The overall purpose of the United Indians project is to provide technical assistance to school districts and tribal organizations who serve Native American elementary and secondary students on identifying and assessing the needs of, and programming for Native American gifted students. The specific objectives for this project are: to develop a position paper on identifying and programming for Native American gifted students and to design and field test a training program for staff serving Native American students within ESD 121 on the abilities and needs of Native American gifted students. These efforts will be focused on schools in Western Washington, particularly within the boundaries of ESD 121 (King and Pierce Counties).

The present position paper is intended to function as a guidepost for the project, to help define the practical and theoretical issues involved in identifying and providing services for gifted and talented Native American Children, and to propose some responses to these issues based upon our experience in Indian education generally, and in particular based upon the author's experience with Native American gifted students with the North Kitsap School District of Poulsbo, Washington.

We have structured this paper around five specific objectives: (a) to provide a theoretical background on the definition of giftedness for Native American students, on identification criteria, and on program design; (b) to relate findings on currently available identification methodologies and instruments to needs of staff and community in identifying Native American gifted students; (c) to provide a brief overview of available research on the learning styles and educational needs of Indian Children: (d) to summarize current practice as reported by gifted projects currently serving Native American students within ESD 121 and those specifically designed for Native American students nation-wide; and (e) through conclusions and recommendations, to relate the findings of the first four objectives 1 - 4 to staff training and to further research and development work needed.

Giftedness and Native Americans

The presently available literature contains a limited number of studies and discussions which directly relate to Native American gifted students. There is a larger body of literature that deals with minority and disadvantaged gifted youngsters; some of the information generated by these studies may be useful to educators of Native American gifted children, if used with a certain degree of caution.

The definition of giftedness is central to discussions about identification, assessment, programming and evaluation for any population of gifted students. For students who come from a culture which is significantly different from that of the majority (Western European) the question of what it means to be gifted will determine not only the way in which those students will be served by a school's gifted education program, but whether they will be served at all.

In 1972, the U. S. Office of Education issued a report on the education of gifted and talented children which recognized six categories of giftedness: (a) the academically gifted, (b) specific academic aptitude, (c) creative, productive, thinking giftedness, (d) giftedness in the visual and performing arts, (e) leadership

221

giftedness and (f) psychomotor giftedness. This definition has formed the basis for much of the current discussion on gifted education for culturally different groups, including Native Americans. Limiting the definition of giftedness to the academic area only seems particularly inappropriate to Native American students, whose experiential background is so rich in areas other than school academics (Roy, 1979).

Because of the great variety of tribal communities and cultures which exist throughout the United States, the specifics of defining and identifying giftedness among Native American children would be difficult to generalize. It has therefore been suggested that criteria for identification be based on the historical and cultural realities of the local community (Locke, 1979), that community members themselves participate in the setting down of these criteria (George, 1979; Dodson & Mitchell, 1978), and that specific tribal values, considered as behaviors, form the basis for gifted identification criteria (Peacock, 1979). Roy (1979) also proposes that definitions of giftedness for Native American children be personally and socially integrative, that they avoid categorization and separation of students from each other, and that they be built upon the symbolic circle of tribal values.

Researchers who have recently investigated the identification of gifted students among minority or disadvantaged populations have raised other questions which must be considered when defining giftedness and criteria for giftedness among Native American children. The psychological impact of being a member of a minority group, as well as the economic disadvantages which many Native American children face, may give them some characteristics in common with other minority and disadvantaged groups (Storlie, 1978; Cummings, 1979). However the generalization of cultural, economic and social differences across groups - the extent to which any similarities of experiences can be translated into identification criteria and ultimately into programming - is at this point an unresolved issue.

As an early and admittedly tentative response to this question, we wish to describe the obstacles, as we see them, surrounding proper identification of and educational opportunity for Native American gifted students, and criteria for the success of any solution to this problem.

Identification and Cultural Relevance

It is generally believed that the ability of a child to achieve consistently above grade level in several academic subject areas is a definitive measure of high intellectual potential. In terms of cross-cultural education, one would have to ask: "In which academic subject areas does the achievement take place, against whose standards is achievement measured, and how is it measured?"

The significance of these questions to those of us concerned with the education of Native American children can be understood with greater clarity if the history of this continent is considered. Our history, which produced a certain social order, might have produced a much different social order had native people retained their dominance here. For example, a measure of high intellectual ability might at this date be the consistent ability of a child to predict the effect of weather changes on deer migration at a particular time of year in a given river drainage area.

For a moment, let us approach this subject of Native American giftedness in a manner which friends of the gifted child will understand instantly. Let us describe (analyze, synthesize and evaluate) the state of the gifted education as it would be in a Native American society.

Children possessing superior intellectual abilities of cognition and convergent production would demonstrate these by knowing the habitats and seasonal migrations of the food animals in the area and by successfully tracking and killing them. Flexibility and fluency might be demonstrated by the complex operations necessary to transform the animal carcass into its multiple uses. These operations include memory of traditions relating to preparation and preservation of game, evaluation of the animal's weight, condition and possible use of its various parts, and synthesis of a variety of skills and knowledge into planning the appropriate uses of the carcass in coordination with a variety of environmental factors and social needs within the tribal group. Children gifted with superior psycho-social abilities might demonstrate these through tribally-delegated leadership roles within the family structure, the village or the tribe. Motivating and coordinating the activities of others in a close-knit tribal community requires assessment of others' personal and social abilities, analysis of each person's formal and informal status and role within the community, and synthesis of these roles and abilities into new efforts and social structures. Those gifted in artistic and performing arts might demonstrate these abilities by an intricate hoop-dance which imitates and reproduces the elaborate patterns and rhythms of the eagle.

Parents of non-Indian children, faced with such a social and educational structure, as it affects their children's opportunities for recognition and advancement, might well feel discouraged and frustrated. "My child cannot seem to do well at hoop-dancing, but she is very talented in ballet. Yet no one cares," a parent might say. Another could add, "Despite the fact that my child does not do well in animal hunting or Native languages and has failed the Figural-Tracking Test, he is very creative with budgets and financial projects at home. But he is in remedial storytelling and no one will refer him on for the gifted program." The situations described would culturally discriminate against non-Native children. However, a few changes in subject area references makes this a very accurate description of a very common experience in the lives of Native American children today. The intellectual operations we wish to look for in Native American children are essentially the same as those used by other high ability children. Developing social structures to accommodate new circumstances, analysis

224

of food resources and their relationship to community needs, and the evolution of dance style within a traditional context all require intellectual processes which transcend cultural context. What we often overlook, however, is the fact that verbal and behavioral manifestations of these intellectual operations are very much culturally influenced.

At the same time, we seem to be burdened with a uniform but antiquated educational system with which to serve a diverse population. As James Olivero put it in his address to the Northwest Gifted Child Association at Central Washington University (1978), "Equal treatment of unequal is unequal." Nowhere is "equal treatment" more unjust than in the identification procedures used to select Native American children for gifted programs; rather than select, they exclude these culturally different children. In the Spring of 1980, of a total of 5150 Native American children enrolled in school districts in King and Pierce counties in the State of Washington, 24 had been identified as gifted.

The dissimilarities between Indian and non-Indian cultures in language and semantic processing, especially in certain abstract and conceptual cognitive modes (Snow, 1977) as well as in the factors of self-fulfillment which motivate behavior (Byrde, 1969) present a complicated problem which Indian and non-Indian educators have reacted to more with intuition than research. Researchers have been willing to acknowledge the uniqueness of each culture, but have not been willing to hypothesize and substantiate what these differences mean in terms of the general characteristics of a gifted child. Thus, directors of programs for the gifted who have sought to include Native American children in programs have had to rely on the "general characteristics" lists (even though they suspect these may be inappropriate), or they go directly to the great equalizer, the intelligence tests or measures of academic ability. Neither of these approaches has been shown to be particularly effective in accurately identifying Native American gifted

NATIVE AMERICAN GIFTED students.

In addition to cultural differences in the manifestation of intellectual abilities, and the inability of characteristics lists and general IQ tests to "find" gifted Native American children, the greatest obstacle to their discovery has been the perception by Native American people of "giftedness." Semantically imagined, the word "gift" within a small Native American community in the Pacific Northwest was interpreted to mean "something to give away." In this cultural community, gift giving was traditionally practiced through the potlatch system. It was truly more blessed (and it gave one greater social status) to give than to receive, and this cultural trait seems to be still intact. One is not as rewarded by acknowledging possession of a "gift" as by the giving of it. The implication for education is that being discovered as having a "gift" and perhaps being in a gifted program is not as rewarding as having given your gift to others. There is a real indication here that a service type of gifted program might be extremely well received by the community and would greatly enhance individual self-esteem.

Another reason often submitted by Native American educators is the one which haunts all gifted and talented children. "We know they have special abilities, so they can make it on their own. It's the less able student whom we must attend to." Only intensive inservice at both staff and administrative levels can rectify this misconception. Meeker (1969), who developed the Structure of Intellect Test based on the Guilford Model, has stressed that only when educators really understand how learning takes place and information is processed in the unique intellect, can we approach the culturally-different gifted child as a total receptor-adaptor of human abilities whose cultural diversity is an enrichment not only to his own self-growth and understanding but to others with whom he shares the world.

With these thoughts in mind, we wish to offer the following reflections on using some typical approaches to identifying Native American students. It has been stated elsewhere in this paper that Native American children are not being served in gifted programs because they are not "identified" as gifted or talented according to criteria in use by the majority of gifted and talented programs in this state and nation. We contend that differences between the majority culture and the Native American culture, in such areas as values, customs, beliefs, experience and acceptable behavior, account for the disparity.

If, as leaders in gifted education generally agree, a multi-criteria approach to the identification of gifted and talented children produces a cadre of eligible youngsters, and if gifted and talented programs are using a multi-criteria approach (rather than relying only on an IQ test) to identification, then more gifted and talented Native American children should become visible. Let us examine the various commonly-used identification tools to determine why in fact this is not true. Each of the reputable educational models for gifted programs has a behavior checklist or nomination form of some type which gives the teacher some clues to the existence of the illusive gifted child in the classroom. The following are statements taken from various rating scales or checklists: (a) above average language development (Dure, 1964), (b) wholesome personal-social adjustment (Buhler and Buirly, 1960), (c) is alert, keenly observant, responds quickly (Kough & DeHaan, 1955), (d) generates a quantity, flow, or large number of questions, guesses, improvisations, explorations, inventions, combinations (Williams).

These statements are the result of research studies with thousands of gifted and talented children and may represent accurate information on observable classroom behavior of non-Native American gifted students. However, it is highly unlikely that a gifted Native American student, sharing the same intellectual processing, language ability and psycho-social development would be identified by these statements.

First, it is erroneous to assume that gifted

behaviors by Native American students are exhibited in the classroom. Recent research with Klallam/Suquamish tribal students suggests that these cognitive and affective indicators are exhibited and recognized in the tribal community and at home, but rarely in a classroom setting. To the former situation, one "belongs"; to the latter, one is at best a "visitor," at worst, an "alien." By the fourth grade, according to the Havighurst study (1972), Native American children have adopted a passive classroom behavior mode characterized by observation rather than participation.

Second, although many of the intellectual operations which indicated giftedness may be present, they may be expressed in forms of behavior which are untranslatable into a "language" school personnel can understand. For example, Joey was a pleasant, quiet fifth grade boy whom the teacher described as continually trying to "buy" friendship from his non-Native American friends. A superior math student, he would finish his work, slip out of his chair, and very unobtrusively try to help the other students. If one should ask for the correct answer, Joe couldn't say "no." When he won a box of pencils in a number quiz he gave them away. This behavior bothered the teacher because (a) Joey often didn't have materials to work with when he needed them, (b) the teacher had no plan or schedule for peer tutors (which is the role Joey was playing), and (c) she felt Joey was helping others "cheat." Was Joey exhibiting personal-social adjustment through such behavior? Would Irving Sato (who has been a strong advocate of psycho-social and leadership giftedness) consider Joey one of the psycho-socially gifted children?

The following statements concerning those with a "gift" or special ability resulted from a consensus-type process conducted among members of the Klallam and Suquamish tribes of Western Washington state. Joey is a member of one of these tribes in which (a) a person with a special ability in social skills will be willing to share whatever he/she has, (b) such a person will help others without embarrassing them, and cares for others, (c) a person with a special ability in leadership is able to recognize problems and figure out how to solve them; brings harmony to others and unites them, (d) a person with a special ability in learning is a contributor who develops her own abilities so that she may be able to share them with others and is one who proves what she knows by what is done, not by just talking about it.

Joey was dealing with his "gift" in ways which were appropriate within his own culture. The teacher was translating his classroom behavior in terms of appropriate behavior in her own culture. Joey was placed in a gifted class and given opportunity to express himself in his own way.

Incidentally, after the initial shock, Joey's teacher became very supportive of the program and enrolled in a class presented by Native American people so that she could become more aware of the Native American culture and serve those students with greater understanding of their needs and abilities.

Although there is evidence that teacher nominations have been less than ideal in accurately identifying gifted students (especially those from culturally diverse backgrounds) they can play an important role in the recognition of gifted students, but are only truly effective when the following conditions are met. The teacher participates with full understanding of the items on a checklist or characteristics sheet, and how they contribute as behavioural indices of intellectual operations to a total picture of students' abilities. This should include a familiarity with the psychological principles and processes on which the truly unique abilities of culturally different gifted students are based. Also, the teacher is sensitive to the possibility of alternative behaviors from culturally different students, which are manifestations of the intellectual operations observed and standardized in the majority culture. It is obvious that a great deal of work must be done to factor out and describe the alternative behaviors of culturally different children. We believe that each cultural community can best accomplish this task for itself. A series of recent studies point to the possibility that teacher nomination can be a positive factor in identifying greater numbers of culturally different gifted and talented students. Cummings (1979) found that use of a locally-devised behavioral checklist by teachers substantially improved the number of minority students who were nominated and eventually identified as gifted. Blackshear (1979) concluded that teacher nomination of culturally different academically gifted students was more effective but less precise as a predictor of giftedness than other indicators used.

Value Attached to Giftedness

In the previous section we questioned the suggested behavioral and intellectual characteristics for identifying gifted and talented students, on the basis of cultural irrelevance. In addition, it is difficult for the teacher to recognize gifted and talented behavior in one culture according to the descriptors of another culture. Using a standardized nomination process with Native American parents or with students themselves often produces the same effect. Parents may not recognize a written description of gifted behaviour as applying their children. The language in which the characteristic is phrased may be so abstract or technical that it is set aside in frustration.

Another problem very basic to the willingness of the parent to participate in a nominating process is the value attached to being identified as "gifted." If "giftedness" is perceived as a "state" or "trait" soley belonging to the majority culture into which a select few "others" are allowed to enter and become isolated then it may not be thought of by the culturally different parent as highly desirable for the child. This was found to be especially true with many Native American people interviewed in the Klallam-Suquamish community. When "giftedness" was interpreted as a state or trait which made one "better" than one's peers, which set one apart from the rest of the community, it was not valued highly.

Authorities on Native American tribal structures report that homogeneous grouping, consensus and harmony are all key universal elements within most Native American cultures. Thus, to identify a person as being special or "better than" is not a process likely to be supported.

And yet, in all cultures there are those individuals who do excel, who have special abilities. In what cultural context do they acceptably exist? In the study with the Klallam and Suquamish Tribes a significant positive cultural context was determined for gifted people which formed the basis of identifying and programming for students: if identification of one's special abilities results in a contribution to others is some way, present or future, then it is a desirable accomplishment. In this case a nominating form was developed with the aid of the community which outlined certain behavior determined to be indicators of giftedness. When Native American parents understood the purpose of the nomination form and agreed with its philosophical base, they were quite willing to take the time and effort to conscientiously complete the form. They also contributed narratives when asked to describe any behaviors they saw in their child that they considered "unusual." One parent wrote, "Sometimes when my girls finish watching a TV show they will rearrange the furniture and 'play' the whole story they saw - each one taking a different part. It really makes us laugh." Another wrote, "My son doesn't get good grades or anything like that, but he always asks a lot of questions about things we don't know anything about. I feel bad that I can't answer him. We have an old dictionary and he reads it like it was a story." Both of these children tested at the gifted level in Divergent Production (Creativity) and Memory on the Structure of Intellect Test.

From this experience we suggest that parent nomination forms for culturally different children will have some validity if: (a) the purpose of the identification and subsequent intervention is fully understood by the parent; (b) the philosophical and ethical goal for such identification and intervention is compatible with the cultural values of the community; (c) the behavior and intellectual operation most descriptive for expressing "giftedness" is determined by the community of which the child to be identified is a member; and (d) the language used to describe behaviors or intellectual operations is common to those using the nomination form.

These recommendations are consistent with the findings of Storlie and Prapuolenis (1978, 1979). Specifically, they found in their study with Flint Community Schools that parental input was an important part of the identification process for culturally different students, and that steps should be taken to make parental nomination more effective (Storlie, 1979). One way to do so would be to include parents in defining the meaning of giftedness for their community and to provide them with some orientation on the identification process and their part in it. We are suggesting that this approach is particularly relevant to reservation-type communities in rural settings.

Multiple Assessment and Identification Methods

In the experience of the authors, one of the most successful programs for finding and developing the gifted potential of artistic Native American students was Project Success, A Washington State Validated Project which originated in the North Kitsap School District in 1974. Briefly, the methods used involved sitting a student down with a variety of art media for regularly scheduled intervals and checking "production behavior" in terms of self-start, flexibility with media, ease and fluency. The products were judged for their originality, elaboration and imagination. The whole assessment often took place without any verbal exchange between the child and the testor other than statements made by the testor to establish rapport and give directions. Ironically, although a number of Native American students were identified as artistically gifted, some of the students could not be admitted to the program because their teachers would not sign a release form allowing them to be "pulled out" of the regular classrooms. The teachers felt that deficiency in academic skills should prohibit participation in gifted art classes.

Another notable effort has been the leadership classes (developed at LaConner, Washington with members of Swinomish Tribe) in which Native American gifted students have been identified by actual participation as leaders in school and community. Native Americans are represented in programs for the gifted in psychomotor abilities (athletics) and in various performing art activities. The inference we draw from the above examples is that when identification procedures are physically or spatially oriented, Native American students seem more likely to be identified. It might also be added that when such classes or activities take place outside of school, school personnel are probably more supportive. Reservation parents, on the other hand, for whom transportation may be a problem, might restrict students from such participation.

Recent research also points to the need for a variety of identification procedures and instruments when working with culturally different students. Blackshear (1979) found that multiple criteria in screening for academically gifted students increased the total number of second-grade black students identified. A two-tiered identification process was used (successive identification of the top twenty percent and then top ten percent as gifted). Instruments employed for the first step included the Comprehensive Test of Basic Skills, an informal creativity test, the local district's Prescriptive Math and Reading Tests, and nominations from peers and teachers. Peer nomination consisted of interviews individually or in small groups, while teachers completed a behavior checklist on each student. The results of the first step for each student were summarized and classified for a final rating score using the Baldwin Identification Matrix. The second step consisted primarily of interviews with each student in the identification pool (top twenty percent).

We have already mentioned the work of Storlie and Prapuolenis of the Educational Testing Service (ETS). The purpose of their study was to provide the Flint Michigan school system with a sound model for developing and implementing a culturally-fair process for identifying gifted children. One of the most interesting features of this study was the use of a representative group of school administrators, school psychologists, teachers, parents and other community members to formulate a working definition of giftedness and to assist in developing and implementing the identification process. The definition worked out by this group included six factors: creativity, intellectual potential, learning ability, motivation, leadership and social/self-awareness, and academic achievement (in that order of importance). Like the Blackshear study, Storlie also used a two-stage approach to identification. The first stage included parent nomination, teacher nomination and a variety of achievement data. A behavior checklist and summary sheet for each child thus placed in an eligibility pool was then prepared and used for the second stage. This second stage consisted of a selection committee's evaluation of each student candidate using a five-point rating scale, and coordinating this rating with placements available in the gifted program and other administrative considerations. The ETS team found that this process was successful in identifying a greater number of culturally different students, that the two-stage process was effective in identifying students who ranked higher with regard to the selection criteria, and that those children selected by this new process did not differ from children previously selected as measured against the six criteria established for this process (thus indicating that standards for the gifted program were not significantly altered).

Those gifted programs in Washington State which

rely heavily on test scores in language ability or reading have a much lower number of Native American students than is justified by their representation in the general population. Given that the Native American population for the state is a little more than 1% of the total population (State Office of Financial Management estimates of 1980 census count), the overall statistic for Native American students in such academic programs is about half that (about .6 of 1%). Progress has been made, however, since then.

There are several alternative approaches which a school district or system could take to solving the problem of under-representation on the part of Native Americans in the ranks of students recognized or identified as gifted and talented: (a) assert that this does not call into question the definition operationalized within the system, and continue with current practice; (b) modify the identification process by using some nomination and selection criteria or tests in different combinations, for example, maintaining national norms as standard for this district but accepting a greater variety of data to meet those norms; (c) make a local effort to define giftedness and the criteria appropriate based on that definition, then pick and choose among available instruments to select those which seem most appropriate to the local definition; (d) restructure the entire nomination and identification process based on a radically different model of giftedness - this may involve adopting a much different set of criteria, tests and procedures, perhaps designing and norming some tests locally, for example, replacing the achievement test and IQ model of identification with the SOI model; (e) use nationally normed tests but compare student performance with the norms for appropriate racial, ethnic, and socioeconomic groups within the district, for example, select those Indian students who test among the top 3% of Indian students within the district.

All of these approaches are practiced in varying degrees by school districts. The approach we are taking in this paper leans more toward approaches 3 and 4 than toward the others. However, each of them must be carefully examined in order for a school system to make an intelligent decision about identification or Native American gifted and talented students.

As we have pointed out, gifted programs systematically fail to identify Native American (and other culturally different) children because they use test instruments and methods which do not allow for difference in language use, comprehension and experience, by using teacher nominations forms in which gifted behaviors or intellectual operations have not been expressed in culturally relevant terms or language, and by using parent or self-nomination forms in which all the above are true.

Besides failure to identify Native American gifted and talented students, the planning and administration of gifted and talented programs within a school system may positively ignore Native American students. The underlying reasons for this become clear when one examines the relationship between the unique abilities of Native American students and the design of most gifted projects. Administrators often do not envision these projects in terms which are consistent with their impression of the abilities of Native American students. One result of this - especially at the building level - is the constant effort by educators to "bring culturally different students into the mainstream." To do this, it has seemed necessary to provide remedial treatment just to bring Native American students "up" to a level in language arts, math, reading and other skill areas in which they can compete with majority culture children who are comfortable and secure in the school's academic environment. Remedial help, then, takes precedence over building on the outstanding strengths of Native American students.

It is not surprising then, that Native American students start resisting the "mainstream" and all its "rewards," including the burden of countless seemingly irrelevant "facts," pressure for high grades (or any respectable grades at all), and intense competition requiring high levels of stress and internal conflict, at the age of 9 or 10. "Mainstreaming" often means sitting with the slow learners, while the gifted and talented student go to the Science Center or Community Arts Center. Kleinfeldt (1973), in discussing her work with Alaska Native children has provided us with some interesting reflections on the ultimate counter- productivity of "remedial" instruction. She points out that it restricts the student's field of learning and fails to draw upon student strengths.

Based on this analysis of now Native Americans have been perceived within the educational system, it is easier to understand why absence of Native Americans from the ranks of identified and selected members of gifted and talented programs has hardly been questioned. It is assumed by many that Native American students are, in fact, not intellectually gifted. As one school principal responded, "If I had any gifted Native American students in this school, they'd be in our gifted program. I don't discriminate." That the school was three miles from an Indian reservation, that the gifted program had been operational for five years, that there had never been any Native American students in that gifted program were facts that this principal never questioned. He had more confidence in the system which identified, selected, treated and evaluated gifted children within his school than he did in the possibility that each cultural or ethnic group might have its own gifted members.

There are several things which might be done to remedy this situation (once it has been recognized that a change is needed). (a) In those school districts where a knowledgeable relationship has been established between school administration and tribal leaders, there is greater probablility that both groups will be more aware of the needs of the children and of how to facilitate the satisfaction of those needs (whether through existing programs or new ones). (b) Exposure of teachers and other public school personnel who have instructional responsibilities for Indian children to Native people in roles of status can be of great help in changing their expectations of Indian children. Unless one has experienced a Native American doctor, lawyer, statesperson or philosopher, one might assume that they do not exist and that roles which require outstanding intellectual abilities are not realistic possibilities for Indian students. Contact on the part of educators with people of this stature in the Indian community - philosophers, storytellers, historians, medicine people, tribal council persons - can not only raise their awareness of the "cultural quality" of a people, but their confidence in and expectations of the abilities of the children themselves. (c) Native American gifted students might have greater accessibility to gifted and talented projects if district and building administrators put a greater emphasis on development of human potential than on conforming human potential to identification and programming systems already established. (d) Greater awareness on the part of Indian education staff working within the school system of the possibility that some of the students they work with may be gifted can help break the alienation reinforced failure and dropout cycle which many capable Indian students face when place in a mainstreaming or remedial situation. Indian education staff are usually quite sensitive to the unique abilities of Indian students, but the realities of skill deficiencies make it seem that these strengths are unexplainable vestiges of tradition and personality that make one smile or wonder, but which certainly are not significant indications of ability or of outstanding future contributions to society. A fuller awareness on the part of Indian education staff of the potential for outstanding achievement which many Indian students hold within them can help these staff members reinforce their abilities with such observations as, "Yes. This child is displaying a sophisticated evaluation skill, or a cognitive awareness, or a divergent creative invention."

Curriculum and Implementation Alternatives and Innovations

Jane was one of four Native American girls in the seventh grade to be nominated for testing in the gifted program. She tested in the 99th percentile in Language Arts on the Metropolitan Test of Academic Achievement. In addition, she wrote a creative essay which was scored highly. Her parents were anxious for their daughter to be part of a program which would encourage her in her studies. She was admitted to the program. Jane, although acknowledged as one of the "brains" in school by her brighter peers, maintained a shyness and reticence which made group activities in gifted class difficult. The teacher tried to pair her up with more "outgoing" students so that she might see that "flexibility" is okay. The creativity that Jane had shown in her early writing, began to conform in a way that the teacher realized was not expressive of her own thoughts. In the third month of the program, the students became involved in producing their own newspaper. They toured a news plant, read about printing presses, editorial styles, bylines, etc.

Each chose a subject and began researching it for focus. Jane had a difficult time deciding on a subject. Finally, at the teacher's suggestion, she chose to do a history of her home area, using as a resource the early journals of the Indian Agent which were on micro-fiche at the Department of Archives to study. One week later, Jane wrote a note to the teacher saying she would no longer be in the gifted program. The parents were contacted and knew of no reason why Jane wished to drop the program but they felt it was her decision. Jane told her teacher later that she just wasn't interested anymore.

Jane's experience is typical of similar situations reported to us. In this case, Jane was available to interview and was willing, as a friend, to share her recollections with us. She liked her teacher, she said, but there was one problem. "Mrs. Brown kept pushing me off to a table with the most obnoxious loud-mouths." Jane also said she felt that she wasn't as capable a writer as the other students because, "When the subjects were handed out, I could never think of anything to write about on that subject." When they went to the Archives to study history for the news article, Jane had read some disturbing things. She had read about children being forced to leave their homes and go to boarding school in Tulalip, Washington. The Indian agent writing the report had been very disgruntled because of the time it had cost him to search out and thrash the students that had been hidden. Jane also read of sickness and sadness. She thought about how she could write about those things in a way that would impact readers as much as it did her. She decided there was no way to do that. At that point, it also seemed unlikely that anyone of her family or friends would be interested in any of the other articles planned for the newspaper project. "I asked myself, 'what are you doing here?'" she said. It was also obvious to her that there was a new separateness between her and her Native American friends. Being gifted didn't seem worth it all.

What was very clear in Jane's account of her experience in the gifted program was the great gulf separating the teacher, and her young student. They might as well have been speaking a foreign language to one another. But for the purposes of discussing curriculum let us analyze what took place in that area. The program was one which "handed out" subjects for creative children to write about. Topics which may have excited the teacher may have only mildly piqued the interest of some of the students, and in Jane's case, did not excite it at all. Jane, at puberty in the seventh grade, was not only conscious that she had no way of including her Native American peers in her activities, but was extremely sensitive to injustices to her people that she had read about. There was a chance here for some very personal expression which could have been shared. But Jane did not feel very warm in the "mainstream." She was convinced that no one would understand. Anyway, why not think that? Had her wishes or feelings been considered in a choice of seat partners, paper topic, or even in picking a subject from the newspaper? Had she been allowed or encouraged to share any of her cultural uniqueness with the others? Did anybody care? Jane probably made a very wise decision when she chose to leave that gifted program.

At the American Indian Gifted and Talented Planning Consortium meeting, in November 1978, Native American educators formulated recommendations for curriculum to be developed for gifted and talented American Indian students, for an expression of the importance for tribal and Native American community involvement in any innovation or curriculum approach and that existing curricula be modified to tribal customs and philosophies. Following is the full text of the recommendations. (a) Establish a clearinghouse for collections of special curricular materials being devloped by public and private agencies for Indian students. (b) Utilize experts in curriculum for gifted and talented Indian tribal and community peoples and other Indian professionals, especially incorporate strong community resources such as elders, parents, grandparents and eminent tribal members who are experts in traditional values. (c) Develop and modify curriculum materials to reflect appropriate cultural aspects and thus to better meet the needs of gifted and talented Indian children. (d) Publish and disseminate exemplary materials to concerned agencies, tribes and Indian communities. (e) Provide training opportunities for curriculum specialists and teachers in local education agencies which have Indian students on the development of appropriate curriculum for Indian gifted and talented children. (f) Convene special institutes for staff of state departments of education, (i.e., special education, gifted and talented education, Indian education, elementary and secondary, curricular area specialists, etc. to meet with state tribal leaders and educators to examine existing state curriculum guidelines and to consider revisions that would encourage more appropriate education for Indian gifted and talented children. (g) Efforts to increase motivation and awareness of the gifted and talented field must be implemented within Indian communities and reservations, along with promotion of parental participation in all phases of program planning.

In June, 1978, Christine Brown, member of the New Directions Gifted and Talented Task Force, Office of Indian Education, made the following recommendation to Dr. Dorothy Sisk, Chairperson of the Gifted and Talented National Task Force: Development of relevant based curriculum material and program design must be established in the ten geographic areas. This will help facilitate Indian students in searching sic their maximum potential. In addition, it is required that careful attention from other cultures does not accommodate the critical need to learn the best from both societies."

Pat Locke, former President of the National Indian Education Association, and a Native American educator who recognized the need for G/T and other differentiated programs for Native American children, has suggested that although the early education years should be devoted exclusively to perfecting the language and culture of the child's own tribe, it is equally important the child learn dual cultures and multi-cultures from the fourth grade onward. The children, by learning the expectations of other cultures as skills, not as values, become contributors to the survival of their own people.

Alford Pemberton, former Chairman of the Education Committee, Minnesota Chippewa Tribe, and member of the Native American Gifted and Talented Task Force, feels that a curriculum plan to complement the activities of the gifted and talented Indian child might include cultural and social awareness, linguistic perceptions and comparisons, family structure and concepts and participation of family life, tribal identification and in-depth comprehension, and self perception and relationship to all of the above.

Shannon County Schools of South Dakota, which serves the Pine Ridge Reservation, implemented a gifted and talented project based on skill building within areas of interests and strengths of the students in art, music, communications and science. Curricula included a variety of media, the use of which centered around the child's culture in a project approach. The instructional strategies included positive reinforcement, small group instruction, self-esteem building, high levels of teacher student rapport, and, perhaps most importantly, culminating activities which included the community. Evaluators were positive in their reviews of the program in 1976 and found that students had not only expanded the range and depth of their own abilities, but had also impacted the community in a positive way. Many of the methods and strategies used by the staff were later incorporated into the regular school program (Huckins, 1976).

The Native American Gifted Project in the North Kitsap School District, Washington State, based curriculum development on Guildford's model, Structure of the Intellect, and the adaption of Meeker's lessons for improving various cognitive operations. The subject areas included Art, Writing, Video Communications and Story Telling. The last area concentrated on developing the skills of oral tradition. Areas had as their objective growth in the intellectual operations of Evaluation, Comprehension, Convergent Production, and Memory. Divergent or Creative Thinking was basic to all activities. Pre- and post-testing on the Structure of Intellect test showed significant gain (statistically significant at the .05 to .01 levels in some areas). In the final report of the project it was noted: "Although it was assumed that development of curriculum materials based on the local tribal customs and interest would act as a motivational force, it was found that these in themselves were not as meaningful to the students when planned and executed in isolation of the classroom. Only when the activities or products were shared with the larger school or tribal community, was the effort and enthusiasm maxmimized. Additionally, it was not assumed that the interaction with the teacher would be of more importance than the strategies and methods used to present and facilitate learning. This was an error in judgment. The teacher to whom the students responded with open fluency and flexibility could have operated independent of any curriculum and still have effected learning we now believe."

Following are staff observations on the curriculum and other needs of students in the Native American Gifted Project (George, 1979): Students need:

- to have time to think and envision before they begin a task,
- an atmosphere that is positive, safe from criticism, teasing, ridicule,
- to believe that it's okay to try; that the process is just as important as the product in terms of personal self-respect.
- to have many experiences in group planning and processing and brain-storming,
- to have individual quiet times for serching the inner self for meaningful experiences,
- to be aware of their own present positive qualities and their potential abilities,
- to have opportunities for service to others, thus fulfilling tribal traditions and achieving a sense of personal worth,
- to explore the values of tribe, family and self and compare with those of non-Indian community, school, friends,
- to practice and experience "life skills" in a scheduled and systematic fashion,
- a physical setting which allows for mobility of movement and the stability of emotional support,
- a variety of hands-on, visual "links" to ideas and concepts being taught,
- to practice problem-solving processes,
- awareness of the creative and intuitive process and how it differs from the convergent process,
- more activities which center on expressing their thoughts and feelings,
- to have some appropriate public recognition of their written and art work (i.e., need to see that what they

do is valued by others),
- to have more experiences in public speaking, story telling, etc.

From the previous quotations and discussions, it is clear that there is some agreement in the following curricula concerns among those who have worked with gifted and talented Native American students. (a) Curriculum, instruction, materials, activities and evaluation should be culturally relevant to the children being served. (b) Curriculum and instruction, while utilizing techniques which relate to higher level thinking skills, creative problem solving, or divergent production should also include convergent production of a product or performance which may be shared with others. (c) Curriculum should contain not only cognitive objectives for skills which will provide the student with a greater understanding and esteem in the "self" as an individual and as a Native American. (d) Curriculum should provide for a variety of experiences and media manipulations to facilitate comprehensions and concept formation about technology, ideas, and processes in the modern world of both Indian and non-Indian people. (e) Curriculum should be flexible enough to allow for student development in and choice of special interest and talent areas, and (f) the program planning of curriculum should not take precedence over student-teacher rapport, a factor which we consider to be the most important element in any program for gifted and talented students.

Each program for gifted Native American students, will, of necessity, begin "where the students are" in terms of their skills, talents, abilities and general academic level. We recommend a well planned experiential, enrichment or exploration approach in the first few months, then, using an assessment approach which identifies areas of strength and weakness (such as Meeker's SOI), building intellectual strengths over a range of subject areas. Intellectual skill building may be accomplished by using as a motivator and vehicle for learning, the students' interest areas which were discovered during the initial exploration period, and intellectual strengths discovered during screening and assessment.

The organization of curriculum and the management system chosen to operate a program will differ according to monetary, time and space, and staff contraints. Some program types which have been used successfully are: gifted resource rooms, individual educational contracts, mentorships, after school interest projects, small group travel and seminars, accelerated subjects, process-based activities, future studies, and creative development. There are doubtless many more. The important element is that the Native American student be afforded the opportunity to utilize his or her unique abilities, understand and be proud of them, and grow toward the promise of the gifts.

Research Training Needs

All of this indicates a need for further work in at least two areas: research and training. There is clearly a need for concentrated and well-designed research efforts to give us more information about the propensities and behavior patterns of gifted Native American students, about the effectiveness and accuracy of various identification methods and instruments in identifying Native Americans, and about the impact of existing curriculum models for high-ability students on Native Americans. Research on these questions is almost nonexistent; we are currently largely dependent for guidance on the expanding body of literature on culturally-different gifted students.

Training and orientation of school staff to the unique needs of high-ability Native Americans using what we do know about the psychology of learning and about the cultural backgrounds of Native American students, will continue to be a significant need into the foreseeable future, particularly in school districts serving high concentrations of Native Americans. Those serving in projects designed to meet the unique needs of Indian students are most often concerned with remediation in basic skill areas and need some awareness of students with exceptional abilities and how to recognize and serve those students. On the other hand, staff working in gifted education projects may require some orientation to the unique needs of Native American students, and how they might best address those needs. The classroom teacher, as a central person in the student's academic development, also needs additional information about the needs of high ability Native American students and how to serve them. United Indians hopes to address some of these needs by developing and implementing in the Puget Sound area of Washington State a staff training package geared to the information and training needs of Indian education directors and staff members. We also hope to develop training materials suitable for classroom teachers and gifted education staff. We undertake this effort in the hope that it will assist those who have the most direct impact on the educational development of Native American children in their efforts to draw out and nurture those children's outstanding abilities.

References

Blackshear, P. P. A comparison of peer nomination and gifted, black primary planning level student, Unpublished doctoral dissertation, University of Maryland, 1979.

Brown, C.(Ed.). Information packet on the American Indian Gifted and Talented Planning Consortium, Washington D.C.: Office of Indian Education, 1979.

Bruch, C. B. Recent insights on the culturally-different gifted. The Gifted Child Quarterly, Fall 1978.

Cummings, W. B. Using alternative criteria to identify gifted children from among culturally different/educationally disadvantaged youth, University of San Francisco, 1979.

Dodson, E. & Spice, M. Workshop Model: approach to alternative programs for the disadvantaged gifted. In National/State Leadership Training Institute on the Gifted and Talented, Advantage: Disadvantaged Gifted. Ventura, CA: Superintendent of Schools, 1978.

George, K. Native American gifted inservice manual. Poulsbo, WA: North Kitsap School District, 1979.

Havighurst, R. J. & Fuchs, E. To live on this earth. Garden City, NY: Doubleday, 1972.

Huckins, R. L. Gifted and talented program in a sparsely populated area: Pierre, S.D.: Division of Elementary and Secondary Education.

Kleinfeld, J. S. Intellectual strengths in culturally different groups; an Eskimo illustration. Review of Educational Research, Summer 1973, 341-359.

Kough, J., & DeHaan, R. F. Teacher's guidance handbook, vol. I, identifying children who need help. Chicago: Science Research Associates, 1955.

LeRose, B. A quota system for gifted minority children: a viable solution. The Gifted Child Quarterly, Fall 1978.

Locke, P. The gifted and talented American Indian child: a first step. In Brown (Ed.), Information packet on the American Indian Gifted and Talented Planning Consortium. Washington, D.C.: Office of Indian Education, 1979.

Murry, S. L. Identifying disadvantaged students for gifted and talented programs. Portland, OR: Northwest Regional Educational Laboratory, 1980.

Passow, A. H. (Ed.), The gifted and talented: their education and development. Chicago. University of Chicago Press, 1979.

Peacock, T. Factors to consider in developing programs for Indian gifted and talented. In C. Brown (Ed.), Information packet on American Gifted and Talented Planning Consortium. Washington, D.C., Office of Indian Education, 1979.

Ramirez, B. Background paper on American Indian exceptional children. Reston, VA: The Council for Exceptional Children, 1976.

Renzulli, J. S. A guidebook for evaluation programs

for the gifted and talented. Ventura, CA: Office of the Ventura County Superintendent of Schools, 1975.

Roy, J. Diversity of tribal customs and philosophies with special recognition and attention concerning the Red Lake Band of Chippewa Indians. In C. Brown (Ed.), Information packet on the American Indian Gifted and Talented Planning Consortium. Washington, D.C.: Office of Indian Education, 1979.

Simons, Barbara-Jone Deve, Handbook for educators of gifted students. Greeley, CO: University of Northern Colorado, 1979.

Snow, A. J., Ethno-science and gifted in American Indian education. The Gifted Child Quarterly, Spring 1977.

Storlie, T. R. & others, The development of a culturally-fair model for the early identification and selection of gifted children. Evanston, IL: Educational Testing Service, 1978.

Torrance, E. P. Dare we hope again? The Gifted Child Quarterly, 1978, 22, 292-312.

Vernon, P. E. Intelligence: heredity and environment. San Francisco: Freeman, 1979.

The author gratefully acknowledges the collaboration of colleague Tom Crawford in this project.

19

GIFTEDNESS ACROSS CULTURES

Nava Butler-Por

A real commitment on the part of educators and society at large to the concept that talent is not the prerogative of any racial or ethnic group, any social class or any residential area . . . may lie untapped in some situations under some conditions, but no population has either a monopoly on or an absence of talents. (Passow, 1972)

The pertinent question which must be asked is how to discover "untapped" talents in children who have been socialized "in a subculture whose values and cognitive experiences are different from those of the dominant culture?" (Getzels, 1969, p. 466). The question of identification and realization of the individual's potential has been of great concern in the past two decades, to education in general and gifted education in particular.

The review of the relevant research concerning this issue reveals the problematic nature of the processes involved in the search for talent. The failure of the traditional intelligence test to discover giftedness (Getzels & Jackson, 1962) and the specific problems of identification of ability among the differently cultured disadvantaged school population have led researchers to investigate the potential of creativity measures as predictors of talent (Torrance, 1973; Gallagher & Kinney, 1974; Butler-Por and Lancer, 1979).

An alternative approach was suggested by Riessman (1962) and Torrance (1979) who maintained that differently cultured children are characterized by different orientations, aptitudes and abilities. This approach suggests the need to extend the research in the area of talent identification to encompass the effects of cultural variables on the development of talent. In this connection, it is interesting to note that Vernon (1975), in a comprehensive discussion of intelligence across cultures, concedes that: "It is probable that Terman and Burt's IQ and the statistician's factors have to some extent held up progress by their inflexibility and their tendency to obscure cultural differences (Vernon, 1975, p. 25). In this case it seems important to ask what are the factors within a given culture that may obscure the ability of the child, a factor which is of paramount importance if he is to reach maximum development and reap the full educational benefits that are provided by the school?

It appears to us that the work conducted by Rokeach (1973) and Feather (1975) on the nature of values in general and in education in particular, suggests that an investigation of the values which are considered important in various cultural groups may contribute toward a better understanding of the effects of the culture on the development of ability. Getzels (1969) for example, stipulates:

Presumably, in a well functioning system the cultural values are internalized by the children through the process of socialization and enter the psychic economy of the individual as cognitive and affective dispositions for value in relevant behavior. The role expectations are defined in relation to the same values that had entered into the socialization process, so that what is required of the child for role performance in the school is congruent with his dispositions for behavior. (Getzels, 1969, p. 466). And he argues: Explicity or implicity, the school requires an achievement ethic with consequent high valuation of the future, deferred gratification and symbolic commitment to success. Not only are these the values of the school, but they are the values of the environment in which most middle-class children are brought up. (p. 491).

GIFTEDNESS ACROSS CULTURES

The study of values in countries such as Israel is of great educational relevance where people from different cultures coexist, interact and educate their children in schools which represent the middle class milieu. It is the purpose of this pilot study to examine the educational values of different cultures and subcultures in Israel so as to gain a deeper insight into the different perceptions of giftedness across cultures.

Sample

The research sample consisted of 72 children and their parents. The selection of children was made from the fourth grade lists of schools in Haifa and the northern region of Israel. The subjects were divided into five groups:

Group 1: Highly gifted middle class children and their parents. The 18 children in this group attend a special class for the gifted in Haifa. Children selected for this program constituted the top 2% of the school population measured on a battery of ability and aptitude tests. The 35 parents are of European origin, and defined as "middle-class" in terms of their socioeconomic status.

Group 2: Middle class children of normal ability and their parents. The 18 children of this group attend a regular class in the same school in which the gifted class is situated. The 35 parents are of European descent and of middle class socioeconomic status.

Group 3: Differently cultured disadvantaged children and their parents. The 12 children of this group attend a school for educationally disadvantaged children, defined as such on the criteria of the Ministry of Education and Culture in Israel: Father's education, income, persons per room and ethnic origin. The 23 parents were mostly first or second generation immigrants from Arab countries.

Group 4: Kibbutz children and their parents. The 12 children study in a regional kibbutz school, drawing its population from five kibbutzim in the

Jordan Valley. The 23 parents are mostly of European origin, and constitute a representative sample of the population of the older kibbutzim.

Group 5: Arab children and their parents. The 12 children attend a village school near Nazareth. The sample consists of the more able fourth graders in the school. The 24 parents constitute a representative sample of this population.

Procedure

The sample was interviewed by means of individual interviews in order to ascertain the significance attached by each participant to values pertaining to education at home and in school. The interview technique was selected as it allows the researcher to explore not only the values that seem important to the subjects, but also what they understood them to mean, how they relate to their overall value system and what value-related behavior is adopted in order to reinforce the values. The interview schedule was constructed on the basis of a funnel system which starts with a broad question and narrows down progressively to more specific points (Cannel & Kahn, 1953). The responses were coded and tabulated separately for each subject on the basis of a content analysis of each interview.

All interviews were conducted within the families in their homes. The child and each of the parents was interviewed separately. At the beginning of each interview the objectives were explained. Care was taken to maintain an open and informal climate throughout each interview.

In order to ascertain the different value systems in the various research groups, it was necessary first to examine which values were considered important by each group. A content analysis of each interview was conducted and the responses were coded and tabulated for each member of the group. The value which received the highest number of responses obtained the highest rank, the remaining values were listed in decreasing order. The following comparisons were coded: fathers of boys (F.b.) with fathers of girls (F.g), mothers of boys (M.b.) with mothers of girls (M.g.), and boys (b) with girls (g).

Results

An analysis of the interviews indicated that ten values were common to most groups, whereas additional values only appeared in one or two specific groups. The results will be reported separately for each group.

Group 1: Highly gifted middle class children and their parents. This group constituted the most representative sample in terms of identification with all the ten values selected for investigation. The values are described below, and for each group, in descending order of ascribed value.

Overall Percentage of Responses for Group 1

Rank	Value	%
1	School achievement	88
2	Social success	77
3	Individuality	77
4	Independance	67
5	Tidiness & Cleanliness	53
6	Material success	43
7	Happiness	40
8	Initiative	40
9	Good Citizenship	21
10	Loyalty	6

School achievement was considered the most important value by all members of this group. It is interesting to note that all parents without exception attributed the greatest importance to this value, and 75% of the children did so. These findings can be interpreted in the light of two main factors. First, this group consists of middle class population which is generally characterized by the high premium it places on achievement. In Israel, achievement norms in relation to children are expressed in and perceived as school achievement. Secondly, the children in this group were participating in a special program for the highly gifted, a factor which served to raise the expectations of parents in this domain. This finding agrees with the previous ones (Butler & Butler, 1979) that despite the emphasis placed in this program on different developmental objectives, parents persist in attributing the greatest importance to school achievement. In addition, if one considers the young age of the children (9 to 10), it is not surprising that a high degree of agreement was found between parents and children.

Social success was valued nearly as much as school achievement. However, it is interesting to note that both parents considered it of greater value for girls. Similarly, more responses were coded for girls than for boys.

Though individuality and independence were highly rated, no significant within group differences were found.

Out of the ten values investigated tidiness and cleanliness was ranked in the fifth place. This finding, though perhaps surprising, can be understood as a belief frequently expressed by parents in the interviews that training at home should affect practices at school. In this connection, it is relevant to mention that the class teacher of this group made a great "educational" issue out of this fact. Parents were more demanding of their boys, a finding which supports the experience of selection procedures for classes for highly gifted children which demonstrated parents' higher expectations and demands from boys.

The analysis of the interviews indicated that material success was related to academic achievement and believed to facilitate the acquisition of a high status academic profession. This value was considered of greater importance for boys. A different picture was obtained for girls. While 50% of the fathers of girls considered it important, none of the mothers responded in relation to girls. Interestingly enough, an identical result was coded for the children: while 50% of the boys attributed importance to material success, none of the girls did.

These findings indicate that there is ambivalence with regard to success of girls. Though school achievement was considered of equal importance for boys and girls, probably as a result of the specific situation of the special class, the aspirations for professional success were congruent with the traditional stereotypic woman's role, and agree with research findings relating to fear of success in women (Horner, 1968; Butler & Nisan, 1975).

Differences in the value of happiness were found between parents and children. While parents valued happiness for their children, none of the children mentioned it. However, in view of the young age of the children, the findings are to be expected. However, it is interesting to note that parents attributed more importance to happiness for boys, a finding which seems to be related to the stereotypic role expectations of women.

Results for initiative were similar to those found for happiness.

Good citizenship was ranked higher by parents in relation to girls. This finding may suggest that parents attribute to girls the traditional role of education at home, as this value is considered an important factor in the educative process in Israel.

Group 2: Middle class children of normal ability. Generally, the value system found in this group resembled that of the previous group.

Overall Percentage of Responses for Group 2

Rank	Value	%
1	School achievement	81
2	Independence	70
3	Social success	66
4	Good citizenship	49
5	Tidiness & Cleanliness	42

6	Material success	42
7	Individuality	40
8	Happiness	25
9	Initiative	25
10	Loyalty	19

No differences were found in school achievement between the previous group and this one. These findings may be the result of the similar socioeconomic status of both groups.

Though independence was ranked equally high by both parents for boys and girls, only 50% of the children mentioned it. The differences between adults and children may be attributed to the characteristics of middle class child rearing practices, which in Israel, at least, do not emphasize independence for the young child.

Social success was found to be fairly highly valued by adults and children. As in the case of the gifted goys, the boys in this group attributed less importance to social success than the girls did.

Good citizenship was coded higher in this group than in the gifted group and parents rated it higher than children. Fifty percent of the children gave this response whereas none of the children in the gifted group did so. These findings might be explained by the more individualistic nature of the gifted child.

Material success received the same rank in this group as in the previous group, however, boys attributed less importance to it than did those in the gifted group. This finding may suggest that success expectations are lower due to the fact that the special class for the gifted is situated in the same school which this group attends. As in the previous group, this value was hardly mentioned by mothers in relation to girls, nor by the girls themselves.

Individuality value was ranked fairly low by all members of this group.

The picture for happiness was similar to that found in the previous group. Fathers similarly valued happiness more for boys than for girls. It may be possible to hypothesize that in this social class, happiness of girls may be conceived as attainable through the fulfillment of this value in the man.

Initiatve and loyalty received the lowest ranks.

Group 3: Differently cultured disadvantaged children and their parents. Compared to the middle class groups, this group was quite different. Only six of the ten values selected for investigation were mentioned. In addition, parents of both sexes attributed a high degree of importance to the values of "respect for parents" and "obedience." It should be mentioned that the expectations of obedience from children is a characteristic of child-rearing practices among oriental people. It will be remembered that most of the parents in this group were of oriental origin. The values coded for this group in are again presented decreasing order.

Overall Percentage of Responses for Group 3

Rank	Value	%
1	Social success	91
2	School achievement	71
3	Material Success	69
4	Independence	34
5	Individuality	34

All the respondents in this group attributed the greatest importance to social success. This finding may be explained in view of the fact that the school operates as a successful community school whose principal is highly committed to this aim.

Though school achievement was ranked second, it is of interest to note the striking difference found between the importance attributed by parents to school achievement for boys and girls. While all parents valued it for boys, only 25% of them valued it for girls. In contrast almost 75% of the girls responded to this value. It seems possible to hypothesize that in this case the girls identify more with the values of the school than with those of the home.

The picture for material success was similar to that obtained for school achievement; however, in contrast to the previous two groups, 50% of the mothers and girls responded to this value. This finding may be understood in the light of the lower income in these families, which makes material success for women necessary.

Independence received a high proportion of responses. While only 30% of mothers attributed importance to independence for girls, 70% of the girls responded to this value.

Tidiness, cleanliness and individuality were ranked low in comparison to other values and in comparison to the previous groups. From the analyses of the interviews it appeared that mothers undertook responsibility for housework, but felt that "if children would clean their room it would be easier."

Group 4: Kibbutz children and their parents. The analyses of the interviews in this group revealed the most striking picture of a society in a state of transformation. The characteristics of the conflicts which arise as a result of a situation in which outside influences impinge on long established and accepted values, becomes evident as one examines both the ranking of the values and their contents.

Altogether nine values were considered of importance. Out of these, seven were common to the other groups, whereas two, "membership in the kibbutz" and "academic profession," were specific to this group.

Overall Percentage of Responses for Group 4

Rank	Value	%
1	Social success	74
2	School achievement	49
3	Individuality	46
4	Independance	34
5	Kibbutz membership	34

6	Loyalty	31
7	Good Citizenship	26
8	Academic profession	26
9	Happiness	3

It is not surprising that in a closely knit society such as that of the kibbutz, social success was ranked in first place. However, it is interesting to note that though both adults and children attributed great importance to social success, mothers considered it more important than fathers, and boys ranked higher than girls. These findings are difficult to explain considering that the social structure of the kibbutz emphasizes peer-group cohesiveness, and children spend most of their time with the peer group. It is important to remember that in three out of the five kibbutzim in this sample, the children no longer sleep in the children's home, a practice which constituted an important ingredient of the kibbutz ideology. Instead, many kibbutzim have adopted the practice of children sleeping in the parents' homes at night. This issue has aroused a great deal of controversy in many kibbutzim. It seems possible to hypothesize that while mothers were more anxious to adopt "home sleeping," they may have also felt more anxiety that this practice would have negative effects on the social education of their children. This factor may have accounted for their responses to this value.

The largest within-group differences related to school achievement. While fathers valued it more than social success, only one mother mentioned it. However, children of both sexes rated it nearly as high as social success. It seems possible to hypothesize that young children are not yet concerned with ideological issues of the adult society. On the other hand, children of this young age often identify with the values of their parents. In this case, the world of the peer group and school may conflict with that of the home.

Individuality was placed third, and was noted nearly as many times as social success. These findings seem to indicate that a gap exists in this group between the values of the subculture and the personal needs of its members. It may be that these findings reflect the transformation of values in a second generation kibbutz population that was reared in the traditional fashion of "communal sleeping" and was later exposed to different socialization practices through the experiences of living in a different society during their service in the army. This encounter between contrasting cultural values may have awakened awareness of perhaps the dormant need for a higher sense of individuality.

Independence, loyalty and good citizenship received fewer responses and failed to reveal consistent patterns, with the exception of loyalty which coded responses for children only, usually in the context of peer relationships.

Membership in the kibbutz and acquisition of an academic profession were specific to this group and mentioned only by parents. These findings are not surprising in view of the fact that children of this age are not aware of these issues. Ninety percent of the mothers responded to "membership in the kibbutz" in relation to boys, which may be interpreted in view of their anxiety that boys would leave the kibbutz upon marriage. Surprisingly, though only one mother responded to the value of school achievement, 30% of mothers valued an academic profession for their children. These findings provide further indication of the gap which exists in this group between the traditional values and ideologies of the kibbutz and the personal values of its members.

The picture for happiness is similar to that found in the differently cultured disadvantaged group, with only the mothers responding to this value. This is incongruent with the general high emphasis on personal development and good interpersonal relationships which was expressed in the interviews. However, these observations may have been made in the context of social adjustment rather than personal happiness. It can thus be understood in terms of the importance attached to social success in the kibbutz.

Group 5: Arab children and their parents. This group differed from the previous ones in two ways: the number of values mentioned was much larger (25 versus 10); and the within-group variance was much smaller. Six values, school achievement, social success, independence, tidiness and cleanliness, material success and loyalty, were common to the previous groups, while the others were specific to this group. As some values were similar it was possible to arrange them into 13 categories. The value system was identified and ranked in decreasing order, as for the other groups.

Overall Percentage of Responses for Group 5

Rank	Value	%
1	School achievement	100
2	Tidiness & cleanliness	97
3	Competitiveness	94
4	Material success	92
6	Sense of humor	92
7	Discipline	89
8	Positive attitude	83
9	Social success	83
10	Independance	78
11	Artistic creativity	78
12	Respect for teachers	75
13	Leadership	67

All respondents without exception attributed the highest importance to school achievement. This finding is of particular significance when one considers that schooling for Arab girls is a fairly new concept. However, as in previous groups, during the interview it was possible to detect the ambivalence that existed toward equality of the sexes in this aspect. For example, several of the fathers mentioned that they attached great importance to intellectual development of boys by the school, while they mentioned the need for artistic development only with respect to girls. Since the results of the content analyses of the interviews in this group indicated that there were hardly any within-group differences, findings will be reported for those values for which differences were found. It should be mentioned that it was more difficult in this group to interview the subjects separately and it is possible that members of the family took their cue from the father.

Differences were found between the parents with respect to independence. While nearly all fathers (11 of 12) responded to this value for boys and girls, mothers gave responses for girls, while only 50% of mothers mentioned independence for boys. This finding may be interpreted in the light of the traditional role of the woman in this culture, which is perceived as responsible for running the home and may have been conceived by the respondents as independence. It is interesting to note that a similar picture was obtained for the children. While all girls responded to this value, only about 60% of the boys coded responses.

Social success was considered by parents of both sexes as more important for boys than girls. While all boys responded to this value, only 75% of the girls did so. These findings may be explained in the light of cultural norms which place social restriction upon girls. It is interesting that despite the fact that girls are restricted in their social activities outside the home, 75% of the girls responded. These findings may perhaps reflect their ambivalence towards these restrictions.

Respect for teachers was only featured in this group. This value is highly rated within the Arab culture and it is surprising that only 50% of the girls so responded, fewer than parents and boys. It may be possible to hypothesize that as the teachers in Arab schools are mostly male (in contrast to the situation in Jewish schools, where most teachers are female) the girls may hereby express some of their objections to the culture's role perception of women, in terms of expectations of obedience to the male member of the family.

The only significant difference that was found in fathers with regard to sex differentiation, was coded for the value of leadership. This value, which received the lowest rank, was considered important for boys by 75% of the fathers, whereas only 50% of the fathers mentioned this value for girls. In contrast, mothers and daughters attributed slightly more importance to this value (75%) with respect to girls than they did for boys. Similar results were found for boys. Such findings are difficult to explain in view of the fact that at least for parents, one would have expected this value to receive a much higher rate, as leadership among the Arab Israeli population is an important issue. However, one possible explanation may be that the results reflect dissatisfaction with the present situation. It may also be that in view of the cultural characteristic of guarding the family privacy, the results are not truly representative. However, it is also possible to conclude, particularly in view of the number and content of the value system, that this society is also in a state of transformation.

Discussion and Conclusions

In general, contrary to our expectations, the findings of this study indicated that the similarities in the value systems of the research groups were more apparent than the differences between the groups. Moreover, it is important to note that the similarities were particularly evident in the area of achievement-oriented values. School achievement, for example, was placed at the top of the value system by three out of the five groups investigated: the gifted group, the normal ability middle class group and the Arab; group while the remaining two groups, the disadvantaged and the kibbutz groups, ranked school achievement in second place. Similarly, social success, a value in Israel which is considered an important ingredient of success in general, and thus constitutes an educational objective both at home and in school, received the highest number of responses in two groups, the differently cultured disadvantaged group and the kibbutz group, and was also ranked in second place by the gifted group and the normal ability middle class group.

It is interesting to note that our findings in relation to expressed values seem to disagree with much of the literature in the last two decades which has emphasized the gap between the two cultures of the whole and the school, particularly among differently cultured populations. Getzels, (1969) for example, says:

> One type of conflict or at least discontinuity, is between the values of the community or of sub-groups within the community and the expectations of the school to which it sends its children . . . . an obvious instance of this is the discontinuity between the orientation giving rise to the so-called culturally deprived or educationally disadvantaged child and the requirements of the school which he is likely to attend. But the incongruities between the cultural values and the school expectations are sometimes more pervasive if less visible than this.

Though our findings appear to contradict those incongruities that are emphasized in the literature, nevertheless, they agree with Getzels' observation that the incongruities are "more pervasive if less visible." If one considers the visible similarities between the different subgroups, it is possible to find a number of reasons which may explain them.

First, considering school achievement, one should emphasize that Israeli society is generally highly achievement-oriented. Though one would have expected this orientation to be more emphasized by the middle class groups, it is possible to hypothesize that the tradition of respect for religious scholarly pursuits which characterize both the Moslem and the

Jewish cultures accounted for the great importance attributed to this value by all subgroups.

Second, although the population of Israel is multicultural, the interaction between the various cultures is great. Most Israelis join the army at the age of 18, where they spend several years in an extremely heterogeneous social situation, undergoing a process of acculturation which often impinges on the socialization practices and values encountered in their previous environment.

Third, the high rate of mobility within the different groups constitutes a continuous threat to the traditional values and ideologies of the various cultures and subcultures. For example, many Arab fathers commute daily from their village to neighboring towns for the purpose of employment. Similarly, members of the developing new towns, often of oriental origin, are employed in the kibbutzim; while members of the kibbutzim are often employed in the towns or serve in the Army and only return home for weekends.

However, while these factors serve to explain the similarities found between the groups in the importance attached to the achievement-oriented values, our findings also indicate the pervasive nature of discrepancies and incongruities which were found. Thus, in investigating a different aspect of the study which related to the within-group differences across the groups, it was found that a high degree of similarity was revealed in the sex differentiation parents made with regard to values considered important for boys and girls. In all groups, achievement-oriented values were coded much higher for boys. Moreover, in the two middle class groups, a similar differentiation was made also for personal values. For example, happiness and initiative were considered by parents to be more important for boys. In addition, occupational and professional expectations for girls were much lower than those for boys. These traditional stereotypic role perceptions were revealed both at the more visible levels of expressed values, and at the more hidden levels of observations made during the interviews.

It is interesting to note that the sex differentiation in values and expectations was also evident in the kibbutz group; these findings reveal the discrepancy between the kibbutz ideology which believes in equality between the sexes and the actual values, expectations value related behavior which were found. For example, several parents observed that the school failed to develop fully the intellectual abilities of their children. Concern was usually expressed for the boys "who may be hampered in their opportunities to attain scientific education and professions later on." One father said: "I don't think that the school really stretches my daughter. If she were a boy I would have sent him to the science enrichment course at the Technion."

The results agree with the research findings concerning the ambivalence felt by women and girls toward success (Horner, 1968; Butler & Nisan, 1975). Moreover, they seem to suggest "that an egalitarian ideology is no guarantee that equality will actually be realized in the perception of its members" (Butler & Nisal, 1975, p. 267). These results have important implications for the education of the gifted, if one considers the fact that participation by girls in the various programs for the gifted in Israel is much smaller for girls than for boys, and it becomes clear that the search for untapped talent should be extended to include not only the differently cultured but also the female child population. Furthermore, it seems that the search for talent should be coupled with efforts toward achieving a significant change in social behavior toward achievement by women.

A different form of incongruity was found within the values system of specific groups. This was particularly noticeable in the Arab and kibbutz groups, a factor which may be attributed to a sharper dichotomy in these subcultures between traditional values and idealogies and those prevailing in the society at large. For example, in the Arab group, the values of obedience to parents and adults received the same number of responses as that of independence and personal freedom. Similarly, in the kibbutz group, the traditional values of the kibbutz such as contribution to the community, working in a kibbutz enterprise, serving other members of the kibbutz, received similar rankings similar to those for such conflicting values as individuality and acquisition of academic professions. These findings may be explained in terms of the relationship between needs and values. Rokeach, (1973) for example, perceived values as transformations of needs which are affected by the societal demands.

Discrepancies were revealed between the values which were expressed by parents and their actual value-related behavior. For example, in the gifted group, individuality was ranked in the third place, yet this value received no reinforcement in the homes. The interviews revealed that children were generally required to conform with the accepted middle class norms of social success, tidiness, obedience and learning useful things in school. Similarly, in the differently cultured disadvantaged group, social success coded the highest number of responses, yet the evidence borne out by the interviews indicated that children were prevented from following outside school social activities and were kept at home to help with younger children and perform other duties.

It appears that further research is needed in the area of discrepancies and incongruities that exist between the "visible" value system and the actual values which are expressed in the socialization practices and value related behavior of different cultures. It is suggested that this form of incongruity is more evident in multicultural societies in a state of transition, and probably constitutes a major factor affecting the identification and full development of the child's talents.

Finally, it seems pertinent to quote Bond who said in his Inglis Lecture at Harvard:

There is "gold in them thar hills", in the rural families of the nation, in the underprivileged regions and races of the nation . . . now possessed for the first time in human history of second generation literacy. This is the gold of high human capacity . . . at no time . . . have the effects of an equalitarian ideal of education so prepared a population for the next possible advancement toward complete equality of opportunity. (Bond, 1959, p. 24)

It would seem that the identification and development of "the gold of high human capacity" is, in the final analysis, a challenge that must be met by education in general and gifted education in particular.

References

Bond, N. M., The search for talent. Cambridge, Mass.: Harvard University Press, 1959.

Butler-Por, N. & Lancer, I. Intelligence and creativity. In A. H. Kramer (Ed.), Gifted children: challenging their potential - new perspectives and alternatives. New York: Trillium Press, 1981.

Butler, R. & Nisan, M. Who is afraid of success and why? Journal of Youth and Adolescence, 1975, 4 (3).

Cannel, C. & Kahn, R. The collection of data by interviewing. In L. Festinger & D. Katz (Eds.), Research methods in the behavioral sciences. New York: Holt, Rinehart and Winston, 1953.

Feather, N. T. Values in education and society. New York: Free Press, 1975.

Getzels, J. W. A social psychology of education. In G. Lindzey & E. Aronson (Eds.), The handbook of social psychology. Boston: Addison-Wesley, 1969.

Horner, M. Sex differences in achievement motivation and performance in competitive and non-competitive situations. Unpublished doctoral dissertation, University of Michigan, Ann Arbor, 1968.

Horner, M. S. Fail: bright women. Psychology Today, 1969, 3 (6), 36-38 and 62.

Passow, A. H., The gifted and the disadvantaged. The

National Elementary Principal, 1972, 11 24-31.

Passow, A. H. There is gold in them thar Hills. New York: Teachers College, Columbia University, 1980.

Reissman, F. The culturally deprived child, New York: Harper and Row, 1962.

Rokeach, M., Beliefs, attitudes and values. San Francisco: Jossey-Bass, 1968.

Rokeach, M., The nature of human values. New York: Free Press, 1973.

Torrance, E. P. Non-test indicators of creative talent among disadvantaged children. Gifted Child Quarterly, 1973, 17 (1), 3-9.

Torrance, E. P. Four promising practices for teaching gifted disadvantaged students. In J. F. Miley et al. (Eds.), Promising practices: teaching the disadvantaged gifted. Ventura, CA: Superintendent of Schools, 1975.

Vernon, P. E., Intelligence across cultures. In G. K. Verma and C. Bagley (Eds.), Race and education across cultures. London: Heineman, 1975.

20

THE TALENTED CHILD IN THE PEOPLE'S REPUBLIC OF CHINA

Susan R. Butler

For nearly 2,000 years the civil service in China has provided a sophisticated organ of government, choosing through a series of anonymous competitive examinations based on Confucian classics. Prior to 1949, the educational system was based on a combination of age-old classical education combined with Western modifications.

Since the founding of the People's Republic of China, educational strategies have varied with the political struggle within the Chinese Communist party. The two strategies, the egalitarian and hierarchical, have many elements in common. The predominance of one over the other reflects the views at the time as to which path China's social modernization should follow. Each period, with alternating emphasis, has provided gains and losses. The victors in each political struggle tend to exaggerate the harmful paths initiated by their opponents. The present emphasis on catching up with the West involves the rapid dismantling of the educational reforms established during the Cultural Revolution, and a return to the pre-1966 school system.

The emphasis on speed of change necessitates the identification and training of the most competent. The key-point school system is presently alive and well, concentrating the best facilities and personnel on the training of the most talented. These special schools, often termed "little treasure pagodas" during the Cultural Revolution, are once more building a meritocracy in the name of modernization. Once this aim has been achieved, the possibility of another change in direction cannot be discounted.

China's development has been retarded by many

factors: its policy of isolation, its foreign occupation, internal political strife, and, more recently, the Cultural Revolution. On October 1st, 1949, the People's Republic of China was established and its leaders set out to heal the wounds of the previous half century. They abolished the feudal system of land ownership and replaced it with collective farming. The leaders inherited a semifeudal and semicolonial Old China, with a large, diverse people and a relatively backward economy.

Liberation and Its Aftermath (1949 to 1966)

During the early years the emphasis was on the rehabilitation and the promotion of stability. The graft-ridden bureaucratic system of local government was replaced by Communist cadres. Rail and road systems were restored, along with a stable currency, a nationwide tax system, a more even distribution of food and clothing, as well as programs for health, sanitation and education. With more than 80% of the population illiterate, the government launched a National Literacy campaign. Women were freed from their subservient position in society, a move which shook the very foundations of the Old China. By the Marriage Act of 1950, Chinese women were given complete financial, marital and political equality. This radically altered the status of women. However, change takes time and in important government jobs, women still tend to hold inferior positions.

When the Communists came to power, the economy was a mixture of peasant agriculture with industry and commerce run by state, foreign and private Chinese citizens. In the peak year prior to Liberation, China had only 207 institutions of higher learning with a total enrolment of 155,000 students as well as 5,892 middle schools with 1,879,000 students and 289,000 elementary schools with 23,680,000 pupils (Jiaoyu, 1980). The pattern, established by the end of the nineteenth century, of encouraging Chinese scholars to study overseas, had (with the exception of the period of the Cultural Revolution) continued. These foreign trained Chinese scholars still form a substantial base at the higher levels of education in China and hence exert considerable influence. Therefore, education in China can best be understood in terms of background knowledge of the helmsman who guided their destiny for over twenty-seven years.

The Influence of Mao Tse Tung

The early education of Mao Tse Tung (1893-1976) was planned to provide him with the knowledge of enough characters to keep the books. His schooling focused on Confucian classics and his teacher belonged to the "stern treatment school" (Snow, 1972, p. 153). Mao's early career included five years at Hunan Normal College. He became involved in setting up a Workers' Evening School, and in 1920 was appointed Director of the Primary School attached to Hunan First Middle School.

His interest in educational experimentation involved him in establishing a self-study University in Changsha the following year "for students who wish to study but either lack financial ability or are dissatisfied with the present school system" (Ch'en, 1965, p. 43). With a deepening involvement in politics, Mao left this position in 1922, but his commitment to education never abated. Mao believed that education should produce well rounded individuals, concentrating on the training of workers rather than specialists. His aim in education was "to enable everyone who receives an education to develop morally, intellectually and physically into a well-educated worker inbued with socialist consciousness."

Basically, Mao believed that everyone was a teacher, that intellectuals could learn from the masses, and that workers and peasants should take part in teaching. He believed that while schools were to pass on knowledge, this was useless unless students also learned from life itself. If education was to produce "revolutionary succesors," youth must integrate with workers and peasants taking part in productive labor, and hence spend time in factories and in the countryside. Here, Mao followed the principles of Marx; he believed that to move towards a Communist Society, the three differences between mental and manual labor, agriculture and industry, town and country would need to be eliminated.

Thus, in the period following the Communists' ascension to power, priority was given to political education as well as literacy.

The Soviet Influence

During the first ten years of the People's Republic of China, Soviet influence was at its peak. Russian teachers taught in tertiary institutes and schools, large student exchange programs were instituted, and massive quantities of written materials were imported from Russia. The Russian influence strengthened the authoritarian and academic type of curriculum with its heavy course content. In the universities which were reorganized along Soviet lines this influence was perhaps greatest. Teachers became the centre of learning, the sole source of knowledge. Stress was placed on engineering and allied subjects, rather than on the humanities.

The Russian influence in these early years encouraged the centralization of economic power. However, this concentration of power became decentralized after the disastrous harvest of the 1960 to 1962 period. The Ministry of Education, in a move towards decentralization, relaxed its controls. The Ministry retained the role of guiding and disseminating information while a variety of forms of education were to be developed to suit local conditions. A combination of teaching and productive labor was introduced into the universities and the entrance examinations became accessible to a greater proportion of children from worker and peasant backgrounds. By 1959, the Ministry of Education had regained most of its responsibilities for planning.

The Soviet withdrawal of technicians in 1960 drew attention to the need for the Chinese to train their own technicians and scientific personnel. In

1962, a foreign language was compulsory for entry to leading universities. Universities generally were stressing basic knowledge and formal coursework, and by 1962 were requiring not more than a month of manual labor. A hierarchy developed in which schools were graded according to their success rates in terms of the number of their students admitted to university. The better schools developed as key-point schools. They were given better resources, and were required to run demonstration classes as well as provide advice for other schools. Many of these were prestige schools of prerevolutionary origin; their curriculum was more academic and did not necessarily include manual labor. This new system was characterized by greater centralization, emphasizing teacher centered classroom learning, a decrease in the time allocated for political study and training, as well as political and extracurricular activities. A standardized curriculum provided by the Ministry was instituted.

The key-point schools flourished with excellent facilities, better trained teachers, new curriculum forms and brighter students. The stress was on science, mathematics and foreign languages, in order to prepare students for entry into the tertiary educational system. Hence China developed a twotrack system of education, one track with the keypoint schools at the center, and the other with a combination of different types of schooling as preparation for direct entry into the work force.

The pattern of schooling immediately prior to the Cultural Revolution, therefore, was basically European with a Russian flavor. It was pagoda like in shape; pre-school kindergartens, specifically in city areas, were provided, for children 3 to 7 years of age, followed by six years of primary schooling, three years of junior school, three years of senior school, and finally with tertiary institutions at the apex of the pagoda. A great deal of the curriculum, especially in the sciences, was directly copied from Russia. Apart from regular schools, there were spare-time schools organized by trade unions and local educational authorities. Factories ran various types of technical courses in conjunction with tertiary institutions. Some agricultural high schools organized productive labor to link their school with a specific work program.

Since the great upheaval of May 4th, 1919, students in China have been routinely involved in political activities and various demonstrations.

The Cultural Revolution (1966 to 1976)

The Cultural Revolution was a time of particular student unrest. Students were encouraged to criticize their teachers publicly and the general respect for teachers was at a particularly low ebb. Mao Tse Tung's thoughts at the beginning of the Cultural Revolution are reflected in a letter to Lin Piao, dated May 7th, 1966:

> While their main task is to study, they should in addition to their studies learn other things, that is, industrial work, farming and military affairs. They should criticize the bourgeoisie. The school term should be shortened, education should be revolutionized and the domination of our schools by bourgeois intellectuals should not be allowed to continue. (Price, 1979, p. 267)

During the Cultural Revolution, there was a move away from hierarchical education, that is, away from special schools and streams of classes to cater to the more talented child. The advent of the Cultural Revolution caused schools to close for two to three years (tertiary institutions recommenced in the early 1970s). The results of the 1966 to 1976 reforms are mixed: the overall result was the reduction of academic standards, course content and the length of schooling. During this time, opportunities were expanded at the base level of the educational pyramid and many inequalities were removed. Authority was transferred from the County Educational Bureau to the communes themselves; the latter increased the amount of schooling available by hiring "minban," that is, local staff to teach. The emphasis was on universal primary education and the expansion of secondary education. Table 1 illustrates the sharp increase in the number of enrolments in primary and high schools.

Table 1

Number of Students Enrolled in Chinese Schools (in thousands)

	1949	1957	1965	1976	1979
Universities	117	441	674	565	1020
High Schools	1268	7071	14318	59055	60248
Primary Schools	24391	4283	116209	150055	146629
Kindergartens		102	162	762	533
Deaf/Mute Schools		8	23	29	32

When the tertiary institutes finally reopened, they emphasized an open door approach to education. Students' qualification for entrance was primarily their ideological suitability, almost regardless of their educational standard. This suitability was decided by superiors and workmates, constituting a method of selection which resulted in varying standards of students entering tertiary institutes. The overall standard of education throughout the country fell considerably and academic education, with its emphasis on "red" rather than "expert," lost its significance. Most high school graduates were resettled in rural areas, practically none were being admitted directly to universities. As a result, students were no longer being motivated to strive for academic achievement.

The Post-Cultural Revolution Period (1976 to 1981)

The death of Mao Tse Tung in 1976 led to a further power struggle within the Chinese leadership. The new leadership, that of Hua Guofeng and Deng Xiaoping, rejected many of the experiments of the Cultural Revolution and embarked on a policy of modernization. Deng Xiaoping and the moderate group had always preferred a more conventional educational model which emphasized high quality academic learning rather than a rural oriented work-study model. Thus the revolutionary zeal of the left-wing Maoist line was replaced by a pragmatic realization that China had to modernize in order to compete with technologically advanced nations. Contrasted with the indecision and delays of the past ten years of unrest, the leadership reviewed its economic position and moved quickly to close the gap between its standards and those of the rest of the world.

The Role of Educational Change in Chinese Modernization

Education was seen as a key ingredient in the new policy of four modernizations (agriculture, industry, national defence, science and technology). The guidelines for this new policy were clearly outlined at the National Educational Work Conference in April, 1978 by the Minister of Education, Liu Xiyao who quoted Chairman Hua's speech at the recent National Science Conference:

only by greatly elevating the scientific and cultural level of the entire Chinese nation and bringing up a mighty contingent of working class intellectuals could the general tasks of the new period be fulfilled and the behest of Chairman Mao and Premier Chou of building a powerful socialist state with four modernizations be carried out. All this requires us working on the educational front to raise at the shortest time possible the quality of education of the schools at all levels and of all types and to develop the cause of education, so as to bring up millions upon millions of labourers having socialist consciousness and mastering modern production skills and to train hundreds upon thousands of specialists in various fields and managerial experts and cadres for modern economy and modern science and technology. (Liu Xiyao, 1978, p. 1)

Along with raising standards for a speedy development is the return to decentralized control, and encouraging provinces, municipalities and autonomous regions to develop new institutions to train their own people in fields needed by their particular locality or region.

The general scheme of education provides for ten years of schooling for city children and eight years in rural areas. The report recommended that Communist Labor Universities, "July 21st Workers Colleges" and "May 7th Colleges" be reorganized and upgraded where necessary to the level of universities or technical institutes. Various types of classes are flourishing, as seen in the improvement of correspondence, evening, spare time, as well as television and radio classes. A television college was to be developed by the Ministry of Education. Agricultural high schools, secondary technical schools, and schools of technology were to be increased, providing both work and study. Attention was to be paid to the rehabilitation of institutes for national minorities, where minority cadres would be trained to disseminate education to remote areas. Special education for deaf mutes and the blind were to be increased, libraries and laboratories throughout the country replenished and teaching techniques improved. Major changes have begun to be made in the area of priority schools and institutions, selection procedures for admittance to tertiary institutions, status of teachers, curriculum, spare time education and productive labor. This is a period of rejection of many educational experiences of the Cultural Revolution which had resulted in an acute shortage of qualified personnel in all fields of work. The country is presently carrying out a massive drive to train millions of people with the standard of education necessary for the success of the Four Modernizations. This was reflected in the speech of Hua Guofeng at the Third Session of the Fifth National People's

TALENTED CHILD IN CHINA

Congress which opened in Beijing on August 28th, 1980:

> We must pay special attention to the use of our intellectual resources and energetically develop our scientific and educational institutions. The level of the development of a country hinges largely on the extent of its use of intellectual resources. The modernization of science and technology is the key to the three other modernizations. Scientific research must anticipate the needs of our economic construction and help solve the scientific and technological problems arising in the course of modernizing our country. . . . The State Council is prepared gradually to devote more funds to science and education in the coming decade and hopes that the governments of the provinces, municipalities and autonomous regions will do likewise. We shall strive in a multitude of ways to bring about more and better results in our scientific and educational work, so that in the course of time we may train generation after generation of workers with socialist consciousness, knowledge of science and culture, occupational skills and good health, as well as large numbers of specialists in all fields such as science and technology, social sciences, organization and management, literature and art, specialists suited to the needs of the four modernizations (in **Beijung Review,** 1980, pp. 17-18)

The importance of education in the total national plan for the Four Modernizations of China is reflected in the new directives seen at all levels of education.

This path is still being followed, as is seen in its confirmation in "On Questions of Party History - Resolutions of Certain Questions in the History of Our Party Since the Founding of the People's Republic of China," a paper adopted by the Sixth Plenary Session of the Eleventh Central Committee of the Communist Party of China on June 27th, 1981. Reference is made to the Cultural Revolution and the ensuing denigration of education, science and culture and discrimination against intellectuals. It is once more confirmed that

> together with the workers and peasants, the intellectuals are a force to rely on in the cause of socialism and that it is impossible to carry out socialist construction without culture and the intellectuals. . . . It is imperative for the whole Party to engage in a more diligent study of Marxist theories, of the past and present in China and abroad, and of the different branches of natural and social sciences. We must strengthen and improve ideological and political work and educate the people and youth in the Marxist world outlook and communist morality; we must persistently carry out the educational policy which calls for an all-round development morally, intellectually and physically, for being both red and expert, for integration of the intellectuals with the workers and peasants and the combination of mental and physical labor; and we must counter the influence of decadent bourgeois ideology and the decadent remnants of feudal ideology, overcome the influence of petty-bourgeois ideology and foster the patriotism which puts the interests of the motherland above everything else and the pioneer spirit of selfless devotion to modernization (in **Beijing Review,** July 6, 1981, p. 37).

Key-Point Schools and Universities

Clearly there must be rapid improvement in the quality and efficiency of education in order for China to reach the technological levels of Western countries. This concern with raising the standard of education is seen in the return of elitist forms of education such as key-point schools, streaming of classes and highly competitive enrolment examinations at the tertiary level. In essence, a double track system of education has been reintroduced. This form of specialized education is in marked contrast to Mao's sense of urgency in moving toward the elimination of differences between mental and manual workers. The key-point schools have more experienced administrators and teachers. They are usually given first choice of graduating teacher trainees. Generally speaking, these schools are given more financial help to enable them to buy reference materials and laboratory equipment. They are able to enroll more capable students through competitive examinations. Often, the teacher-pupil ratio is lower than in ordinary schools.

With the establishment of key-point schools in March, 1978, eighty-eight universities were also designated as key-point institutions. Most are long established institutions such as Peking (Beijing), Tsinghua and Futan as well as more recent tertiary institutes such as Kiangsi Communist Labor University and the Tachai Agricultural College. Universities in China are free to most students, and they provide medical care, dormitory living and a stipend.

As of 1979, National Academic Examinations for entrance to tertiary institutions are set by the National Ministry of Education and administered by the local Educational Bureau under the direct supervision of the party committee. Marking scales are provided by the examiners and strict marking procedures are adhered to. Intake quotas are allocated by national administrators to the various institutes, taking into account regional differences. All examination results in the various subjects are made public along with the results of physical examinations. There is a right of appeal available to all students. Science students are assessed on technical subjects and arts students on arts subjects. The examinations include five subjects with a total score of 500. Foreign language constitutes 30% of the overall total. The minimum mark for entry to the Physics Course at the University of Beijing is generally 400 but students coming from country areas who may be slightly disadvantaged are given some leniency and may enter with slightly lower marks, approximately 370 or 380.

A method of expanding student numbers has been the admission of day students, who have scored at least 300 out of 500 in their examinations but were not admitted with the first batch of entrants with the highest scores. These students enroll as full day or evening students and pay approximately 25 yuan a term. Most classes are held in the evening due to lack of sufficient space at the tertiary institutes. These students who enter on a self-paid basis will receive a graduation certificate but will have to apply for a job individually. That the system favors children living in the urban areas is accepted as a relic of history. It is hoped that raising the level of education in rural areas would increase the level of production and hence, the possibility of the government providing more tertiary education. This, however, appears to be a long shot.

The reintroduction of the examination system has been praised by some for encouraging students to study; others complain that the system is becoming too examination ridden. In order to encourage and identify the most talented, newspaper advertisements are published during the month of May asking for those talented in various areas (music, art, and academic) to present themselves for examinations to be held in various capital cities. In addition to this are various types of contests such as mathematics, which were criticized during the Cultural Revolution but had been reintroduced in 1978. Physics and chemistry contests recommenced in 1979.

The Encouragement of Excellence in Chinese Education

The Chinese University of Science and Technology in Hofei, Anhwei Province, has established a special class of highly talented young people, mostly in their early teens. These students attend classes in physics, mathematics, foreign languages and other subjects. These children are China's youngest university students. The age range is approximately eleven to sixteen. The students were chosen on the basis of interviews and investigations, held by university staff, of a larger group of young people recommended as outstanding by teachers and local cadres from all parts of the country. Some candidates were middle school students sitting university entrance tests. Special preparatory courses have been designed for individual and group needs prior to allowing them to attend regular university classes.

As part of a move toward excellence in education, new textbooks have been introduced at primary and middle school levels throughout the country, under the direction of the National Ministry of Education. This is creating a greater degree of centralization than that which had existed prior to the Cultural Revolution. Although there is an ideological orientation to this material, the political content has been very much reduced. A greater range of subjects is provided at the high school level, including classical Chinese.

China's recent changes in attitude to the outside world have had a direct impact on the courses of study. As it moves away from its traditional isolationist position, China is sending students abroad for training, as well as encouraging visits by overseas scholars. Students are selected for overseas study either by sitting for stringent examinations, or by being recommended by senior staff members from their particular institutes. The problem of sending students overseas at this point in time is the serious shortage of students and teachers with adequate foreign language skills to benefit from several years of overseas training.

Role modeling continues to be a method used in encouraging the facets of character deemed important. The encouragement of excellence in education can be seen in the deliberate television coverage of young people having great talent in specific areas such as art, mathematics, science and other attributes important to current Chinese ideals. China is trying to cope with the serious problem of attempting to provide appropriate education for talented youth who will inevitably have the task of administering the modernization program of the government. Only the very talented are able to go on to tertiary education. The problem of educated youth sent to the countryside during the Cultural Revolution remains; in many cases they are unable to return to their city of origin due to economic factors and the scarcity of educational opportunities and employment.

Priority has been given to the regular educational system and more specifically, to the system of key-point schools and tertiary institutes. Part time educational programs have been encouraged to raise their academic standards. Some part time courses are now requiring either a particular educational level for entry or else the sitting of specific examinations. The examinations held at the end of these courses are used partly for decisions or promotion.

Academic excellence in research is being encouraged and new research units are being opened in specific areas. This is reflected in a new interest in "educational engineering," that is, the study of the first years of a child's life and environmental influences. This will involve research into the importance of education. How can the innate ability of children be fully tapped and how can a child's strong points be cultivated to the fullest extent? There is also a move in the direction of providing home education to assist the maturational processes of children. It is believed that parents have been inclined to stress academic progress and neglect moral education. This service aims at correcting the parents' approach and helping to balance the attitude of parents who are either too lenient or too strict.

Related Issues

China is faced with approximately seven million graduates from middle schools each year. Of these, three million are unemployed. These graduates, termed "youth waiting for employment" generally remain at home and study, attempting to pass tertiary entrance examinations the following year. This creates serious problems, as many young people prefer to work in large factories run by the state. The pay is generally higher because of bonuses and fringe benefits and the job is secure for life. When parents retire from factories, their children generally replace them. It is realized that the country needs more service workers, such as barbers, nurses, waiters and waitresses, cooks, and various other technical personnel. Due to century-old concepts, many do not like to take on these jobs as they feel they are inferior. The government is trying to provide further vocational training at the middle school level rather than generalized training. Unlike middle school graduates, graduates from higher education and vocational and senior technical schools are more likely to obtain employment upon graduation.

Cadres have not been forgotten. Back in the early 1950s, Mao Tse Tung advocated that cadres (political leaders) should be both red and expert - red referring to high political consciousness, and expert referring to vocational proficiency. Most cadres have attained the educational level of senior middle school or college. Three million have received a college education, while more than five million are engaged in scientific or technological work (Beijing Review, June 2, 1980). Crash courses presently provide training for approximately eighteen million cadres. At the national level, the ministries are running cadre training schools, while the universities are offering specific courses. Further courses are being offered by all departments at the central and local level, as well as various enterprises, industry, television colleges, evening schools, correspondence courses, special training classes, seminars and symposiums. There is a move to retrain cadres whose technical knowledge is inadequate and to select a larger number of young cadres from graduates of universities or secondary technical schools. This represents a shift from selecting cadres from among workers and peasants with little education. The Party demands that the cadres adhere to the Socialist role, be competent with professional knowledge and vocational skills, and be in the prime of life. They are required to be able to shoulder heavy tasks and to work at the grass roots level to gain practical experience in production and management.

Conclusion

The style of teaching in China is basically that of regurgitation of between revolutions material, infused with the little current Western data that has managed to seep through. Due to the confusion and cultural isolation during the Cultural Revolution, much factual knowledge and many ideas are outmoded compared with real Western modernization. China's size negates rapid dissemination of knowledge. Chinese students returning from Western institutions may find themselves meeting with resistance in their attempt to implement contemporary foreign technology. The drought of foreign materials during the Cultural Revolution, followed now by a flood of new materials on all fronts, must have its impact. The Communist educational policy has had numerous sudden shifts in direction related to political changes. The gifted have been directly affected by these policies; the conflict finally reached its peak when schools were closed during the Cultural Revolution and academic excellence underwent subsequent degradation.

The death of Chairman Mao and the reinstatement of Deng Xiaoping led to the abandonment of Cultural Revolutionary policies, and a return to those of the early sixties which established priority provision for the more capable. Mao believed that education was the means to produce revolutionary successors and the continuation of the revolution. Deng Xiaoping and the more moderates hold that education provides the means of training the technical and scientific expertise needed for China's modernization.

The changing educational policies have reflected the different interpretations of the nature of socialist development. Those who believed that socialism was best served by increasing production favored issues of quality and academic standards, while those who favored revolution preferred the immediate extension of education to the general population, compromising academic standards. The radicals rejected examinations as favoring academically motivated upper classes, and believed that students' political development was the aim of education. The moderates prefer examinations to select the academically talented, stressing that scientists should concentrate on their particular expertise.

The problem remains that, in an effort to achieve modernization, priority is being given to the key-point system and the development of tertiary education, largely at the expertise of the needs of the countryside. There is still a discrepancy between theory and practice; although China is striving towards modernization, very little has changed in terms of basic rote memorization within the classroom context. This situation is probably influenced by the fact that the Chinese language itself requires mastery of a vast number of characters.

It must be remembered that 85% of the Chinese population live in rural areas. Their support is essential to the continuation of any system of education. The problem remains as to how best to deal with the educated youth sent to the countryside during the Cultural Revolution. This lost generation feels disadvantaged and bitter.

While China is rapidly making up for time lost during the Cultural Revolution, the dilemma still remains as to how China can train its most talented people, yet avoid an intellectual elite in an egalitarian society. Perhaps when sufficient modernization and economic growth have been established, the more radical line of combining productive labor and education will once more prevail and the Marxist vision of Communist education become a reality.

References
Beijing Review, Nos. 22, 27, 38 (June 2, 1980; July 6, 1981; Sept. 22, 1980).

Ch'en, J. Mao and the Chinese revolution. London: Oxford University Press, 1965.

Jiaoyu Education Zhongguo baike Nianjian. Yearbook of the Greater Encyclopedia of China, 1980.

Price, R. F. Education in modern China. London: Routledge & Kagan,Paul, 1979.

Snow, E. Red star over China. Harmondsworth: Penguin Books, 1972.

Tse Tung, Mao. On the correct handling of contradictions among the people. In Four essays on philosophy. Peking: Foreign Languages Press.

Xiyao, Liu. Report of the National Educational Work Conference. Peking: Ministry of Education of the People's Republic of China, 1978.

21

ATTITUDES TO PROVISION FOR GIFTED CHILDREN: THE CASE OF THE USSR

John Dunstan

Giftedness is for many an emotive term because it implies some superior quality or qualities which not everyone possesses. This prompts the question of the necessity, desirability and legitimacy of special provision at the school level; differentiation raises the spectre of discrimination. Furthermore, such provision has obvious implications for resource allocation, and in times of financial stringency its supporters are compelled to argue for it with particular persuasiveness. Yet much of the scholarly discussion on gifted children seems to fight shy of wider problems and to take place in a sociopolitical vacuum. The present paper is a preliminary contribution toward the filling of the gap. The study of attitudes, an important concern of social science, is of intrinsic interest. What follows is an attempt to survey and to classify attitudes relating to special provision for gifted and high ability children and young people.

Since individuals' stances vary so much according to their interpretation of giftedness, it is necessary to define the term. For immediate purposes I shall use the narrow definition of high ability expressed in actual achievement. Lest some react to this by abandoning this paper in disgust, let me hasten to add that this is by no means to be regarded as a qualitatively superior definition but rather as one which serves as a starting point for the classification of attitudes and which will lead ultimately to what might well be thought a better one. The epithet "actual" is unavoidable because if the ability is not demonstrated the question of provision for it may not arise.

JOHN DUNSTAN

Provision for Gifted Children in the USSR, 1958-1973
The educational context. Although this paper is
primarily concerned with Soviet attitudes to provision
for gifted children rather than the provision itself, it
is appropriate to outline how that provision arose and
indeed the context in which it operated. In the 1950s
the highly academic orientation of the Soviet general
school, geared to admission to higher education at a
time when competition for entry was becoming much
more intense and when the effects of the lowered
wartime birthrate on the future workforce were
increasingly discernible, came to be regarded as
incompatible with socioeconomic needs. Young skilled
workers were urgently required, but school leavers
were often prepared for this neither physically nor
mentally. So the school was vocationalized, at first
experimentally in the mid-1950s, and then violently
under the Khrushchev legislation of December 1958.
The seven year period of compulsory schooling was
increased to eight years (four primary, four middle).
The youngest children did two periods of manual work
per week, the fourteen year olds five, the oldest ones
twelve; and the senior course was extended from two
years to three in order to contain the increased load.
There was also an expansion of the vocational and
technical sector as well as part time and evening
courses of all types. The reform had ideological
motivation as well as pragmatic: it was intended to
reassert the importance of the Marxist principle of
labor as one of the three primary components of the
educational process in the broadest sense and the one
which had been particularly neglected for some twenty
years.

It soon emerged that there were those who felt
apprehensive about the new trend. The swing away
from cognitive considerations and academic priorities,
epitomized in the 1958 proposal to introduce two years
work experience as a preliminary to entering higher
education, evoked a reaction in people concerned about
the country's continued economic progress. Soviet
science and technology had had an impressive record,

culminating in the successful launch of Sputnik I. On the other hand, the rate of economic growth was falling, it was necessary to move away from the utilization of Western experience and towards independent research and innovation, and the American reaction to the Soviet space achievements promised to intensify the great contest. There was not only a need for young skilled manpower; if one looked beyond the confines of the country into the international arena with its uncommitted third world spectators, the first priority was for highly trained specialists to enable the USSR to take the scientific and technological lead.

Such views gathered strength during the early 1960s as the poly- technical reform of Khrushchev lost momentum and collapsed almost completely. There were inadequacies all round: poor planning, shortages of personnel and equipment, superficial and narrow training, overburdening of the pupils. The curriculum was pruned in 1964 and vocational training in school ceased to be mandatory in 1966. Conative and to some extent affective goals began to be displaced by cognitive ones. Though his education policy was just one of many reasons why Khrushchev had to go, it seems very appropriate that on the day after his downfall in October 1964 an extremely high-powered commission first met to determine the future content of secondary education.

It is interesting to see how the minority viewpoint of 1958, which was predominantly concerned with ensuring the replenishment of the Soviet scientific leadership, turned into a majority stance, but with a much wider academic remit, by the middle of the next decade. The debates centered in the Curriculum Commission's activities of 1964-66 suggests parallels with the American experience of the 1950s. Again we think of Bruner, whose discussion of **The Process of Education (1977)** underwent its first foreign translation - into Russian. Again there was the call for vital concepts to be determined and for superfluous material thereby to be jettisoned from overloaded syllabuses in the name of scientific advance and the national need.

And scientific advance, it was now said, required the efficient teaching of all children. The new emphasis was very much on knowledge and on cognitive development, and the upbringing goals which in the next few years were to be increasingly stressed were those with obvious cognitive relevance, notably to resist anti-Soviet ideologies and attitudes by the ability to go to the heart of the matter and mobilize material from related areas, so as to out-argue one's adversaries and convince one's weaker brethren of the error of their ways.

The massive restructuring of the curriculum elaborated by the Commission and initiated by a decree of November 1966 took nearly a decade to implement and thus passes beyond the time limit which we have set ourselves. But before we turn to consider provision for gifted children against this shifting background, we have one final overlapping trend to mention which has since emerged predominant at the present. The shortage of young skilled workers and the excess of 17 year olds with unrealisable expectations of higher education were problems on which the Khrushchev reform had only marginal effect and which quickly reasserted themselves. By the late 1960s they were once again the focus of attention, and the action taken to deal with them constituted a reversal of the Khrushchev technique: by a decree of April 1969 senior stage secondary education was injected into the traditionally despised vocational schools with 15-plus entry. This sector has since been steadily expanded, being also one of the four avenues to compulsory 10-year education, which was enacted in 1977. A reinvigorated interest in the vocational aspect has concomitant highlighting of affective goals, paramount concerns being not only ideological and labor upbringing but also moral education. The curriculum debate has lately been renewed, though in a somewhat lower key, and reflects the general school's current preoccupation of preparing young people realistically for jobs.

The development of provision for the gifted.
Such is the background against which important
developments in provision for unusually able children
came to the fore during the 1960s. Most of these
developments were something quite new for the Soviet
school. One particular type of provision, however,
could boast a pedigree of well over 200 years.
Russia's first ballet school had been founded in 1738
after the Empress Anna had imported a French dancing
master, one Jean-Baptiste Landet, to start a ballet
school for pages and choristers, surviving to this day
as the famous Leningrad (Kirov) Ballet School. In the
early 1970s it was one of around a hundred full time
secondary schools for artistically gifted children; there
were about five such schools for the fine arts to every
three for music and two for ballet (Dunstan, 1978).
They then comprised nearly 8% of the special schools
which we are considering. These figures do not
include colleges with 15-plus entry offering medium
professional training. They are heavily selective,
taking an average of about 3% of original applicants.
They are normally justified by the argument that
artistic talents must be nurtured intensively for
everybody's sake and that only by specialized teaching
and facilities can this be ensured.
Supporters of special provision for outstanding
gifts of other kinds found these schools a useful
precedent. The closest analogy was perhaps athletic
talent, and here the matter possessed a more overtly
national and international dimension: the football
(soccer) school established in Tbilisi, the capital of
Georgia, in 1946 was followed by a number of sports
boarding schools in the 1960s. Thus it is hoped to
produce athletes who will prove to the world the
superiority of the Soviet system on occasions such as
the Olympics. The political role of international sport
is a fact, to deny which is foolishness. About 1970
there were eighteen or more of these schools (Dunstan,
1978) or almost 1.5% of all special schools for children
with particular abilities. Although some were in great
demand, others had had a checkered career and a few

had actually closed; despite their official backing, it seems that there is a fairly widespread view that resources should be more equitably husbanded and that a career in sport is ideologically dubious if not frivolous.

The growing concern in the early 1960s about the international implications of Soviet domestic policy, mentioned in the previous section, may well have contributed to the creation of an atmosphere conducive to the development of the sports schools. The same may be said of schools specializing in a foreign language from the second year, if we are thinking in terms of diplomats and translators, but it is also possible to see them as one of the few positive outcomes of Khrushchev's vocationally oriented reform. Starting as a pilot scheme in the RSFSR in 1948, the language schools were greatly expanded by a decree of May 1961. The preamble to the decree specifically mentioned the growing importance of knowledge of foreign languages because of the USSR's increasing international contacts. Ten years later they constituted the largest group of special schools, numbering at least 600 (about 47.5% of the total) (Dunstan, 1978). It would, however, be misguided to think of them as schools for linguistic geniuses; they were supposed to be available for any children whose parents wanted them to have intensive language training, and the admission procedures, though including tests of imagination and the ability to reproduce the sounds of the foreign language and a physical examination, were fairly informal. On the other hand, they were perceived to offer something special, demand tended to exceed supply, and thus the ability range was likely to be superior to that in most "mass" schools.

Arguments about national need were particularly relevant to the creation and preservation of the two kinds of special provision which remain to be mentioned. The whole question of establishing special schools and classes had been thoroughly aired in the nationwide debate preceding the Khrushchev reform of

December 1958. It succumbed to egalitarian pressures, but various eminent people, notably scientists, who had played an active role in those discussions, soon took up the cause again; a leading opponent of the idea (Academician Lavrent'ev, head of the USSR Academy of Sciences' Siberian Section) changed sides; the 1961 Party Program promised science the new status of a driving productive force, and leading scientists thus increased their political stature; and it is probable that the disastrous effects of the Khrushchev reform upon the quality of admissions to higher education added weight to their arguments. So from 1962-63 we see the emergence of the _fiziko - matematicheskie shkoly_ or FMShs, boarding schools specializing in mathematics and science (usually physics), attached to and partly staffed by a higher educational institution, and offering along with the general subjects a very high level of specialized teaching to their rigorously selected 14 to 16-year-old entrants (about 2% of those initially interested). Including the four original FMShs in Moscow, Leningrad, Kiev and Novosibirsk, by 1970 there were some eleven such schools over the whole country. Their purpose was unashamedly to produce a scientific and technological elite.

It was mentioned above that a significant change came about in Soviet secondary education in the mid-1960s. Cognitive considerations came to the fore, and for a brief period national need was seen predominantly in those terms. But it was a far more holistic view of national need than in 1958 when different sorts of national need were pitted against each other. By 1964-65 the pace of differentiation by types of schools had slowed down: economists were saying that special schools were too expensive and the supply of good teachers was running out. The November 1966 decree can be interpreted in part as an act of compromise: it was a symbolic statement of "this far and no further" to those who saw differentiation in terms of separate institutions, yet a guarantee to them of their existing territorial rights against egalitarian encroachment; and simultaneously it was an assurance to the egalitarians that at least for the overwhelming majority of young people, special interests and abilities would be catered for without prejudice to the basic general education program and without socially divisive structures. Such, at any rate, was the intention. How were these respective aims to be achieved?

Another of the few successes of the Khrushchev reform was that a number of general schools had developed unusually good vocational programs in the senior forms in such areas as computer programing. Called "mass schools with a special profile," they were explicitly permitted to continue under the November 1966 decree, but the phrase "a certain number" did not augur marked expansion. In the Russian Republic they grew from 222 in 1967-68 to 323 by the early 1970s (Rutkevich & Filippov, 1973), which is a large percentage increase but in reality modest enough, from 1% of all the republic's secondary schools to about 1.4%. Over the whole country they reached a total of 536, representing some 42.5% of all special schools by 1971.

In contrast to this guarded legitimation of special profile schools, the decree had no inhibitions in providing for the development of options (electives) from form (grade) VII in order to deepen pupils' knowledge and develop their varied interests and abilities. Comment in the press made it clear that they were to be the main vehicle of special provision, and being additional to the common compulsory course they would not prejudice it. In 1973-74, 54% of the school students in the top four years were enroled in options. Although options had to contend with certain difficulties, such as whether all pupils or only those more obviously capable of profiting from them should attend, their right to exist was undisputed. In accordance with the general trends of the 1970s, their potential vocational function came to receive increased emphasis.

Finally, the strengthening of cognitive goals reflected in the 1966 decree was also to be seen in the official blessing bestowed on differentiated teaching techniques, such as flexible ability grouping within the mixed ability class - though this has provoked egalitarian rumblings - and in the impetus given to academic extracurricular activites. Traditionally the only means of catering for special talents among the mass of children, school societies and part time schools and clubs for art, music, sport, crafts, etc., outside the school were supplemented as the 1960s drew on by an increasing variety of academic extracurricular facilities such as correspondence and summer schools organized by universities and institutes. The long standing Moscow Mathematics Olympiad (academic contest) was put on an all-Russian basis in 1961 and an all-Union one in 1967, now covering physics and chemistry also. While such facilities may periodically be criticized on organizational grounds, they are inherently immune from attack on social ones and so enjoy general approval.

Attitudes to Provision for Gifted Children (Note 1)

The extent of special schooling. Although we have not so far gone out of our way to stress the diversity of opinion about special provision for high ability children that exists in the Soviet Union, this must by now be becoming apparent. The strong post-revolutionary tradition of the unified school common to all children was breached by the late 1950s only to the extent of 26 special full time schools for the artistically gifted and a small handful of other experimental schools. Fifteen years later, numbers had risen to nearly 1300, with a greater range of establishments.

This is an impressive increase in absolute terms, but seen as part of the Soviet school system, the special schools appear in a rather different light: about 1970-71, schools for the arts comprised an estimated 0.06% of all general day schools and 0.23% of general day schools with the senior course; sports boarding schools, 0.01% and 0.04% respectively;

language schools 0.34% and 1.36%; maths and physics boarding schools less than 0.01% and 0.02%; and other special profile schools 0.31% and 1.21%. They thus totaled 0.73% and 2.86% respectively (Note 2). In other words they were and indeed still are, relatively speaking, very few. This means that if they are perceived to offer something worthwhile they must be highly selective, and that fact alone must cause problems in a vast country with an ideological commitment to equality which, however much infringed, is unmistakably part of popular consciousness. Their relative fewness may itself suggest opposition to them and the likelihood of a quest for less objectionable alternatives.

Hostility and support. Opposition indeed there was, as well as strong support. Controversy was very fierce in the closing months of 1958 and continued to be heard throughout the period under review, though becoming more muted towards the end. This was surveyed with detailed examples in relation to specific types of provision in my book, **Paths to Excellence and the Soviet School** (1978). Hostility and support may be expressed in terms of a typology of attitudes to provision for giftedness: whether one's concern is predominantly directed toward the individual child or toward the wider society, and whether or not one favors special treatment should attributes be displayed. It may be useful to elaborate this typology with a few comments on its Soviet applications.

Hostility might be societally oriented, with the expression of fear about the creation of privilege, prejudice to collectivism as a broad social goal, and the prolongation of the division of labor. The notion of the purposeful, harmonious collective is fundamental to Soviet education and social organization, and the importance attached by Marxism to the abolition of the division of labor needs no gloss. It might be individually oriented: concern might be voiced that the youngster's personality development would be impaired, that prognostic or diagnostic difficulties could cause him intolerable stress. Here the traditional though now diminishing Soviet abhorrence of mental testing is perceptible. It might represent a combination of these objections: the endangering of the great collective which is Soviet society in this case operates through a series of concentric circles with the individual at the center, individual and group interact, and damage to one is damage to the other. All in all, special provision involving any sort of selection or exclusion might be deemed a travesty of education. We need to remember that in the Soviet usage education is often interpreted in an extremely broad sense with far more emphasis attached to the affective domain and the interplay between affective and cognitive aspects than is usual in many other systems.

Of course, hostility might be expressed without giving reasons, and the same was true of support. Other supportive attitudes might be societally oriented, stressing standards and national need, advocating more efficient vocational guidance and preparation for higher education in the interests of the economy and society, and presenting equality of opportunity as a social good with social benefits. If we recall the economic and political climate in the USSR around 1960, we can see the relevance of this approach. The facilities in question might be argued for in similar terms, as educational laboratories whose findings were to be applied for the enhancement of the whole system. Nail up a board saying "Experimental" in the Soviet Union and you can do all sorts of things. Individually oriented supporters might see equality of opportunity in terms of maximizing the child's chances of personal development, which might well not take place without intervention, and they might call for improved career guidance for the same basic reason. Here one can discern the influence of a tendency in Soviet pedagogy and psychology which was important during the 1920s, was eclipsed in the 1930s, and re-emerged gradually in the period reviewed: an interest in the child as an individual, extending incidentally to the study of abilities. Finally, approval might combine both societal and individual orientations: more efficient teaching and a more sensitive pedagogy based on a concern about the fulfillment of both obvious and hidden potential are presumably in the interests of the individual and the society alike.

Methodological problems. That there was such a range of attitudes to the problem in the Soviet Union gradually became clear as the earlier study took shape. But the assessment of their relative importance remained, at the end of the work, a matter of hunch and informed guesswork; and it was rather crude. Could anything be done at first to crystalize and then to refine it? So the above typology was developed as a conceptual tool, in the hope that the complex of interrelated issues might then be perceived more clearly, and comparison facilitated. Especially if some form of quantification could be applied, it ought to highlight dominant attitudes at different times, and thus indicate change, prompting possible explanations.

Very real problems, however, confront the Western student of social change in the USSR. True, ever the last twenty years or so Soviet sociologists have been setting to work again, and more empirical research is available than one might think; but they do not appear to have turned their attention to our topic. It was Oskar Anweiler (1979) who pointed out that no systematic Soviet study on it existed - none at all, from any disciplinary standpoint. If it is a hot potato, how much hotter for the Western scholar.

Nearly all Western work on the USSR is written on the basis of data which have been collected from the Soviet press, learned journals and so on, and which therefore have potentially been subjected to purposeful editorial intervention and censorship. Thus further difficulties spiral: the material is already affected by its authors' perceptions and prejudices; it may be editorially biased; and the foreigner then brings his own perceptions and prejudices to bear on it. But let us not be deterred by this recipe for inaction. The first of these three difficulties for researchers and research designers, subjectivity is an occupational hazard. So we press on, consoled by the fact that awareness of danger is the best prophylactic.

In the case under review it was decided to count the instances of expressions of opinion on the subject of provision for high-ability children in material gathered for the period 1958-73 and then to explore how far an analysis of them could go. The crucial question here, since it could not possibly be claimed that all expressions of opinion recorded in print had been located, was one of representativeness; and it was unanswerable. The most that could be said was that the material was spread fairly evenly over the 16-year period, and that there was quite good continuity and representativeness of bibliographical sources (Note 3).

Thus the data had their limitations, and it would be foolish to claim a high degree of scientific reliability for the results achieved. On the other hand, evidence of any kind was preferable to no evidence at all, as long as one treated it not as conclusive but, at most, as indicative. With these caveats it was felt worthwhile to proceed.

Procedure

Method and rationale. The raw material gathered for **Paths to Excellence** was re-examined and mentions of provision for high ability were extracted and initially recorded and cross referenced by type of attitude, period, and type of provision. In general, only original Soviet sources were used; foreigners' reports and comment were not included unless they cited specific Soviet individuals not otherwise noted. The initial attributions were then checked three times, mainly to give further thought to borderline cases.

Attitudes were classified as hostile, supportive and neutral. With rare exceptions, each source was registerd once only; but occasionally a single article might sum up a debate by citing several contributors with differing viewpoints, who were then listed individually, and very occasionally indeed a single contributor might present both sides of a case with equal cogency, in which event two entries were made. "Neutral" is therefore to be understood not as "objective" but as "indifferent" or "devoid of evaluative comment" (Note 4). Hostile and supportive attitudes were further broken down, according to their orientation, into societal, individual and unspecified. At the same time, stances straddling the societal-individual divide were noted: "combined," whether hostile or supportive, means either that societally and individually oriented attitudes were separately discernible, or that the argument put forward had both societal and individual implications. "Unspecified" means that general support or opposition was expressed without explanatory comment.

The four year (sometimes eight year) periodization was chosen in the expectation that change would thereby become more apparent, but there is some historical justification for the division. The year 1958 saw a great debate on polytechnism, harbingering the Khrushchev reform, and an important secondary debate on special provision for gifted children. The period 1962-65 brought the rundown of the reform and the rise of the special schools. The completion of the work of the Curriculum Commission and the resultant decree entitles us to regard 1966 as a watershed year. In 1966-69 there followed the initial implementation of the curriculum reform and moves considerably to extend the remit of special provision. The years 1970-73 betokened a re-emergence of the vocational principle which also began to affect the character of some major types of such provision.

The forms of provision envisaged in the basic analysis were as follows: unstated special schools; special schools for the arts; special sports schools; language schools; mathematics and physics boarding schools; mass schools with a special profile; and differentiation (i.e., a differentiated approach to teaching, in ordinary schools; although this included various organizational forms, it tended to be advocated or rejected on principle). All the above schools ranked as general (i.e., not technical) day schools. "Unstated" refers mainly to 1958 and to what were then conventionally labeled "schools for gifted children." Since all these categories of provision were controversial, it was decided that "differentiation" should exclude options (electives); their right to exist was undisputed and to have included the considerable amount of material on them would have unnecessarily inflated the support for differentiation. Extracurricular facilities were also omitted because of their general acceptability.

One further point should be mentioned. After the initial calculations were completed, the scope of the enquiry was extended to take heed of the occupational groups of contributors of material, and finally the major sources themselves, since in the USSR these tend to represent broadly indentifiable interests of one kind or another.

Towards an analysis of attitudes. A total of 382 expressions of attitude, including neutrality as defined above, were recorded over the sixteen year term. The basic results are summarized in Table 1 by period and Table 2 by type of provision.

The most striking feature of Table 1 is that expressions of support overall (nearly 60%) greatly outweigh those of hostility (some 25%), yet we have seen that just before the end of our period, special schools probably comprised under 3% of all general day schools with a senior course. One's first thought might be that this merely reflects a high degree of consensus about the desirability of provision for children of very high ability; since special schools tend to be smaller than average, one is forcibly reminded of the view of some Western psychologists that perhaps 2.3% of the population can be classified as of very superior intelligence (IQ 130+). Apart from the controversial nature of psychometry, however, this reaction leaves too much unsaid. Given the traditional (although not ubiquitous) Soviet suspicion of the notion of general intelligence, might not all this support have led us to expect a greater amount of provision so as to cater

Table 1

Summary of Expressions of Attitude to Provision for Gifted* Children in the USSR, 1958-73, by Period

Period	Hostile	Neutral	Supportive	Total
1958-61	44	5	61	110
%	40.0	4.5	55.5	100
1962-65	15	9	67	91
%	16.5	9.9	73.6	100
1966-69	21	20	59	100
%	21.0	20.0	59.0	100
1970-73	17	23	41	81
%	21.0	28.4	50.6	100
Total	97	57	222	382
%	25.4	14.9	59.7	100

*Throughout these tables, "gifted" is used elastically; although the Soviet discussion is sometimes conducted in terms of giftedness (odarennost'), reference is more often to a high level of ability (sposobnost') or abilities.

---

adequately for special talents, consequently covering up to 5% of the school population (Vernon, Adamson, Vernon, 1977)? Indeed, given the traditional abhorrence of privilege in Soviet schooling, once the dam had been breached why stop there?

The point is that much more cognizance should be taken of conflict. A general study of educational developments over this period leaves one with the feeling that the table understates the extent of actual hostility; and it is in the nature of things that advocates of change are more vociferous than those who resist it. The base from which the build up began was extremely low, provision for special intellectual abilities was virtually unprecedented at this level of education in the USSR, there was enormous resistance for various reasons from all sectors of Soviet society to the notion of departure from the principle of the unified school (Dunstan, 1978), and consequently an immense propaganda effort had to be expended in order to achieve relatively modest though disproportionately significant results. We must remember, however, not to see the matter solely in terms of special schools; as Table 2 shows, nearly one quarter of expressions of support concerned differentiation, and that principle triumphed resoundingly, at least in theory, in 1966.

It is not remarkable that hostile attitudes were at their most numerous at the beginning of the period (40%), when the idea of a radical departure from tradition was broached, or that supportive ones peaked in 1962-65 (73.6%) when conative concerns were ceding to cognitive ones and special schools were just beginning to ride the crest of the wave of official acceptability. By 1970-73 the matter had become less topical and controversy had subsided, the facilities had evidently come to stay, and we note an increase in neutral, matter-of-fact treatment of them (28.4%, overtaking hostile comment).

Table 2 is constructed differently to show the relative importance of various types of provision in exemplifying different attitudes. It reveals that the most discussed types of provision were, in descending order of frequency of reference, maths and physics boarding schools (FMShs), mass schools with special profile, differentiation, and, after a considerable gap, unstated special schools. Over a quarter of all references and nearly a third of supportive ones concerned the FMShs, reflecting not least the frequent infatuation of the press with the "schools for future Lomonosovs" (Note 5). The rather low representation of the arts schools is hardly surprising, considering

Table 2

Summary of Expressions of Attitude to
Provision for Gifted Children, USSR,
1958-73, by Type of Provision

School Type	Hostile	Neutral	Supportive	Total
Unstated	34	1	10	45
Special, %	35.1	1.8	4.4	11.8
Arts	5	10	23	38
%	5.2	17.5	10.1	9.9
Sports	2	6	9	17
%	2.1	10.5	3.9	4.5
Language	5	10	10	25
%	5.2	17.5	4.4	6.5
Math-Physics	15	13	73	101
Boarding, %	15.5	22.8	32.0	26.4
Special	17	15	49	81
Profile, %	17.5	26.3	21.5	21.2
Differen-	19	2	54	75
tiation, %	19.6	3.5	23.7	19.6
Total	97	57	228	382
%	100	100	100	100

their unique pedigree, and that of the sports boarding schools, still lower, may be due to their slightness of development before the second half of our period - even by 1973 they had only passed the 20 mark and to ambivalent Soviet attitudes to professionalism in sport. The FMShs were even fewer, but enjoyed unparalleled kudos.

The one really astonishing feature of Table 2 is the ostensible lack of public interest in the language schools. It must be remembered that they comprised the largest group of special schools, slightly larger than the special profile mass schools, yet the latter are over three times more conspicuous. Indeed, relatively, though not absolutely, expressions of attitude hostile to the language schools (5.2%) exceeded supportive ones (4.4%), and of no other type of provision could this be said. This most interesting phenomenon cannot be explained with certainty. But a possible explanation is latent official concern about their public image. Also, the censor may have been at work.

Set up originally on utilitarian grounds, as we have seen, language schools soon became greatly sought after because they were thought to offer something special. The claim that they were not initially intended to be selective (except in the mild sense of excluding children physically unlikely to cope) sounds genuine, but demand alone was enough to cause them rapidly to become so. Proven ability in a foreign language was never the major criterion for admission that it was in music or physics for schools with those profiles; in any case, with recruitment at the age of six or seven it could scarcely have been so, except perhaps for those whose parents had paid for them to be taught a foreign language in nursery school. So what counted most often was parental aspirations and savoir faire. Straws in the wind suggest that the authorities became very unhappy about the unseemly scramble for places at institutions which came to be uniquely redolent of the officially anathematized grammar school or lycée. Criticism started to appear in 1966, according to our data, but in absolute terms was even more limited than approval. Presumably it was not thought desirable to encourage public discussion of the schools and the dubious behavior they engendered, all the more so since (as with special profile schools) the children of the intelligentsia and thus of the influential tended to be over-represented in them (Note 6).

Paucity of data causes us regretfully to abandon further discussion of the language schools, for our part; and the same applies to arts and sports schools. Table 3 breaks down Tables 1 and 2 into the four categories of provision on which information is fuller. Little additional comment, however, is needed. Expressions of attitude to unstated special schools are naturally bunched at the beginning of the period because it was only later that individual types expanded and attracted more notice. Of the 32 expressions of hostility, 27 date from 1958, reflecting the general indignation then articulated at the proposed departure from the unified schools structure. Already, however, there was evidence of support for particular kinds of provision, which in the case of the mathematics and physics boarding schools and the special profile schools peaked in the period immediately following their respective official recognition; they could now be extoled with the confidence born of legitimation. But the need for continued support suggests that they were by no means immune from criticism.

The category "differentiation" presents a dissimilar picture: here support was strongest before the 1966 decree and opposition apparently increased immediately thereafter (the data indeed refer to 1967 and 1968). This somewhat contradictory situation may be explicable partly by the umbrella-like character of the term and partly by the educational climate of the early to mid-1960s. Between 1956 and 1963 there was considerable canvassing, led by eminent educationists but ultimately unsuccessful, for a form of differentiation known as "furkatsiya" (furcation), that is, branching of senior stage of general schooling into groups of special subjects. In 1964-66 the Curriculum Commission was at work and differentiation within general schools, usually conceived as a more flexible approach to the class unit and the individual pupil, was in the air. But the 1966 decree legitimated special intensive classes and sometimes, especially in 1967, this led to proposals for, and experimental instances of, forms of differentiation on the basis of pupil performance, which evoked howls of protest (Dunstan, 1978). Moreover, mixed ability teaching by groups, while officially commended, also met with resistance on egalitarian grounds (sometimes perhaps a rationalization of unwillingness to change).

In Table 4 an attempt is made to break down expressions of hostility and support yet further in accordance with the typology. Over the whole period, it appears that hostile attitudes were predominantly individually oriented (55.2%), and supportive ones more societally (45.2%) than individually directed (39.9%), though in the latter case the difference was slight. It should be noted that over a third of contributors in each instance took a broader ("combined") view, but for immediate purposes of comparison have been regarded as sharing the two orientations equally and thus not materially affecting the picture. Individual-hostile and societal-supportive attitudes were particularly in evidence in the first half of the period, while in the second half the individual and the societal drew closer together, somewhat blurring the picture. Can an interpretation of these patterns be offered?

The most likely explanation is that people simply adapted themselves to the prevailing economic and political climate. Let us first examine this in relation to support. About 1960, as has been mentioned above, national need became a paramount consideration. This was a major cause of the curriculum enquiry of the mid-1960s. In its turn, however, the enquiry opened out the interest in individual abilities and talents. This had been present earlier, but it had been neglected and was much narrower in concept, whereas by the end of the decade it was being translated into action.

As to opposition, we suggest that in 1958, although public debate had become much freer, the atmosphere was scarcely relaxed enough for more than a little public pillorying of existing institutions (special arts schools) for the alleged contravention of basic

Table 3

Expressions of Attitude to Provision for
Gifted Children, USSR, 1958-73, by Period
and Selected Type of Provision

Type	Hostile	Neutral	Supportive	Total
Unstated Special Schools				
1958-61	32	1	7	40
1962-65	2		2	4
1966-69			1	1
1970-73				
Total	34	1	10	45
%	75.6	2.2	22.2	100
Math-Physics Boarding Schools				
1958-61	1		4	5
1962-65	6	4	32	42
1966-69	3	4	25	32
1970-73	5	5	12	22
Total	15	13	73	101
%	14.9	12.9	72.3	100
Special Profile Schools				
1958-61	5	1	11	17
1962-65	1	1	9	11
1966-69	6	10	16	32
1970-73	5	3	13	21
Total	17	15	49	81
%	21.0	18.5	60.5	100
Differentiation				
1958-61	3	1	19	23
1962-65	5	1	21	27
1966-69	10		10	27
1970-73	1		4	5
Total	19	2	54	75
%	25.3	2.7	72.0	100

principles of social justice. It was easier to criticize proposed but nonexistent schools on these grounds. But objections mostly found expression on the much more personalized level of the potentially detrimental effects of the given schools on individual boys and girls, and continued to do so for some time. By the early 1970s the situation was changing. There had been well over a decade of relative freedom in educational debate and sociologists had been able to devote a fair amount of their attention to educational matters. New kinds of special schools for children of high and very high ability had now existed in sufficient numbers and over a sufficiently long period to justify a stocktaking exercise which was to raise some fundamental social questions. Moreover, since in the wake of the curriculum reform differentiated methods had penetrated at least some of the mass schools, certain of these questions were beginning to acquire wider significance.

Table 4

Expressions of Attitude to Provision for Gifted Children, USSR, 1958-73, All Types of Provision, by Period and Orientation

Orientation	Societal	Individual	Unspecified	Total
Hostile				
1958-61	13.5	22.5	8	44
1966-69	8	13		21
1970-73	9.5	7.5		17
Total	34.5	53.5	9	97
%	35.6	55.2	9.3	100
Supportive				
1958-61	21.5	17.5	22	61
1962-65	35.5	26.5	5	67
1966-69	26	28	5	59
1970-73	20	19	2	41
Total	103	91	34	228
%	45.2	39.9	149	100

Such were the general trends in attitude orientation, but did they vary much between different types of provision? For closer examination of this we turn to Table 5. Here the basic periods are octennial, partly to present a more straightforward juxtaposition of data, partly to reduce the number of very small quantities, and partly to highlight the contrast on either side of the watershed years 1965 and 1966. Again, expressions of the combined perspective have been divided equally between societal and individual. Among hostile attitudes, we note that the individual orientation (55.3%) exceeded the societal (34.1%) throughout but was less marked in the second octennium; that this reflects the increase in wider concerns mentioned above seems probable, despite the meagerness of the material. Societal-hostile views were never a majority orientation for any of these types of provision. It is noteworthy, however, that opinion with regard to differentiation within the mass school was evenly divided.

Turning to supportive attitudes, we find that the societally directed outstripped the individually oriented in the first octennium (with the exception of differentiation), while in the second eight year period this feature was slightly reversed. Among the advocates of mathematics and physics boarding schools, considerations of national need were still just strong enough to prevail during the second period, despite the general retreat from such positions. After 1966 the individual-supportive stance generally gained ground with the widened interest in pupil potential opened up by the curriculum reform. Its predominance throughout both periods in the case of differentiation within the mass school is not surprising when one reflects that such a connection is, after all, intrinsic.

Let us turn now to scrutinize contributors to the debate, enumerated in Table 6. The high proportion of retrievable occupations (nearly 70%) is due mainly to the fact that in the USSR writers of published letters and articles usually state their occupation. The sample is heavily biased towards the education professions,

Table 5

Attitude to Provision for Gifted Children, USSR, 1958-73, by Main Period, Selected Type of Provision and Orientation

	Hostile			Supportive		
	58-65	66-73	Total	58-65	66-73	Total
Unstated Special Schools						
Societal	10.5		10.5	4	1	5
Individual	15.5		15.5	3		3
Unspecified	8		8	2		2
Total	34		34	9	1	10
Math-Physics Boarding Schools						
Societal	1.5	3.5	5	21.5	18.5	40
Individual	5.5	4.5	10	10.5	16.5	27
Unspecified				4	2	6
Total	7	8	15	36	37	73
Special Profile Schools						
Societal	0.5	4	4.5	10	11.5	21.5
Individual	5.5	7	12.5	5	14.5	19.5
Unspecified				5	3	8
Total	6	11	17	20	29	49
Differentiation						
Societal	3.5	5.5	9	16.5	4.5	21
Individual	3.5	5.5	9	22.5	9.5	32
Unspecified	1		1	1		1
Total	8	11	19	40	14	54
All Four Types						
Societal	16	13	29	52	35.5	87.5
Individual	30	17	47	41	40.5	81.5
Unspecified	9		9	12	5	17
Total	55	30	85	105	81	186

% for All Four Types		
Societal	34.1	47.0
Individual	55.3	43.8
Unspecified	10.6	9.1

educationists, psychologists, teachers and administrators at all levels together constituting 37.4%, and if we add scientists and other academics this rises to 58.9%. Given this particular issue, the bias towards the world of education is understandable, and has probably been increased by extensive use of the educational press; the Soviet man in the street is accustomed to listen respectfully to the experts, but in this case it is a pity that his voice cannot be more clearly heard.

The contributor groups having been identified, Table 7 proceeds to examine the distribution of attitudes of the three major ones. All these groups at first displayed the high level of hostility which characterized the start of the sixteen-year period, but thereafter educationists and psychologists, though predominantly supportive, were somewhat more critical of special provision than teachers and far more than scientists; the overall ratios of hostility to support were respectively 1:2.1, 1:2.9 and 1:6.6. The educationists' considerable backing for such facilities in the years leading up to the curriculum reform gave way, it seems, to much dissatisfaction with some of its immediate consequences. The scientists, on the other hand, remained staunch advocates of special provision once the rift in their ranks was healed by Academician Lavrent'ev's conversion to the FMSh idea in 1961 (Note 7). Reading their remarks, one feels how much more pragmatic they tended to be as a group than their educationist colleagues. On this issue at least, "education workers" appeared relatively more responsive to ideological principle.

When the attempt was made to break down these attitudes further according to orientation, it was again bedeviled in part by very small quantities; nevertheless certain observations can be made and conclusions

Table 6

Contributors to Coverage of Provision for Gifted Children, USSR, 1958-73

	1958-61	1962-65	1966-69	1970-73	Total	Average
Educationists and Psychologists						
	26	30	16	9	81	21.2
Scientists						
	12	19	19	11	61	16.0
Teachers						
	15	7	8	3	33	8.6
Educational Administrators (Union or Republic level)						
	5	5	11	2	23	6.0
Academics (note a)						
	3	2	12	4	21	5.5
Supreme Soviet Deputies						
	12				12	3.1
Party Officials						
	6	2	1		9	2.4
Others (note b)						
	15		4	5	24	6.3
Unspecified						
	16	26	29	47	118	30.9
Total						
	110	91	100	81	382	100

(a) Either unspecified or other than educationists, psychologists and scientists; (b) local educational administrators, workers and skilled workers, and sportsmen and commentators (6 each); government ministers, enterprise directors and students (2 each).

---

drawn (Table 8). Were the combined perspective to have been listed separately, it would have predominated overall at about 40% of expressions of attitude; but once again it was split equally to swell the two contrasting ones. The individual orientation was strongly in the lead (56.4% against 30.8%) with

Table 7

Expressions of Attitude to Provision
Gifted Children, USSR, 1958–73,
by Period and Major Contributor Group

	58-61	62-65	66-69	70-73	Total	%
Educationists and Psychologists						
Hostile	8	7	5	3	23	28.4
Neutral	2	2	5	1	10	12.3
Supportive	16	21	6	5	48	59.3
Total	26	30	16	9	81	100
Scientists						
Hostile	5		1	2	8	13.1
Neutral						
Supportive	7	19	18	9	53	86.9
Total	12	19	19	11	61	100
Teachers						
Hostile	6		2		8	24.2
Neutral		2			2	6.1
Supportive	9	5	6	3	23	69.7
Total	15	7	8	3	33	100

regard to hostile views but less so in respect of supportive ones (44% against 41.5%), mainly because of the scientists. This group showed a greater tendency to societally directed support than the other groups, probably because such arguments (plus the societal element in the combined ones) would carry most weight with the Party and government leadership whom they hoped to convince, although after 1966 they were not unaffected by the movement towards wider differentiation.

It is of interest that, alone among all three groups and both divisions of attitude, supportive campaigning by scientists received at least as much attention from 1966 onwards as before that year,

Table 8

Attitudes to Provision for Gifted Children, USSR, 1958-73, by Main Period, Major Contributor Group and Orientation

	Hostile			Supportive		
	58-65	66-73	Total	58-65	66-73	Total
Educationists and Psychologists						
Societal	4	3	7	15	3.5	18.5
Individual	9	5	14	15	6.5	21.5
Unspecified	2		2	7	1	8
Total	15	8	23	37	11	48
Scientists						
Societal	1.5	1	2.5	13.5	12	25.5
Individual	1.5	2	3.5	9.5	12	21.5
Unspecified	2		2	3	3	6
Total	5	3	8	26	27	53
Teachers						
Societal	1.5	1	2.5	3	4.5	7.5
Individual	3.5	1	4.5	7	4.5	11.5
Unspecified	1		1	4		4
Total	6	2	8	14	9	23
All Three Groups						
Societal	7	5	12	31.5	20	51.5
Individual	14	8	22	31.5	23	54.5
Unspecified	5		5	14	4	18
Total	26	13	39	77	47	134
% for All Three Groups						
Societal			30.8			41.5
Individual			56.4			44.0
Unspecified			12.8			14.5

presumably because the sort of provision that they favored (mathematics and physics boarding schools and mass schools with special profile) required constant backing in the face of continued opposition. Table 5 is relevant here, although we know from Table 3 that in the 1970s a more sober outlook came to prevail.

We have already remarked that educationists and psychologists and to a lesser extent teachers, though mainly supportive, nevertheless seem to have had a significant number of people among their ranks with serious misgivings about, or objections to, special provision. In the case of the educationists most of all, hostility was more clearly individually oriented than societally, although several combined these concerns. It is regretted that the response from the chalkface was so slight; there is other evidence that teachers in particular were unenthusiastic about mixed ability teaching through groups, and one has a strong suspicion that many of them treated the slogan "a differentiated approach to every pupil" as an irritating exhortation from the ivory tower.

To draw this section to a close, we examine some of the vehicles that carried our data. Serial publications in the USSR can be identified with particular organizations: thus **Pravda** is the Communist Party newspaper, **Izvestiya** that of the government, **Uchitel'skaya gazeta** that of the Ministry of Public Education jointly with the education workers' union, **Sovetskaya pedagogika** is the monthly journal of the Academy of Pedagogical Sciences, and **Narodnoe obrazovanie** that of the Ministry of Public Education. Together they accounted for 57.1% of the materials. In Table 9 we discern something of the relative importance of this issue among them and the line they took on it.

The hostility/support ratios were: **Sovetskaya pedagogika,** 1:4.8; **Izvestiya,** 1:3.3; **Pravda,** 1:2.2; **Uchitel'skaya gazeta,** 1:1.9; **Narodnoe obrazovanie,** 1:1; and others (not shown), 1:2.3, which approximates to the mean for all contributors. **Uchitel'skaya gazeta,** with its readership of teachers, educationists and

Table 9
Expressions of Attitude to Provision
for Gifted Children, USSR, 1958-73,
by Period and Selected Printed Sources

	58-61	62-65	66-69	70-73	Total
Pravda					
Hostile	7	1	1	2	11
Neutral	1	1	1		3
Supportive	12	6	5	1	24
Total	20	8	6	4	38
Izvestiya					
Hostile	8	3		1	12
Neutral	1	1			2
Supportive	10	16	8	5	39
Total	19	20	8	6	53
Uchitel'skaya gazeta					
Hostile	13	1	4	5	23
Neutral	1	3	7	9	20
Supportive	18	9	6	11	44
Total	32	13	17	25	87
Sovetskaya pedagogika					
Hostile	2	1	1		4
Neutral			1	3	4
Supportive	6	8	5		19
Total	8	9	7	3	27
Narodnoe obrazovanie					
Hostile		3	3		6
Neutral			1		1
Supportive	1	3	3		6
Total	1	6	6		13

administrators was naturally exercised over the matter, and, alone of the publications cited, maintained its interest throughout the period; though predominantly supportive, it also displayed minor but significant degree of hostility which we have come to expect particularly of the educational rank and file. The part newspaper **Pravda** and the government one **Izvestiya** were equally involved in the heated debate at the start of the period, but whereas for the former the issue rapidly receded into the background, the latter was advocating special schools (mainly FMShs) still more vigorously in 1962-65, and with greater coverage than any other paper mentioned. Concern about economic development may explain this support, but not the different interest shown by the two main papers.

The enthusiasm of the government newspaper and the moderate support of the national teachers' newspaper contrast oddly, in different ways, with the attitudes of the two sections of the education leadership respresented by **Narodnoe obrazovanie** and **Sovetskaya pedagogika.** If **Izvestiya** expressed strong majority approval at national government level for special provision, at least by 1962-65, encouraged no doubt by the powerful scientific lobby who found ready access to the paper's columns, the national educational administration exemplified by **Narodnoe obrazovanie,** who would have to find the resources for implementing the new policy, had very mixed feelings about the matter. Perhaps they preferred to play it down. Leading educationists, on the other hand, writing in **Sovetskaya pedagogika,** tended to be markedly in favor of special provision until they became preoccupied by other concerns at the turn of the decade.

This enquiry has once again demonstrated for the period under review the falsity of the old stereotype of the Soviet Union as a cowed society unquestioningly implementing policy decisions formulated on the Party heights. Some areas are, of course, a good deal more sensitive than others; but in education there is generally public participation in policy formulation, and different groups may have different interests and accordingly express different opinions. As time passes and circumstances change, they may become more vociferous or less so. Even when some of them have their way and the desired outcome is enshrined in law, there may be practical impediments to its realization, and opposition may continue to surface occasionally. Indeed, the groups themselves may be extremely diverse entities. Despite their known affiliations, the newspapers and journals cited in Table 9 all put forward widely ranging views; the same is true of the professional groups appearing in Tables 7 and 8. But, to make a point which the tables do not show, the position is even more complex than this; apart from its orientation, support or hostility within a given group may possess a multifaceted character. Advocates of facilities for high ability children may favor a broad sprectum of such provision; they may advocate a particular form or forms of it; or they may express strong general or particular support while singling out some aspects for criticism. They may even change their minds. The present study is not designed to show these complexities, but rather to indicate and explain general trends and orientations in attitudes; for purposes of generalization such refinements are unimportant, but we should perhaps remember that they exist.

Finally, it is necessary to put the topic in perspective. After this concentrated scrutiny one might be forgiven for thinking that it was a major national talking point for years on end. But as soon as one reflects that an intensive search produced only an annual average of about 24 references, one realizes that this was not so. The nearest it came to be such was late in 1958, and even then it was only one of several issues in the polytechnization debate. Nevertheless, its ideological implications invest the relatively few contributions with an importance that might be difficult to attach to much greater numbers on a less controversial matter.

Summary and Conclusion

Over the whole period 1958-73, expressions of support for special provision for gifted children in the USSR greatly outnumbered those of hostility, while hostile attitudes, though present throughout, were most conspicuous at the outset. This is explained by the low starting base, by the strong ideological objections which were provoked by proposals radically to alter the status quo, and by the immense effort which had to be expended not only to overcome initial resistance but thereafter to contain it. It thereupon slowly decreased, firstly as interest shifted to more accessible forms of provision, and subsequently as the emergence of other curricular concerns brought a less partisan mood.

As the epitome of academic excellence, the mathematics and physics boarding schools occupied the center of the stage in 1962-65, amidst far more cheers than catcalls, but thenceforth had to share it with mass schools with a special profile and the issue of differentiation of the ordinary school. In contrast, language schools evoked so little publicity, although they formed the largest group of special schools, that there are strong grounds for thinking that discussion was discouraged; what there was evinced an unusually high ratio of hostility to support. The backing received by special profile mass schools after legitimation in 1966 was not matched by that for mass school differentiation, most likely because of the width of breach of egalitarian principle which the latter seemed to imply, official policy notwithstanding.

Classifying attitudes in closer accordance with the typology, one concludes from Table 4 that overall hostile attitudes were in the main individually oriented, and supportive ones primarily societally oriented, in addition to which it should be remembered that a good third of contributors combined these orientations. But these attitudes were more distinct in the first half of the period than the second, presumably because at the earlier stage national need was a paramount consideration, while the latter stage saw a much greater interest in individual abilities, promoted by the curriculum reform. Conversely, in the earlier period criticism based on implications for the individual was easier than on societal grounds, whereas by the early 1970s sociologists had gained more confidence and much differentiated provision was ripe for stocktaking.

The debate was dominated by educationists and scientists and to a lesser extent by other workers at all levels of education. In general, scientists were highly supportive, and educationists and teachers noticeably more critical, though still mainly in favor. The less satisfactory outcomes of the curriculum reform gave educationists food for thought. Combined (societally and individualy oriented) perspectives predominated; apart from that, teachers' and educationists' attitudes were chiefly individually directed and those of scientists societally directed, though the quantitative differences between the two contrasting orientations were too small to make much of this.

As to the press, the government organ showed a significant amount of support for special provision and the leading education research journal was clearly in favor, contrasting markedly with the divided attitude of the journal of the education ministry, responsible for implementing policy changes, and to a lesser extent with the moderate support of the education ministry and union paper. Overall, a great diversity of viewpoints was apparent, and circumstances might cause attitudes to change.

Afterword. In conclusion, let me issue a plea, make a suggestion, and ask a question. The plea: when studying the problem of provision for gifted children, it is essential to consider the wider context. If this seems platitudinous, let us just reflect how much discussion of the subject takes place in a political vacuum. Developments in the USSR showed that the failure and success of attempts to implement a program were intimately linked with contemporary educational policy in general, with ideological imperatives, and with changing sociopolitical and socioeconomic circumstances. It is likely that this will be applicable elsewhere, even in a very different social system. If it is not heeded, the probability of being able to achieve very much will be slight.

Next the suggestion: if we wish to bring about change, we must evaluate and re-evaluate the current political-economic situation and develop and adjust our strategy and tactics accordingly. The question of special provision can be argued either way, but for immediate purposes let us assume that it is the desideratum. It is probably easiest to win this when one can reason convincingly that it is in the national interest. In the USSR it was the combined-supportive and societal-supportive stances that predominated, probably because they brought the better results. As was advanced at the beginning of this paper, the combined-supportive orientation arguably has the virtue of being socially unifying and focused more on potential than achievement; in spirit at least, it is universalist. As such, it comes to meet all except really hard line egalitarians. But it is its societal-supportive element, I suspect, that most influences tough minded governments. The powerful scientific lobby seem to have been the chief instigators of that amazing breach with tradition in the Soviet Union of the 1960s. Educationists tended to be individual-oriented in their attitudes, and, not to mention their unimpressive disunity, it is doubtful that their individual-supportive stance carried much weight with the political leadership. Is there a moral in that for us?

And lastly the question: how far indeed can we learn from the Soviet experience? To revert to the last point, for example, it may be that an individual-supportive stance would after all be more effective in a society less collectively-oriented than the USSR. We need further studies of the relationship between context and dominant attitudes and policy-making and implementation on this issue of special provision for clever children. We need them for other countries, and preferably on a superior data base to what has perforce had to be used because of the peculiarly intractable problems of Soviet area research. Only by bringing such studies together will we be able to generalize safely about the most effective means to achieve our goals.

Notes
1. I am grateful to my colleague Dr. Philip Hanson for his comments on this section of the paper.
2. Derived by setting unit totals against totals for general day schools in **Narodnoe Obrazovanie, nauka i kul'tura v SSSR** (Moscow: **Statistika,** 1977), pp. 26-27.
3. Notably, **Current Digest of the Soviet Press,** its weekly index to **Pravda** and **Izvestiya,** and the French **Bulletin signaletique du Centre National pour la Recherche Scientifique: Philosophie: 3e partie** for virtually the whole period; **Annual Education Bibiography of the International Bureau of Education,** 1958-1969; the Library of Congress **Monthly Index to Russian Accessions,** 1959-1968; **Ezhegodnik knigi SSSR,** 1958-1967; **Literatura po pedagogicheskim naukam,** 1964-1973; **Soviet Studies Information Supplement** (later **ABSEES**), 1964-1973.
4. The idea of neutrality presented a problem. If the sources had been much more numerous, it might have been felt necessary to distinguish between "objective" and "non-evaluative" in a different way. In the circumstances, since truly objective appraisals were minimal, it was thought more useful to register the two orientations, for example, the same balanced account might be both societal-supportive and individual-hostile. Nonevaluative or indifferent comment was deemed worthy of note since it comprised a significant part (14.9%) of total mentions; without it the sample would have seemed excessively polarized and restricted.
5. M. V. Lomonosov (1711-65), scientist, poet, lexicographer, founder of Moscow University, and the archetypal Russian genius.
6. In the early 1970s, children from white collar workers' and specialists' families formed 58.5% of the

pupil complement at special schools, and 32.5% at ordinary schools (**Vysshaya shkola kak faktor izmeneniya sotsial'noi struktury razvitogo sotsialisticheskogo obshchestva** (Moscow: Nauka, 1978, p. 65).
7. For debates on the desirability of maths and physics boarding schools see pp. 116-123. Dunstan, 1978.

References

Anweiler, O. Review of J. Dunstan, Paths to excellence and the Soviet school. International Review of Education, 1979, 25, 564.

Bruner, J. S. The process of education. Cambridge, Massachesetts: Harvard University Press, 1977.

Dunstan, J. Paths to excellence and the Soviet school. Windsor, Berks, U.K.: NFER Publishing, 1978.

Rutkevitch, M. N. & Filippov, F. R. Social sources of recruitment to the intelligentsia. In M. Yanowitch & W. A. Fischer (Eds.), Social stratification and mobility in the USSR. While Plains, New York: International Arts & Science Press, 1973.

Vernon, P. E., Adamson, G. & Vernon, D. F. The psychology and education of gifted children. London: Methuen, 1977.

22

THE GIFTED IN A DEVELOPING SOCIETY: THE NIGERIA CASE

Henry Olajide Oluyele Coker

Academics and practitioners of education, psychology, political science and public administration should, indeed, be jointly involved in the search of identification techniques and various strategies to be of assistance to the gifted. All these fields have certain commonalities in the pursuit of excellence. Political scientists are interested in alternative public policies, the democratic and antidemocratic ecological variables of such policies, public opinion and pressure groups, political culture, modernization, power authority, and the entire public policy process of the political system (a la Easton) which entails demand, support, conversion process, and decision or outcome. These are concepts, ideas and issues of political science which are pertinent to public policy on the gifted and talented - an educational and psychological area of concern.

Similarly, public administrators are concerned with public policy process, administrative discretion and responsibility, innovation and its management, development administration, recruitment and selection of public personnel and the like. The search for the most appropriate method of testing and recruitment of the ablest and the talented under a merit system continues, from culture to culture, in the field of public administration. Creativity is a preoccupation of this discipline because of its bearing on administrative discretion, innovation and initiative. I see these as being of equal concern to disciplines interested in the talented and gifted in the developed and developing societies.

This paper is intended to explore the circumstances or ecology of public policy on the gifted in Nigeria. It will examine the educational policy of the country and the place of the gifted under such a scheme. The thesis of the paper, however, is simply that political, professional, public and administrative neglect has conspired against a functional public policy on the gifted in Nigeria whose primary attention is the achievement of universal free and compulsory education.

It is generally agreed that public policy concerning gifted children has usually undergone four phases. First is the recognition of the need for giving additional care (beyond the usual for the regular children) to the gifted child. The second phase concerns attempts to develop the appropriate, peculiar curricular methods and techniques of teaching to meet the needs of the talented. The third is evaluating the methods and techniques used to see if the needs are met. The fourth involves strengthening the program at work which entails correcting deficiencies. While such a political culture like the Anglo-American has already reached the third and fourth phases, Nigeria's preindustrial political system is presently at the first phase. This stage of development in Nigeria with respect to the gifted will therefore be the focus of this pertinent paper. The questions of why, how and what next become pertinent.

The Concept of the Gifted

A chat with some colleagues when tossing with the idea of presenting this paper validates some commonly held assumptions. More than seventy-five percent of the fifteen professionals, from varied disciplines, were of the view that a call for a public policy on the gifted would be elitist, a political device that would be perpetually dominated by the existing ruling elite and a subjugation of the masses into permanent inferior education. Goetsch came to similar conclusions in his findings in the United States in 1940. Such a general consensus in an academic community should not be seen as an indictment of the future of Nigeria's technological advancement.

Webster's Dictionary defines the gifted as having a natural ability or aptitude; talented; notably superior in intelligence. Abraham (1958) has warned that there is no such thing as an accurate composite of a gifted child. Webster's definition, however, is a close approximation of the conventional, layman's view of the gifted.

Conceptual definitions from various scholars in the field range from those who equate giftedness with high intelligence quotient to those whose preference is in characteristic traits of the talented.

The American Psychology and Guidance Association (1961), offers a definition based on the Intelligence Quotient Scores of 115 or above for a talented child on a Stanford-Binet Intelligence Test. Such a child may at the same time have other special abilities which are not a variables into his classification into being a gifted child. Furthermore, he cites the Cleveland experiment where IQ 130 and above was the standard entry point for school enrolment as opposed to IQ 125 and above used in other parts of the United States. The disparity on the minimum score is noteworthy. Some psychologists might argue it is insignificant. The principal objection to the IQ measurement, I believe, is the cultural factor which has not been taken into consideration especially in a multicultural society such as Nigeria. Again why settle on 115? What of the scores of 110 or 140? Or does the variation in scores take the cultural factor into consideration. It is being suggested, for instance, that a TEDRO-Nigeria-Binet Test "if standardized" could be a more reliable test of Nigerian gifted children. The author did not suggest any minimum score (Nason, 1958); Nason runs away from some specific figure. To him the criterion is for the child to have "a very high score on general intelligence test."

Some resort to descriptive definitions of the phenomenon of "the gifted." Fair (1970) observes that the talented child is a pupil with an exceptionally high potential in one or more general or specific areas, whose potential cannot be adequately developed except with "special provisions within the curricular, extra-curricular, and counseling programs." Goddard (1928) simply says that the gifted child is at least a child of high intelligence (Hollingworth 1942). Witty (1951) defines it in functional terms, one whose performance is a potentially valuable and consistently remarkable. As with most descriptive definitions, they raise more problems than they offer solutions. What is "exceptionally high potential?" How high is "high intelligence"? How does Hollingworth arrive at her "top one percentage"? Nevertheless, they offer some concrete ideas about performance, human activity and potential. These ideas illuminate our notion of activity or potential activity, of the functional aspect of the talented.

The method of itemizing variables to define a concept is an easy way out in social sciences. However, sometimes it proves fruitful. To this end the unique role of the teacher in identifying the talented in his class cannot be overstated. Teachers according to Durr (1964) are to be equipped to look for such characteristics as above-average language development, persistence in attacking difficult mental tasks, the ability to generalize and see relationships, unusual curiosity and a wide variety of deep interest. As for parents, they are to detect certain peculiar traits which only parents can identify (Durr, 1964). They are to answer such questions as the following. Does he have a retentive memory? Does he show unusual interest in a number of relationships? Does he understand complex sentences? Love (1967) hastens to caution that rightly answering these questions does not always denote the gifted trait, nor is a gifted child bound to possess the listed characteristics. Dehaan (1961) envisages a school program, an institutional approach, rather than a teacher or parent individual type.

The main problem here is the amount of parochialism displayed by all these authors, in the cultural bias of most of the characteristics. The

331

general view of Love is that all parents are literate enough to identify the characteristics. Which of them are we to consider crucial enough to identify the gifted - since not all questions are to be answered? How does Durr intend to administer tests fo find out above-language development in a multi-linguistic society as Nigeria? What happens in Nigeria where the lingua franca is an alien, colonially introduced language which the majority of parents do not understand or speak? These are questions relevant for the Nigerian experience as it moves from the first phase into the other crucial ones. It is an attempt to alert us to anticipate possible problems and focus our research to this end.

Classical Approach to the Talented in Nigeria Society

Tradition recognizes the exceptionally brilliant in the Nigerian value system. Nigerian schools in the past had a special way of coping with talented children. Three methods in which they were motivated and compensated can be identified - grouping and streaming, accelerated or double promotion, and enrichment. The tradition which began in colonial days utilized the accelerated/double promotion method. Gifted children who might have to stay nine to ten years in primary school, for instance, spent only seven to eight. Such a child had no special curriculum. He simply went ahead of his age group pursuing the class course program and taking the same examinations as the rest of his new class.

Such a system of compensation was not institutionalized. The colonial government had no policy in this regard; neither did the mission schools. In fact, it was considered solely at the discretion of the teacher and the headmaster of the particular school. The parents had no input into such decisions. The child faces enormous problems in the context of Nigerian society. Olayinka points to the social gap created in terms of age differentiation. He also noted that in certain courses, like mathematics "which build progressively on a sequence of knowledge and skills, the practice of making a child skip a class, 'tends' to create a gap in the child's knowledge (of Mathematics)." Perhaps the most devastating effect, to me, is peer rejection or nonacceptance "especially if the child's teacher inadvertently plays up the child's superiority to the rest of the class." In our superstitious society the exceptionally brilliant might be considered an "abnormality" by his peers. He could be seen as a wizard, a product of some witchcraft, a user of "juju" or some magical powers. Rather than earn respect and legendry he might end up being an outcast, feared and considered harmful.

His own personality may temper or aggravate this type of dysfunctional characterization. If he were helpful to his colleagues, sociable and approachable he could be better understood. However, judging from my personal experiences, those talented classmates in my class in the primary school days were in most cases anything but sociable and approachable. They were indeed enigmatic, feared, unpenetrable personalities. Only when they reached high school and took public international examinations (like Cambridge School Certificate or London Matriculation) did they really earn the respect and appreciation they deserved. An added problem is that their achievement is limited by our form of educational system which often limits opportunity. The anecdote given above may be unscientific but that was a personal experience and personal perception, shared by my classmates about the few talented pupils in our primary school days.

Nigeria's Contemporary Educational Policy: The Legal and Constitutional Environment

Most of our uninstitutionalized, ad hoc and unspecific arrangements on the gifted in the past continue virtually unchanged. The continuity of the status quo in this regard is better understood within the context of our educational system and governmental policy, which in turn is an outcome of the broad national and constitutional objectives and policy. The Third National Development Plan (1975 to

1980) identified five national objectives, to establish Nigeria firmly as a united, strong and self-reliant nation, a great and dynamic economy, a just and egalitarian society, a land of bright and full opportunities for all citizens, and a free and democratic society. These objectives are reaffirmed in the current Fourth National Development Plan (1981 to 1985).

They fall within the context of Chapter II of the new Republican Constitution of 1979 which stipulates the fundamental obligations of the government in the section entitled the "Fundamental Objectives and Directive Principles of State Policy" found in Sections 13 to 22 of the 1979 Constitution of the Federal Republic of Nigeria. Section 18 spells out its Educational Objectives:

1. Government shall direct its policy towards ensuring that there are equal and adequate opportunities at all levels.

2. Government shall promote science and technology.

3. Government shall strive to eradicate illiteracy and to this end Government shall provide -

     (a) free, compulsory and universal primary education,

     (b) free secondary education,

     (c) free university education, and a

     (d) free adult literacy program.

These general objectives and directive principles are in fact enforced by law. In other words, no government, federal or state, can be taken to court for inability to implement a policy of free, universal and compulsory education at all levels if it considers it not financially practicable. It is an ideal to be pursued by the governments of the federation. Nevertheless these ideals have policy implications.

Perhaps the most controversial part of the Constitution which has the greatest policy implication for our educational policy and programs is in section

14, paragraphs (3) and (4). Paragraph (3) specifically requires that:

> The composition of the Government of the Federation or any of its agencies and the conduct of its affairs shall be carried out in such manner as to reflect the federal character of Nigeria and the need to promote national unity, and also to command national loyalty thereby ensuring that there shall be no predominance of persons from a few states or from a few ethnic or other sectional groups in that government or in any of its agencies.

Similar requirements are demanded of the Government at state and local levels in their compositions, the conduct of their affairs, and of their agencies. The requirements are rooted in our basic social, political and economic diversities, that exist in spite of the need for political unity. The experiences of our fragile and fragmented political system, the series of political crises, a devastating civil war, a long period of authoritarian military rule have combined to temper the ethnocentric, divisive and centrifugal tendencies of our political system. These are the legal and constitutional frameworks of our educational policy.

National Educational Objectives and Priorities
Education enjoyed high priority in Nigeria's development planning, ranking third to fifth in various National Development Plans since the 1962-68 Plan. In the current Plan, it ranks first in some State Plans. The Federal Government is basically committed to the creation in the country of an educational system capable of ensuring that every citizen is given full opportunity to develop his intellectual and working capabilities for his own benefit and that of his community. The nation seriously believes that education is a very powerful instrument of social change in the process of dynamic nation building. In

the National Development Plan of 1975-80 and the current Plan. (1981-85), the Governments of the Federation, believing seriously that education is the cornerstone of their development plans set certain education objectives and programs. The objectives of the Third Plan (1975) are:

1. to expand facilities for education aimed at equalizing individual access to education throughout the country;

2. to reform the content of general education to make it more responsive to the socioeconomic needs of the country;

3. to consolidate and develop the Nation's system of higher education in response to the economy's manpower needs;

4. to streamline and strengthen the machinery for educational development in the country;

5. to rationalize the financing of education with a view to making the educational system more adequate and efficient; and

6. to make an impact in the area of technological education so as to meet the growing needs of the economy.

These objectives determine and set out the priorities of the Government educational policy. They have very important policy implications for the various levels and sections of education in the country. Since education is a concurrent subject in our federalism, the emphases vary from state to state. The various political parties in the Federation have some specific programs or party planks on education. For instance, the National Party of Nigeria (NPN) which is the ruling party at the centre believes in what is generally described as "qualitative education" which its opponents describe as "elitist". Its election manifesto claims that an NPN Government "shall work towards providing free and qualitative primary education, free and qualitative vocational education, free and qualitative University education in accordance with the provisions of the Constitution" (Graf, 1980). It sought also to improve teacher training schemes, teachers' conditions of service, and teaching techniques. The rival political party, the Unity Party of Nigeria (UPN) has a "mass education" policy which has been labeled "qualitative" by its NPN opponents. Its election manifesto emphasizes free, universal, compulsory education at all levels of education. It eliminates the method of entrance examination into secondary schools. The party planned to "ensure for the masses of our people access to free and compulsory education at primary, secondary levels, free education at postsecondary levels. . . ." The remaining three political parties share similar or a hybrid of these two views on education. The general theme is free education at all levels, but none has a party program for the talented and gifted children, except if one interprets "equal opportunity to all" to include the exceptional children.

The Problems and Growth of Education in Nigeria

Nigeria's educational policy must contend with a number of her basic problems derived from the need for unity in diversity. The policy's place for the gifted in her educational system is a consequence of these contending problems and priorities. A number of bottlenecks have been identified in our education system. (Graf, 1980). The first is the structural imbalance in the educational system of the country whereby ninety percent of school enrolments in the formal school system are in the primary school level as against ten percent in the other levels. In developed societies the ratio is generally 60:40 for primary and other levels (secondary and postsecondary) of the educational system.

The second problem in our educational system is the low level of enrolment at each level of education. In 1971, for instance, one in every three children was in primary schools and one in every sixteen was enroled in secondary schools in the nation. This manifests itself in the illiteracy rate in the nation. Similarly, a higher illiteracy rate is found among adults. The Government recognizes now the paramount need for adult education and programs for nonformal education to cope with its manpower needs.

The third, and the most difficult, problem to tackle is the geographical imbalance in the distribution of educational facilities. This is a product of a colonial policy which neglected the Moslem northern provinces of the country by barring the missionaries (who were agents of development) from the North for political and administrative expendiencies. In 1926, there were 3,825 primary schools in the south with total enrolment of 136,630 children. In the north however, there were only 125 primary schools and no secondary schools, and a total enrolment of 5,120. In 1956, the Primary School totaled 13,412 while the secondary schools totaled 159 and total enrolment was 2.27 million in the south. Correspondingly in the north there were 2,045 primary schools recorded and a further 14 primary and 14 secondary schools which gave total enrolment of 179,712 was recorded. The situation has not changed. This educational lag has continued to affect administrative and economic aspects of the nation.

To effect changes in this direction the Third National Development Plan stated that there is lopsidedness in the geographical distribution of educational facilities. Consideration of justice and equality demand equalization of such opportunities such that every Nigerian child should have comparable opportunities for self development and fulfillment irrespective of where he lives and the economic and social circumstances into which he was born. Programs for "catchment areas" and for the "disadvantaged areas" have been developed to cope with the problem.

Another educational problem is lack of adequate, trained teaching staff at every level. This consequently lowers the quality of education and, in view of high enrolment rate under the program of free universal education, it makes the classroom over congested. This has led to a teacher to pupil ratio of 1:40 or 1:46. Compounding this is the declining number of schools as against increasing enrolment at the primary level as a result of the free education scheme and government's effort of merging schools for quality and economic purposes. The situations at secondary, teacher training and vocational, etc., sectors are similar.

The final and most relevant problem is the neglect of special education in Nigeria. The Government recognized this problem especially with respect to "providing for children who are handicapped as a result of disabilities such as blindness, deafness and dumbness."

Special Education and the Talented in Nigeria

Conceptually, special education can be equated with exceptional children education. This implies grouping the handicapped together with the gifted since they both need special techniques, curricula and treatment. The Federal Government of Nigeria (1975) has this "process" approach in creating the Special Education Unit in the Ministry of Education. The Unit caters to children and adults who possess learning difficulties because of different sorts of handicaps: blindness, partial sightedness, deafness, hardness of hearing, mental retardation, social maladjustment, physical handicap due to circumstances of birth, inheritance, social position, mental and physical pattern or accident in later life.

The common problem of these is that they are unable to cope with "normal class organization and method." The second category of clientele is the specially gifted children who are intellectually precocious and find themselves insufficiently challenged by the programme of the normal school and who may take to stubborness and apathy, in resistance to it. The Government consequently embarked on a universal primary education for "the handicapped and the exceptionally gifted."

This policy of dichotomy and fusion was to enable the Government to focus on certain purposes and objectives on Special Education. They include, first, efforts to give concrete meaning to the idea of equalizing educational opportunities for all children, their physical, mental, emotional disabilities notwithstanding. Secondly, it is to provide adequate education for all handicapped children and adults so that they may play their roles in national development. Lastly, the policy is to provide opportunities for exceptionally gifted children to develop at their own pace in the interest of the nation's economic and technological development.

In other words, the principle of equal opportunity for all Nigerians formed the basis of special education for those who could not profit by the normal school system because of their handicap or their exceptional intelligence or creativity. A National Council on Special Education was created to include representatives from four Ministries: Health, Education, Social Welfare and Social Development, and Labour, to plan for the gifted and the handicapped. Furthermore, the Federal Ministry of Education set up a Committee to coordinate with the other relevant Ministries on the activities of Special Education.

Suffice to say that all the efforts of the Federal Government have been devoted exclusively to programs for the handicapped to the detriment of gifted and talented children. Gifted and talented children in our society suffer from neglect at governmental, academic and public levels. In spite of the policy statements in the National Development Plan (1975) its expansion in the Policy on Education, the Federal Government has embarked on no concrete activites, created no committee to coordinate or plan for the gifted. The Third National Development Plan (1975) planned for a vote of over eight thousand million dollars on Special Education. There is no record of the amount which was used in the area of giftedness. The 1977 Policy on Education reiterated the Government's commitment to the gifted. It stated that the various Ministries of Education in the Federation "will, in consultation with the appropriate bodies, provide special programs for the gifted children, but within the normal educational set up." Also "the education of the handicapped and the gifted children will be free at all levels up to the

University level where possible."

These policy statements have not been programatically followed up with respect to the gifted. But, in the area of the handicapped, the Government took over or subsidized privately owned institutions, set up functional National Advisory Councils to plan and coordinate nationally for the blind, the deaf and dumb, and other disabled groups in the nation. In some cases individuals afflicted with a certain disability were made chairmen of a council. The Government developed children's clinics (for the handicapped) as part of the hospital complex, gave special scholarships to the teachers and students of the handicapped at both Nigerian and overseas institutions, has embarked on adapting certain techniques, like the Braille for the blind which is being translated into Nigerian main languages. What is more, the handicapped (for example, the blind, the deaf and the dumb) win public sympathy especially through their occasional nationally televised entertainment programs.

There are no concrete programs for the talented, but certain activities of Government perform these functions of identification and compensation. The first is through the central examination system of Nigeria like the West African Examinations Council's General Certificate of Education and School Certificate for Secondary and postsecondary levels, the Common Entrance Examinations for entrance into Federal Government Colleges and national essays like the John F. Kennedy's Essay Competition. This system of international and national competitions assist in identifying and compensating gifted children.

In addition, only a small percentage of admission into Federally owned secondary schools are actually based on merit, especially since the Government commenced its "Unity School System." This system is meant to inculcate nationalism and national integration. Our central examination method also encourages rampant cheating in examinations. The second indirect function of government activities is the scholarship scheme whereby a small percentage of awards - at

341

secondary, technical, and University levels - is based on merit for studies within and outside Nigeria. Special knowledge or distinction in one's field of study does give the person or child the opportunity for Government support. The trouble with the scholarship schemes in Nigeria is that other criteria, as well as merit, determine who gets what and in what field a scholarship will be awarded. For instance, the criteria of "federal character," of "catchment areas" or "disadvantaged areas" can and do displace merit of the talented children in the nation.

The Problems of the Talented in Nigeria

In examining the overall policy aspects on the talented in Nigeria, certain environmental and institution factors seemed to have conspired against a policy or any set of programs for talented and gifted children. There is dearth of literature on the Nigerian experience (or lack of concrete experience) in the gifted and the talented children by Nigerian or foreign authors.

The Departments of Psychology and Education have no Departmental Units currently involved with gifted-oriented research (except the fledging one at the Faculty of Education, University of Ibadan, where very little work has been done as compared with work on the handicapped). Dr. Olayinka's article is one of the very pioneering efforts in this field.

Second is the Government's blatant disregard of its formulated policy arising from the merging of the handicapped with the exceptionally gifted. Ideally, the two have certain commonalities, but they have grown separately and unevenly. They have different political bases for support, and therefore cannot but be rivals as long as they are both grouped into a special Education Unit in the Federal Ministry of Education.

Third (and a consequence of the second) is the lack of political power, or even influence, by the gifted to generate public awareness and government action. The strength and indeed the power of its counterpart in the Special Education Unit arises from the demand and support of such pressure groups as the Nigerian Society for the Blind, the Nigerian Society for Nigerian Deaf and Dumb, the Nigerian Soceity for the Disabled, etc., the Nigerian Union of Teachers, the Parents-Teachers Association, various related academic associations, and other interest groups. Power to help in the formulation and implementation of public policy is crucial for any public organization in terms of support, survival, expansion, the annexation of other interest units or functions, and in the political education over its interest. Simply put, the gifted and the talented children as an issue lacks a political base, hence it is suffocated (and given no room to grow) by the activist rival - the handicapped.

The fourth problem is the lack of public interest in the gifted. Some people see them as abnormal in the negative sense, wayward, dysfunctionally precocious. Some see them as certain mystics, and oddities. Public enlightenment programs are needed to enable the public to appreciate the need to identify and encourage the gifted. This in turn will help in the fashioning of a public policy on the gifted. It will help Nigerians to appreciate the creativities of some of our talents.

Conclusion

There is a paucity of academic, state and public interest in gifted children. The situation is unfortunate in a developing society, blessed with relative wealth (at least as compared with the other developing societies) and faced with enormous problems of nation building which demand the talents of the nation.

There are a number of constraints on the evolution of the public's awareness on the gifted. They include constitutional and institutional problems; the structure of government, lack of pertinent interest articulation by the academics, the officials and relevant social groups, lack of public awareness and appreciation of creativity and talent, and the nontechnological and nonscientific or noninvention orientation of a society which has become more dependant on imported technology and invention which kills challenges, innovation and creativity in our society.

I believe the following steps should be taken to move Nigeria from the first phase of policy development on the gifted.

1. A well coordinated program of public enlightenment for the understanding of and appreciating of the gifted as well as for early identification and planning for gifted children.

2. A separate Division or Unit for the gifted and talented, distinct from the handicapped group of exceptionals.

3. The need for Government effort to search for talents in all disciplines, arts and activities, and the development of policies to be effectively implemented whereby their talents and creativities will be utilized in the nation-building efforts and for international export.

4. The Universities should embark on serious research to generate interest and find solutions to some gifted-related problems like testing and learning strategies of the gifted children. The various disciplines of education, psychology and the social sciences in general, including political science and public administration, should work together in this endeavor.

5. Finally, international articulation for and research on the gifted should continue to critically examine on a cross-cultural comparative basis, pertinent issues of the gifted and talented society. The World Council for Gifted and Talented Children has a crucial role to play in this area.

References

Abraham, W. Common sense about gifted children. New York: Harper and Brothers, 1958.

Almond, G. Political development. Boston: Little Brown, 1970.

American Psychology and Guidance Association: Guidance for the academically talented student.

Washington: National Education Association, 1961.

Coker, H. O. The merit system: a comparative study of Ghana and Nigeria. An unpublished dissertaion for the Doctorate of Public Administration. Albany: State University of New York, 1977.

Dehaan, R. F. Guidlines for parents of capable youth. Chicago: Science Research Associates, 1961.

Durr, W. F. The gifted student. New York: Oxford University Press, 1964.

Easton, D. The political system. New York: Alfred A. Knopf, 1960.

Federal Republic of Nigeria. Policy on education. Lagos: Federal Ministry of Education, 1977.

Fair, J. Talented youth committee township high school. Evanston, Illinois: 1970.

Geotsch H. B. Parental income and college opportunities: Teachers College contribution to education, No. 795. New York: Teachers College, Columbia University Press, 1940.

Goddard H. H. School training for gifted children. Chicago: World Book Company, 1942.

Graf, W. D. Elections 1979. Lagos: Daily Times, 1980.

Hollingworth, L. S. Children above 180 I.Q. Chicago: World Book Company, 1942.

Love, H. D. Exceptional children in a modern society. Dubuque, Iowa: William C. Brown, 1967.

Nason, L. J. Academic achievement of gifted high school students. Los Angeles: University of Southern California Press, 1958.

Olayinka, M. S. The education of gifted children and its challenge to Nigerian parents and laymen.

Witty, P. Gifted children. Washington, D. C. Heath and Company, 1951.

23

GIFTEDNESS IN CONTEXT

Ahmed Yussufu

As educational systems around the world become more sophisticated and broader in terms of adapting to individual needs of the children and adults they serve, the exceptional child has come more and more into the focus of educational planners. Exceptional children, whether they be handicapped or gifted, require more help from their respective cultures and societies if they are to gain their full potential in today's world. But in dealing with exceptional children, the handicapped have made far better strides in developmental planning than that of gifted and talented children. Thus, the lack of recognition and developmental planning for the gifted and talented children throughout the world accounts for the greatest brain-drain to developed and developing nations alike in wasted manpower and much needed talent.

However, there are many factors that must be considered by those who wish to tap this rich source of talent. These factors are precisely the ones that either encourage and motivate the gifted and talented child or inhibit and suppress him. These factors may have subtle differences from one culture to the next, but in a broad sense they all fall into the broad categories presented here.

Definition

Definitions of talented children vary widely the world over. Some experts say that they comprise the top 2% of all children, while others state they are the top 5% or 10%. In countries where IQ testing assessments are done, authorities sometimes state that they are those children with IQs above 140, while others, still, say it is those above 135, 130 or 120. Still another definition is that they are children who range in the top 5% on tests of creativity. For our purposes, however, and in far simpler terms, let us say that gifted and talented children are those who are clearly superior to their peers in academic excellence, creative talent or both.

Specific tests of intelligence, creativity and achievement are frequently used for identification purposes of these children. But these tests are not available in many countries of the world as they are not culturally sensitive. Even in those countries where they are to be found, as tests and a study by Barbe (1967) has shown, as many as 70% of potentially gifted children will not be found by these methods alone.

For these reasons and many others, many countries are using the more observable behavior of these children rather than that of formalized testing. While the checklist of behavior that might be attributed to these children is long and they vary somewhat depending on the culture, they basically include such items as curiosity, inquisitiveness and persistence, independence, sustained interest, interest in one or more fields, the ability to learn quickly, the tendency to set higher goals than those of his age mates, to behave counter to accepted traditions, do unexpected things, and have generally superior problem-solving capabilities.

When properly nourished, inspired and motivated, these children can be not only a joy but also productive. Unfortunately, many factors and variables are negatively constructed to inhibit such children. It is these factors and variables I wish to talk about today.

Culture and Socialization

Socialization is one of several major classes of variables that affects literally every aspect of our lives. Likewise, cultural attitudes which establish the definition of normalcy, the quality of formal and informal education, their organizational settings and the larger context of how each member works within the society, may predetermine who will and will not be recognized and helped as a gifted and talented child or adult. One cannot underestimate the importance of socialization and culture in every aspect of fundamental learning we all go through. For the exceptional child, they may impose both positive and negative reward systems that develop or suppress the potentialities of the child. We must remember that almost all educational and socialization systems are geared to the accepted notion of normalcy and therefore the "normal" child. Thus the exceptional child, whether advanced or retarded, is often left standing in the cold.

An international opinion supported by research has accepted the idea that intelligence quotient is not a fixed or static thing. Many experts now accept that the gifted and talented potential of many children is not a genetic phenomenon, but rather the acquisition of superior talents through many variables such as early training and socialization, and cultural approval.

One may break down these variables into informal and formal groupings. The informal aspects of culture include those institutions such as the family unit and the peer group, as well as cultural attitudes and accepted sex roles. The formal aspects include institutions such as the educational system and religion, as well as broad organizational settings and such things as national goals for development.

Informal Aspects

The child's earliest experience with the process of socialization is in the informal aspects and institutions of the given culture. Thus the family unit becomes the first and foremost variable in the development of all children. But these are closely followed by the sex-role and cultural attitudes they learn within the home as well as the increasing peer-group influence as they continue to grow.

The family unit, and in particular the parents, seems to have the earliest impact on the potentialities of a child. Studies have shown that the gifted and talented child is often the first born who receives the greatest amount of early stimulation and adult interaction in his environment. Other studies indicate that intelligence capacity seems to drop as the family size increases and the amount of adult interaction decreases with younger children.

As studies in developed nations show us today, the earlier the stimulation to the environment of the child's emerging world, the more likely he is to have a superior capacity for learning and talent. Decreased activity and stimulation leads to decreased capacity.

Other influences found in the home will also greatly encourage or suppress a child. The cultural attitudes of which talents and giftedness are acceptable and which are not influence the direction in which a gifted and talented child may drift. Parental attitudes that are more often than not internalized, such as responsibilities and life goals, determine how the child may view his own talents and use them in a positive or negative manner.

Sex roles within given cultures seem to have a greater impact than has previously been thought. This is particularly true in those cultures which are male-dominated and female-passive. Many studies have shown acceptance of certain talents and giftedness in relation to cultural attitudes of sex roles (Torrance, 1962). One study showed that girls who are gifted seem less expressive than gifted boys in the public arenas, such as school, but not in the more private area of written expression suggesting some sex-role inhibitions (Gallagher, 1965). Such sex roles continue to be important in every culture to a greater or lesser extent. Thus a girl may have superior talents in the arts but not in mathematics which has classically been seen as a male domain. These attitudes continue despite the many studies that show equal abilities in almost every area regardless of sex when socialization is geared towards this attitude.

The larger context of cultural attitudes is more difficult to define, but they are as persuasive in determining which children and adults are seen as gifted and talented and which ones are not, especially in early childhood. A child with superior mathematical abilities who can build a computer or who has superior leadership abilities is often given greater opportunities than a child whose abilities may one day only build a better mouse trap. Those gifts and talents that will later fit into the achievement goals of the larger society will be talked about later under national goals. It is enough to say here that they have considerable influence on the development or suppression of certain talents.

Social status and peer group influence becomes increasingly important as the child grows. Social status of gifted and talented children seems partly a function of age. In the elementary (primary school) years they often hold superior status within their peer groups (Gallagher, 1958; Pielstick, 1963). Through secondary school years they seem to suffer a reversal in socal status. Value preferences of secondary students were found to be negative towards "brilliance" unless they were balanced by interest in athletics or by nonstudious attitudes (Tannenbaum, 1962). Social status throughout adult life is probably more influenced by the adult's own good adjustment to life and the cultural attitudes towards his chosen field. Certainly within socioeconomic class groupings, the higher the social class, usually the higher chance of appropriate opportunities for the gifted and talented child. But this is not always the rule and generalization of this should be carefully avoided.

Social acceptance of high IQ persons seems to be less than the person in the 125-150 range. This suggests the cultural feeling that extreme superiority in any given field more often isolates the person due to cultural mistrust and aversions of such people.

Formal Aspects

While the informal aspects of culture and socialization pervade every part of our lives, what have been presented above are the more discernible and easily identifiable elements that have a great impact on the early development of any child, but especially the gifted and talented child.

Let us now turn to the formal aspects. These are, of course, much easier to study due to the formal structure by which they exist within cultures, and therefore a great deal more is known about them and their effect on gifted and talented children.

The first, and the most important, is the educational and academic system under which these children will receive the majority of their formal training, but, religious institutions, organizational patterns of the culture or society, and official national goals will equally influence the course of these children.

The educational system is often described as pressure chambers for conformity with teachers lacking sensitivity to value the original and novel performance of the exceptional student. This, coupled with the many requirements and the reward system found in most educational systems, most certainly inhibits novelty and originality of most gifted and talented children. The system of reward and failure with countless tests, grades, selection processes, syllabi, single text use, etc., largely predetermine which children will receive extra help and stimulation within the school environment.

Many educators argue that the specific courses that children may take have far less impact on them than the teachers with whom they have contact. However, many studies, in Terman's classic **Genetic Studies of Genius,** seldom dealt with the kind of educational experience that might have made the difference in individual creativity. However, it seems correct to assume that by broadening the educational experience, these children will be more easily identified and helped.

Bearing in mind the differences between cultures, in 1962 Torrance did a study across six cultures for intellectual fluency or originality, and all presented very different developmental curves. However, an interesting aspect was that all curves had a slump or dip about the fourth grade. The explanation for this has been that the child comes face to face with an inflexible curriculum and a school program that places emphasis on conformity and standardization. It is, thus, at this critical moment that most educators and school systems fail to offer to their gifted and talented children the stimulation and motivation that will enhance and develop them. This may also be a large contributing cause to the large number of them who grow to be chronic underachievers.

In relation to high creative students and high-intelligent students, there have been some interesting studies. These seem to largely reflect attitudes of the culture through teachers. Here again we may see the essential awe and mistrust of highly exceptional children by teachers. Getzels and Jackson (1962) stated that the "creative" student is characterized by more intellectual risks and less social conformity than the usual high IQ student. High creative students often have a kind of rebellious approach to society, while low creative, high intelligent students are found to be more conformist and dedicated to school achievements (Yamamoto, 1964; Wallach & Kogan, 1965). Thus it is not surprising when a study by Getzels and Jackson (1962) suggested that teachers might prefer conformist gifted students to high creative and talented students. Such teaching attitudes are, of course, the reflection of the pervasive attitude of the culture, but the damage they can do probably exceeds that of any other formal institution.

Little information is available on the effects of organizational procedures within schools such as streaming and grouping on nurturing creativity. It is known that different kinds of scheduling, grouping arrangements and program flexibility are needed to reconceptualize the educational system to be functional and helpful to these students.

Such formal institutions as social class, nationality and religion have in the past born great weight in fostering intellectual giftedness. However, Smith (1964) showed that when these factors are controled, association between desirable traits and giftedness was not evident; but while they continue to have influence upon the given opportunities of children, they are important in the culture that favors certain institutions and not others.

The organizational pattern and setting that will be found broadly throughout most formal and informal aspects of any given cultures also have an effect upon the development of the child. In those systems which are hierarchical in nature and are based on single, authoritative leadership, independence is much more suppressed, especially in those that may challenge the conformity of the culture. In those cultures where independence is encouraged and leadership is based on broad group processes, originality is more likely to be encouraged.

Finally, the establishment of essential National Goals have had a particular effect on gifted and talented persons, especially within developing nations where such goals are the guidelines for development. In a study done in Ghana and Thailand, those rated as high achievers within the country were those who had a direct impact upon furthering the stated National Goals. Here we can see how a preferential bias towards certain types of talents and giftedness may largely exclude the majority of other children who have talents, but these are not deemed important to the task of national development and leaves them without further opportunities.

One last comment here, before I close, on the vast number of underachievers who are to be found in every culture and society: where the exact blame lies for underachievers is unclear. Some studies suggest that such things as poor parental/child relationships (Pierce, 1961) or a punitive home environment (McGillivray, 1964) contribute to underachievement. Yet other studies suggest the large role that inflexible and over-standardized educational systems have upon these wasted talents. Whatever the cause, the social consequences that have incurred by underachievers - fail to persist in frustrating situations, seek thrills and excitements, show greater feelings of hostilities, seek

353

out peers with similar negative feelings for schools
(Marrow & Wilson, 1961) and may show withdrawal
from academic studies (Perkins, 1965) present special
problems. To be sure, not all poorly adjusted children
and adults are underachievers, but a great many of
them are. The wastage of intelligence and creativity
as well as the delinquent and negative behavior can
cause a social burden that need not be there. Broader
attitudes within cultures as well as more flexibility
with the formal institutions would help lessen this
social problem.

The Situation in Kenya

Now I would like to look at Kenya in the context
of what I have spoken about so far. When one looks at
giftedness in Kenya, one can easily see the influence
and the role our National Goals play as well as the
impact of cultural and ethnic motivations. Our National
Goals try to emphasize the need for excellence and
diversity among our talented and gifted persons.
Through Government policies, we try to bring greater
educational and social opportunities to enhance their
potentialities. Though our emphasis is primarily towards
those who will pragmatically help us meet our national
developmental needs, within our limits we have tried
to encourage other talents as well.

Through the striking differences portrayed in
types of giftedness and talents between ethnic groups,
geographical locations and religious groupings, we can
see the strong cultural and ethnic motivations to
certain talents. This includes our world ranking
high-altitude runners and track and field athletes from
Rift Valley, and footballers and boxers from Western
and Central parts of Kenya.

Other areas which are strongly influenced by
these tribal motivations are the numbers of fine
artisans and craftsmen of traditional crafts of both
national and international reknown, Kenya believes very
strongly in maintaining its traditional past and as such
encourages the fundamental and traditional arts of its
various cultures such as Akamba wood carvers and

basket weavers, Kisii soap-stone carvers and many others. In this way we have seen ever increasing degrees of excellence in native art forms. One cannot exclude either music or dance which has strong ties in most African cultures. To promote this talent in Kenya, we have annually organized Music and Drama Festivals which embrace all age groups and cultures. These are begun from grassroots levels and continue up to national competitions. We encourage originality of material in music, drama and dance. As a result of these national festivals, superb talents from various parts of the country have emerged.

Kenya has tried to promote academic giftedness in its formal education system as well. This is done in the classroom, and the selection through ability groupings process to National Schools for Higher Education that more fairly offers opportunity to different cultures, geographical locations and socioeconomic levels of Kenya's indigenous population.

The Kenya Government spends much time and money on those areas where environmental deprivation has led to low academic performance. In such areas as Kenya's arid northern desert region, the Government supplies boarding school facilities and free food and milk programs in the hope of decreasing the environmental deprivations caused by the nomadic life styles and harsh existence in the arid areas.

Another area we might look at is the effect that government public education has had as well as mass media through radio and press in bringing the larger world to the public. Today we see the influx of new ideas and new experiences which emanate from such exposures. This has helped to break down some old cultural views and allow new talents to emerge among our young people. This is a phenomenon that is being experienced by most developing nations.

Conclusions

In-depth studies of the writings of highly creative and intelligent persons show they are ultrasensitive and more complex and suggest that they suffer in trying to come to grips with their talent, especially in the face of the cultural desire for conformity. The broadening of cultural variables and aspects that will allow more of these children and adults to seek opportunities appropriate to their talents is no easy task and one that will require many, many years to accomplish.

But the formulation of Government policy based on National Goals within Kenya and other countries is helping to broaden the cultural experience and views. If we are to utilize the vast amount of talent within our reach, this process of broadening cultural variables must be encouraged to continue despite the limited resources we have. It is important that each country, particularly those that have not defined appropriate programs to cater to their people of exceptional qualities, ensures that such programs are formulated for the fulfillment of these various individual talents. The social benefits of such involvements are likely to have dramatic impact upon every member of society, and not only on the gifted and talented. However, the gifted and talented persons who achieve appropriate training can dynamically motivate the society at large.

References

Ebel, R. L. Encyclopedia of educational research, 4 ed. New York: MacMillan, 1969.

Barbe, W. B. Identification of gifted children. Education, 1967, 88, 11-14.

Gallagher, J. J. (Ed.). Teaching gifted students: a book of readings. Boston: Allyn & Bacon, 1965.

Getzels, J. W. E., Jackson, P. W. The meaning of giftedness. Education, 1962, 82, 460-464.

Marow, W. R. & Wilson, R. C. Family relations of bright high-achieving and underachieving high school boys. Child Development, 1961, 32, 501-510.

McGillivray, R. H. Differences in home background between high achieving and low achieving gifted children: a study of one hundred grade eight pupils in the city of Toronto public schools. Ontario Journal of Educational Research, 1964, 6,

99-106.
Perkins, H. V. Classroom behavior and underachievement. American Educational Research Journal, 1965, 2, 1-12.

Persell, C. H. The qualities of research on education: bureau of applied social research. New York: Columbia University Press, 1971.

Pierce, J. V. Personality and achievement among able high school boys. Journal of Individual Psychology, 1961, 17, 102-107.

Pielstick, N. L. Perception of mentally superior children by their classmates. Perceptual and Motor Skills, 1963, 17, 47-53.

Schubert, J. G. Impact of participant training on the attainment of development goals: the methods and procedures for assessment of impact. Washington: U.S. Agency for International Development, March, 1976.

Smith, R. M. Industrial arts activities for children with individual differences. Journal of Industrial Arts Education, 1964, 23, 21-24.

Torrance, E. P. Ten ways of helping young children gifted in creative writing and speech. Gifted Child Quarterly, 1962, 6, 121-127.

Wallach, M. A. & Kogan, N. Cognitive originality, physiognomic sensitivity and defensiveness in children. Durham, North Carolina: Duke University, 1965.

Yamamoto, K. Creativity and unpredictability in school achievement. Journal of Educational Research, 1967, 60, 321-325.

24

REACHING THE UNREACHED:
A VIEW FROM THE UNICEF PERSPECTIVE

Danica Adjemovitch

So many of the children in this world are gifted or talented in some way, and yet, how many of them are given the opportunity to develop their precious gifts and talents? I am not only thinking of bare survival. I am thinking of the lack of stimulation, the limited understanding on the part of families, communities, even in some instances of educators, in awakening the latent potential in every child. "Reaching The Unreached" serves as a descriptive working title for this paper. It is also a phrase which aptly epitomizes a variety of effective approaches, whether long-term or short-term, including those which UNICEF has developed in order to reach the largest number of the world's unreached children, in as many ways and on as many levels as possible.

I will attempt to address some of those aspects which have particular relevance to the broad theme of this conference. In doing so, I will refer to the aims of the International Year of the Child (IYC) and to significant developments in IYDP (appositely enough, 1981 has been declared by the general assembly of the United Nations as the International Year of Disabled Persons) in terms of their effect of the optimum development of every child's potential.

IYC

Many people have actively participated in the International Year of the Child, which commemorated the twentieth anniversary of the U.N. declaration of the rights of the child. Our hope was, and still is, that the activities and impetus given to the cause of children will continue with vigor, with vision and with steadfastness of purpose throughout the years to come.

IYC was not intended to be just one calendar year, focusing for an ephemeral period of 365 days on children's needs and problems. It was conceived to serve as a rallying call and as an urgent invitation to the world community to renew and reaffirm its concern for the present condition and for the future of all its children - not by words alone but by deeds that will improve the situation of children nationally and internationally on a long-term basis. Every year must be the year of the child.

Children born in 1979, the International Year of the Child, will be twenty-one at the end of this century which marks the end of one millennium and the beginning of another. What will they have to say about their first twenty-one years? How will our commitment to them be judged?

What we do know is that of the 122 million children born in 1979, one in every ten is dead. This adds up to the tragic figure of 12 million children. "Almost all of those 12 million children died on the knife edge of poverty; a poverty so absolute that the bare necessities of life are beyond its reach; a poverty so stubborn that a trebling of world output has failed to loosen its grip on one-fifth of the world's people; a poverty so unnecessary that it mocks any pretentions to planetary civilization" (Grant, 1981).

"The state of the world's Children - 1981", a report by James P. Grant, Executive Director of UNICEF, puts forward the belief as well as the evidence that, for the first time in history, the world is possessed of the resources and the knowledge to mount a decisive push against mass hunger, ill-health and illiteracy. The question no longer revolves around our capacity to achieve this goal but rather about our wisdom and our will to do so - simultaneously sobering and encouraging words.

IYDP - Some Facts And Figures

At least one child in ten is likely to be born with or to acquire a significant disability. In the developing areas of the world, this means that we can easily find at least 120 million children under the age of fifteen with disabilities.

Based on a study of the situation of handicapped children recently carried out by Rehabilitation International with UNICEF assistance, certain generalizations were posited as valid for the great majority of children living in developing countries (Acton, 1979). I shall try to touch upon a few.

One generalization concerns the dire implications resulting from the combination of disability and poverty. Either factor may cause the other. In combination, they have the lethal capacity to destroy the lives of individuals with impairments and to impose upon their families burdens too crushing for them to bear.

Furthermore, when programs to assist in the development of the community actually reach it, the benefits go last and least to those families who are burdened with both poverty and disability. This is a consequence of many factors within the family, the society and the fragility of human compassion. But in the end, it is usually because the family with a disabled member has been, to some degree, rejected from the mainstream of community life and resources - and the development plan provides no mitigation for this social reality.

Another disquieting finding brought out the abysmal lack of accurate information about disability, its causes and consequences, and about what can be done to counteract them. The study also brought out the appalling wealth of existing misinformation, prejudice and fear. These factors all combine to produce attitudes and social behavior that are in themselves important causes of disability and of handicapped lives in developing countries. For instance, children with even minor impairments are often stigmatized as crippled or blind or deaf, and thus shut off from the very support and stimulation that would have enabled them to develop and function in society.

At least 90% of whatever rehabilitation services

exist in the developing areas are based on models from the industrialized west and are operated by staff trained in those models. This international cooperation and assistance has taken place almost entirely in the past 30 years and has produced some islands of excellence - centers, schools and programs that are performing as well as the models from which they were derived. It has also produced workers of great dedication and skill.

However, two crucial problems remain. First, the totality of existing services reaches, at best, only a few thousand people in those areas where it is estimated that there are at least 300 million with disabilities, not counting the additional increase of two million disabled persons each year. Second, it may be questioned whether the concepts of rehabilitation services which have evolved in the industrialized west are necessarily appropriate for areas with quite different economic and social situations.

Thinking along these lines leads inexorably to the question of prevention. All too often this aspect is neglected or treated as a separate crusade instead of as an interlocking and interacting component within the continuum of prevention, rehabilitation and social action.

This separation of prevention from rehabilitation has proved to be a major mistake in the approach to disability (Acton, 1979). The human experience is a progressive development which starts before conception, when the characteristics of the mating partners may or may not produce impairment, and terminates at death which too often is the culmination of a progressive reduction of capacities, a process which in other contexts we call disability. Everyone is faced with the prospect of impairment; everyone is likely to suffer a diminution of capacity during his or her lifetime but whether or not it will be called a disability depends on the culture more than on the incapacity. Programs developed in the industrialized world and urged upon developing countries are not based on these realities. Instead, they evolve from the idea that an impairment is a special event, requiring that the individual be immediately removed from the normal stream of development and performance, and introduced to the blessings of our buildings, equipment and professional personnel.

The most important asset for any program for disability prevention and rehabilitation is the family, and in most developing areas the ties and functions of the family are strong components within the social context of the individual (Acton, 1979). Therefore, high priority must be given to activities that will overcome the superstitions and fears of the members of the families of disabled persons, instruct them in procedures they can follow to prevent disability or assist in the rehabilitation process, and acquaint them with the sources of help that already exist or may soon become available. Successful work at this level, by remaining with the existing social framework of the individual's life, can do much to maintain normal human development and performance, whether or not the impairment can be eliminated or reduced.

We are only slowly beginning to learn that a child or an adult with a disability is also a person endowed with a family, with traditions, with customs, with tastes and appetites, with fears and apprehensions, with pride and ambition, and with a culture through which these elements are integrated. Yet, this panoply of support systems rooted within the family, the community, and the individual with the impairment has so far been largely ignored.

UNICEF awareness of these factors is acute and is reflected in the basic services concept, the promotion and support of primary health care, and in concern with enabling children to realize their full potential. In the course of the International Year of the Child, the policy to promote child mental health was adopted by the executive board in 1979 - a policy whereby the preventive and rehabilitation aspects are viewed as a single subject having interacting components that could be addressed to primary health care (UNICEF, 1980).

UNICEF's Regional Program for Early Childhood Stimulation

According to the report by Robert Hepern, of the High/Scope Educational Research Foundation on Early Childhood Programs in Latin America, the potential contribution of early childhood education to national development still remains unrealized in 1980. At the end of the seventies, less than 10 percent of Latin America's young children were enrolled in such educational programs, and of this group many were not those most in need of social services. Almost 25 percent of Latin America's population - 80 million children – are six years of age or younger. An estimated 50 to 65 million of them are growing in environments characterized by poor hygiene and unsanitary conditions, inadequate housing, insufficient nutrition and lack of parental or caretaker attention because parents and older siblings often go out to work in order to meet basic physical needs (United Nations, 175b, World Bank, 1975, 1978).

Most young children in Latin America are profoundly affected by poverty, both physically and emotionally. More than 50 percent suffer from the effects of protein deficiency. Nutritional anemia affects 10 to 20 percent of them directly and perhaps twice as many when the indirect effects on pregnant and nursing women are considered (Bengoa, 1973; Berg, 1973; Pollit, Halpern & Eskenasy, 1978). Infant mortality rates, though considerably lower than in previous years, average 84 per 1,000 live births, and are even higher in urban barrios and rural areas.

The psychosocial development of young children growing up in this kind of setting is hindered by many of the correlates of poverty. Malnourished children exhibit apathy and reduced responsiveness to the environment, irritability, withdrawal and an inability to carry out tasks, as do the children who have had persistent diseases or infections. Other grim effects of poverty include lags in cognitive development and in readiness for formal schooling.

Against this background, UNICEF developed their

THE UNICEF PERSPECTIVE

Regional Program for Early Childhood Stimulation, which was started by Ms. Carmen Naranjo, a dynamic and inspired educator. While "early stimulation" encompasses any activity which enhances the child's physical and psychological development, it also requires that an adult communicate with the child through gestures, humming, speech and all other forms of human expression. The techniques are simple to teach and to learn and can be communicated to parents through extension of the activities of health, welfare, or educational institutions which care for children. These techniques can be applied anywhere, and the only prerequisite for their success is a real interest in the child's development and a willingness to monitor the child's growth. The mother's involvement is essential in the early months, and the father and other family members all need to become increasingly involved.

UNICEF Action in Central America

At the request of the governments of six Central American countries (Costa Rica, El Salvador, Guatemala, Honduras, Nicaragua and Panama), UNICEF inaugurated in 1978 a program concerned with all aspects of young child stimulation and development. The encouraging results of the program have led to its extensions and it has attracted attention all over Latin America from individuals and institutions active in research on child development. The program, by its nature, concentrates on seminars, workshops and instructions and, within different countries, embraces different activities. However, two national programs already existed in the area, one in Panama under the auspices of the Panamanian Institute for Special Enablement (Instituto Panameno de Habilitacion Especial) and the other in Costa Rica under the Mental Health Department of the Ministry of Health (Departamento de Salud Mental del Ministerio de Salud). It is these two programs which served as the nucleus for UNICEF's regional program, concentrating on children between the ages of 0 and 6.

The program developed a variety of thrusts. In Costa Rica, for example, it conducted specific research on the benefits of breast-feeding and rooming-in at maternity hospitals, and on child-rearing practices. In Panama, it worked on a standard program of early stimulation and helped plan mother-and-child welfare policies. In Guatemala, it designed a system of informal instruction in all-round child development for the Indian population. In Belize, assistance was provided in defining policies relating to the preschool age groups. In El Salvador, consultation was offered to research institutions and in establishing children's centers for migrant farm workers.

The program's cornerstone rests on cooperative action with local communities, many of the preschool child care centers are staffed by young volunteers, others by mothers turned teachers. A widely distributed publication entitled "Make a little effort" (Un pequeno esfuerzo) brought about a grandmothers' movement in Panama which encouraged many older women to come forward and offer to look after children. They called themselves Donas Marias, after the main character in the story.

As the Donas Marias exemplify, putting early stimulation techniques into practice does not require the launching of sophisticated and costly programs. It calls instead for extending the already existing activities of the health, education and welfare authorities. By inviting community participation in the teaching and application of simple techniques of early stimulation, government institutions will find that they are promoting an improvement which can rally support from all sections of society.

Reaching the Unreached in the Philippines

Here is a vivid example of what UNICEF has accomplished in the Philippines. The project itself is called "Reaching The Unreached" (RTU) and revolves around the concept that it is best to invest in training the disabled child towards self sufficiency today rather than devoting hard won earnings to buy a wheel-chair tomorrow.

In countries where a large proportion of the rural population live in poverty, the disabled child often gets trapped between overprotection and negligence. All too often, the child with impairments is regarded and treated as "abnormal" by the family and the community, and thus, may grow up without truly growing and may only become an ever-increasing burden on the family. Josephina almost became such a burden. Her story is vividly told in the UNICEF booklet **Reaching the Unreached.**

At the age of ten months, this little girl was described as virtually a wilting head of lettuce in the arms of her mother. And though her body showed nothing but bones beneath her skin, she gave the impression of being boneless because she could not even hold her head up. Her eyes were lifeless and she would not respond to talking, or smiles or sound. The colorful empty shampoo bottles her mother gave her as toys did not interest her either. Believing that an impaired child was something of a curse, Josephina's mother shielded the infant from the public eye, while accepting the burden as the will of God. Resigned to taking care of an invalid for as long as she lived, yet having no one to help her with the house-keeping, Josephina's mother cooked meals, scrubbed floors, washed dishes all with one arm while holding Josephina with the other. This situation continued until RTU workers set to work. Gradually, Josephina started responding to the field worker's tickling. A very simple no-cost intervention technique involving muscle stimulation. The child was rolled over, encouraged to stand up, tossed in the air while her worried mother gazed in fear lest the child's bones break. Startled at first, Josephina got used to the exercises and to her mother's surprise, did not even mind when the field worker began gently kneading her arms and legs. Josephina's mother was helped to understand that muscles can waste away if left inactive and thus, cause permanent disability. Thereafter, upon instruction from the field workers, the tickling became a daily therapeutic ritual for mother and child. Four months later, Josephina had put on weight. She began running about the house in a walker with a string of brightly colored beads to play with, and became as responsive as any normal child her age. What is even more encouraging was the mother's attitude towards her child. Hostility was replaced by amiability towards the field workers and the neighbors, and her shame and guilt by justifiable pride in her daughter's progress.

Josephina's case illustrates that disability, or increasing disability can be prevented by educating parents in simple methods that bring positive results. The objective of the project is to change the attitudes of the able towards the disabled, rather than maintain the old approach of making the disabled adjust to the able. This is, in itself, a major new development and calls for painstaking efforts in order to involve not only the family but also municipal and community leaders in every step of the project. It calls for concerted community action and public education focused on measures to prevent disability such as appropriate child rearing practices, the value of nutrition, good environmental sanitation and regular prenatal care. This approach is to the advantage of all children, whether in the developing or the industrialized world. The potential of giftedness in every child will be fostered and enhanced thereby.

References

Acton, N. Disability and the developing world, presented to the Brookings Symposium on disability and the developing world, Washington, D. C., September 1979. International Rehabilitation Review, 1980, 2.

THE UNICEF PERSPECTIVE

Grant, J. P.   The state of the world's children 1980-81.   UNICEF.

UNICEF.   Childhood disability: the prevention and rehabilitation.   April 1980.

PART 5

CURRICULAR CONSIDERATIONS

The largest number of participants at any meeting about the gifted is likely to be teachers looking for improved techniques and materials to serve their gifted pupils. Most such meetings do a good job satisfying this need, especially at the introductory level. However, a world conference is an expensive and probably inappropriate forum for a predominance of such activities except as local professionals may be newly exposed to the expertise of those attending. While the Fourth World Conference did, therefore, devote nearly a quarter of its 147 sessions to workshops, only one of these is reported here.

The opportunity was taken to pause for reflection, to consider the nature of what it is we would teach gifted children and how we do it. The first three papers are at a relatively general level. The Minister of Education and of Colleges and Universities, in Canada's most populous and industrialized province, Bette Stephenson reflects on the role of government and legislative leadership in bringing about programs for the gifted. World Council Honorary Director Harry Passow proposes a conceptual framework for curriculum for the gifted, and four kinds of curricula which must be considered.

The six concluding papers look at more specific questions and may be grouped according to two of Passow's four curricular categories. First, with regard to general education, Pierrette Massé and Françoys Gagné examine the evolution of the ideas of enrichment and acceleration from their perspective of encouraging the development of gifted curriculum in the world's second-largest French-speak city, located in North America. Also, Her Majesty's Inspector Tom Marjoram reviews particular concerns at the relatively neglected secondary level and Gilbert Nicol proposes the International Baccalaureate as a suitable program for many gifted adolescents. Edward de Bono and Norah Maier presented two workshops on the CoRT thinking skills program, and these are summarized. Second, illustrative of specialized education, Harold Don Allen introduces a mathematics fraternity for school children, and Véronique Rossillon and Marguerite Castillon du Perron relate an enrichment program in the arts. The subliminal covert curriculum was conveyed by Alan Kramer in Chapter 8. The nonschool educative settings curriculum dominates the majority of papers in this volume.

25

LEGISLATIVE LEADERSHIP AND
THE EDUCATION OF THE GIFTED

Bette Stephenson

I join with the delegates to the Fourth World Conference on Gifted and Talented Children in expressing a deep appreciation for the sponsorship of this presentation by Phi Delta Kappa - the honor society in education which is devoted to the development of leadership in education.

Departments and Ministries of Education must be vitally concerned about leadership This was perhaps why Dr Bruce Shore, on behalf of the organizing committee of this Conference, invited me to address the general topic of the role of political and governmental leadership in serving the educational needs of gifted students. There has been considerable interest in Ontario's Bill 82 with regard to the gifted and I have been asked to recount some of the background to the legislation and the aspirations that go with it. I shall, therefore, provide a sketch of the developments which led to the passage of Ontario's special education legislation and conclude by focusing on its implications as they concern Ministry of Education personnel, school boards, teachers, and pupils.

The theme for the Fourth World Conference is "Many Views of the Gifted for the Advantage of All Children." May I begin with the final phrase of this theme: "of All Children"? For more than one hundred years, the overriding philosophy of all governments of Ontario has been that all children who have a right to attend school in the province should have opportunities to excel and should receive educational programs designed to meet their needs, interests, and capabilities. Many school boards throughout Ontario reflected this belief by developing excellent programs to accommodate the educational needs of exceptional students, although existing legislation did not specifically require them to do so. Such programs, however, were not being enjoyed by all children who had special educational needs because of physical, mental, emotional or learning exceptionalities. Consequently, the Ontario Ministry of Education designed a comprehensive plan for special education in 1972 to rectify this situation. The Yellow Book, as it was called, did not burst upon the educational scene like a newly launched rocket, indeed, rather than taking off it sat; but, following some revision, it was refueled to become the basic vehicle for the implementation strategy now underway.

The events which led up to Bill 82 may be of some interest to those who are currently considering legislative action in respect of the education of exceptional students. In the early 1970s, teachers, professional organizations, and parents' associations were debating, sometimes very vigorously, the notion of a "zero-reject" policy in education. Within the context of this activity, members of the Association for Bright Children (ABC) and the Council for Exceptional Children (CEC) were strongly advocating the inclusion of gifted children in all developments that might ensue concerning exceptional children.

In the mid 1970s, the Ontario Ministry of Education began to review the implications of "mandatory" legislation, particularly in light of the passage in the United States of America of the Education of All Handicapped Children Act and its subsequent Regulations. There were several Private Members Bills introduced into the Ontario Legislature over two or three Sessions at this time and in 1978, in the Speech from the Throne, the Ontario Government indicated its intention to proceed towards "responsibility" legislation. This term is, I believe, preferable to either "zero-reject" or "mandatory" because it recognizes that with rights to opportunity comes a responsibility to provide appropriate educational opportunities for all children and youth who are our teachers, parents, taxpayers and citizens of tomorrow.

During the spring of 1979, draft legislation, in the form of an Amendment to the Education Act, 1974, was circulated to all school boards, professional and parent associations and other ministries of government. Much encouragement was received but a number of concerns were also expressed. The draft legislation was revised on the basis of the input received and in May of 1980, I introduced in the Ontario Legislature, Bill 82 - An Act To Amend the Education Act, 1980. The following month the Bill received second reading and during the summer and fall it was extensively debated in committee. On December 2, the Bill received third reading and on December 12, 1980, it was given Royal Assent and became Chapter 61, Statues of Ontario, 1980.

When I introduced Bill 82 in the Ontario Legislature on May 23, 1980, I stated that the principle is one of universal access to public education. The concept is simply that an educational system which is supported by the taxation of all citizens, has an obligation to be of service to all children, exceptionalities notwithstanding. Among these exceptionalities we list "intellectual" which includes "giftedness." A student identified as gifted is entitled to have access to a special education program. Such programs should help to maximize the potential inherent within this population of students. Our legislation defines a special education program as one which is based upon and modified by the results of continuous assessment and evaluation and includes a plan containing specific objectives and an outline of educational services to meet the needs of the exceptional pupil. If the statistics are correct, and I believe they are, we can no longer afford to let large numbers of able students drop out of our schools because of lack of challenge and relevant learning.

In essence then, Bill 82 states that effective September 1, 1985 all school boards in Ontario will be responsible for providing special education programs for all exceptional students, including the gifted. In all fairness, however, I must admit that legislation is only as valuable as its successful implementation. Thus, to assist school boards and teachers with the development of appropriate special education programs and educational services to accommodate the unique needs of exceptional pupils, a comprehensive plan for implementation was prepared. A Steering Committee of senior Ministry officials was established to give leadership and direction to the planning for successful implementation of the legislation. During the school year 1980-81 an initiating team worked closely with the Steering Committee to plan and operationalize an extensive pilot project which involved twenty-one school boards, representing the many different geographic regions and varying degrees of expertise in special education.

A major objective of the pilot project was to determine the material and human resources which would be required to provide for the students assessed as being in need of some form of special education. A planning guide was developed by the Ministry's Special Education Branch to assist school boards in this endeavor and revisions and refinements have now been made to this instrument, based on the experience of the pilot boards. One of the most gratifying outcomes of the pilot process is that in Ontario we now have school boards helping school boards in ways which simply were not happening hitherto. On October 1 and 2 of 1981 the Ministry of Education sponsored an invitational conference on implementation to launch the phase-in of our legislation from the present to 1985. Representatives from all school boards throughout Ontario were invited and the Pilot Boards, the Initiating Team and the Steering Committee shared their experiences, the lessons they have learned and the planning expertise they developed during the pilot year.

To assist the Initiating Team and to work directly with school boards, regional teams have been established in each of the six Regional Offices of the

Ministry throughout Ontario. These Regional Teams will continue to provide leadership in the planning and delivery of special education programs. To bring practical experience in special education to the Regional teams the Ministry of Education has seconded Francophone, Anglophone and Native personnel to work directly with teachers, consultants, principals, and supervisory officers at the school board level. This form cf face to face assistance is greatly appreciated by these professionals. Here again it is people helping people that is making the difference. In addition to the Board Planning Guide, the Special Education Branch of the Ontario Ministry of Education has developed and will make available a number of other resource documents. These documents include a Special Education Information Handbook for the use of school administrators and a Special Education Instructional Materials and Resources Manual for teachers.

The many teachers of gifted children are the key to the success or failure of any Bill 82. For them leadership at the classroom and school level is a fundamental issue. To help make that leadership successful in gifted education in Ontario, teachers can expect to receive assistance with identification processes, curriculum development and program implementation. There are other resources also available to the teacher of gifted children. In addition to the support and professional development assistance provided by the Ministry of Education and their own school boards, teachers in Ontario are offered a wide range of Special Education courses at the preservice and the in-service levels through the faculties of education of our universities. Gifted education is one of the options available. In addition, the Ontario Institute for Studies in Education in Toronto offers courses in this area at the graduate level.

At the present time, we are discussing with the faculties of education the degree of specialization that is desirable in particular areas of exceptionality. Whatever the outcome of these discussions, one thing is clear. The rather intensive dialogue in which we have been engaged with the faculties of education over the past two years on the subject of Special Education has helped them to plan for the next four. They are aware of the job that has to be done in providing special training and they are willing to do it according to the best information available.

During the planning stages of Bill 82 the Government of Ontario recognized that substantial additional expenditures would be required for implementation. A commitment was made to provide the additional financial resources that would be required. Funding for Special Education will be increased each year to a total additional amount of $75 million by 1984-85. The Ministry of Education is in the process of revising the current Special Education funding mechanism and intends to fund Special Education programs and services for the gifted in the same manner as other Special Education programs and services.

Having just referred to matters financial, is this indeed the bottom line? How do all the things I have mentioned relate to the individual gifted child? I would like to conclude by focusing for a moment on the actual case of a youngster whose name is Omar. During the kindergarten screening process and subsequent assessments he was diagnosed as being in the upper superior range in mental ability. During his first year at school he could read fluently and comprehend at a sophisticated level. A gift in mathematics was manifested in his ability to multiply and divide decimal fractions and compute simple square roots. His parents were consulted and a team of resource personnel was invited to complete further assessments and assist his teachers to develop learning objectives. These would become the framework of an individual education program that would encompass both acceleration and enrichment. Implementation strategies were designed, materials were obtained and teaching resources were flexibly utilized to meet Omar's educational needs. A program to remedy a speech problem was designed and implemented by a speech correction teacher. Omar was found to be lacking in social skills so his classroom teacher, with resource assistance, ensured that there was a focus on his social development. To accommodate his giftedness in mathematics, a program in logic and computer science was designed by an enrichment teacher. To challenge him in the area of reading he was cross-graded with a grade five class.

All this happened in a school that was not a Pilot Board school and that has no direct contact with the Steering Committee or the Implementation Team. It came about because there was a caring principal who was keenly interested in the emotional, social, physical, and intellectual growth and well-being of his students. It came about because the sensitized school board made available to the classroom teacher the skills of appropriate resource people. It came about because Omar's parents were interested in his school programs. Throughout Ontario there are many Omars. In some parts of the Province the intent of Bill 82 has been practiced for many years. In others the financial and professional resources were lacking. Bill 82 will make the difference for the Omars who have not until now enjoyed equality of educational opportunity.

Ontario has embarked on a journey which is as exciting as it is worthwhile. We do not expect the road to be always straight and even, but we do think our carefully planned approach will help smooth the way because it is based on the principle of school boards, administrators, teachers, support staff and parents working together to develop the best educational provision for pupils with special needs. We have provided direction but we have also sought to reach out into each local community through the planning process to involve all those agencies and organizations with a significant interest or involvement in Special Education.

I have great hopes for the future because I see us moving forward together. Bill 82 has been the catalyst for this and we all know very clearly what our destination is. It evokes in all of us a deep sense of occasion for it is the realization of a concept that has its origins in the very roots of Ontario's history - equality of educational opportunity. Perhaps the most exciting prospect of all is the enrichment that this can bring to our Province's education system. The new opportunity afforded exceptional pupils should not, must not, be perceived to be at the expense of their regular classroom peers, for this is a false and harmful perception. Our exceptional pupils and the instructional techniques we develop to help them learn should be a positive influence on the system as a whole. The extent to which we appreciate this will determine the extent to which we are capable of maximizing educational opportunities for all our children.

26

THE FOUR CURRICULA
OF THE GIFTED AND TALENTED:
TOWARD A TOTAL LEARNING ENVIRONMENT

A. Harry Passow

Only a relatively few educators quarrel with the Marland Report statement: "These gifted and talented are children who require differentiated educational programs and/or services beyond those normally provided by the regular school program in order to realize their contribution to self and society" (Marland, 1971, p. 9). There are those, such as Samuel Strauss (1981), who believe it is:

> both foolish and wrong to select certain youngsters (by procedures far from valid) as "gifted" and lavish attention upon them by placing them in special schools, special classes or special programs. There is little evidence that such special treatment succeeds in its purported mission, and plenty of evidence that future scientists and scholars do not need such stimulation. Better to devote the resources to encouraging the average youths (p. 159).

In my view, there is a good deal of evidence that differentiated programs and services are needed if potential of the gifted and talented is to be realized. In an article which appeared in the December 1955 **Teachers College Record,** I wrote:

> We cannot leave the talented child to his own devices, for the evidence is mounting that, while some individuals do emerge despite lack of education and guidance, many others do not. Nor should there be raised a false conflict between

education for all children and special provisions for education of the talented. The Education Policies Commission recently (1955) wrote, "To educate the gifted at the expense of educating the vast majority of children would deny American Principles. Nevertheless, to neglect the gifted would equally deny American principles and also endanger national welfare by a wastage of talent" (p. 168).

The issue is not whether or not gifted and talented children need differentiated programs and services but rather what constitutes a differentiated program and differentiated services. What constitutes differentiated? What constitutes a program?

A look at programs and practices as described in various current publications shows considerable diversity. Epstein (1979) observed:

Differentiated education for the gifted and talented can take almost an infinite number of forms. Programs are about as varied as are the gifted and talented children themselves. Local districts should design them to meet the needs and use the resources of the local community (p. 6).

The curriculum has been defined as a changing assemblage of opportunities for educative experience. The process of curriculum development involves many kinds of decisions: what is to be taught, to whom, when, how, under what conditions, by whom; and how are the results to be evaluated? The elements of curriculum which must be ordered and reordered into opportunities for experiences include: goals and objectives, content, learning activities, teaching strategies, material and personnel resources, evaluation, organization, time and space.

Differentiated education is essentially a curriculum problem and decisions about program design and the arrangement of educative experiences are guided - following the traditional Tyler-Taba curriculum model - by studies in three areas: the nature of gifted children (their needs, characteristics and persistent problems), the nature of society (its heritage, culture, present and future needs for persons with high level abilities), and the nature of knowledge (including the disciplines and their unique functions). As with all curriculum-design problems, decisions on the program design stem from philosophic commitments, value systems, theories of learning and development, convictions concerning resources, beliefs about the nature of schooling and the functions of the school.

Despite the tremendous variations which exist among a group of gifted and talented children, they do have many characteristics which differentiate them from other learners. Clark (1979), for instance, has described these differential characteristics in five areas: cognitive, affective, physical, intuitive, and societal, emphasizing that "an analysis of those characteristics can provide us with a model for organizing educational programs" (p.162). Such lists of differential characteristics are useful only as a frame against which to study the nature and needs of the specific population for whom differential experiences are being planned. In Clark's (1979) schema, the differentiating characteristics "create related educational needs that make demands upon school programs in terms of modifications in classroom organization and methodology" (p. 163).

While all aspects of the educational process - goals and objectives, content, teacher-learning activities, resources, evaluation procedures, time, and space - can be differentiated, it is only as the differentiation is integrated and articulated that those learning experiences and engagements take on real meaning.

We have often oversimplified the nature of differentiation, sometimes reducing it to an argument of acceleration versus enrichment of curriculum. Aside from the problems of there being many different forms and styles of acceleration and enrichment, there is, as

FOUR CURRICULA OF THE GIFTED

Martin Dishart (1980, p. 26) noted, a larger issue.

> It should not be necessary to either enrich or
> accelerate a curriculum in order to use it for the
> gifted. This is also true when "acceleration" is
> defined as simply putting the gifted child one or
> more grades ahead in the same program with
> classmates who are older instead of gifted.
> Educational programs for the gifted should be
> based upon the needs of the individual learners
> rather than upon making up for the program
> deficits in a curriculum for the nongifted. There
> is a resultant difference between enriching or
> accelerating an inadequate or inappropriate
> curriculum and designing an adequate and
> appropriate curriculum for use in the first place.
> Although all curricula should be modifiable for
> individual learners, the gifted need more than
> either patched up or souped up hand-me-down
> curricula. An enrichment supplement does not
> really correct a curriculum that is weak, dull, or
> redundant for the learner. And such a curriculum
> pushed faster does not correct its faults even if
> the learner achieves content acceleration. There
> are curricula which are simplified enough and
> slow enough for handicapped learners. <u>Why not
> develop curricula which are enriched enough and
> accelerated enough for gifted learners</u>?

Thus, Dishart criticizes much of our efforts at
differentiation as "enriching or accelerating an
inadequate or inappropriate curriculum" and challenges
us to "develop curricula which are enriched enough and
accelerated enough for gifted learners." Some years
ago, I intended to argue in similar fashion when I
wrote:

> Enrichment of education for gifted students
> consists of providing experiences which are
> appropriate and adequate in terms of each
> student's unique nature and needs.

Appropriateness and adequacy can be judged only in terms of clearly defined goals for students with various kinds and degrees of giftedness (Passow, 1958, p. 219).

A good deal of what is labeled "program for the gifted" is indeed "patched up or souped up" even when not connected with hand-me-down curricula. It is often fragmented and unrelated to experiences which have preceded and those which follow these learning activities. Scope and sequence - two significant terms in the lexicon of the curriculum planner - are conspicuously absent in many curricula for the gifted and talented. There are even those who argue that attention to scope and sequence will crystalize learning activities and eliminate the spontaneity and creativity which should be part of the learning experiences for the gifted and talented. It should be added that scope, sequence, articulation and cumulative learning are not necessarily attended to in the so-called regular curriculum at all times.

In designing differentiated curriculum for gifted and talented children and youth, there are really four curricula which all students experience and which must be considered. There is the **general education curriculum** which is aimed at providing the knowledge, skills, insights and attitudes required of all individuals to participate effectively in society and which provides the foundation on which specialized talents can be nurtured and developed. Second, there is a **specialized curriculum** which is aimed at the knowledge, skills, insights and attitudes which will enable the individual to identify and develop areas of specialized talents and gifts and become a creative, productive gifted or talented person. Third, there is a **subliminal/covert curriculum** which provides both affective and cognitive growth and development from the school and classroom climate and the transactions which take place within those educational environments. And, finally, there is the **nonschool educative settings curriculum** in which considerable education and socialization take place.

FOUR CURRICULA OF THE GIFTED

Obviously, these "four curricula" are seldom distinct and separate since the subliminal/covert curriculum is omnipresent. Elements of the specialized curriculum may also be nurtured through general education curriculum experiences.

The basic argument advanced here is that differentiated education for gifted and talented children and youth does not take place only in those programs we label "gifted education" but in the total learning environment which such individuals experience. Although there are many varied operational conceptions of the nature of giftedness, almost all of them agree on certain characteristics which suggest that the gifted and talented have the potential for interacting with learning opportunities in qualitatively different ways even when those opportunities lack challenge and richness. While it is important that we attend to the specialized curriculum in which individual talents are nurtured, these talents cannot be fully nurtured unless we consider the total educational and socializing experience the individual is provided. If this sounds like an echo of the "education of the whole child," it is because it is the education of the gifted individual with which we are concerned - his cognitive, affective, physical, intuitive, and social domains which interact to produce the potential for gifted behavior.

The general education curriculum is sometimes called the basic curriculum, the required curriculum, the core curriculum, or by other similar labels. All of these labels imply that there is some basic set of learning experiences which all youngsters need if they are to function adequately in a society. At the most basic level, they are the basic skills of literacy, numeracy, citizenship, etc. At another level, general education involves, as Ward (1961, p. 35) has put it, "those experiences serviceable in educating and training common higher mental processes . . . such as reasoning, judgment, abstraction, and understanding per se . . . ." Ward points to the relationship between general education and specialized education ("vocational training" as he calls it):

General education enhances the understanding of nature, and of man and his institutions and ideas. ... This cultivation of understanding contributes pervasively to man's functioning as a citizen, a member of a family, and a friend or foe of given causes. It may contribute, and should, to the manner in which a person perceives his vocation and the use which he makes of his particular talents .... It is the wholeness of the talented engineer or architect for which the common school is properly responsible, the education and elaboration of his pervasive modes of thought and behavior ....

It is the general education curriculum which provides the foundation or base on which specialized talents can be nurtured and developed. It provides the substantive content and the cognitive and intuitive processes which are necessary for functioning as a "consumer" in society and on which the specialized curricular experiences can build if the individual is to function as a "producer" in society. It is the general education which contributes to what Maslow (1954) calls "self-actualization."

Whether the general education curriculum is provided for in a regular class, a pullout program, a special class or any other kind of organizational arrangement, clearly modifications and adaptations are needed and differentiation is required. Smith and Renzulli (1979, p. 12) suggest a "systematic plan for compacting and streamlining the required curriculum." Their plan is aimed at relieving "gifted students of the boredom that often results from unchallenging work in basic skills areas," and guaranteeing "that the child has standard competencies necessary for later achievement," and at providing the time needed for the pursuit of acceleration or enrichment activities. The basic premise of the Smith-Renzulli "compactor" notion is "that gifted students should not be required to relearn material that they mastered two or even three years ago, nor should they be required to spend large amounts of time on basic activities that ordinarily can be learned in a fraction of the time required by other students." The Compactor form is used to analyze the child's abilities, interests and learning styles; to describe procedures for compacting material; and to detail "alternative approaches to providing advanced level experiences . . . for students who have been helped to master the required curriculum in a more economical and efficient manner." This is one proposal for differentiation of the general education curriculum, with the differentiation in the form of acceleration or enrichment activities.

Educational experiences may be differentiated in at least three ways: breadth or depth, in tempo or pace, coming at an earlier developmental stage or in less time than is usual; or in kind, being of a different nature from the usual experiences. Where qualitative differences in learning occur, it is the interaction of the special characteristics of the gifted and talented student with the substance and processes of the curriculum which result in the learning differentials. Different disciplines and content, different processes lend themselves to curricular adaptations differently.

The specialized education curriculum is aimed at nurturing the special talent areas of the individual. It consists of those engagements and learning opportunities which enable the individual to identify and begin to develop the skills, knowledge, insights, values and understandings needed to realize one's potential. In very few talent areas is one's potential developed fully in the elementary and secondary school; sometimes it is only identified and nurturing barely begun. David McClelland (1958) once observed:

> Suppose we could locate that sleepy boy in the back row, the potential poet; what would we do for him? . . . The plain fact of the matter is that we do not know what we would do: we do not know enough about what goes into the making of a poet. We may know somewhat more about

what goes into the making of a scientist or a professor (based on IQ tests and academic training); but we still know far too little to be confident about how to develop talented performance out of talent potential (pp. 23-24).

While there is still a good deal that we do not know about developing talented performance out of talent potential, we do know some things about which we can be confident. Studies like Anne Roe's **The Making of a Scientist** (1953) or Getzels and Csikszentmihalyi's **The Creative Vision** (1976) provide some insights into what scientists and artists experienced in developing their potential. Or, Paul Brandwein's **The Gifted Student as Future Scientist** speaks of "Activating Factors" - "opportunities for advanced training and contact with an inspirational teacher" (p. 11).

Brandwein writes of an operational approach in which all students take ninth grade science. Those who show any signs of distinguishing themselves in science (high achievement, great interest, willingness to do extra work, etc.) are given an opportunity to work in laboratories during their free periods before, during or after school. In the second year, students are selected for a special science class. Selection includes those students who have shown ability in science, but, in addition, any student who plans to make science a career may apply. Students selected for the class are given an opportunity to:

1. Engage in some "original" research work on the high school level. Each student is under the close guidance and observation of a teacher.
2. Learn laboratory techniques (histological, bacteriological, analytical chemistry, work with glass, etc.).
3. Learn the expert use and operation of laboratory equipment of all types (analytical balance, microscope, electric oven, autoclave, etc.).

4. Gain special skills in shopwork, including handling of common materials, wood, metal, etc.
5. Engage in library research. Required reading includes college texts in biology, physics, and chemistry and other pertinent materials.
6. Take adequate training in mathematics. This includes a special class which may go as far as the calculus.
7. Prepare exhibits of their work for demonstration before other students, at science fairs, or local exhibitions.
8. Prepare reports of their work (in their senior year) in writing for the school science journal or for other journals.
9. Engage in seminar activity at regular meetings of the Forest Hills High School Science Society and the Mathematics Honor Society. Students who have shown competence in science are eligible for election to the society. Students who offer the best reports of their work will in turn be invited to submit their work at a Biology Congress . . . or to exhibit their projects at the Science Fair. . . .
10. Engage in the Annual Science Talent Search of the Westinghouse Educational Foundation.
11. Take a course in college physics (using the calculus). This course was organized by a group of students who are part of this program (Brandwein, 1955, p. 11).

Brandwein's approach to the special education portion of science education - the effort to select and give special training to individuals who show promise of becoming scientists of the future - assumes further education and training at the college and graduate or professional school levels. The analog to Brandwein's operational approach can be used in any area - there is the knowledge, content and substance of the discipline; its special methodologies and processes; its modes of problem definition; the exercise of creativity, innovation, and originality found in any area of specialized talent. The specialized curriculum will not, in my view, develop poets, musicians, scientists, mathematicians, and other specialized talent areas but should activate and motivate the commitment and the development of the competencies and affective behaviors required for nurturing such talents. It should start the development of talented performance out of talent potential at a level commensurate with the maturation and development of the individual.

The subliminal/covert curriculum is one to which we have not paid much attention. Discussing the importance of school climate and environment in connection with desegregation and integration, Charles Pinderhughes (1967) observed:

> What the pupils are learning from one another is probably just as important as what they are learning from the teachers. This is what I refer to as the hidden curriculum. It involves such things as how to think about themselves, how to think about other people, and how to get along with them. It involves such things as values, codes, and styles of behavior. . . .

Self-concepts, attitudes toward more and less endowed peers, willingness to "be different," task commitment and perseverance, acceptance as an "acceptable" of specific kinds of talents and talent areas, willingness to participate in the school's system of rewards and punishments - these are just a few of the things which pupils learn from each other and from the climate in which they find themselves. Is the pursuit of excellence an accepted goal, accepted by teachers, students, and the community? What concept of excellence is being pursued?

Behavioral nuances on the part of teachers, parents, and adults affect student perceptions of the gifted and talented. Singling out gifted students for special attention can result in a perception of an elite group with all of the negative consequences which can accompany such perceptions, or such actions may be accepted as a normal approach to individualization, depending on how such arrangements are made. The social consequences of ability grouping are not inevitably negative and detrimental either to the gifted or others. Psychological problems may or may not emerge as a consequence of special programs for the gifted. The climate of the classroom and the school, the interpersonal relationships therein, the structured and unstructured learning environments, the formal and informal transactions are powerful mediators of cognitive, affective, and intuitive growth. Moreover, this subliminal/covert curriculum has a powerful impact on the more formal curricular experiences of students. Whether, to what extent, in what ways, and how committed individuals will be participating in, grasping or designing learning opportunities depends on the climate created for the pursuit of excellence. More formal counseling and instruction may emerge from needs uncovered in this area, for example, values orientation, personal guidance, group counseling, leadership training, and ethics. Attitudes toward giftedness and talent held by those identified as in need of differentiated services and programs as well as those not so identified have a profound affect on motivation, involvement, performance, and behavior. We have not attended to this hidden curriculum adequately. In a world, including our educational world, dominated by the average and mediocrity with only lip service to the notion of individual differences, the environmental climate is a strong influence on the quality of learning and the pursuit of excellence.

As for the nonschool educative settings curriculum, many institutions and agencies instruct directly, systematically and deliberately. As Cremin (1980) has pointed out, traditionally, only the school is thought of as having a curriculum:

> but the fact is that many institutions have curricula that are quite explicit and well defined. Every family has a curriculum. . . . Every church and synagogue has a curriculum. . . .

Every employer has a curriculum. . . . One can go on to point out that libraries have curricula, museums have curricula, Boy Scout troops have curricula and day care centers have curricula, and, most important, perhaps, radio and television have curricula - and by these curricula I refer not only to programs labeled educational but also to news broadcasts (which presumably inform), to commercials (which teach people to want) and to popular dramas (which reinforce certain common myths and values). (p. 19)

Education and socialization take place in many different settings and the cognitive and affective growth of the gifted and talented are affected by those informal, unstructured curricula, as well as the more formal. These learnings are brought to the school and, unfortunately, seldom taken into account in planning more formal curricula. How giftedness is perceived and treated in the home and community, for example, results in formation of self-concepts, attitudes, commitments, etc. . . . Which talents will be valued and supported is affected by the family's value system and its structure.

Aside from these more or less informal curricula, there are many personnel and material resources in the community's nonschool educative agencies which can be used to enrich, challenge and thus differentiate programs and services for the gifted and talented. Community- centered experience-based learning extends the base of the classroom and makes the whole community the learning environment.

Experience-based learning opportunities often represent a form of "learning by doing in a reality setting" and frequently involve mentor or intern relationships. By extending the learning environment into the community, the school can enrich the resource base - both human and material - which is available to the gifted and talented individuals. Formal and informal arrangements, structured and unstructured can be found in museums, libraries, laboratories, service agencies, government, industrial and commercial organizations, etc. . . . In many instances, gifted and talented students are so advanced in their areas of specialization that school-based resources tend to be more limiting than enriching.

Whether or not gifted and talented students receive "credit" for community-centered experience-based activities is less of an issue than the arrangements which are made for mediating such experiences.

In a 1955 article titled "Concerning the Nature and Nurture of Genius," Pressey studied the careers of exceptionally gifted persons and noted that all seemed to have had: (a) excellent and early opportunities for abilities to emerge and to be encouraged by families and friends, (b) access to early and continuing individual instruction and guidance, (c) opportunities for regular and sustained practice in their areas of giftedness together with opportunities to progress and develop at an individualized pace, (d) participation with other performers (not necessarily of the same ability level) which provided a basis for continuing stimulating relationships, and (e) stimulation by frequent and increasingly strong success opportunities (pp. 123-129). Pressey's observations deal with environmental influences and a pervasive climate for nurturing talent.

There are many valid and valuable "programs for the gifted" to be found across the country. These involve various kinds of modifications and adaptations, instructional and administrative, aimed at providing differentiated programs or services for gifted and talented. Many of those programs do indeed provide for richer, more challenging learning for the gifted and talented. They do constitute differentiated learning environments but are not, in the sense being advanced here, total learning environments. Gifted and talented individuals are learning in many different settings and are experiencing many different curricula. Four curricula of the gifted and talented - the general education, the specialized, the subliminal/covert, and the nonschool educative setting - have been identified as a challenge to educators of the gifted. Dishart (1980) has asked: "Why not develop curricula which are enriched enough and accelerated enough for gifted learners?" I am suggesting that if we are to develop adequate and appropriate curricula for gifted and talented students, we must attend to all of the curricula which such individuals experience and not just the specialized curriculum on which our efforts have been focused to date.

References

Brandwein, P. F. The gifted child as future scientist. New York: Harcourt, Brace and Company, 1955.

Clark, B. Growing up gifted. Columbus, Ohio: Charles E. Merrill, 1979.

Cremin, L. A. Change in the ecology of education: the school and other educators. In T. Husen (Ed.) The future of formal education, Stockholm: Almquist and Wiksell International, 1980.

Dishart, M. Book review: The gifted and talented - their education and development. Educational Researcher, 9 (5), March 1980.

Epstein, C. B. The gifted and talented: programs that work. Arlington, Virginia: National School Public Relations Association, 1979.

Getzels, J. W. & Csikszentmihalyi, M. The Creative Vision: A longitudinal study of problem finding in art. New York: Wiley, 1976.

Marland, S. P. Jr. Education of the gifted and talented. Volume I: Report to the congress of the U. S. of the U. S. Commissioner of Education, Washington, D. C.: U. S. Government Printing Office, 1971.

Maslow, A. H. Motivation and personality. New York: Harper and Brothers, 1954.

McClelland, D. C. et al. Talent and Society. Princeton: Van Nostrand, 1958.

Passow, A. H. Talented Youth: our future leaders. Teachers College Record, 1955, 57 (3).

Passow, A. H. Enrichment of education for the gifted. In N. Henry (Ed.). Education for the Gifted, 57th yearbook, Part II, National Society for the Study of Education. Chicago: University of Chicago Press, 1958.

Pinderhughes, C. Racial isolation in the public schools: A Report of the United States Commission on Civil Rights. Washington, D. C., U. S. Government Printing Office, 1967.

Pressey, S. L. Concerning the nature and nurture of genius. Scientific Monthly, 1955, 81.

Roe, A. The making of a scientist. New York: Dodd Mead, 1953.

Smith, L. H. & Renzulli, J. S. A teacher's handbook for individualizing instruction for the gifted. New York: New York City Teacher Center Consortium, 1979.

Strauss, S. The gifted and non-gifted. Chicago: Saturn Press, 1981.

Ward, V. S. Education of the gifted: an axiomatic approach. Columbus, Ohio: Charles E. Merrill, 1961.

27

OBSERVATIONS ON ENRICHMENT AND ACCELERATION

Pierrette Massé & Françoys Gagné

The majority of authors who write about giftedness classify special educational services under three main categories: enrichment within the regular class, acceleration, and grouping into special classes. This typology is so well known that Passow familarly calls it the "trinity of adaptations" (1979, p. 446) for this particular group of pupils. If we examine the definitions for each of the three parts of this trinity, we find a superficial agreement among the authors. Most consider the grouping in a special class as "the organization of students into administrative and instructional units in order to facilitate the attainment of educational objectives" (DeHaan & Havighurst, 1961, p. 103). Also, authors generally define enrichment as the opportunity for the gifted or talented pupil to study more extensively or in greater depth an educational content which may or may not be part of the curriculum (Tempest, 1974). Finally, along with Pressey (1949) we usually perceive acceleration as the possibility to get through the various steps of the school process faster or earlier than expected.

Underneath this superficial agreement there are, however, important divergences and sometimes even contradictions among the authors. Thus, when identifying the contents outside the curriculum offered to gifted or talented pupils, they refer to supplementary enrichment (Durr, 1964), cultural enrichment (Stanley, 1976), or augmentative changes (Passow, 1979a). When referring to the fact of more extensively covering some subjects on the curriculum, Durr (1964) uses the expression horizontal enrichment, De Haan and Havighurst (1961) speak of broader, extensive or lateral enrichment, whereas Passow

(1979a) suggests changes in extent, depth or intensity. In short, the least we can say is that there is no lack of semantic creativity.

Those divergences, of which we just gave a few examples, would be minor if they applied only to their titles. Unfortunately, they often reflect important differences in the conception of special services to be offered to this school subpopulation. Thus, some authors, such as Marland (1972) or Passow (1979a), consider enrichment as simply a type of intervention or an administrative measure, among others, designed to satisfy certain specific educational needs of gifted or talented children. On the other hand, DeHaan and Havighurst (1961), Durr (1964), Kaplan (1974) and Sumption and Luecking (1960) perceive this concept as the keystone of school programs intended for these pupils.

So, what is enrichment? What form should it take? Should we give it this focal character favored by some authors? If so, where do we situate acceleration or grouping in relation to this pivot concept? In order to find the answers to those basic questions on the education of gifted or talented pupils, we first asked ourselves what should constitute educational services specifically intended for this "exceptional" clientele. This led us to a differentiation procedure of educational experiences with respect to any marginal school population. When we applied this procedure to gifted or talented pupils, we were inevitably forced to redefine enrichment and to specify its various forms. Those new definitions finally allowed us to determine the role of acceleration and grouping in relation to enrichment. This document will proceed through the various phases of our search for a more precise concept of educational services adapted to gifted or talented pupils.

The Differentiation Process

In works on giftedness written during the past twenty years, considerable importance has been given to the principle of "differentiation" of the various educational interventions related to gifted or talented pupils. To better understand the exact meaning of this term, let us first distinguish between the regular program and a special program. What is a regular program? It is simply the educational program followed by the vast majority of children, those who do not belong to any of the marginal groups of children called "exceptional." As for a special program, it is usually a more or less substantial adaptation of the regular program in order to meet the specific needs of a marginal subpopulation. A special program will be deemed appropriate only if it satisfies specific educational needs within this marginal population, that is, needs that are exclusive to this population, shared with no other marginal group. In this case, and in this case only, can we speak of a differentiated educational program.

But how can we identify the specific educational needs of a marginal population? The answer is simple: those needs arise directly from the specific or differential characteristics of the population concerned. The differentiation of an educational program with respect to a marginal population is therefore achieved in three consecutive steps: (a) identify the characteristics of the population concerned, (b) then, determine the corresponding educational needs, (c) finally, develop the appropriate means to meet these specific educational needs, that is, create a differentiated program. This development of a differentiated educational program for gifted or talented pupils should normally follow these three steps.

First Step: Differential Characteristics

Does this school clientele have distinct characteristics which can be interpreted as specific educational needs? This time the answer is not so simple: since Terman's research in California at the beginning of the century (Terman & Oden, 1951), the findings of which were corroborated in various countries at several years' interval (cf. Lovell & Shields, 1967; Parkyn, 1938, cited by Shields, 1968), it has been generally recognized that gifted or talented children distinguish themselves from the average on a myriad of differential characteristics. The latter have been inventoried by Renzulli, Hartman and Callahan (1975), each characteristic being based on at least three studies, often carried out at different times. That inventory was made into a set of scales to identify gifted or talented pupils (Renzulli, Smith, White, Callahan & Hartman, 1976).

So the problem does not lie in finding differential characteristics in those pupils, but rather in extracting from this plethora a limited number of more general characteristics directly related to learning, since only those will generate specific educational needs and therefore require a differentiation of the school program. We tried several methods to solve this problem. First, by examining the various modifications to the school programs favored by authors for gifted or talented pupils, we discovered the characteristics ascribed to those pupils which could justify such modifications. We also looked for the characteristics most frequently mentioned and formally identified as being the most discriminating. Finally, we listened to much testimony from parents and teachers.

As a result of this search, we were able to isolate four differential characteristics of a cognitive nature which were particularly likely to influence the content and the methods of educational experiences intended for gifted or talented children. We did not take socioaffective differential characteristics into account because research in this area is still too incomplete and vacillating, and because these characteristics have less impact on school programs.

Rate of learning. One of the main cognitive characteristics of gifted or talented children is, no doubt, their rate of learning. As Keating says (1979, p. 217), "it is quite obvious that it is the rate at which they are able to acquire and integrate new information." Gold also states (1965, p. 135), "Gifted children as a group differ from others in learning ability: they learn faster and remember more, and they tend to think more deeply with and about what they learn."

Ease in the face of complexity. A second characteristic is mentioned almost as frequently as the first one, and could even explain the latter: it is the ease with which gifted or talented individuals face problems which appear quite complex to other people of the same age. In the area of cognitive skills, this ease is evident with regard to abstract concepts or complex logical reasoning. Gallagher (1975) even considers this second quality as the main differential characteristic of gifted or talented individuals: "If there is one factor common to all young people we call gifted, it is their ability to assimilate abstract concepts, to integrate them more efficiently and to use them in a more appropriate way than the average individual" (p. 19).

Diversity of interest. All research indicates that gifted or talented children demonstrate a vast curiosity in all kinds of fields, striving to understand the workings of objects or persons. This perpetual questioning denotes a great diversity of interests. Ziv (1977) considers it the main differential characteristic, stating that "The thirst for knowledge constitutes the most outstanding feature of the gifted child" (p. 36). This thirst for knowledge frequently results in a wide range of knowledge (National School Public Relations Association, 1979).

Depth of specific interest. At a very young age, gifted or talented individuals often show a marked interest in some specific spheres. Several studies mentioned by Renzulli (1979), in a detailed review of writings on this subject, illustrate the deep involvement of those individuals in a chosen field. He considers this last trait essential to giftedness.

To summarize, it is evident that gifted or talented children distinguish themselves from the regular school clientele mostly by their fast rate of learning, by the ease with which they master the most complex problems or develop the most advanced skills, by the diversity of their interests, and by the depth of some of their specific interests.

Let us note, however, that these four differential characteristics may not manifest themselves to the same extent in all gifted or talented children; they are partially related to the individual's degree of giftedness or talent. Their manifestation may also depend on the stimulation the individual receives from his educational, social or cultural milieu.

Second Step: Specific Educational Needs

In order to develop a differentiation of school programs which will be suitable for gifted or talented pupils, we must translate into specific educational needs the differential characteristics identified in this subpopulation. In this case, it is a relatively simple operation, since the fast rate of learning of gifted or talented pupils implies their need for a faster presentation of the instructional contents. Their ease in the face of complexity indicates their need to develop and exercise the most complex mental processes (analysis, synthesis, evaluation, divergent and creative thought, etc.) and the most advanced skills. The diversity of their interests points to their need for more extensive and more varied stimulation. Finally, the depth of some of their interests is evidence of their need to more thoroughly develop some fields of interest.

Differentiation is enrichment. As already stated, educational experiences are deemed differentiated only to the extent to which they satisfy the specific needs of the clientele concerned. In the case of gifted or talented pupils, such educational experiences must be differentiated from the regular program in four ways corresponding to the four specific needs of those pupils. Thus, experiences which are differentiated by a more dense rate of learning, by the development and exercise of more complex mental processes or more advanced skills, and by the availability of more extensive, varied or in depth knowledge, constitute more enriching experiences.

Enrichment, therefore, is the differentiating principle of educational experiences for gifted or talented pupils. To put it another way, enrichment is the most effective means of satisfying the specific educational needs of this particular group of pupils.

Enrichment

In view of the arguments submitted, enrichment must be defined as

an increase in density, complexity, diversity and depth of educational experiences for gifted or talented pupils, in order to meet their specific educational needs.

In terms of a direct response to their specific needs, enrichment must be considered the differentiating principle of the educational experiences intended for this target population. A program which is differentiated to suit gifted or talented pupils must be viewed as

a structured set of means (formulae, projects, administrative measures, etc.) for the purpose of enriching the school life of gifted or talented pupils.

Whereas this last definition is close to that of Fox (1979), the first one differs to some degree from the usual concepts, and therefore calls for a few comments.

As defined, enrichment may assume four different forms:
1. enrichment in density, by accelerating the rate of presentation of educational contents,
2. enrichment in complexity, by developing and exercising the most complex mental processes or the most advanced skills,
3. enrichment in diversity, by opening the door to a

larger variety of knowledge, or

4. enrichment in depth, by allowing the pupil to explore in depth a field of interest.

Here are a few examples of those four forms of enrichment. Half-time regular curricula and continuous progress without acceleration are perfect examples of enrichment in density. When secondary level pupils, gifted in biology, perform under supervision an assignment on the physiological factors involved in obesity or cancer, then we refer to enrichment in complexity. Enrichment in diversity is often achieved at the primary level by introducing subject matter outside the curriculum, for example, history of music, ancient civilizations, theory of evolution, astro construction or operation of common objects, etc. Finally, enrichment in depth allows the young amateur politician to write his own French compositions on this theme, to present a paper in English on the workings of Parliament, to go deeper into the political aspects of the period studied in his history course, etc. To summarize, enrichment in density refers to the rate of learning, enrichment in complexity is directly related to the processes or skills involved, and enrichment in diversity and in depth deals with the content of learning.

However, each of those forms of enrichment only partially meets the specific educational needs of gifted or talented pupils since those needs are concomitant: they apply at the same time to their rate of learning, their ability to develop more complex skills or mental processes, and their varied and advanced interests. To completely respond to their needs, these must be met simultaneously, that is, their educational experiences must be increased concurrently in density, complexity, diversity and depth. It is possible, of course, for some differentiated experiences to emphasize one form of enrichment over another. This emphasis however must not ignore the need to apply every dimension of enrichment if we are to completely respond to the needs of the gifted or talented.

We would like to point out that all pupils do not

require the same amount of enrichment. Indeed, their needs vary according to their degree of giftedness which is why the exceptionally gifted pupil will probably require longer periods of enrichment or more intensive enrichment than other gifted pupils.

We are not the only ones attempting to identify the various forms of enrichment. Durr (1964) distinguishes three, which he calls horizontal, vertical and supplementary. DeHaan and Havighurst identify two types: the first is indifferently called "intensive," "vertical" or "in depth," and the second also bears several titles: "in extent," "extensive," "horizontal" or "lateral." Passow (1979) mentions four types of modifications to the regular program: horizontal, vertical, reorganizational and augmentative. And Stanley (1976) recognizes four types of enrichment which he mischievously calls "busywork," inappropriate, cultural and appropriate.

Among the numerous dimensions and names given to enrichment by various authors, it would eventually be possible to trace the ones which correspond to the forms and titles we ourselves have applied to this concept. Thus, one might think that what other authors call supplementary, in extent, lateral or even cultural enrichment, corresponds to what we refer to as enrichment in diversity. But when, for example, an author talks about horizontal enrichment, what specific need of the gifted or talented is he trying to meet? Does he want to allow this pupil to progress at a faster rate, encourage him to develop and exercise more complex mental processes, authorize him to explore in depth a field of interest, or open the door to a larger variety of knowledge? Here is the root of the problem. All possible transmutations between the authors and ourselves are partly conjectural since none of them have explicitly followed our method of differentiation of a school program to suit a marginal population. Each author promotes various forms of enrichment for gifted and talented pupils, none of which is derived directly from the identified differential characteristics and specific needs of those pupils. That is why we felt the need to undertake a more thorough procedure of differentiation of the educational experiences destined for this particular clientele. This allowed us to arrive at four dimensions of enrichment, to which we have given titles corresponding to the specific needs recognized in gifted or talented pupils. Unfortunately, the dimensions and words advocated by other authors only allowed us to assume certain priority needs which they recognized in such pupils.

Additional Information on Enrichment

Enrichment: means and aim. The two definitions we have just set forth confirm that enrichment is both a means and an aim: it is the best means of meeting the specific educational needs of gifted or talented pupils, and at the same time it is the aim of the various components of a special program. Among the most popular means of enrichment are full time or part time special classes, activities outside the regular hours, summer courses, tutors or mentors, resource centers, skipping, thematic clubs (journalism, astronomy, computers, etc.) and many others. As Ward (1965) so well emphasized, however, we must not mistake the whole for the part; just as one swallow does not make a summer, a single means does not constitute a "program." In practice, a program is usually the result of the combination and adaptation of various means.

Enrichment is not a program. Some authors speak of "enrichment programs" which are often compared to grouping or acceleration programs. This concept of enrichment as a form of response among others to gifted or talented pupils does not seem appropriate to us. In view of our definition of enrichment, any program truly differentiated for those pupils must aim at some form of enrichment in relation to the regular program.

Enrichment: a specific objective. By stating that enrichment is the differentiating principle of educational experience intended for gifted or talented pupils, we imply that enrichment is exclusively for them. This statement echoes Gold's concept: "an educational program . . . which on the whole being uniquely suited to the gifted is both unnecessary for and impossible of accomplishment by students of lesser ability." (1965, p. 136). But it contradicts Passow, who considers that enrichment is "the essence of good education" (1958, p. 193), or Renzulli who claims that "enrichment is not the exclusive property of persons interested in the gifted and talented" (1979a, p. 15). It is true that any individual in a learning situation increases his knowledge and skills, but in terms of a modification to the regular program, that is, from a normative viewpoint, enrichment becomes a measure intended specifically for this particular clientele - the gifted or talented.

Quantitative or qualitative enrichment. Our definition of enrichment as a four-dimensional increase of the educational experiences for gifted or talented pupils might lead one to believe that such experiences must differ quantitatively from those of other pupils. Actually, this is not so. Gifted pupils do not need "a little bit more of the same thing" but rather educational experiences which are qualitatively different from those in the regular program. Thus, the increase in density is achieved through more advanced learning content, the increase in complexity through the development and exercise of more complex mental processes or more advanced skills, and the increase in diversity mainly through the introduction of subjects not on the regular curriculum. Those modifications are much more qualitative than quantitative, as was suggested by several authors such as DeHaan and Havighurst (1961), Gallagher (1975) and Kaplan (1974). These qualitative modifications do not imply that gifted pupils should not master the regular program contents and develop the basic skills, just like other pupils, but rather that they must be allowed to go beyond those prerequisites and develop their potential to the fullest. It is therefore necessary to maintain a connection between the regular program and the special training offered to the gifted or talented.

Enrichment and teaching approach. This qualitative aspect of enrichment further implies that the teacher must modify and adapt the teaching approach. Indeed, since one of the functions of enrichment is the development and exercise of the most complex mental processes or the most advanced skills, the teaching approach must focus on such development and exercise rather than on the transmission of knowledge. According to Bloom's taxonomy (1956), the cognitive objectives of learning are the analysis, synthesis and evaluation of the study contents rather than simply their knowledge, understanding or application. The teaching approach must necessarily be modified to meet those higher objectives; this applies to every function of enrichment. That is why Gallagher (1975) considers that, whereas a modification of the learning environment is not always essential to the differentiation of school programs for gifted or talented pupils, differentiation always necessitates a transformation not only of the study contents but also of the teaching methods needed to transmit those contents.

Enrichment and cognitive development. The emphasis on highest mental processes and most complex skills to meet the enrichment needs of gifted or talented pupils does not mean that we should forget the necessity of developing other aspects of their personality. The objectives of emotional and social development in education are just as valuable for this particular group of pupils as for others. We must keep in mind that because of their superior skills, gifted or talented pupils will eventually play an important role in society (or may already have done so). One of the functions of education is to prepare them to play that role adequately. On the other hand, the possibility of gifted or talented pupils overdeveloping their cognitive skills should not entail the unilateral development of the emotional and social aspects of their personality. This fear of hypertrophied development seems to apply mostly to academically talented pupils. We readily accept that pupils who are talented in music, dance or gymnastics can perfect their particular skills, but we are more reticent in allowing pupils talented in literature or science to increase their skills and cultivate their interests in these subjects.

Enrichment and pupils' interests. Enrichment constitutes a response to the specific needs of gifted or talented pupils only if it is closely linked with their particular interests. Thus, a pupil wanting to progress more rapidly in mathematics or to further develop his interest in astronomy would not have his need fulfilled if given "enriching" experiences in arts, computer or physics. We should therefore avoid enrichment experiences for gifted or talented pupils which correspond to the educators' interests, or to their idea of what should be an enriching experience, rather than to the specific needs and interests of those pupils.

Acceleration

Some enrichment experiences are designed to increase the density of educational experiences for gifted or talented pupils, therefore to increase their rate of learning. This concept of "increased rate of learning" immediately suggests acceleration since, by definition, to accelerate means "to increase the rate of." Yet, increasing the rate of learning does not automatically have an accelerating effect on the pupil. Consider, for example, pupils who participate in a special program made up of half time academics and half time music. During the academic half time, those pupils cover the usual program in half the time allotted in regular classes; yet they do not move on faster from one grade to the next; they complete their primary level in say six years, which is the norm, therefore, they do not accelerate their rate of going through the regular school process. Those pupils, nevertheless, covered the usual program in fifty percent less time than the pupils in regular classes. Thus they had the advantage of an increased rate of presentation of learning contents and therefore of an acceleration of their rate of learning.

In order to make a clear distinction between acceleration of the learning rate and acceleration of the pupil's progress through the regular school process, we will use the term "acceleration" only in cases where the pupil progresses through the various levels of the school system more rapidly than the norm, and we will call enrichment in density the planned increase in the rate of presentation of learning contents. This approach differs from that of DeHaan and Havighurst (1961), Passow (1979), and Renzulli (1977), who do not make a clear distinction between acceleration of the learning rate and acceleration of the pupil's progress through the regular school process. It is however similar to Durr's (1964) and Stanley's (1976), although the latter does not give a clear definition of acceleration.

As mentioned earlier, authors generally agree on the following definition of acceleration: the possibility for the gifted or talented pupils to go through the school process more rapidly or more precociously than expected. This concept, although similar to ours, does not situate acceleration in relation to enrichment which, as we have seen, must be the differentiating principle of educational experiences designed for gifted or talented pupils. Hence, we define acceleration as

> a characteristic of certain means of enrichment, which corresponds to an advancement faster than the norm, either by subject or by grade.

Let us now make a few comments on the two main components of this definition.

Acceleration: a means of enrichment.

1. There are various means of enriching the school life of gifted or talented pupils, some of which are accelerative and others not. This is why we consider acceleration not as a means but as an accessory component which characterizes some means of enrichment. Acceleration therefore is not an aim in

itself: it only represents an attribute of certain means which, in the area of education of the gifted or talented, always involve enrichment. Any means with an accelerating component must also provide enrichment by contributing to an increase in density, depth, extent or complexity of learning. The child who skips a grade, for example, is seeing a content which is denser, deeper, more varied and more complex than if he had followed the regular schedule. In this sense, we might even add that the regular program itself becomes enriching for this child if he goes through it earlier than the norm and thus satisfies some of his specific educational needs.

2. There are numerous means of enrichment of an accelerating nature. Acceleration is not just skipping or starting early; it can also mean continuous progress, more advanced courses, exam credits, combined classes, etc.

3. Except for one, all those means result in a reduction of the time normally required to complete one or more steps of the school process. "Acceleration refers to the time element in education" (DeHaan & Havighurst, 1961, p. 98). The only exception is early entry to Kindergarten or grade 1: it is no more than an early progression through some steps of the school program.

4. Some of those means, such as getting into grade 1 earlier than normal, are not preceded by any form of enrichment in density. Others are accompanied by enrichment in density, such as combined classes, while some are subsequent to the enrichment experience, as, for example, advanced placement. Thus some forms of enrichment in density almost automatically entail acceleration. This is not always the case, however, as shown in the example of academic half time, mentioned earlier, which allows time for enrichment in depth, extent or complexity.

Acceleration: faster advancement than the norm.
1. The term advancement describes both an advancement and an administrative measure authorizing this advancement and giving it official approval. "The

main distinction between enrichment and acceleration is therefore administrative" (Keating, 1979, p. 218). This statement echoes DeHaan and Havighurst, who claim that a distinction must be made between enrichment and the various administrative measures which make it possible (1961, pp. 82-83).

2. Stanley (1976) recognizes that advancement may involve one or more subjects, in the case of exam credits or more advanced courses, for example. It may also apply to all subjects in a particular grade, such as early starting or skipping.

3. The accelerating component only applies when it corresponds to advancement which is more rapid than the norm. Even if a child enters grade 1 precociously and then goes on precociously through the whole school process, acceleration only applies to the grade 1 since it is only then that there was an increase of educational experiences, when acceleration took on its full meaning (i.e., a characteristic of a means of enrichment).

4. Acceleration must be defined in relation to a norm, that is, in relation to the hypothetical rate of progress of an average pupil, within a subject or from one grade to another. Compared with the established norm, acceleration might appear to push the talented pupil, or risk forcing him to advance too rapidly; yet for this pupil, such progression is normal since it corresponds to his own rhythm, which is more rapid (DeHaan & Havighurst, 1961, p. 98). Acceleration therefore does not force a talented pupil to progress more rapidly than his or her norm. It only releases the brakes imposed within a normative system by lessening or canceling the deceleration (according to Sanderlin's expression, 1973, p. 115) to which the pupil was subjected within that system.

Conclusion

Giftedness is just beginning to arouse interest in French Quebec. Our initial steps in this field consisted of numerous readings and discussions on the main concepts formulated mostly by North American authors. Our observations led us to reexamine some of their theoretical substrata and to look at a few divergent points of view. The present document is the fruit of those observations; its overall objective was to

1. establish the concept of enrichment and its dimensions on the basis of a rigorous method of differentiation of the educational programs intended for gifted or talented pupils,

2. relate the functions of enrichment to the specific cognitive characteristics of this target population,

3. confirm the role of enrichment as the priority aim of interventions suited to those children, and as the best means of responding to their distinct educational needs, and

4. demonstrate that there is no contradiction between enrichment and acceleration, but rather than they are closely linked, to the extent that educational means with accelerating components are designed to enrich the school life of the gifted or talented.

We hope these observations have pointed the way toward a more structured grouping of the various concepts found in writings on giftedness.

References

Bloom, B. S., Taxonomy of educational objectives. Handbook I: cognitive domain. New York: McKay, 1956.

DeHaan, R. F., & Havighurst, R. J. Educating gifted children (2nd ed., rev.). Chicago: University of Chicago Press, 1961.

Durr, W. K. The gifted student. New York: Oxford, 1964.

Fox, L. Programs for the gifted and talented: an overview. In A. H. Passow (Ed.), The gifted and the talented: their education and development; the seventy-eight yearbook of the National Society for the Study of Education. Part I. Chicago: University of Chicago Press, 1979.

Gallagher, J. J. Teaching gifted children (2nd ed.).

Boston: Allyn & Bacon, 1975.

Gold, M. J. Education of the intellectually gifted. Columbus, Ohio: Merrill, 1965.

Kaplan, S. N. Providing programs for the gifted and talented: a handbook. Ventura, California: Office of the Ventura County Superintendent of Schools, 1974.

Keating, D. P. The acceleration/enrichment debate: basic issues. In W. C. George, S. J. Cohn, & J. C. Stanley (Eds.), Educating the gifted: acceleration and enrichment. Baltimore: Johns Hopkins University Press, 1979.

Marland, S. P. Education of the gifted and talented. Report to the Congress of the United States by the U.S. Commissioner of education. Washington, D.C.: U.S. Government Printing Office, 1972.

National School Public Relations Association. The gifted and talented: programs that work. Arlington, Virginia: National School Public Relations Association, 1979.

Passow, A. H. The meaning of enrichment. In N. B. Henry (Ed.), Education for the gifted. The fifty-seventh yearbook of the National Society for the Study of Education, Part II. Chicago: University of Chicago Press, 1958.

Passow, A. H. A look around and a look ahead. In A. H. Passow (Ed.), The gifted and the talented: their education and development; the seventy-eigth yearbook of the National Society for the Study of Education. Part I. Chicago: University of Chicago Press, 1979. (a)

Passow, A. H. Secondary schools: program alternatives for the gifted/talented. In J. J. Gallagher, J. G. Gowan, A. H. Passow, & E. P. Torrance (Eds.), Issues in gifted education. Ventura, California: Office of the Ventura County Superintendent of Schools, 1979. (b)

Pressey, S. L. Educational acceleration: appraisal and basic problems. Bureau of Educational Research Monographs, no. 31. Columbus, Ohio: Ohio State University Press, 1949.

412

Renzulli, J. J. What makes giftedness: a reexamination of the definition of the gifted and talented. Ventura, California: Office of the Ventura County Superintendent of Schools, 1979. (a)

Renzulli, J. S. The enrichment triad model: a guide for developing defensible programs for the gifted and talented. Mansfield Center, Connecticut: Creative Learning Press, 1979. (b)

Renzulli, J. S., Hartman, R. K., & Callahan, C. M. Scales for rating the behavioral characteristics of superior students. In W. B. Barbe & J. S. Renzulli (Eds.), Psychology and education of the gifted (2nd ed.). New York: Halsted (Wiley), 1975.

Renzulli, J. S., Smith, L. H., White, A. J., Callahan, C. M., & Hartman, R. K. Scales for rating the behavioral characteristics of superior students. Mansfield Center, Connecticut: Creative Learning Press, 1976.

Sanderlin, O. Teaching gifted children. New York: Barnes, 1973.

Shields, J. B. The gifted child. London: National Foundation for Educational Research in England and Wales, 1968.

Stanley, J. C. The case for extreme educational acceleration of intellectually gifted youths. Gifted Child Quarterly, 1976, 20 (1), 66-67.

Sumption, M. R., & Luecking, E. M. Education of the gifted. New York: Ronald, 1960.

Tempest, N. R. Teaching clever children, 7-11. London: Routledge & Kegan Paul, 1974.

Terman, L. & Oden, M. The Stanford studies of the gifted. In P. Witty (Ed.), The gifted child. Boston: Heath, 1951.

Ward, V. S. Educating the gifted: an axiomatic approach. Columbus, Ohio: Merrill, 1961.

Ziv, A. Counselling the intellectually gifted child. Toronto: Guidance Centre, Faculty of Education, University of Toronto, 1977.

28

THE SECONDARY SCHOOL CURRICULUM
AND THE GIFTED CHILD

D. T. E. Marjoram

The School Curriculum

The school curriculum, and particularly the secondary school curriculum, is currently receiving a good deal of attention. On 25 March of this year the Department of Education and Science in London published "The School Curriculum." This document deals with the needs of all children, primary and secondary, and essentially pleads for breadth, coherence and relevance. It contains the passage:

All pupils should be encouraged throughout their school career to reach out to the limit of their capabilities. This is a formidable challenge for any school, since it means that the school's expectation of every pupil must relate to his individual gifts and talents. It is as necessary to meet this challenge for the ablest as for those who learn slowly and with difficulty or who have special educational needs, whether they are in ordinary or special schools; no groups' needs should be subordinate.

Her Majesty's Inspectors' (HMI) earlier publication, "A View of the Curriculum," proposed that "There is a need for greater and much more explicit consensus on what constitutes five years of secondary education up to the age 16." That consensus must take account of many things including these:
1. that the needs of the handicapped, the less able, the gifted, the culturally deprived and the culturally different vary enormously;
2. that in a climate of falling rolls and diminishing resources those agreed essential curriculum components

can and must be maintained. This paper offers a tentative view about one small, though very important characteristic of that necessary consensus - curricula for the gifted.

The Importance of Approach

Most of those who have written on curriculum for the gifted - Gallagher (1975, 1965), Passow (1976), Stanley (1976), Tannenbaum (1972), whether or not they advocate segregation by ability, stress methodology and mode of approach, agree that the gifted need scope to relate abstract ideas, innovate, pursue notions and topics in depth. Professor Evyatar at the World Conference in Jerusalem 1979 spoke on "Pattern and the Gifted Child." He quoted research on the predilection of children to look for taught patterns and the beneficial effects of work aimed at searching for unfamiliar relationships and patterns. Children will not innovate or travel unfamiliar paths when well trodden paths and established formulae are at hand. A problem-solving element is essential in the teaching of most, but especially for the very ablest. Evyatar has also shown that art for young mathematicians may be ultimately more beneficial than more mathematics. Professor Getzels (1981), in another address at the same conference, described his own research in nurturing creativity through "problem-finding" classroom activities. "To solve a problem is not always the most difficult thing - it is asking the right question that matters."

Professor Passow (1981) holds the view that there is too often a tendency to concentrate on the "gift" and pay insufficient attention to the other needs of the gifted. The important thing, claims Passow, is to create conditions in which a talent can best grow naturally. One of the worst things is "over-teaching" - it can be more harmful than neglect.

My own paper on creativity put forward the view that the most truly creative work is not usually the product of total freedom which can be bewildering or even limiting. Careful preparation, quality-stimuli, often form the best springboard to outstanding work.

The Need for Breadth of Content

The halls of fame are peopled with many who achieved greatness in fields other than those for which they were intended or first trained. Examples include Galileo, Mendel, Swift, Trollope, Baden-Powell, Delius, Rontgen, Marconi and Sibelius. Some, like Rodin, Grieg, Tolstoy, Wordsworth, Chesterton, Leibig, Einstein, Turner, Monet, were thought to be slow or inept or clumsy as children and would not have been considered in need of a special form of curriculum.

In any case, some subjects are such that a late start is no bar to ultimate mastery. Anyway, very few tests are reliably predictive and many children are unpredictable. Many research studies have underlined how difficult it can be for teachers and parents to recognize giftedness in their own charges. On the other hand it is not uncommon to find it recognized in those who don't possess it.

This would seem to argue strongly for a broad curriculum for all so that as many options as possible remain open. Experience in each of the main areas of language, mathematics, science, esthetic development, modern language, should continue until 16 though the gifted pupil must, of course, be able to opt for further languages, or sciences or humanities via the optional portion of the school program.

Differentiation within the "Core"

Moreover, as the HMI "View of the Curriculum" emphasizes, there is a need for skilful differentiation of depth and difficulty of treatment of those subject areas, notions and topics common to the curriculum of the least and most able.

Let us look briefly at each of these areas and consider how differentiation within such a framework or core might apply to each component. (For greater detail see the HMI Discussion document No. 4 Appendices (HMSO).

Language

The ablest undoubtedly need courses and materials devised for individualized learning which provide open minded opportunities that stretch and challenge. There needs to be room for choice and space for the private activities of reading and writing. Opportunities inside and outside the classroom need to be numerous and varied - drama groups, presentations, theatre and visits. There should be writers' groups which are either self-selective or self-sufficient. Resources such as magazines, libraries of quality, school book shops, poetry readings and competitions all help. But resources alone are insufficient. Bright pupils need advice and encouragement to extend their range and positive teacher intervention. The appropriate text at the right moment is all important. Systematic extension of reading skills broadening the experience can make very considerable demands on teachers' own skills and knowledge. The crucial issue is how to find acceptable ways of bringing the appropriate pupils and teachers together or even how to make sure that the appropriate teachers are in the schools to begin with.

Mathematics

Mathematical potential is often revealed by precise communication. Gifted pupils can have a wide vocabulary and a gift for selecting the appropriate word. Their language may be impressively concise as well. They may reveal themselves in other ways - the original remark, the unexpected question, the leap to the abstract, the distrust of intuition, a persistence and desire for perfection. They may detect ambiguity or imprecision in the teachers' own mathematical language.

Gifted young mathematicians want to generalize, set the particular fact in a general setting, relate one problem to another quite different one. What will happen they ask themselves, or their friends, or the teacher, if we change the numbers, if we work in a different base, if we use letters instead of numbers, if we turned it upside down or reflected it or enlarged it, if we did it in 3 dimensions instead of 2, if we tried it with irregular figures as well as regular ones, if we imagined it drawn on a balloon?

The appropriate provision for such pupils can take many forms. It can involve the encouragement of individual reading and giving the right problem at the right time. There are other more fundamental strategies such as providing accelerated courses, intensifying the amount of set work covered in a classroom or by homework or pushing on more rapidly with the main line of the course with some pupils. Some teachers prefer to provide extra enrichment for pupils' mathematical studies by forms of supplementary tuition or by club activities outside lesson time.

Science

Those who are gifted in science can see the relevance of what is learned in science lessons to situations outside the laboratory. They have the capacity to leap ahead or jump steps in an argument and to detect faulty logic, to perceive the direction of an investigation and to anticipate realistic outcomes. They can connect scattered or disparate data into coherent patterns, pursue persistently an investigation until all reasonable avenues have been explored. Many have the ability to hold a problem in the mind and analyze it.

As far as provision for the gifted child in science is concerned the most important factor is to meet teachers who can identify his or her gifts and elicit the appropriate responses. Crucial is the teacher's knowledge of the subject, as well as enthusiasm and level of expectancy. Equally important is the sheer craftsmanship of marking and the teacher's ability to assess progress, plan ahead, be able to put a good book in the hands of the pupil, suggest what he or she thinks about a particular way of tackling an experiment, or send the pupil to see an "expert" the teacher knows.

In the VIth form, pupils gifted in science can often develop narrow interests. If allowed, they tend to choose more sciences in general studies options: electronics, photography, astronomy, heredity, rather than compensatory elements. My science HMI colleagues emphasize that a balanced framework for all VIth-formers is necessary so that mixed art and science groups can discuss together aspects of the major areas of human experience - scientific and mathematical as well as literary, historical and esthetic.

Modern Languages

The child who is gifted in modern languages is often not identified by objective tests. An interesting study in Exeter a few years ago in which senior modern language teachers were asked to nominate highly gifted linguists, who were then tested, revealed that some of them had very moderate Verbal Reasoning Quotient scores. Linguistic talent spotting therefore depends very upon the quality of the teacher examining with care the work of the pupils and looking diligently for signs in everyday efforts. The gifted pupil is likely to do work which is not only careful and accurate but which also shows signs of a fellow feeling for the language. To some extent the gifted pupil "becomes" French while using the language, whereas the merely able pupil uses French efficiently, but without identifying with it.

In the study of literature, the gifted linguist shows insight and fellow feeling in the use of individual words and the organization of word patterns to a marked extent. Indeed there are examples of authors who have acquired sufficient command of a second language to be accepted by the second culture as a major contributor to it. Conrad, Nabokov and Koessler have not only acquired a foreign language but empathized with it to the point of metamorphosis into the very foreigner they begin by merely imitating.

As far as provision is concerned, in many schools inadequate attention is accorded to the skills of writing and reading, particularly to rapid silent reading which is essential for the development of the gifted linguist. It is not common for local education authorities to make special arrangements for gifted children in modern languages, but a few have organized short intensive residential courses for able school pupils with a special interest in languages. In one authority district which is fortunate in having attractive residential centers and enthusiastic advisers, a number of intensive courses have been offered which have proved very popular and successful. At one of them it was reported "the linguistic progress of the pupils was remarkable in pronunciation, comprehension, confidence, fluency and accuracy. From a sticky start on a Friday evening, progress was made to uninhibited and animated discussions on Sunday afternoon with most of the pupils."

Esthetics and the Arts

Esthetic thinking pervades the curriculum and there are those who have a natural sense of style and knowledge to go with it which makes them connoisseurs in many areas of esthetic expression. However, as far as schools are concerned, the major vehicles for esthetic thinking are music, art, drama; to a lesser extent literature; and for some mathematics. Clearly we haven't time to look at curricular provision in all those subjects but it is worth making a few comments about music and art, where problems of adequate curricular provision and organization can arise.

Music

The pupil gifted in music is likely to possess an instinctive sense of style, an understanding of what music is about and a natural physical and intellectual rapport with a chosen instrument. Moreover, these characteristics can develop at a very early age and, indeed, if a child's bent is towards performance in the modern competitive world, an early start must be made, particularly as a pianist or string player. Few of the virtuosos of today were not competent players by the age of five. A tape in my possession of a nine year old playing the Bach E-flat prelude for piano and Clare McFarlane's playing of the Bach E-major partita in the Young Musician of the Year Competition underline how difficult it is for the ordinary school to begin to cope with musical giftedness of this order, particularly in performance skills. In this area, more than in any other, except perhaps ballet, therefore, the problem of curricular provision may sometimes only by resolved by transfer to a special school. However this does not absolve the ordinary school from making robust efforts to provide high quality musical opportunities and stimulus for those who for one reason or another cannot go to a music school. Most local education authorities provide peripatetic teaching, weekend master classes or they run youth orchestras, some of which are of outstanding quality. It must not be thought, however, that it is easy to cope with performance skills in other subjects. The gifted young artist, poet, craftsman, mathematician, soccer player will always look for and respond to spectacular mastery in teachers and wise teachers will cultivate this as part of their pedagogical repertoire.

Art

Whereas in music and ballet there are considerations of physical development and habit formation which are essential from an early age, the same cannot be said of the visual arts, and there are noteworthy examples in this country of ordinary maintained schools which make outstanding provision for the able young artist.

Artistically Gifted Children

These children have an interest often amounting to an obsession with visual recording, matching the world around them to images which they create. They have an ability to depict in a way which is illuminating or revealing, seeing or emphasizing unexpected relationships between colors or shapes. They have, or readily acquire, the draughtmanship, manual and physical skills or techniques they need to convey their message. They are sensitive to the quality of the materials and tools they use. What do they need from school? First of all they need recognition and an acknowledgement that the gifts they possess do make them, not better or worse, but different. They then need opportunity - and sufficient time - to choose and to practice in their chosen field. Their practice and achievement should be challenged and appraised with vigor and frankness by teachers and there is no doubt about the beneficial effect on the artistically gifted of specialist teaching. Its absence may be a major hindrance to the early recognition of artistic talent and its development. Gifted young artists need an enriching environment - an introduction to the culture and history of their chosen art, access to books and periodicals in variety for study in breadth, travel to galleries and museums, the opportunity to meet adult and experienced practitioners of their art, and the chance to work side by side with other gifted pupils in outside clubs or classes.

Much of what has been said or recommended above would, if carried out by the intelligent acquisition of resources and by the thoughtful, flexible school and classroom organization, greatly improve not only the lot of the gifted but also the teaching of other children. In planning curricular provision for the gifted then, while we must retain breadth - for every gift can only be fully illuminated against the back-cloth of the whole of human knowledge. Nevertheless, within that broad, coherent core, there needs to be much choice and variety. The content itself has to be graded from the simple and concrete to the abstract and difficult. The methodology should span the range of careful, patient, structured teaching for the less able to the "studied neglect" of the most gifted, so that they can get on and try their own wings. All this calls for careful organization of resources and time. It calls for teaching of high quality, skilful assessment, careful record keeping. Maybe that implies a need for improved initial teacher training and more in-service training.

Viewed in this way some might argue that there is a case for development away from the curriculum conceived as parcels of knowledge and skills defined by examination syllabuses and labeled with subject names towards the concepts of "modes of thinking" whereby the commonality of the core curriculum would lie mainly in its ingredient areas of experience - the esthetic and creative, the ethical, the linguistic, the mathematical, the physical, the scientific, the social and political, and the spiritual. We might even begin to ask such questions as why weaving is often found in the school curriculum but chess is seldom represented.

Summarizing, then:

1. early prediction can be dangerous when it involves early specialization or dropping subjects which are difficult to resume later; curriculum for the gifted should not be too narrow;

2. differentiation, choice, quality, opportunity for innovation, all need tobe provided within the common areas of experience which comprise the curriculum core;

3. flexibility of organization and ready access to varied resources, human and material both inside the school, are vital;

4. some examination syllabuses are too packed with facts and allow too little scope for initiative. Questions, particularly open questions, are better than closed questions or didactic approaches, particularly for gifted pupils. "Studied neglect" can do less harm than over-teaching. The gifted need space and time for contemplation. I should like to pursue this need for contemplation a little further. Those children whose gifts may ultimately place them in positions of influence and even power can be solitary, reflective, introspective. Some of them have religious or spiritual needs; some may need to develop moral sensitivity and responsibility. Schools must consider how these things as well as social and political awareness can be built into the program for all and particularly the ablest.

I cannot conclude without saying that in England difficulties lie in the path of realizing these ambitions.

The current economic climate is giving pause for thought in every area of education. Falling rolls are decreasing the size of schools and will progressively diminish the flexibility needed to provide small withdrawal sets and ad hoc group work. Unemployment is causing great anxiety among young people and makes it more difficult even for able youngsters to plan ahead confidently. Educational legislation has led to the setting up of an Assisted Places Scheme - which may help the very ablest; it has also produced post-Warnock legislation, whereby more handicapped pupils than formerly must be catered for in maintained schools, with possible diversion of already straightened resources. More optimistically, it is still quite possible, given careful planning, and good will, to solve those problems while holding course and conserving what is best. Indeed, it is essential that we do.

References

Berman, A., Evyatr, A., & Globerson T. Mathematical patterns and gifted children. In A. H. Kramer (Ed.), Gifted children: Challenging their potential, new perspectives and alternatives, New York: Trillium Press, 1981.

Evyatar, A. Enrichment therapy. Educational Research, 1973, 15, 115-122.

Gallagher, J. J. Teaching the gifted child, 2nd ed. Boston: Allyn and Bacon, 1975.

Gallagher, J. J. (Ed.). Teaching gifted students: a book of readings. Boston: Allyn and Bacon, 1965.

Getzels, J. W. & P. W. The meaning of giftedness. Education, 1962, 82, 460-464.

Getzels, J. W. What is giftedness? Different approaches. In A. H. Kramer (Ed.), Gifted children: challenging their potential new perspectives and alternatives. New York: Trillium Press, 1981.

Passow, H.A. Nurturing giftedness: ways and means. In A.H. Kramer (Ed.), Gifted children challenging their potential, new perspectives and alternatives, New York: Trillium Press, 1981.

Passow, A. H. & Tannenbaum, A. J. Some perspectives
for the mid-70s. Education of the gifted and
talented. National Association of Secondary
School Principal's Bulletin, 1976, 60, 3-12.

Stanley, J. C. Youths who reason extremely well
mathematically: SMPY's accelerative approach.
Gifted Child Quarterly, 1976, 20, 237-238.

Tannenbaum, A. J. A backward and forward glance at
the gifted. National Elementary Principal, 1972,
51 41-53.

29

RESTORING A CHALLENGE
TO SECONDARY EDUCATION

H. Gilbert Nicol

Our gifted youth have been described variously as one of our most wasted resources and the most neglected of our handicapped population. Their plight has created new fields of inquiry and argument for social scientists and led to convocations such as this conference, attracting those concerned from throughout the world.

Yet there is apparently little agreement on who the gifted are - the 130-plus IQ is a hazardous basis, created to serve bookkeeping bureaucrats more than educators - or whoever they are, how best to respond to the needs of those in secondary education. Partly as a result of this, there has been much greater activity on behalf of the very young where the bright and precocious more easily capture our attention and affection and the support of funding sources.

This emphasis on the younger age group also has more practical reasons. In the lower school levels, there is less diversity in subject specialization and more opportunity to organize classes in which children can explore their hidden potential. In the upper grades, those concerned for the gifted - and here I enlarge this group to include all students who find neither sufficient challenge nor a sense of direction and purpose in their education - are confronted with the problem that confronts almost all our high schools today.

The problem, as I would state it, is that secondary education, in reaching out in all directions, has obscured its essential purpose and in the process abandoned the challenge of achieving excellence. Like many modern cities, education has grown far and wide while its core has deteriorated and convenience and comfort have become the standards of achievement.

In initiating the study that produced the recent reform of the curriculum at Harvard, Henry Rosovsky, dean of the Faculty of Arts and Sciences, could have been speaking as well for our high schools when he wrote in 1964, "At the moment, to be an educated man or woman does not mean anything. It may mean that you have designed your own curriculum. It may mean that you know all about urban this or rural that. But there is no common denominator. The world has become a Tower of Babel in which we have lost the possibility of common discourse and shared values."

Christopher Jenks has described the development of the Harvard core curriculum as going back to complexity and said that what we should want of young men and women is the ability to think clearly and to act rationally on the basis of thinking rather than on the ability to respond quickly to varied stimuli.

Despite our efforts to tailor high school education to the special needs of students and to make it exciting and relevant for them, substantial drop out rates continue, having reached as high as 23%.

Twenty percent of our high school graduates are deficient in language and numerical skills. Since 1970, inferential comprehension in reading of 17-year-old high school students has declined, as have their abilities in expository writing and mathematical reasoning.

Nearly one half of recent high school graduates have been found to consider their high school experiences as neither valuable nor even fairly useful. And as many of those in high school today do not consider the work hard enough.

To darken further this gloomy prospect, our schools are often burdened with curricular changes that have social or political ramifications without having academic or intellectual underpinnings. And, as one of President Carter's departing administrators remarked, "If you think you can see light at the end of the tunnel, you must be looking down the wrong tunnel."

Much of the distress that today surrounds us in

education reflects our looking for answers to uncertain questions, trying to solve problems that have not been clearly stated. It is quite human for us to focus on concerns of which we are most aware and to neglect those that lie hidden deeper in our consciousness. We leave that to our theologians and philosophers. We are passengers on the Titanic arguing about seating arrangements as the ship goes down.

Our problem, of course, is: How do we impart learning to young people in such a way that they are equipped to live in a world a quarter of a century away in time? I leave to the modern day H. G. Wells, George Orwell and futurists at large the realm of precognition. As a matter of fact, I am not much concerned with what the future will be like, only that it will be at least somewhat different. We should be concerned not only with educating young people to live in today's world but in preparing them to adapt to tomorrow's world, the world they will be most a part of, the world of 2016 and 2031, when they will be at their most productive.

It is abundantly clear that many and perhaps most of our students and teachers are able and willing to accept greater challenge. Our response is not a matter of financial resources, but our determination to face the realities of the future. Our schools cannot hope to keep pace with the swiftly expanding fields of knowledge, but we must recognize our young people's ability to learn and our teachers' willingness to teach.

The high school today has become a way station through which our children pass to achieve some other destination - employment or further education - or simply to teach the school leaving age. In less than fifty years, the high school diploma has been transformed from a credential of achievement to merely a ticket of admission to some other opportunity. We do not ask the high school graduate, how well have you learned to acquire knowledge, but how much knowledge did you acquire, what job did you get or to which college or university were you admitted?

More often than not, this way station - epitomized by the comprehensive high school - is filled with a bewildering array of vending machines among which the student may either wander aimlessly sampling this and that, or select only from those for which he or she has acquired a taste. A number emerge quite well educated, despite, more than because of the system, but too many leave little better equipped for the future than when they arrived.

For the past four years, as the representative of the International Baccalaureate Office for Canada and the United States, I have traveled back and forth across both countries, listening and talking to secondary school people and others in education about a program that was devised to enable young men and women to move easily from secondary schooling in one country to university studies in another. This is the reason the International Baccalaureate program was developed; but it has elicited interest in both our countries, particularly Canada, principally as a program for the academically talented and highly motivated.

The IB, as it is known, is an elite program because its rigorous standards demand excellence, an essential quality of all educational endeavors. Any standards in education that are not measured in terms of excellence are not standards at all. Those who condemn this elitism must condone mediocrity, which has no place in education.

I will describe the International Baccalaureate program for two reasons. First, it represents many of the highest standards achievable by young people between the ages of, roughly, 16 and 19. Because of this, it is accessible only to a relatively small portion of students. The second reason is because the focus and general design of the IB program can be used to serve all students without sacrificing the standards of excellence that encourage students to reach beyond their grasp. I am describing this particular program because it so clearly spells out those principles that should be reflected in your thinking as you seek opportunities to respond to the needs of the highly motivated and academically talented.

The program is a comprehensive and cohesive curriculum of general education that responds to the need for greater challenge on the upper secondary level and for new opportunities to achieve excellence in education. Designed and administered by the International Baccalaureate Office, a Swiss foundation in Geneva, the curriculum encompasses traditional courses of study, incorporating multicultural perspectives. It is based on international standards of achievement in developing all the main powers of the mind through which man interprets, modifies and enjoys his environment.

Each candidate for an IB Diploma is required to become proficient in language and mathematics - the two most important tools of communication and analysis, and the students must learn, as Thomas Arnold wrote, "about things and their forces and men and their ways."

The objectives to be achieved in each subject offered by the school in the program are set forth in a syllabus that provides guidance without specifying the teaching methods to be used. Thus, each teacher is free to work with the students in his or her own style. Both the syllabuses and examinations are prepared and administered under the direction of a multinational team of examiners. They are designed to emphasize the philosophy of teaching - how the historian or physicist acquires knowledge rather than what they know - and thereby accommodate the diverse traditions to be found in the 35 countries where today more than 150 schools offer the program. The program is offered in both French and English and examinations can be arranged in any other language.

During the last two years of secondary school, the IB Diploma candidate studies six subjects, three of them for approximately five periods a week for two years and three for half that total time over one or two years. From the courses being offered by the school, the candidate selects one from each of the following areas:

Language A, the language and its literature of the school or that native to the student including a study of world literature in translation from at least two other cultural areas; in Canada and the United States this is most often English or French.

Language B, the second area, is a second modern language, distinguished from Language A in not requiring the same depth and breadth of cultural understanding or literary analysis. The requirement that a second language be studied serves not only an essential practical need in an increasingly interdependent world but the need to analyze the relations between the elements of a sentence and grasp the various ways in which ideas are translated into words. U.S. Congressman Paul Simon reports that tests show students who study another language do better in all academic areas and students in the lower fourth of the academic scale show even more gain from language studies than those in the upper fourth. This echoes the work of Wilder Penfield at McGill, arguing that language learning influences all learning abilities by enhancing intellectual capacity.

In the Study of Man, the student chooses among history, geography, economics, philosophy, psychology or social anthropology. Experimental Sciences offers the choice of biology, chemistry or physics.

The fifth requirement is mathematics. We are rightly concerned about monolingualism, especially the paucity of opportunities to learn non-western languages, but we should be equally concerned about the erosion of mathematics as a requirement for graduation and the inadequacy of that which is taught. The computer era is here yet whether we think of them as toys or useful tools, we seem oblivious, in terms of mathematics, that the computer is already a fact of life for everyone. Teaching computer technology will prepare students for this generation of computers; teaching mathematical reasoning will prepare them for the generations to come.

As a sixth subject, the student may select art, music, a classical language, an additional subject offered under languages, study of man, experimental sciences or mathematics.

To date, 17 schools in Canada and 34 in the United States have adopted the IB program. They are in small towns and large cities scattered across the continent: from Bridgewater, Nova Scotia, to San Francisco - from Edmonton, Alberta, to Harlingen, Texas. Thirty-five are public schools; the 16 independent schools include 6 also serving multinational communities.

The IB serves all kinds of schools: rural and inner-city; comprehensive and academic; magnet schools; schools with 60% or more of their students from minorities in the population, and schools serving affluent neighborhoods and international communities. Students enroll in the IB program simply on the basis of how ready and eager they are to learn, to seize the opportunity for upward mobility that has always been the hallmark of public education in both countries.

Therefore, let us consider what the IB represents for a school adopting the program. We must agree that there is little that is unique in the IB. The program is a new application of general education theory which has been extolled and opposed for centuries. Characterizing the teaching of the sophists, Aristotle said, "The teaching they gave to their pupils was ready but rough. For they used to suppose that they trained people by imparting to them not the art but its products, as though anyone professing that he would impart a form of knowledge to obviate pain in the feet, were then not to teach a man the art of shoemaking, or the sources whence he can acquire anything of the kind, but were to present him with several pairs of shoes of all sorts; for he has helped him to meet his need, but has not imparted to him any art."

More than twenty centuries later, Dorothy Sayers calls for a return to the Aristotlean philosophy. "We have lost the tools of learning that were so adaptable to all tasks," she writes. "Instead, we have merely a set of complicated jigs, each of which will do but one task and no more, so that no one ever sees the work as a whole."

Whatever the reasons for a school's adopting of the IB program, the program's impact on the school and school district has already been shown to have implications beyond serving the academically talented and highly motivated. By offering students a concisely defined curriculum leading to a diploma, the IB is reestablishing a goal and a sense of the intrinsic value of secondary education. This affects not only those students enrolled for the IB examinations but their fellow students, giving them all a better sense of the meaning of excellence in education.

It is equally important that the IB gives students and teachers a thrilling sense of the university of education as they follow the same courses of study preparing them for the same examinations as their peers in Brazil and Swaziland, Belgium and the United Kingdom, India and Japan.

Those who condemn it as elitist, in the pejorative sense, cannot comprehend that excellence in academic achievement can be as important to the entire student body and school community as are sports teams and programs in the performing arts.

With well defined structure and requirements, the IB program - as would any similar upper secondary level program - serves in the lower grades as a beacon toward which students set their course in selecting subjects that will best prepare them for the challenge. Usually not aware of their post secondary goals, 7th and 8th grade students can focus on the means for equipping themselves to be able to choose among whatever options they may later have. Earlier interest in foreign languages and more advanced mathematics are examples of the choices made.

Probably an even stronger implication in the reorientation toward learning skills is the effect on teachers. Some may at first be reluctant to participate, but they soon join those enthusiastic to respond to a new challenge. Again and again, IB schools are presented with the problem of selecting among those who want to teach an IB subject.

Too often we hear of teacher burn-out and increasing numbers of poor teachers. A spokesman for a teachers' union in one of the States remarked that if the governor did not approve a tax increase he would be unable to pay teachers more and thus be unable to achieve his goal of excellence in education. I dispute this mercenary view of teaching.

A recent study of government aid to independent schools in British Columbia - aid which was used mostly to raise teacher salaries - reported preliminary findings after two years that parents and students consider the teachers to be less committed. Often teachers are not paid enough, but just as often they want more intellectual incentives and challenge as much as or more than money, which I assume most of us also want.

Most of all our teachers yearn for recognition of their intellectual prowess. New York Times Editor Fred Hechinger recently commented on the publicity given a university scholar's scientific theory supporting the biblical account of the Exodus and the fact that the same theory had been generally ignored when advanced seven years earlier by a high school teacher. Wrote Hechinger, "If there is scant likelihood that a teacher's creative explorations beyond the high school syllabus will be taken seriously, what are the chances that people with serious intellectual interest and potential will go into, or stay in, school teaching? As a result, schools will become more and more intellectually barren."

In Maryland, a teachers' committee determined Aristotle's "Poetics" and Machiavelli's "The Prince" to be too difficult for 10th graders and a teacher who insisted on assigning portions for optional extra credit was suspended. When teacher burn-out is referred to, it connotes among other things, boredom. The principal cause of boredom is lack of academic challenge. Certainly none of the teachers preparing students for the IB examinations complain of boredom and teachers and students are brought closer together in the common cause of mastering the external examination.

Why do we offer our young people during these crucial years between 13 and 19 so little opportunity for learning and so much opportunity to accumulate information and acquire knowledge - which as Alfred North Whitehead remarked, "Keeps no better than fish"?

It is easy to blame the universities for not requiring a measure of learning for admission, but no school or board of education has as its principal mission preparing students to enter college or find immediate employment. Their mission is to educate, period; and by educate, I mean to provide each student with all the learning arts he or she can reasonably be expected to have the ability to develop and use.

The need to provide all students with a means for learning in the major disciplines is critical at a time when the percentage of high school graduates immediately entering a college or university is declining. According to the United States Bureau of the Census, 65% of those entering a college or university in 1970 had been graduated from high school that year; by 1977 the percentage was 54%. This 17% decline over eight years represented a gradual decrease in each year except 1972, a decline that continued despite changing economic conditions and the end of the Viet Nam era draft deferment in 1974. Thus, more than ever, the high school affords many young people the last opportunity to acquire the learning skills essential to their continued intellectual growth and ability to make the most of future opportunities.

Given the ability to learn commensurate with his or her potential, each and every student is then equipped not only to acquire new knowledge but to nurture and develop the capacity to learn, no matter the field of endeavor, and to pursue this interest in a world greatly changed from today's. This surely is the essence of education as distinguished from training. Such education is not opposed to but supportive of meaningful vocational training. This is particularly so in light of reports from the United States Bureau of Labor Statistics that, in January 1981, 53% of the workforce was in white collar jobs, representing a 33% increase over the past 20 years. General Motors has begun the organized and intensive recruitment of liberal arts majors. An internal study at AT&T reported that liberal arts graduates progressed more rapidly in management than did business and engineering majors, making a strong showing in managerial skills.

There is another popular trend in the United States introducing at all levels of education courses on how to think. This is suspect: another typical quick fix approach, implying that thinking can be independent of content. I wonder if knowing rules of inference independent of content is terribly valuable. We are preparing young people to live in a world which we see through the glass only darkly, but we can assume that once a person has learned to think within the major modes of learning the capacity to think will have been developed to the point where changing or new content will be acceptable challenges. We know nothing about the physiology of learning, yet we do know that thinking is an infinitely expandable process. When the contents of what we learn to think about are comprehensive and cohesive, our powers to think will be applicable to content areas previously unknown.

None of this is meant to suggest that the IB program is a palliative for the academic malaise that pervades secondary education. Instead, at a time of eroding public confidence in secondary education, I suggest that schools adopting the IB or a similar general education program are signaling a disposition to return to Thomas Jefferson's faith in education as the proper religion of a democracy and the belief that schools and education in general should be a causative agency and not a reactive or reflective agency in the making of a social organization. The abundant evidence produced in recent years of how schools are failing our young people is persuading educational leaders to doubt the wisdom of their well intentioned (although misguided), less exacting approach to the education of young people and to return to the demand, rigor and strength which characterized the curriculum less then twenty years ago.

Whatever path our young people follow after they leave high school, we have served them well only if we have helped them learn to think. Only if they can think in the different modes of learning can we say we have prepared them to respond to those future needs of which we know so little.

In the closing chapters of his "Memoirs," Jean Monnet wrote, "Some people refuse to undertake anything if they have no guarantee that things will work out as they planned. Such people condemn themselves to immobility. 'Tomorrow is another day,' my father used to say, with a zest which my mother, in her wisdom, did her best to calm. 'Sufficient unto the day is the evil thereof,' she would reply. They were both right. Day to day effort is needed to make one's way forward; but what matters is to have an objective clear enough always to be kept in sight."

In commending a liberal arts program with rigorous standards as the rational response to the needs of the academically talented at the secodary level, I suggest this approach as offering both a practical and achievable objective and a means for serving the ambitions of all students and teachers. There is no better way to fulfill your destiny than through your faith in the ability and willingness of your students and all students to reach - sometimes beyond their grasp - but always to reach for excellence.

30

TEACHING THINKING TO THE GIFTED

Edward de Bono and Norah Maier

The education of gifted and talented children and students has progressed through several evolutionary stages. At the first World Conferences, our major preoccupation was with definitions and identification procedures; the third conference began the examination of programs. The focus on the content of curricula for the gifted led to a demand for a qualitatively differentiated approach for this group. Suggestions that skills be the basis of such a curriculum (Tannenbaum, 1981), that idea scope be examined (Gallagher, 1981), and that problem finding be included (Getzels, 1981) arose. The proposal that thinking be a separate subject on the curriculum for the gifted was also made (Maier, 1981). Since then, "thinking" has become an enrichment component, a complementary study, or a subject in provisions and programs for the gifted (e.g., at the University of Toronto Schools).

The time has come that direct and deliberate attention to the development of thinking skills is more worthwhile than the acquisition of yet more knowledge. The information explosion, and the development of sophisticated mechanisms for processing that information has made it more important than ever to focus on the basics underlying all processing. Inadequate thinking skills can handicap even those who possess a vast storage of facts and data. There is a considerable danger in the traditional educational belief that a highly intelligent individual, supplied with adequate information, will exercise a high degree of skill in thinking.

In fact, high intelligence may not be associated with a high degree of thinking skill. The work done at the Cognitive Research Trust at Cambridge has also shown that skill of thinking can be improved by direct attention and the learning of simple operating methods. The more intelligent a person, the greater the need to pay particular attention to his thinking skills; there exists a danger of being trapped by one's own intelligence. We have coined the phrase "intelligence trap" to designate this danger. One of the elements of intelligence is the speed of scanning in the brain; gifted children seem quicker at understanding and processing information. However, this can develop into the habit of jumping to facile conclusions, or being satisfied with the first logical answer. A narrowness of mental processing develops here which precludes the search for alternative approaches or solutions. The reward system employed in the conventional classroom encourages the development of this trap.

We stretch brilliant minds by giving them ever more difficult and complex problems. Although such challenges work well for motivation, they may develop an impatience with the simpler steps which more advanced operations necessitate. The result is a type of superficiality which is quite surprising in a mind otherwise exhibiting a wide curiosity. At the University of Toronto Schools we have found that a twelve year old in Grade 7/8 must already learn to reign in the speed of his mental processing. Given a problem situation to consider for the precourse test, the majority of children offer a solution or take a position immediately, then follow it up with thinking steps. It is clear that this is not only reactive thinking, but also defensive thinking. It is a mental habit which leads to rationalization, not clear reasoning. The task of the educator in such cases is to slow down the cognitive process in a deliberate manner, to offer the child tools which permit him to examine a given situation from all sides before applying judgment.

A parallel trap can be found in the affective domain of the child. It is the "ego trap." The child that stands out in the earlier grades is so often rewarded for being right, for correctly pointing out fallacies in other answers, for seeing something that no one else has seen. This ego involvement is being clever and being seen to be clever; it makes the development of a wide range of thinking skills very difficult. A skilled thinker needs to detach his thinking from his ego so that he can observe his thinking in action and note its failure. The desire to be right - the fear of being wrong - develops a caution that is detrimental to cognitive growth. Moreover, it channels the thinker to stay on tracks that are guaranteed to bring him known success. This dependence on precedent is based on the assumption that what worked before will work again. Indeed, at the junior and secondary level of education, a mind which outpaces others in the processing stage can continue to be successful. In higher education, however, this skill may become a weakness if it is not accompanied by a broad scope in the initial stage of thinking, that is, the perceptual stage.

It thus helps to distinguish between how we look at things, perception, and how we move on from what we perceive, processing. Logic merely processes something that has been perceived: perfect logic can thus perfectly service an inadequate or even biased perception. Children who have been identified as bright or gifted are often done so on the strength of their verbal and mathematical performance. However, flawless verbal and mathematical reasoning can follow a very superficial view of the problem or situation. It is also accompanied with the tendency to be satisifed with a single approach so that the gifted child rests content with the first "right" answer he or she comes across. In the limited scope of elementary and secondary education, especially if the child is grouped with other children of average ability, no problem may arise. In later stages of learning, such rigidity prevents the learner from even seeing the necessity of discovering alternative approaches. Frustration and impatience are then directed toward the processing stages; error is sought in the analysis, not in the original perception. A block-arranging experiment on some academic staff illustrates this point. Many of the academics took a first step which was right, and then a second and third step, both of which were right - and then they were at an impasse. They insisted on going forward since they knew they had been right at each stage. Many of them took a long time to solve the problem and some of them gave up. The same problem given to school children is often solved in a few seconds. The children start by taking the same steps but, as they find themselves getting nowhere, they go back to the beginning and try a different approach. The Harvard academics accepted that great fallacy of thinking: "If you are right at each step, there is no need to go back."

A correlate to this becomes a limited creative scope. Playing it safe, fearing to take a risk, a child is more likely to be a game player than a game designer. The convergent cognitive processes which are necessary to succeed in conventional schooling may stifle the development of divergent perceptions. This is pronounced where the intellectual performance is used to fulfill the affective needs of the ego. Intelligent children are quick to learn the rules of the game and to play according to those rules. At school, the brighter children quickly learn what school is all about, how to succeed, how to pass exams, how to please the teacher, how to impress their peer groups. In later life, the same facility at observing the mechanics of a system permits them to learn the rules of their profession, industry, or corporation. Though this must basically be an advantage, it becomes a disadvantage when flexibility is called for. A person who too quickly adopts the "culture" of his surroundings may not realize how this culture fashions and restricts his thinking thereafter. Yet the present need, at all levels of activity, is this very ability to find alternative approaches, alternative solutions, in fact, alternative problems. A focus on developing the ability to handle open-ended situations will service the practical future of the individual. In a mathematics textbook, there is no point in thinking beyond the right answer since you cannot be more right than right. But life does not consist of problems set out in mathematics textbooks. In everyday situations, one answer will not do. One carries on thinking to find a better solution, and then on from there until a decision or action has been taken. To teach thinking is to teach its use.

The teaching of thinking has been approached in a number of ways. There is a discussion approach, which sees children verbally processing some interesting topic in the hope that the thinking employed in that discussion can be generalized into a direct thinking skill. In actuality, the point to point drift of our natural thinking style, as well as the reactive idea generation of oral exchange, has little effect on developing thinking skills beyond the ability to assess evidence. Although minor debating skills may emerge, fast talking is not fast thinking. Furthermore, attention is focused on the content rather than on the process of thinking. The transfer to other matters does not take place.

Problem-solving or decision-making procedures constitute another approach. Many of these programs revert to the classical model of logical processing in their objective of developing the reasoning power of the child. While this type of training is useful in general, it is dangerous to the child with an above average ability for the above reasons. The questionable transference between the ability to solve hypothetical situations or complex mind puzzles, and the ability to think effectively in real life situations, must be circumvented. A focus on the point of entry in our thinking, on the perception part of thinking, is the approach we take at the Cognitive Research Trust and in the CoRT Thinking Program (de Bono, 1982).

CoRT thinking isolates tools which directly represent a perception aspect of thinking. They are attention directors which cover a wide range of operations in applied situations. Each of the tools is practiced, quite formally and deliberately, on a large number of different situations. The program is designed to remain simple because it must lead to a development of a wide range of thinking skills employed in a practical manner. Efficient rather than descriptive or philosophical thinking is the aim.

The focus is on thinking as a deliberate process rather than a combination of inspiration and information. Very little information is given in the applied practice exercises. The situation is often deceptively simple. This leads to occasional disorientation on the part of gifted students. They are so accustomed to being presented with complex problems or volumes of information that the self reliance necessary for providing the total context for the thinking operation unsettles them. The more aggressive type reacts by discarding the whole exercise. It verifies his feeling that it is quite an insult to ask him to "learn to think" in the first place. Slowly, the example of peers who have likely had less confidence in their skills, and who have in fact often sought better ways to deal with a problem, convinces him that it is not a matter of learning an idiom, but of directing one's thinking beyond mere content. Finally, the gifted pupil comes to realize that although the thinking situation itself is very simple, he is required to bring sophistication to it. He has to create both the context and also his own thinking within this context. It is at this point that interest grows.

The program consists of six units. Each unit comprises one broad area of mental activity. CoRT I develops the general skill of suspending judgment. This is organized around ten lessons, each of which is constructed to develop a breadth in the perceptual range of the student. PMI (considering the Plus, Minus, and Interesting aspects of a situation or decision) leads the student from the narrow classification of positive and negative aspects. Students quickly see that this tool expands to include those ideas which would have seemed incorrect or off-topic in conventional terms. Yet, they discover that the additional category initiates and permits the relevance of innovative ideas. They come to recognize that the serialist processing of information into positives and negatives eliminates ideas that are generative and creative. The "Interesting" category in this skill leads students to the speculative track of thinking. Projective, rather than reactive, thinking tools develop the mental position of anticipating rather than reacting to things or events. Another lesson, C&S, considering the Consequences and Sequel of a decision in short (one to five years), medium (five to twenty-five years), and long (over twenty-five years) periods, leads students into the habit of mapping out the detailed consequences of an action before taking it. Examining the alternatives, possibilities and choices (APC), or considering all factors (CAF), provide the tools for a wide scanning of any matter before the narrowing process of selection begins.

Gifted students are quick to recognize the possibility of mental paralysis inherent in a broad perception of alternatives. They are disturbed by the acceptance of all ideas no matter how irrelevant, and rightly so. The ultimate goal is to equip the individual with all the tools which lead to efficient thinking. For this purpose tools are introduced which contract the first stage, achieving a wide perceptual scan, with a variety of selective instruments to facilitate decision-making and action. After an examination of aims, goals, and objectives (AGO) and other people's viewpoints (OPV), students practice the skill selection by discovering one's first important priorities (FIP).

The six units of the program cover sixty thinking tools and are identified as follows: CoRT I - Breadth; CoRT II - Organization; CoRT III - Interaction; CoRT IV - Creativity; CoRT V - Information and Feeling; CoRT VI - Action. The sixty lessons may be organized in a two and a half year period if structured according to weekly lessons of forty to fifty minutes. The level of application sweeps from the elementary to adult education. The units lend themselves to individualized programming because they are independent of each other rather than cumulative. This discreet characteristic permits the individual instructor to apply that unit which suits the particular needs of the group.

At the University of Toronto Schools, a combination has been developed which arose out of a discovery of the peculiar needs of specific stages of development. Consequently, Breadth and Organization are taught in Grades 7 and 8, Interaction and Information and Feeling in Grade 9, and Creativity and Action in Grade 10.

Interdisciplinary studies arise from such a program. As these tools underlie most operations in the thinking area of any subject, they provide the vehicle for synthesis which most education systems have been seeking. Because the thinking operations learned are simple and basic, their application across the board of subject areas is possible. Transfer is now not a matter of content but of skeletal mental attitudes. It follows that such a transfer may escape the academic idiom of the school and reach beyond it to the world of action. Passive understanding and description is the conventional role of the learner. In this perceptual approach to thinking, the learner acquires the instruments for active application and life-long learning.

Special attention should be paid to the unit on Creativity (CoRT IV). It is in this section that gifted students are presented some lateral thinking techniques. It was necessary to create the neutral label "lateral thinking" to describe the change from one way of looking at things to another. Even people designated as "highly creative" get locked into a single way of seeing something. This type of perception may be considered different and original because it diverges from the established way of seeing something; however, with time, this perceptual track may become as rigid as any conventional one. This accounts for some of the narrowness in certain types of creative production. Thus, even the highly creative can use tools which will help them to deliberately explore ways of connecting hitherto unconnected ideas or discovering novel combinations. The gifted need this training in the process of changing concepts and perceptions in order to balance the highly developed critical faculty which education fosters in them.

Criticizing ideas is not necessarily generating ideas. Children are given basically the same techniques as adults to escape from personal or established ways of looking at things. In a lesson on "Concept Challenge" they are led to test the uniqueness of concepts. This may lead to other ways of doing things. "Dominant Idea" asks them to discover the dominant idea in any situation in order to escape from it. They practice the use of ideas not for their own sake, but for the ideas they may lead to in a lesson on "Stepping Stone." Finally, they are made aware how "Random Input" can generate a creative process which works on the mental patterns created by knowledge and experience and shapes a new approach. Once more, this expansion of creative perception must be followed by a contraction towards application and action. Students are made aware of the "Requirements" which may influence the creation of ideas for a particular purpose. Likewise, they are asked to examine whether an idea fits the requirements, and the advantages and disadvantages of its application in a lesson on "Evaluation." Lateral thinking, then, attempts to shift the exercise of a critical intelligence to that of creative intelligence. Although there is more immediate satisfaction in the former, the gifted should become aware of the long term use of creative production. It is one more method to move beyond the complex, closed problem-solving approach to the speculative, open ended track of thinking.

The teaching of thinking to the gifted can thus effect several changes in their education. It prepares them to become creative producers instead of passive consumers of knowledge. It frees them from a curriculum which only draws on their strengths, rather than also combats their weaknesses. It gives them the tools for self-directed learning. Equipped with the basics of perception, the gifted child, adolescent, or adult can respond positively to the changes that beset him day to day. Constructive action, rather than passive contemplation or criticism, results from the confidence that one can think effectively. What more should educational services provide for this group of intellectual exceptionality than an opportunity to navigate, rather than drift through, the future?

References

de Bono, E. Thinking. In N. Maier (Ed.), Teaching the gifted, challenging the average. Toronto: University of Toronto Guidance Centre, 1982.

Gallagher, J. J. Differentiated curriculum for the gifted. In A. H. Kramer (Ed.), Gifted children: challenging their potential; new perspectives and alternatives. New York: Trillium Press, 1981.

Getzels, J. W. Problem-finding and the nature and nurture of giftedness. In A. H. Kramer (Ed.), Gifted children: challenging their potential; new perspectives and alternatives. New York: Trillium Press, 1981.

Maier, N. Thinking: a curriculum subject for the gifted. In A. H. Kramer (Ed.), Gifted children: challenging their potential; new perspectives and alternatives. New York: Trillium Press, 1981.

Tannenbaum, A. J. A curriculum framework for differentiated education for the gifted. In A. H. Kramer (Ed.), Gifted children: challenging their potential; new perspectives and alternatives. New York: Trillium Press, 1981.

31

EXTRACURRICULAR MATHEMATICS: INCENTIVE FOR THE TALENTED

Harold Don Allen

The extracurricular, so-called in one form or another and to varying purpose and degree, has roots deep in Western education. The playing field, the track meet, school dramatics, oratory and debating, singing and instrumental music, student publications, and sundry "clubs" of an academic, special interest, or social nature all developed and proliferated in recognition of and in response to a diversity of inclinations and needs. Mathematics, as an elective extracurricular activity, has early origins on this Continent, but the main thrust of its organized development has significantly been in the last 25 to 30 years.

Among school subjects, mathematics has a particular ability, at whatever level, to challenge, occupy, develop and capture the imagination of the abler student. One finds Shoesmith, a mathematics club innovator, eloquent on this point as early as 1933. At secondary and even upper elementary school level, however, it may be in individualized and small group effort, beyond the strictly curricular, that this challenge is most felt. Accordingly, for the gifted and talented among today's youth (though, to an extent, potentially for all), the growth and elaboration of the school mathematics club, mathematics day, mathematics fair, and individual and team mathematics competition, would seem to be and are of disproportionate educational significance.

Early instances of mathematics-related activity extending beyond the schoolroom exercise can be traced to the bygone era of spelling bees and other curriculum-related interschool and intercommunity rivalry, and involve the "challenge question," as it was commonly known. A mathematical problem, "practical" or otherwise, would be attempted and solved by one class or school, then sent to another as a challenge. Quite possibly, parents and others in the community became involved. One accessible source for such problems would be the miscellaneous, sundry, or promiscuous exercises which served to conclude school arithmetic of this period. Thus, the spirit of the challenge question is represented in these two nineteenth century problems, the first from Frederick Emerson, **North American Arithmetic** (Boston, 1837):

If 12 oxen eat up 3 1/2 acres of grass in 4 weeks, and 21 oxen eat up 10 acres in 9 weeks, how many oxen will eat up 24 acres in 18 weeks, the grass being at first equal on every acre, and growing uniformly?

and the second from Benjamin Greenleaf, **National Arithmetic** (Boston, 1867):

A servant draws off a gallon on each day, for 20 days, from a cask containing 10 gallons of wine, each time supplying the deficiency by the addition of a gallon of water; and then, to escape detection, he again draws off 20 gallons, supplying the deficiency each time by a gallon of wine. How much water still remains in the cask?

Still other "challenges" no doubt arose from problems "making the rounds" at the time, much as my students have labored over this elementary but difficult question of more recent origin:

Three routes link towns A and B. The shortest route is direct, in a straight line, and a 30 minute drive. The second route is by way of town X, to one side of AB, over straight roads from A to X and from X to B. This route takes 35 minutes. The third route is by way of town Y, to the other side of AB, over straight roads from

A to Y and from Y to B. This route takes 40 minutes. X and Y are both 25 km from town B, and roads from X and Y meet at B in (to keep the mathematics simple a right angle. Find the speed at which the vehicle is being driven.

The school mathematics club is a phenomenon of this century, but a search of the literature confirms that successful clubs have been in active existence for more than 75 years. "To study certain interesting matters connected with mathematics which do not properly find a place in the usual classroom work," the first such club was established at Shattuck School, a private school in Faribault, Minnesota, in 1903 (Newhall, 1911, p. 500). Other such clubs have adopted, or commentators have cited, markedly similar aims, "to round out and supplement the mathematics courses in the high school" (Russell and others, 1924); "to allow the pupil to explore and discover . . . the many interesting and worthwhile pleasures" associated with mathematics (Reed, 1925); "to develop an appreciation of mathematics, a greater interest in it, and a broader understanding of the subject than can be secured in regular classroom work" (Steward, 1930); and (an ambitious but worthy extrapolation) "to bridge the gap between text book study and actual application" (Sweedler, 1936). Although one finds a modest upsurge in interest in school mathematics clubs in the years immediately following World War II (see, for example, Owen, 1952), the elaboration of school contests and interschool meetings had not yet begun. A statement of mathematics club objectives from this period (Boyd, 1953) underlines needs of society and the potential of the abler secondary student: "to inspire and develop the capable student toward creative research in mathematics" and to familiarize the student with fundamental branches of mathematics "with the view in mind of possibly motivating that student to pursue subsequently this branch of knowledge on a professional level, thus, perhaps alleviating our shortage of mathematicians."

For Americans, in particular, the late 1950s, the dawn of the space age, was characterized (it will be recalled) by markedly renewed interest and concern relating to mathematics and science "electives" as such and to imaginative approaches to the identification, motivation, and development of mathematical and scientific talent. Phenomenal growth in school mathematics clubs, mathematics and science fairs, and regional and national contests and competitions date from this period. Already solidly established and enjoying institutional support of the American mathematics and mathematics education communities, Mu Alpha Theta (MATh), the national organization of secondary school and junior college mathematics clubs, was in a unique position to provide necessary and welcome leadership and coordination. Subsequent development of school mathematics clubs in North America (and, to an extent, abroad) accordingly may be identified in the main with the growth and maturation of Mu Alpha Theta, its publications, services, and regional and national activities.

"To engender keener interest in mathematics, to develop sound scholarship in the subject and promote enjoyment of the subject among high school and junior college students" were the ambitious but wholly praiseworthy aims of Mu Alpha Theta when its constitution appeared in **The Mathematical Teacher** in May, 1957. The cosponsorship of the Mathematical Association of America and the National Council of Teachers of Mathematics was noted by Mu Alpha Theta at its inception and continues to the present time, extending to representation on the Mu Alpha Theta governing board.

As a national society of mathematics clubs, Mu Alpha Theta has exerted leadership in school extracurricular mathematics primarily at two levels, the chapter (there currently are 1200) and the individual member (presently numbering 27,000). Chapter affiliation in Mu Alpha Theta is granted a school or college club only after investigation and approval of the school mathematics program and the mathematics qualification of faculty. Correspondingly, in its criteria for individual membership at national level, Mu Alpha Theta functions somewhat as a school mathematics honor society. Minimum standards of general scholarship and of mathematics coursework and attainment are stipulated in the national constitution. Individual chapters may set even higher standards before recommending a candidate for full membership. Associate membership typically is accorded interested students who are working satisfactorily toward national minimum requirements.

To the mathematics club, its faculty sponsor, and its student executive and membership, Mu Alpha Theta currently provides a wide range of support and services. A quarterly publication, **The Mathematical Log,** sent in bulk to chapters, offers expository writing, problems and challenges, program ideas, opinions, and news and photographs of national, regional, chapter, sponsor, and student activities. Also, affording the exceptional student a unique opportunity to publish and share mathematical findings of general interest, occasional collections of student papers are edited and released to chapters as **Mathematical Buds.** Other Mu Alpha Theta publications include a **Handbook for Sponsors** (1978); a compilation of background reading, **Topics for Mathematics Clubs** (prepared by nationally recognized authors and released in collaboration with The National Council of Teachers of Mathematics, 1973); and a diversity of more specific, mathematics-related publications, such as Richard V. Andree and Josephine Andree's, **Logic Unlocks.** (A well-known writing team, the Andrees were the driving force behind the establishment and early development of Mu Alpha Theta.) Chapter charters, individual membership certificates, club banners, patches, seals, and jewelry items popular with students also are available from the national office. Since 1968, national conventions of Mu Alpha Theta have been held on United States university campuses during the summer vacation period, each attracting several hundred students and sponsors. Support also has given by national office to mathematics contests and to regional, state, and local Mu Alpha Theta meetings.

No one formula has characterized the successful school mathematics club. Some Mu Alpha Theta chapters have functioned virtually as honor societies, according recognition to top mathematics students in each graduating class. Others have been strongly "service" oriented, providing tutoring, organizing mathematics field days, contests, and other events, and raising funds to send "math teams" to state and regional competitions. The heart of most clubs' activity has been weekly to monthly meetings of full and associate members, approaches to a successful meeting also being richly diverse.

Accordingly, what are the types of mathematics club programs most likely to be popular at secondary school level? Faculty sponsors have been giving careful consideration to this question since clubs were begun on this continent, early in the present century. The answers have little changed with the years. In his pioneer article in **School Science and Mathematics** (1911), Newhall described in considerable detail a variety of activities and approaches, giving further attention to the aptness of topics and questions from recreational mathematics (1916). Other early commentators on school extracurricular mathematics have included Snell (1915), Shoesmith (1916), Webster (1917), Wheeler (1923), and Reed (1925) - Reed also providing a comprehensive overview of the scattered literature to that time. Worthwhile extensions and bibliographies subsequently were produced by Hoag (1931) and Anning (1933). Other sources of useful "math club" ideas have included Dalton, on student-presented programs (1966); the Mu Alpha Theta "handbook" and "topics" publications; and, of late, the "Clubs" department of **The Mathematics Teacher.**

A conservative but not unsuccessful approach to club program has been for a teacher, commonly the faculty sponsor, to use meetings to develop, for interested students, an area of mathematics beyond what could be done in the classroom - a series of presentations in, typically, calculus fundamentals, "modern mathematics," or computer mathematics, for a self-selected, well-motivated group. On the other hand, from early writings (for example, Newhall, 1911), it is evident that faculty sponsors have been quick to recognize the importance of students "working up" and presenting their own material, with help, as needed, from faculty and library sources.

Among mathematics-related topics to "work up" and deliver, perennial favorites have included old algorithms, biographical notes on mathematicians, "magic" squares and cubes, logic, paradoxes and fallacies, cryptography, probability experiments, games of chance, finite geometries, noneuclidean geometries, recreational topology, linear programming, diophantine equations, continued fractions, nomograms, "outdoor" mathematics, and other mathematical applications. One finds, too, a recurring preoccupation with topics at the limit of ready comprehension - the infinite, the infinitessimal, "imaginary" numbers, fourth and higher dimensions, properties of the tesseract.

"Activity"-type meetings also evidently have enjoyed continuing popularity, including construction and investigation of such mathematical models as the skeletal icosahedron and Moebius band. Origami, with its relation to symmetry, also has provided worthwhile programs.

Skits, plays, poems, and dialogues receive frequent mention in earlier literature.

Other activity reports have included a mathematical party, wall and ceiling decorations and also table decorations being constructed by club members, a mathematics assembly, and also a mathematics banquet. I once was privileged to attend a Mu Alpha Theta dinner at which the principal speaker was a high school teacher who doubled as a professional magician. Considerable insight was offered into how mathematics underlies some elementary but impressive "magical" effects.

Competitive games such as nim, hex, and sprouts and solitaire games and activities such as tangrams (and its variants), polyominoes, hexaflexagons, and life also are of demonstrated interest and value as club programs, as are a diversity of commercial puzzles and games having a mathematical foundation.

Mathematical specialties, mathematical applications, or career opportunities in mathematics and related fields, have been discussed at club meetings by visiting lecturers from universities, business, and industry. "Field trips" to computer centres, science museums, airports, and similar facilities, also are reported to have been well received.

Individual competitiveness and team spirit both have provided a basis for worthwhile club programs, with "problem solving" sessions and "math bowl" type playoffs. A source of particularly good problems has been the Annual High School Contest of the Mathematical Association of America. Mu Alpha Theta currently is a cosponsor of this contest. Useful guidelines for "math bowl" organization are provided in Mu Alpha Theta's **Handbook for Sponsors** (pp. 50-58). Further, in current practice, no "math meet" is considered complete without a "Rubik's Cubathon" in which individuals race to "restore" identically scrambled puzzle cubes.

Additional insight into the kinds of mathematics that can effectively enrich the curricular and extracurricular may be gleaned from titles of **Mathematical Log** articles selected by a succession of editors. Thus, leafing through twenty years' issues, one chances upon, among others, "The Semiotics of Mathematics" **(Mathematical Log,** 24:3, Spring 1980); "On the Importance of Uniqueness of Prime Factorization" (15:1, September 1970); "Mini-lessons in Number Theory" (13:3, April 1969); "Puzzles, Tricks, and Mathematical Reasoning" (15:3, April 1971); "Be a Lightning Calculator" (4:2, January 1961); "Symmetric Continued Fractions" (9:3a, April 1965); "The Pascal Triangle and All That" (15:2, December 1970); "The Fundamental Theorem of Algebra" (10:3, April 1966); "Group Theory" (13:2, December 1968); "Planar Ternary Rings" (15:1. September 1970);

EXTRACURRICULAR MATHEMATICS

"Number Systems with Negative and Rational Bases" (17:1, September 1972); "Some Basic Properties of Functions" (17:1 September 1972); "Some Basic Properties of Functions" (14:1, September 1969); "The Consistency of Axiomatic Systems" (16:1, September 1971); "The Mathematical Concepts of Infinity" (12:1, September 1968); "Linear Programming" (8:2, February 1964); "Finite Geometry" (9:1, September 1964); "The Right Angled Triangle" (11:2, Winter 1966-67); "Area of an Ellipse" (20:1, September 1975); "Flexicells" (16;3, April 1972); "Spirolaterals" (21:2, January 1977); "Icosahadron Puzzle" (21:3, April 1977); "Polyhedral Lampshades" 26:1, Fall 1981); A Glimpse of Toplogy" (11:2, Winter 1966/67); "A Problem in Cypher Analysis" (10:3, April 1966); "Opportunities in Quality Control" (12:3, Spring 1968); "A Glimpse into Game Theory (18:1, September 1973); "Investigating Palindromes" (25:3, Spring 1981); "An Elucidation of the Fourth Dimension" (10:2, February 1966); "Mathematics and Youth in the Last Third of the Twentieth Century" (13:1, September 1968).

Students who gain the most from school mathematics clubs very likely are those who put the most into them - their organization, their activities, their competitions. Such students tend to be present in disproportionate numbers at Mu Alpha Theta national conventions. As a speaker, editor, and fellow-participant on such occasions, I've been privileged to live and interact with several thousand such students. For me, such observation effectively shatters any stereotype as to the mathematically active and able among today's youth. Genuine love of mathematics, high competitive spirit, and keen and articulate alertness need not override or preclude good fellowship or the desire for a good time. Skipping a Disneyland excursion to "bone up" for Math Bowl competition is frowned upon, and anything but the rule.

As **Mathematical Log** editor, I've received and saved hundred of letters from sponsors and students, and gained useful insight into the kind of challenge that captures the imagination of the most able. Perhaps because they are relaxed with mathematics, these students enjoy playing with it. Challenge them (as one instance) to represent 49 with four 3s and elementary mathematical operations through factorial (which is difficult), and they'll find a way; ask for 65 (which, with suitable restrictions, may be impossible), and they'll try the harder, and be the better for it. I encourage these students to browse in the mathematics sections of school and community libraries, and in bookstores. Recreational Mathematics and Theory of Numbers are two recommended headings. I refer them to old **Scientific Americans** (often available secondhand), for the fine expository writing of Martin Gardner in his section, "Mathematical Games," to **The Journal of Recreational Mathematics;** to **School Science and Mathematics** for its splendid "problems" section; to **Games** and **Four-Star Puzzler,** for novel and imaginative competitions frequently having a logical or mathematical foundation; and to the many Dover Publications paperbacks in mathematics and the sciences. Theory of Numbers is, of course, unique both in the richness of its history and in its ability to pose deep, challenging questions - some unsolved - in language that a child can understand.

The secondary school mathematics club, as evolved, can offer something extra and worthwhile for all students, but is especially important for the ablest. Coffield, in a recent **Mathematics Teacher** contribution, very well summarizes advantages to the faculty sponsor, normally the key person in club operation, and benefits to the student.

The school mathematics club sponsor, Coffield points out, can enjoy discussing mathematics without the concern of classroom managment, get to know some students better, see students in a different and relaxed setting, try out a novel lesson that might (be used) with a regular class, see students grow mathematically, and refresh some little used advanced mathematics skills.

The student, in turn, should gain the opportunity

to share ideas and experiences in mathematics, solve problems in groups, mingle with students of different ages, demonstrate leadership qualities, and express an interest in mathematics without dealing with negative peer pressure.

"One of the best methods of combining honor with opportunity for superior pupils is in mathematics." This is as good a characterization and appraisal of the secondary school mathematics club (and of Mu Alpha Theta) today as it was of the formative local club of fifty years ago (Shoesmith, 1933, p. 30). Indeed, after 25 years of intensive leadership and coordination from Mu Alpha Theta and the mathematics and mathematics education communities, the North American record of extracurricular mathematics - the clubs, meets, fairs, contests, and conventions - in identifying, challenging, and giving recognition and support to the mathematically able is less widely appreciated than it should be - but, we submit, is indeed impressive.

References

Andree, R. V. & Andree, J. Logic unlocks. Norman, Oklahoma: Mu Alpha Theta, University of Oklahoma Mathematics Department, 1979.

Anning, N. High school mathematics club, a radio talk over WJR. Mathematics Teacher, 1933, 26, 70-76.

Boyd, J. R. A mathematics club for the able. In J. A. Brown & H. T. Karnes (Eds.), Mathematics Teacher, 1953, 46, 43-45.

Coffield, P. W Give 'em a good clubbing. Mathematics Teacher, 1980, 73, 112-114.

Dalton, L. C. Student-presented programs. Mathematical Log, 1966, 10, 3.

Dalton, L. C., & Snyder, H. D., (Eds.). Topics for mathematics clubs. Reston, Virginia: National Council of Teachers of Mathematics and Norman, Oklahoma: Mu Alpha Theta, 1973.

Hoag, R. Sources of program material and some types of program work which might be undertaken by high school mathematics clubs. Mathematics

Teacher, 1931, 24, 492-502.

Huneke, H. V. What is my alpha theta? In L. C. Dalton (Ed.), Mathematics Teacher, 1980, 73, 528-529.

Huneke, H. V. National high school and junior college mathematics club. Mathematics Teacher, 1957, 50, 372-373.

Kalin, R. Handbook for sponsors. Norman, Oklahoma: Mu Alpha Theta, 1978.

Newhall, C. W. A secondary school mathematics club. School Science and Mathematics, 1911, 11, 501-5-9.

Owen, E. L. A high school mathematics club. In J. A. Brown & H. T. Karnes (Eds.), Mathematics Teacher, 1952, 45, 457-460.

Reed, Z. High school mathematics clubs. Mathematics Teacher, 1925, 18, 341-363.

Russell, D., Gulden, S., & Derby, M. Mathematics clubs. Mathematics Teacher, 1924, 17, 283-285.

Russell, D., Gulden, S., & Derby, M. Mathematics club programs. Mathematics Teacher, 1928, 17, 350-358.

Shoesmith, B. I. Mathematics clubs in secondary schools. School Science and Mathematics, 1915, 16, 106-113. Shoesmith, B. I. What do we owe to the brighter pupil? Mathematics Teacher, 1933, 26, 20-32. Snell, C. A. Mathematics clubs in the high school. Mathematics Teacher, 1915, 8, 73-78.

Webster, L. M.. Mathematics clubs. Mathematics Teacher, 1971, 9, 203-208.

Wheeler, A. H. Mathematics club program. Mathematics Teacher, 1923, 16, 385-390.

32

A FRENCH APPROACH TO EDUCATION FOR GIFTED CHILDREN

Véronique Rossillon & Marguerite Castillon du Perron

Description of the Center

In France, school attendance is compulsory between the ages of 6 and 16. Except for a few variations, the programs and schedules are the same for all children. The system is more or less successful because, except in the case of children who are unable to attend a normal school, it does not take into consideration the varying rates of learning. Although the reform which introduced the "college" for children aged 12 to 16 provided for special help for slow children as well as more extensive and more enriching programs for the gifted, such provision is not being applied evenly; in fact its application is difficult since the necessary means have not yet been supplied.

Realizing that support for intellectually gifted children was insufficient, and in the hope of being useful to the Education Nationale by creating a model of extensive and enriched education, the association Jeunes Vocations Artistiques, Littéraires et Scientifiques opened in Paris, in October 1978, a center of activities and recreation for children aged 5 to 15. The center operates outside regular school hours on Wednesdays and Saturdays, from 2 to 6 pm. During the holidays, the Association also organizes a cultural trip in France or in some other country.

In October, the members are grouped into small teams of no more than 8 or 9 children, according to their age, their knowledge, their tastes and affinities. Two series of four sessions are planned for the year, each session lasting an hour and a half and devoted to research and creation, that is, two sessions on Wednesday and two on Saturday; there is a change of programs in February. The children must attend the center on both Wednesday and Saturday since the sessions are complementary and form a balanced program.

Overall, candidates for the Jeunes Vocation center are referred to us by their parents, directors of schools,institutions or medico-pedagogical services. The entrance exam consists of interviews with parents and the child, as well as a series of tests. In general, the tests used are Wechsler's intelligence scales, the collective scale of intellectual level of l'Institut d'etudes demographiques and of l'Institut d'orientation scolaire et professionnelle, and various tests in logical reasoning. In principle, a child is accepted if his results place him in the top centile of the population (135 IQ on the standardized scale), but we take into account the method used to arrive at this IQ and the sociocultural milieu. We demand less of those who have not had the opportunity to broaden themselves. The center also admits children who appear gifted in drawing, whatever their tests results. With the exception of the latter, and based on Wechsler's scale, the IQs of the 63 children who attended the center since 1978 are as follows:

Lower than 122:	1
123-127:	3
128-132:	11
133-137:	21
138-142:	13
143-147:	6
148-152:	4
153 plus:	4

There are 46 boys and 17 girls. Overall, they come from families of employers, technicians, teachers, top or middle executives and members of the liberal professions.

The programs comprise disciplines studies in school as well as subjects unknown to the pupils, but all subjects are treated in a nonbookish manner.

A FRENCH APPROACH

Sample Activities (February 1981)

Age	Wednesday	Saturday
13-14	Computer	Music
11-12	Physics & Chemistry	Mathematics
10-11	Woodwork	Biology
9-10	Theatre	Games
7-8	Ancient History	Ancient History
6-7	Newspaper production	Knowledge of Paris
5	Mime	Various activities
13-14	Geography	Biology
11-12	Astronomy	Drawing
10-11	Physical chemistry	History & Legends
9-10	Drawing	Writing workshop
7-8	Wood sculpture	Games
6-7	Theatre	Mime

We will now give you a more precise idea of some of the activities performed at the center and of how the sessions are conceived and animated. We will also impart some of our instructors' thoughts.

Workshops

History. The sessions devoted to history are of a very unusual nature.

One set of workshops deals with ancient civilizations. Over a period of 18 months and in 42 sessions, the 6- to 8-year-old children started off with australopithecus and only got as far as the Median wars. To their delight, they climbed zigurrats and pyramids, covered the heads of Pharaohs and of the beautiful Cretan called "la parisienne," compared cuneiform writing and hieroghyphs, sailed on the Tigris and the Nile, and cried for Helen of Troy.

Here are a few remarks made by our instructor,

Madame Zeigler, after six months with a 6-to 8-year-old group studying the Sumerian period: "I feared the program would not be appropriate for their age, or that the pace would be too tiring; apparently this was not so. By alternating periods of study, reflexion, manual or physical activities, the afternoon went by without any sign of fatigue. However, I read or told a story during the last half-hour. . . . Odd: while listening to a record, the boys become quite agitated after ten minutes, whereas a story or reading brings about extraordinary calmness. . . . Worth reporting: the abundance of documents brought by each child - books and even photograph albums related to the subjects under study. . . . To conclude, the children seem happy; this is demonstrated by their regular attendance and their active participation. Parents do not find them more tired than before they started attending the center. Nicolas's mother told me that on those days, he comes home calm and in a good mood, contrary to other days. I think the children have the impression of being in a house of their own and that they are happy to be together. . . .

"How do you bring ancient civilizations to life? By allowing the children to look at things of the past (visits to museums, photographs, slide projection); by telling them about the lives of the people concerned (as soon as my story becomes too abstract their attention vanishes: I have to describe the characters, give them a name); by having them reproduce (drawing, modeling) a few works of art (thus art and history become associated in their mind). I trust that once we are able to materialize time with the use of a 'graduated' tape the children will get some idea of the chronology and, with the help of a map we are preparing together, they will visualize the space where the events took place. If I happen to find a record, a song, a poem, an article or a tale to illustrate the subject, I shall use it. Music of course will have to be more recent: it is difficult to find music from 3000 years B.C."

A second set of history workshops dealt with

history and legends. Some 8- to 9-year-old children were introduced to history through a different approach, less archeological than poetic. A storyteller delivers all the treasures of old legends related to real or imaginary events, about which she gives the children pertinent and precise information. Thus they get acquainted with Charlemagne by being told about the death of Roland at Ronçavaux, with the trouveres and troubadours through the legend of William of Orange, with the crusades through the narratives of chroniclers who blend reality and imagination.

Following the narration of intriguing adventures or mysteries which elicit questions, the storyteller clarifies certain epochs and problems, filling the gaps in their knowledge. Thanks to the Templars they learned about France under the reign of Philippe le Bel, and thanks to the Teutonic Knights we tackled the eternal Polish problems.

"It took about two months to achieve minimal homogeneity in this group of nine children. Each one worked only for himself. Gradually, I saw a few pairs being formed. By January the group was integrated and the change was spectacular. I noticed, however, that things run a lot smoother when a child is missing; perhaps eight is the ideal number. . . . As for work, it seems rather difficult to me to do anything serious until the children are accustomed to one another; then, everything is relaxed and they appear very happy. They are still at an age where the marvelous, the legends, are more enticing than history, so we must strive to maintain a balance."

Writing. Although related to languages and literature, the art of enjoying or writing poetry is not practiced in school.

"The writing workshops represent one of our most sensitive attempts. The children grumbled about history and geography, but at the very word poetry they were up in arms - or else they had a grim idea of the subject. 'What's the use of poetry?' ask the boys. Oh yes, I wrote a poem for my cousin's marriage, sighs a ten-year-old girl, producing a few sentimental lines. Let us mention that not one single child brought a poem worth of the name, which makes one wonder about spontaneous creativity."

Of all our instructors, our poets are probably the ones with the most thankless task. Like other educators, they deal with children who tend to be superficial, are more interested in quantity than in quality, confuse intelligence and knowledge; but they also find in most children a weakness in syntax and orthography which interferes with a true understanding of what they read. "This weakness is due to the fact that those children really belong to the pictorial civilization" claims one of our poets; "the reference is no longer the verb, but the picture, hence the increasing loss of quality and mastery of writing which is a linear effort, as opposed to imagery which is a global effort."

To help the children understand poetry, our instructors attempted in their own way to shake up the everyday language of the children: truisms, automatic associations, cliches, pleasant platitudes, catch-all words, all were systematically trapped and eliminated. The sentence was demolished so that the world could come out in all its strength and singularity. Let us here quote one of our staff instructors, a teaching college graduate, accredited in classical letters, a writer and poet. "We first tried poetic games in the form of contraints which allowed them to grasp the existence of the word, its substance, its aesthetics, its use and its semantic value: le Fictionnaire - catalog of words that cannot be found, rhyming sentences, storytelling devices, free words: anagrams, palindromes, combined words, etc., creation of an artificial language, words in the city, poetic arts anthology, metaphors, and surrealism and poetic writing: automatic writing."

The play on words enabled the children to appreciate the material available, use it in a novel way, and criticize their own work. Now partially freed of old conventions, they are able to more or less consciously express their feelings. We are finally coming down to the very conditions of the creative act.

The children still look upon writing with mixed feelings, of course, but they write with much more conviction. It should be realized that we are not simply looking for talent; we are trying to free the emotions and the imagination. Within a very short time, the children were writing poems such as these:

> J'écris pour convoquer le monde
> Et que la terre soit ronde
> J'écris comme un fou qui ne cherche rien
> J'écris aussi parfois pour les chiens
> Et les mots jouent leur va-tout
> J'écris pour que vous soyez comme moi
> C'est-à-dire fou, n'est-ce pas?
> (boy, age 12)

> La fenêtre de ma mansarde
> Buvait d'un oeil avide
> La plus mince parcelle
> De cette animation
> Qui telle la chaleur
> S'elévait lentement
> Jusqu'à la plus lointaine des étoiles
> Elle capturait tout
> De la rumeur si sourde
> Qui monte d'une grande ville
> Elle revait longtemps de s'envoler au loin
> Et lorsqu'elle sortait de se revérie
> Elle pleurait longtemps de ne pouvoir le faire.
> (boy, age 9)

> La mort
> Seul point net
> Du sablier du temps,
> Ombre de pierre,
> Vapeur flottante lumineuse,
> Porte sombre sur l'ennui,
> Fenêtre ouverte sur un mur,
> Barrage de larmes ou de mystère,

Lien d'acier unissant la magie et l'horreur,
Cordon de cuir ou corde du pendu
Soudant le rien et l'absolu,
Triomphe de l'illogique
Equivalent de la vie,
Sommeil liquide,
Noir vaporeux de clarte,
Chat en robe longue
Telle est la mort.
(girl, age 11)

Theatre. Our objective is not to stage charming playlets for year-end ceremonies, nor to put children in the limelight. The trio formed by Jean Davy, former member of the Comedie francaise, his wife Odile Mallet and his sister-in-law Geneviève Brunet have all the qualifications.

"When I found myself at the beginning of the year facing those bright eyed children," says Geneviève Brunet, "so passionate and curious but terribly individualistic and competitive, each one wanting to be first, convinced of their own superiority and trying to speak before the others, I was slightly but very interested. Since the theatre involves team work and discipline, the first thing those children had to learn was how to live in a group; also, I did not want them to view this art as third rate acting or childish play; through the theatre, I hoped, they would come into contact with life, literature and art.

"At first I considered adapting to their young age, but on my first contact, and despite their lack of discipline, I changed my mind; their sharp understanding, fine intelligence, quick reflexes, and their desire to know the reasons for doing things, persuaded me to use the same teaching approach with them as with young professional actors. So I started off with the usual relaxation exercises. Lying on the ground, eyes closed, in complete silence, they learn to remain quiet, not to speak, not to move, and to identify with an inanimate object, to 'become' a lump of clay which gradually comes to life from within, without any outward sign. The children gladly go through this exercise, which channels their vitality and develops their concentration. For quick relaxation, I then follow with what I call 'the jumping cry' (la cri saute): each child in turn takes off and as he jumps, he utters the loudest possible cry without contracting his larynx. This requires strength and spontaneity, without any concern for aestheticism, and it is excellent for overcoming timidity, the desire to show off, the fear of being judged - the usual trappings of the theatre. Even those who at first refuse to do this exercise soon allow themselves the joy of this liberating cry.

"The next important step is to make them understand that theatre is an art not of initiation but of recreation, that one must learn not to 'pretend' or copy, but to feel and become. Through a series of progressive exercises, the children learn to rouse their imagination, develop their inner sincerity, and avoid trickery, affectation, grimacing. They increase their powers of observation, their concentration and their discipline, as well as the speed of their reflexes. They must then learn to re-experience sensations and feelings based on memories and personal experiences, despite their youth (memory of a sad day, a happy day, a burn, etc.).

"It is obvious that this self-improvement work, although done collectively, is extremely beneficial; in fact it is particularly necessary for children who, because of their giftedness, tend to isolate themselves from their environment. I have seen them blossom out, become more calm and more interested with each session, and more dedicated to an art heretofore unknown to them.

"After staging a text or one of LaFontaine's fables, in which they all participated as one of the characters, we were able at the end of the term to produce the first act of Moliere's 'Bourgeois Gentilhomme,' each child having chosen a role. Following a first reading where I found them to be a particularly receptive and passionate audience, I had the pleasure of discovering in front of me a small group of actors among which, thanks to the preliminary exercises, there were no lazy or third-rate actors, where everyone belonged. No shrinking from work, terrific cooperation: in two sessions they knew their lines and the stage was set.

"It would have taken a whole term to be able to produce a show, but the results would have been astonishing. These children who were too individualistic, too self-centered and undisciplined, became within six months a cohesive and attentive group, no longer determined only to have a good time but also to build and produce a piece of work in which each has his own role, and everyone must stand aside and exercise self-control. They did their best to do justice to an author who had beocme alive and close to them, feeling they were his accomplices."

Mime. Let us go even further. These children, some of whom might become characterial, give up all purely intellectual activity in order to let their inner self speak, allow their fantasies to explode, and learn to control them. Edith, a mime who stages her own shows and is on her way to becoming as famous as Marceau, tries to make the children realize that each part of their body works separately and is under their control. She also tries to make them discover the aspect of unpredictability in interpretation. Her sessions include, according to circumstances and the children's ages, limbering-up and body control exercises, introduction to dancing, evocative mime and the study of masks and clowns.

Woodwork. Because the children too often harm themselves by developing their intelligence at the expense of their body and sensitivity, we encourage them to express themselves through woodwork. A carpenter and a sculptor (teacher at Ecole Boulle), each run a workshop. During the first semester this year, a group of 10- to 11-year-old children accomplished the following. In their first exercise, by joining and gluing wood trimmings of various shapes and types, the children built a structure on the theme

"fantastic architecture." They were involved in:
- a choice of shapes and types of wood,
- preparation of parts by eventually sawing them to arrive at the desired dimensions,
- sandpapering, joining and gluing,
- identification of various types of wood, beech, walnut, oak, etc.,
- developing a shape, harmonizing the volumes, and
- concern for balance between execution and creation. Overall, this exercise was appreciate and well executed.

Their second exercise, research and creation of a simple mobile using animal shapes of their choice, included the added objective of a study in chromatics. The subject was quite well understood but the work was done too fast and therefore the results were mediocre. This is probably due to the fact that the children were more interested in quickly completing a project than in the step-by-step operation. As for the chromatic part, the results were deceiving: since the children had never painted a "volume," they had difficulty in seeing the relationship between volume and color. I should have given them an intermediate exercise. The failure is therefore mine. For the second semester, younger children (8 to 9) were given other assignments. In the first exercise, drawing their inspiration from photographs found in books on animals, the children executed a drawing which was then transposed on wood with a burin. Prints could then be made from the woodcut. This exercise allows the child to see the evolution of his original drawing through a three-step technique. The objectives included:
- understanding the process,
- being in contact with the material and its exigencies (against the grain, crosswise),
- becoming familiar with balanced movements: holding the burin in the left hand, striking with the right hand, or vice versa, and
- becoming aware of the dangers of a sharp tool.
This was positive in the sense that every child was interested, even if the end product did not look too

great. The exercise must be looked upon as getting acquainted with woodwork, not merely as "making a beautiful engraving." It takes years to master this trade, but it was important for the children to become aware of it. One of my sculpture teachers at Ecole Boulle used to say, "Ten good plans are not worth one mediocre production."

The second exercise, the construction of an inlaid box, involved five steps.
- study of a square shape made up of unequal triangles,
- construction of a laminated box,
- preparation and sawing of small plates and traingles,
- gluing of the parts on the laminated box, and
- sandpapering and finishing.
The preparations for this work being diversified, no one tired of it; also it is pleasing since it combines creation and usefulness.

Drawing. Through drawing we sought to bring out the sensitivity and critical sense which are so important to be developed in the intellectually gifted child. Most of the children who come to the center have had access, more or less, to drawing courses in their schools. In general, they had learned nothing, except that the time devoted to this subject is always to little to achieve anything. The teaching of art in France is generally too lackadaisical to foster much progress in the pupils. There again, one runs into the eternal problem of the alleged "creativity" of the child. As in poetry, we have never seen children arrive at the center who, without having seriously worked at their drawing, gave us the impression of being able to express their views and of having talent. On the other hand, once we teach them things as elementary as different kinds of pencils or shading, apparently hopeless and uninterested, they come into their own.

Here are some observations on two groups, first of a group of eight children, aged 8 and 9. "They were a large group and heterogeneous. The first theme, 'a community forest,' was intended to reassure those who felt less artistic.   After examining some pictures, each child designed a tree, drew it in India ink, and located it on a background.   Everyone seemed interested in the structure of trees and, overall, attention was held through several sessions.   On the other hand, few seemed concerned with the collage once their individual involvement was over.

"The second topic was a still life composed by the children themselves.   They had to call on their observations and use color in suggested ways. Remarkably, the youngest children's concentration was fixed for the three-quarter hour sessions.   Use of a very dilute wash enabled them to concentrate on the drawing without the difficulties presented by black and white work.   It seems that the children were able to cope with the difficulties and taste the delights of artistic skill.

"The group of 12 and 13 year olds was, in this semester, at a similar level and ready to work.   The theme of 'mankind' was chosen for its versatility and richness.   The first topic, a pencil rendering of a modern sculpture chosen by the child, then sketching sessions with a live model or ancient sculpture, focused awareness on the structure of the body and on learning to look and to simplify.   The modeling of 'Aphrodite au collier' was designed to enlarge experience in three dimensions and to produce a concrete tactile pleasure while eliminating elaborative details.   The visit to the Rodin Museum was a focal point of the experience, for history, modern art, and with regard to technique."

Music.   We had no vision of replicating the conservatories which flurish in every Paris neighborhood.   Neither did we seek to make students play any intrument or systematically learn solfege, nor to create a choir or orchestra.   We especially wanted children who had not developed a musical ear or taste to discover the profound joy which music can give them throughout their lives.   For those who would never study music, we hoped to give a thirst to listen, the need to know more than work, daily life and silence, that there is rhythm and harmony in every creation.

Our collaborator, Olivier Greif, well known French composer, declared, "Musical sensitivity has always seemed to be related to a certain openness at the intuitive level. The child who enjoys listening to music dares to leave the often reassuring shield of intellectual analysis, dares to trust a world of sound. We should rejoice in the child who enjoys and knows how to listen.

"At the beginning of the year I began by bringing more records than scores, but I soon noted that the children listened infinitely better with the live music. Where ten seconds of recorded music lost their attention, ten minutes of live music did not seem too long. The child is attracted by all that goes with making music, from the movements of the musicians to the different scores. It seems easy to awaken interest in children with the right bias: to simply place beauty in front of them is not always the most effective way to experience it.

"Even the children's ability to listen to recorded music improved considerably since the beginning of the year. Six months ago, I could not hold their interest more than a minute. Now, we frequently listen to works or parts of works for 15 to 20 minutes without feeling a decline in the intensity of their interest.

"The development of their receptiveness to twentieth century interested me considerably, ever since the first session when I made them listen to an excerpt from the third part of Debussy's La Merr (1903-1905). It brought nothing but grins, mocking, and incomprehension. Placed in its context, in its stage of musical evolution with works that precede and follow it, it speaks and becomes evocative. Now, we listen to Berlioz, Boulez, Xénakis, Cage and it all seems natural."

Mathematics. A mathematician, university professor, entrance examiner at the Ecole Polytechnique, tried "with new materials to carry out demonstrations and solutions previously done." With few exceptions, he worked with groups of boys some

A FRENCH APPROACH

of whom were not more than five years old. Two children stood out among them, one, 13 years old, derived on his own theorems of which he had never been told. His level would have permitted admission to the Ecole Polytechnique had he been old enough. The other, 12 years old, was actively interested in conic sections (ellipses, hyperboles, etc.) and transformations of time.

Fascinated by the harmony of the work of Euler and of triangles, he quickly understood the difficulties of location of points on polar coordinates.

Mr Vauthier touched on all the branches of mathematics: number theory, algebra, infinity, probability, geometry, logic and fundamental theory.

Two groups of children evolved: the "actives" and the "passives." "The 'passives' divided further into those who really did not want to try to follow the conversation or to make an effort to find something, and the others who latch on to a result and seek to cling to it. I do not know if I have awakened any career aspirations, but at least I may have shown that mathematicians are not necessarily crazy. "The 'actives' break down into two groups. The first engage the proposed theme, pull it forward, ask questions and answer most of them, wish for an extension of the topic, and seek out new knowledge. These are the traditional 'math whizzes' who comprehend rapidly but who can be criticized for thinking that a problem is solved when the answer is known rather than trying to create original solutions. The others take a proposed problem or theme and monopolize it, transform it into something else and propose solutions. Their involvement is undeniable but they are incapable of fitting themselves to a discipline. They are, a priori, less scholarly than the first group and achieve less success because they have to create their own path through the mathematical thicket.

Astronomy. A young researcher working on his thesis, poet and musician in his spare time, enchanted a group of eleven and twelve year olds. His approach was not to fill them with numbers and facts, rather to

474

bring them to liberally ask metaphsysical problems, to give them materials with which to ponder the expansion of the universe.

"The children showed the strong influence of current popularization of astronomy which adopts the methods of zoology: show a wide variety of objects, evolutionary history of galaxies, etc. - all generally accompanied by long lists of numbers which don't give the slightest feeling for the discipline. Offering no possiblity for understanding representationally, they directly address our sixth sense, mathematics. And, surely, it is this extrasensorial aspect which most delights the majority of children; it makes them dizzy with quantities, throwing about distances to the farthest galaxies.

"It is very difficult, I realized, to involve elementary school aged children in research. Facts, figures, but little effort to analyze, to synthesize; for example, historical stages in knowledge are neglected. Also, despite any efforts, I could not bring about interesting reflection on such major issues as the place of people in the universe. Cosmology is out of reach.

"During the astronomy and astrophysics sessions, we often confronted the issue of 'common sense' in the unfolding of physical phenomena, as likely at the scale of the universe as at the atom. Where we suggested theory, the children imposed experience. It is known that the extremes of scale of the universe make little 'common sense.' This inability to extrapolate knowledge from daily life disturbs children who do not seem to have the maturity to accept the extreme fragility of positions we espouse with the benefit of our daily experiences. It seems desirable to help some of these children to analyze, to escape the limits of the encyclopedia. At least two of them resented the need or the call to do so. Many of the others got the taste of science; let us help them to forge an awareness."

It seems that our instructor tapped a profound reaction with this group of twelve to fourteen year olds. In one semester he established a personal relationship with each of the children; an atmosphere was set up which they accepted. It is clear that they now understand what is being discussed rather than stopping for a few minutes while they conjure up some images. In place of scientific data, numbers, and the dry description of the universe which they had, it became evident that it is necessary for them to be preoccupied with the existence of this universe. Their vision is enlarged. They are bothered and concerned. That is what we wanted.

The Instructors

The difficulties experienced by our instructors can sometimes be discouraging. We sought to bring the children into contact with high level specialists in every domain, rather than teachers, even though they sometimes meet that qualification, too. We also wanted to know that our mathematician devoted himself to pure mathematics for half his time, that our poet actively set up a poetry journal and published, that our astronomer devoted his life to research. Further, we prefer to give these children male teachers. Two thirds of them were boys, the majority of their class teachers were female, and the children had little opportunity to dialogue with men. We ask the teachers to establish a platonic relationship with the children. Our ideal is that the young Alcibiades meets Socrates but especially not the scholasticism of Madame de Genlis.

It is easy to imagine the qualities necessary to work at the center: humor, balance, generosity and love of children, pedagogical sense, general culture, and competence in one or more desired fields. It is nice to be famous, but not indispensible. The ideal instructor is difficult to find, but we have discovered several. Some come so close to perfection that we would be disheartened to lose them.

After three years, our instructors are becoming a team. They sympathize with the children, carry the relationships beyond the center, but are only beginning to foresee the children benefiting from common efforts. We realize it will take them a while to get used to the original approach of the center and many have barely begun to go to the trouble of transforming themselves from professors to master teachers. This prompts us to change our team as little as possible. Nevertheless, such immobility would go against our purpose of multiplying the children's chances of meeting outstanding people. The solution appears to be to keep the best, not to hesitate to introduce new faces, or other activities, and to renew essential activities with different people.

The twenty-three instructors (in 1981) included two university professors, five preparatory classes in the "grand écoles" and secondary schools, four university researchers and assistants, two elementary teachers, three university students, and seven professionals, including three actors, a sculptor, woodworker, mime, and composer. Fourteen were men and nine were women. Each led one or two one-and-a-half hour sessions a week, and they met every Wednesday or Saturday afternoon during recess to get to know each other better, to exchange views, or to extend a discussion with the children. We are proud that these free moments passed together have contributed greatly to the friendly and relaxed atmosphere at the center. Every month everyone gathers around a large birthday cake.

A Resolutely Humanist Program

Our program is global. It addresses the total personality of the child to enable each to develop aptitudes in harmony, to bloom, and not to waste a part of his or her being.

It encourages intellectual curiosity while responding to children's questions and urging them to ask others, critical ability, the spirit of comparison and not the disorganized accumulation of facts. "Much better a head well made than a head well filled" (Montaigne).

It seeks to favor the awakening of sensitivity and a balance between body and spirit.

A FRENCH APPROACH

It encourages sociability, putting the children in contact with masters they can admire, permitting contact with other children with whom they can talk and perhaps form friendships, helping them to appreciate qualities other than intellectual which they often tend to scorn.

It imposes certain constraints, avoids amateurism and the facile, and stands off superficiality and dilettantism.

It is not a question of shaping all the children in a single mold, nor forcing them to a common level or to a common model, but to let the sparks fly, to permit each to affirm his or her creativity, to draw from within whatever will feed the imagination, to gather the ability to really create artistic, literary or scientific works or new human relationships.

Our program is complete. It aims to open the most diverse domains for the child. It encompasses letters, arts and sciences. It appears desirable that the children explore varied domains and that they do not limit themselves to their favorite activities, so that they can become truly cultured. It lets the children out of their bird cage and makes them capture the richness of the world.

It is coherent. Whatever the initial theme, the projects inevitably lead the children to penetrate many subjects to have the sense that the fences established by convention between different disciplines can be arbitrary.

Our program is financially nondiscriminating. It ignores financial status, present or anticipated. We want to free the child from worry about income, permit not yielding to any imperatives but those which arise from the sciences and techniques, which provide the means to discover one's real vocation and the freedom to choose it.

A Program Adaptable to All Children

This program is, in fact, a model for education, since it seeks to give each child all opportunities to harmoniously develop his or her abilities. It seems easy with gifted children: they are more curious, learn more quickly, concentrate better. Once again it is necessary to state that their shine is sometimes only on the surface, their culture often ends with their effort, their tastes are selective, and they are not always comfortable when presented with a new dish. "Chemists" who are not interested in the fabrication of blue crystals, "paleontologists" who limit themselves to describing dinosaurs' pelvic bone structure, and avid readers who never open anything but the same scientific journals display a quasipathological obstinacy, remain focused on themselves, and refuse dialogue.

This same quality is evident in most children. All gain from working in small teams, being the respected students of outstanding masters, benefiting early from a broad, general culture, enjoying work well done, acquiring critical skills, determining their own future so that it does not necessarily commit them to a particular occupation.

Most of the activities of the Centre Jeunes Vocations can be offered to all children, with the exception the certain very abstract disciplines such as astrophysics. One goes more or less according to the abilities of each. Why penalize the majority of children by offering them teaching and recreation of lower quality on the pretext that their appetites appear more measured? It is merely a question of regulating the quantity and pace.

A Program Adaptable to Many Countries

Outside school. The Jeunes Vocation program is easily adaptable, and we are prepared to bring our materials to anyone who requests them at our Paris office, and to meet with any interested visitor. Our files and reports are also at their disposal.

Jeunes Vocations was created by a parents' association which finances the center with the help of the Fondation de France. The families of the children who attend the center contribute fees which cover about one fifth of the expenses which principally comprise honoraria for the instructors, maintenance and heating of the house. One could imagine less costly arrangements employing already existing sites, volunteers, parents, retired people or students, for example.

In schools. We think that programs resembling ours could suit other countries and that they could be adapted to other teaching systems, complementing regular or special programs according to the local context. On the other hand, our model - as an education system itself - could be adapted with adjustments by any school.

The Work Accomplished Can Serve All Educators

We are trying to understand how intellectually gifted children learn, in order to know how to teach them and what they are well suited to learn.

What are their rates and rhythms of learning? Is each accelerated in intellectual maturation, that is, do they pass more quickly than others through different stages of development, do they acquire abstract and logical thought sooner?

Why do some subjects especially interest them? Do they exhibit a particular type of creativity or are they subject to current styles and their prejudices?

Do their interests correspond to a profound choice or do these children lack information and are the interests fixed before having had access to alternative domains? What happens when they are initiated to new domains?

We are seeking to serve gifted children. Meanwhile, we are devising study and creativity sessions at the center as a psychopedagogical experiment whose practical and theoretical conclusions could serve the teaching of all children. Consider the writing workshops. In reality, it is a question of implanting a pedagogy of poetry which presents new communication situations for the contemporary child. For this child, at first, there is an image, but not yet a verb. If we wish to pass on dialogue to future generations, it is necessary as of now to reconcile the child and the word.

Recall also the mathematics sessions, of which one of the goals, and not the least, was to discover that mathematicians are not distant, boring, or neurotic.

Finally, and this question equally concerns all children, what is creative spirit and where does it go if it has no place to be exercised? Can we say a child is inherently creative if one understands this term to be the ability to imagine new relations, to create an original work? Is it not necessary to help the child to nourish the imagination and to express sensitivity, to become familiar with the history of humanity and great works, to learn to free oneself from existing ideas, to acquire techniques and skills, to achieve a sense of effort and perseverance so as to open the doors to creative production?

Conclusion

We do not boast of being original. Perhaps we are, nevertheless, if to be original is to stay within bounds and wisdom, not be impressed by fashions, and to accompany the children in the discovery of a twentieth century humanism which can also be a humanism for tomorrow. It seems essential to us that children should be able to benefit from the long accumulated experience and traditions of mankind. And so, may they only be able to draw on the resources and energy necessary to develop themselves soundly, avoid uniformity and verbalism, surmount the explosion of science and the techniques to discover, in the end, their calling.

CONTRIBUTORS

Miss **Danica Adjemovitch,** formerly Senior Technical Officer, International Year of the Child Secretariat, United Nations, New York.

Dr **Harold Don Allen,** Professor of Education in Mathematics, Nova Scotia Teachers College, Truro, Nova Scotia, Canada, and editor of **The Mathematical Log,** newsletter of the high school mathematical association Mu Alpha Theta.

Dr **Susan R. Butler,** Professor of Education at the University of Sydney, Psychologist at the Royal Alexandra Hospital for Children, Sydney, Australia, frequent visitor to and author of curricular materials on the People's Republic of China.

Ms **Nava Butler-Por,** School of Education, University of Haifa, Haifa, Israel.

Dr **Glenn F. Cartwright,** Associate Professor and Director of the Computer-Based Instructional Research Laboratory, Department of Educational Psychology and Counselling, and Centre for Teaching and Learning Services, McGill University, Montreal, Quebec, Canada.

Dr **Henry Olajide Oluyele Coker,** Senior Lecturer in Political Science, University of Lagos, Lagos, Nigeria (keynote speaker).

Ms **Dorothy Coleman,** National Association for Gifted Children, London, United Kingdom.

Dr **Dewey Cornell,** Psychological Clinic, The University of Michigan, Ann Arbor, Michigan, United States of America.

Dr **Edward de Bono,** Cognitive Research Trust and Cambridge University, Cambridge, United Kingdom, lecturer and author of several books on creative thinking and the "CoRT" curriculum; Dr **Norah H. Maier,** University of Toronto Schools, Toronto, Ontario, Canada (keynote workshop).

Dr **Martin Dishart,** Director of the Psychological Services Centre, South Ohio, Nova Scotia, Canada, and former Director of the Mid-Atlantic Regional Educational Laboratory, Baltimore.

Dr **John Dunstan,** Centre for Russian and East European Studies, University of Birmingham, Birmingham, United Kingdom.

Ms **Alyce Faye Eichelberger,** Taristock Psychiatric Clinic for Children and Parents, London, United Kingdom; Mr. **Tom Greener,** Headmaster, Day maladjusted School of the Inner London Education Authority, London, United Kingdom.

Dr **Joan Freeman,** psychologist and author, Senior Lecturer at the University of Manchester, Manchester, United Kingdom.

Dr **Françoys Gagné,** Professor of Psychology, Université du Québec à Montréal, Montreal, Quebec, Canada; Mme **Pierrette Massé,** consultant on programs for the gifted, Commission des Ecoles catholiques de Montréal, Montreal, Quebec, Canada.

Ms **Karlene George,** Consultant, Gifted Technical Assistance Project, United Indians of All Tribes Foundation and Norter Kitsap School District Native American Gifted Project, State of Washington, United States of America.

Dr **Albert Jacquard,** geneticist and demographer, Institut national d'Etudes démographiques, Paris, France (keynote speaker).

Mr **Earl C. Joseph,** Staff Scientist - Futurist,

Sperry-Univac Corporation, St. Paul, Minnesota, United States of America.

Dr **Margot Lagesen King,** psychologist and consultant, King Research and the University of Wisconsin-Platteville, Platteville, Wisconsin, United States of America.

Dr **Alan Kramer,** National Supervisor for Enrichment Programs, Department for Gifted Children, Ministry of Education and Culture, Jerusalem, Israel.

Mr **D. T. E. Marjoram,** Her Majesty's Divisional Inspector of Schools, London, United Kingdom.

Mr **H. Gilbert Nicol,** Executive Director, International Baccalaureate of North America, New York, New York, United States of America.

Ms **Alanis Obomsawin,** Abenaki singer, song writer and poet, producer at the National Film Board of Canada, Montreal, Quebec, Canada (keynote speaker).

Mrs **Margaret Parker,** Executive Director, Kootenay Centre for Gifted Children and the Kootenay Learning Centre, Kaslo, British Columbia, Canada.

Dr **A. Harry Passow,** Jacob H. Schiff Professor of Education, Teachers College, Columbia University, New York, New York, United States of America.

Dr **Arthur Robinson,** psychiatrist, Arhus Psychiatric Hospital, Risskov, Denmark.

Ms **Véronique Rossillon** and Ms **Marguerite Castillon du Perron,** Jeunes vocations artistiques, litteraires et scientifiques, Paris, France.

The Hon. Dr **Bette Stephenson,** Minister of Education and Minister of Colleges and Universities of Ontario, Toronto, Ontario, Canada.

Dr **Richard E. Tremblay,** professor, Ecole de psycho-éducation, Université de Montréal, Montreal, Quebec, Canada.

Dr **Klaus K. Urban,** special educator, Universitaet Hannover, Hannover, Federal Republic of Germany.

Dr **Burton L. White,** psychologist, author, lecturer and Director, Center for Parent Education, Newton, Massachusetts, United States of America (keynote speaker).

Dr **David Willings,** professor, Faculty of Administration, University of New Brunswick, Fredericton, New Brunswick, Canada.

Mr **Ahmed Yussufu,** Ministry of Basic Education, Nairobi, Kenya.

EDITORS

Dr **Bruce M. Shore,** Associate Professor, Department of Educational Psychology and Counselling and in the Centre for Teaching and Learning Services, McGill University, Montreal, Secretary of the World Council for Gifted and Talented Children, Organizer and Program Committee Chairman of the Fourth World Conference on Gifted and Talented Children.

Dr **Françoys Gagné,** Professor, Department of Psychology, Université du Québec à Montréal, Member of the Program Committee of the Fourth World Conference on Gifted and Talented Children.

Dr **Serge Larivée,** Associate Professor, Ecole de psycho-éducation, Université de Montréal, Member of the Program Committee of the Fourth World Conference on Gifted and Talented Children.

Dr **Ronald H. Tali,** Associate Professor and Chairman, Department of Administration and Policy Studies in Education, McGill Univerity, Montreal, Chairman of the Finance Committee and Member of the Organizing Committee of the Fourth World Conference on Gifted and Talented Children.

Dr **Richard E. Tremblay,** Associate Professor, Ecole de psycho-éducation, Université de Montréal, Member of the Program Committee of the Fourth World Conference on Gifted and Talented Children.

THE WORLD COUNCIL
FOR GIFTED AND TALENTED CHILDREN

The World Council logo on this volume and its predecessors reflects the sponsorship of World Conferences on Gifted and Talented Children by the Council since its founding after the 1975 Conference:

London	1975	Montreal	1981
San Francisco	1977	Manila	1983
Jerusalem	1979	Hamburg	1985

Membership in the World Council also brings the newsletter **World Gifted** and the journal **Gifted International.** Copies of the selected proceedings of the three previous World Conferences may be ordered from Trillium Press. For further information on membership and other services please write to:

The World Council For Gifted and Talented Children
Box 238, Teachers College, Columbia University
525 West 120th Street
New York, New York, U.S.A. 10027

Executive Committee
James J. Gallagher (U.S.A.), President
Dan Bitan (Israel), Vice-President
Ron Day (Australia), Treasurer
Bruce M. Shore (Canada), Secretary
Elena Konstat (Mexico)
Jean-Charles Terrassier (France)
Klaus K. Urban (Federal Republic of Germany)

Editor, Gifted International
Dorothy Sisk

Secretariat
A. Harry Passow, Honorary Director
Milton J. Gold, Executive Secretary
Beverly Goodloe-Kaplan, Associate Executive Secretary